T0235374

Lecture Notes in Computer Science   9275

Commenced Publication in 1973
Founding and Former Series Editors:
Gerhard Goos, Juris Hartmanis, and Jan van Leeuwen

More information about this series at http://www.springer.com/series/7408

Márcio Barros · Yvan Labiche (Eds.)

Search-Based Software Engineering

7th International Symposium, SSBSE 2015
Bergamo, Italy, September 5–7, 2015
Proceedings

 Springer

Editors
Márcio Barros
Federal University of Rio de Janeiro State
Rio de Janeiro
Brazil

Yvan Labiche
Carleton University
Ottawa, ON
Canada

ISSN 0302-9743   ISSN 1611-3349 (electronic)
Lecture Notes in Computer Science
ISBN 978-3-319-22182-3   ISBN 978-3-319-22183-0   (eBook)
DOI 10.1007/978-3-319-22183-0

Library of Congress Control Number: 2015945149

LNCS Sublibrary: SL2 – Programming and Software Engineering

Springer Cham Heidelberg New York Dordrecht London

Printed on acid-free paper

Springer International Publishing AG Switzerland is part of Springer Science+Business Media
(www.springer.com)

Message from the SSBSE 2015 General Chair

It was my pleasure to welcome all SSBSE 2015 delegates to the beautiful city of Bergamo in Italy. After Benevento (2009) and Riva del Garda (2012), this was the third time Italy hosted SSBSE. Italian researchers have been active from the inception of this event and the interest in search-based approaches to software engineering has seen a steady growth in Italy as well as outside Italy in recent years. The city of Bergamo is structured in two levels. The lower city (in Italian, "città bassa") is more modern and dynamic, while the famous upper city ("città alta"), built up on the hills, boasts a stunning historic center with an extremely rich heritage of art and history. The two cities are separated by the powerful Venetian Walls.

For the third time in its history, SSBSE was co-located with the ACM SIGSOFT Symposium on the Foundations of Software Engineering (ESEC/FSE), offering participants a unique opportunity to be exposed to the most recent advancements in the wide software engineering area and in the specific area of search-based software engineering.

The organization of SSBSE 2015 was the result of a collective effort and as General Chair of the symposium I am grateful to all the people who contributed. It was my pleasure to have the possibility of working with them. The Program Chairs, Márcio Barros and Yvan Labiche, were able to put together a great Research Track, including new stimulating research directions and results that span all areas of software engineering, from software design and construction, to verification and validation. Shin Yoo and Leandro Minku attracted a high number of excellent submissions in the Challenge Track, featuring three whole sessions in this edition of the symposium. My gratitude goes to Federica Sarro, who managed the papers submitted to the Graduate Student Track and to the Short Paper Track. The program includes two outstanding keynote speakers, Prof. Kenneth A. De Jong from George Mason University and Dr. William Langdon from University College London. The high quality of the program stems from the reviewing activities carried out by the members of the Program Committee and, last but not least, from the research work of all the authors. I wish to thank them all.

I would also like to thank the Publicity Chair, Yuanyuan Zhang, the Web Chair, Roberto Tiella, and the Local Chair, Angelo Gargantini. I am grateful to Springer for publishing the proceedings of SSBSE 2015. The Steering Committee of SSBSE, chaired by Mark Harman, provided invaluable guidance and suggestions; previous General Chairs, Gordon Fraser and Jerffeson Teixeira de Souza, gave me extremely useful tips. Coordination with the ESEC/FSE General Chair, Elisabetta Di Nitto, was crucial in maximizing the synergies between the two events. Annalisa Armani and her colleagues at Fondazione Bruno Kessler constantly assisted me in the financial and logistic organization of the event.

Financial support from the sponsors, Fondazione Bruno Kessler, Huawei, and CREST, was fundamental for keeping the registration fees low and ensuring at the same time a rich and exciting social program, including a banquet in the upper city of Bergamo. A special thank you goes to Huawei, for sponsoring two best paper awards in the Research Track and one best paper award in the Graduate Student Track, and to CREST, for sponsoring the Challenge Track award.

September 2015   Paolo Tonella

Message from the SSBSE 2015 Program Chairs

On behalf of the SSBSE 2015 Program Committee, it is our pleasure to present the proceedings of the 7th International Symposium on Search-Based Software Engineering, held in the beautiful city of Bergamo, Italy. SSBSE 2015 continued a strong tradition of bringing together the international SBSE community in an annual event to discuss and to celebrate progress in the field.

This year, SSBSE matched last year's record number of submissions, totaling 51 submissions, all tracks included. Authors from 15 countries and all continents submitted their work to the symposium: Europe (Belgium, France, Germany, Italy, The Netherlands, Norway, Sweden, Switzerland, the UK), Asia (China, India), America (Brazil, Canada, the USA), Oceania (Australia), and Africa (Algeria). We would like to thank them all, regardless of acceptance or rejection, for making the review process and the conference very interesting for everyone. Specifically, we received 26 papers to the research track, 13 papers to the challenge track, eight short papers, and four student papers. At the end of the review process, where each submitted paper was reviewed by at least three SBSE researchers, 12 papers were accepted to the research track, all submitted papers were accepted to the challenge track, four short papers and two student papers were accepted.

We would like to thank the members of the SSBSE 2015 Program Committee. Their continuing support has been essential in further improving the quality of accepted submissions and the resulting success of the conference. We also wish to especially thank the General Chair, Paolo Tonella. Paolo and his team managed to keep the organization of every single aspect under control, making the conference a special event to all of us. In addition, we want to thank Federica Sarro for chairing the student track and the short paper track and we would like to thank Shin Yoo and Leandro Minku for chairing the challenge track, which attracted twice as many papers as in the previous year.

In keeping with a successful tradition, SSBSE 2015 attendees had the opportunity to learn from experts from both research fields of search and software engineering, in two outstanding keynote talks. This year, we had the honor of hosting a keynote on co-evolutionary algorithms from Prof. Kenneth De Jong, who has been influential in the evolutionary computation research community. Furthermore, we had a keynote on genetic programming for software improvement from Dr. William Langdon, who is well-known for his extensive expertise and experience in designing and implementing genetic programming systems.

We hope that with these proceedings, anybody who did not have the chance to be in Bergamo will have the opportunity to feel the liveliness of the SBSE community.

September 2015

Márcio Barros
Yvan Labiche

Organization

General Chair

Paolo Tonella   Fondazione Bruno Kessler, Italy

Program Chairs

Márcio Barros   Federal University of Rio de Janeiro State, Brazil
Yvan Labiche   Carleton University, Canada

SBSE Challenge Tracks Chairs

Shin Yoo   University College London, UK
Leandro Minku   University of Birmingham, UK

Short Papers and Graduate Student Tracks Chair

Federica Sarro   University College London, UK

Organizing Committee

Angelo Gargantini   University of Bergamo, Italy
Yuanyuan Zhang   University College London, UK
Roberto Tiella   Fondazione Bruno Kessler, Italy

Program Committee

Shaukat Ali   Simula Research Laboratory, Norway
Leonardo Bottaci   University of Hull, UK
John Clark   University of York, UK
Thelma Colanzi   State University of Maringá, Brazil
Massimiliano Di Penta   University of Sannio, Italy
Arilo Claudio Dias-Neto   Federal University of Amazonas, Brazil
Robert Feldt   Blekinge Institute of Technology, Sweden
Gordon Fraser   University of Sheffield, UK
Mathew Hall   University of Sheffield, UK
Colin Johnson   University of Kent, UK
Marouane Kessentini   University of Michigan, USA
Fitsum Kifetew   Fondazione Bruno Kessler, Italy
Dongsun Kim   University of Luxembourg, Luxembourg
Claire Le Goues   Carnegie Mellon University, USA

Raluca Lefticaru	University of Bucharest, Romania
Zheng Li	Beijing University of Chemical Technology, China
Phil McMinn	University of Sheffield, UK
Tim Menzies	North Carolina State University, USA
Leandro Minku	University of Birmingham, UK
Justyna Petke	University College London, UK
Pasqualina Potena	University of Alcala, Spain
Simon Poulding	Blekinge Institute of Technology, Sweden
Xiao Qu	ABB Corporate Research
Marc Roper	University of Strathclyde, UK
Guenther Ruhe	University of Calgary, Canada
Christopher Simons	University of the West of England, UK
Jerffeson Souza	State University of Ceará, Brazil
Angelo Susi	Fondazione Bruno Kessler, Italy
Jerry Swan	University of Stirling, UK
Silvia Vergilio	Federal University of Paraná, Brazil
David White	University of Glasgow, UK
Xin Yao	University of Birmingham, UK
Yuanyuan Zhang	University College London, UK
Mel Ó Cinnéide	University College Dublin, Ireland

Additional Reviewers

Andrea Arcuri	Scienta, Norway, and University of Luxembourg
Wesley Assunção	Universidade Federal do Paraná, Brazil
Muhammad Rezaul Karim	University of Calgary, Canada
Dipesh Pradhan	Simula Research Laboratory, Norway
Renata Rego	Federal University of Amazonas, Brazil
Shuai Wang	Simula Research Laboratory, Norway

Steering Committee

Mark Harman (Chair)	University College London, UK
Andrea Arcuri	Scienta, Norway, and University of Luxembourg
Márcio Barros	Federal University of Rio de Janeiro State, Brazil
Massimiliano Di Penta	University of Sannio, Italy
Gordon Fraser	University of Sheffield, UK
Claire Le Goues	Carnegie Mellon University, USA
Jerffeson Souza	University of the State of Ceará, Brazil
David White	University of Glasgow, UK
Yuanyuan Zhang	University College London, UK

Sponsors

Supporters

Contents

Short Papers

Graduate Student Papers

Invited Talks

Co-Evolutionary Algorithms: A Useful Computational Abstraction?

Kenneth De Jong[(✉)]

George Mason University, Fairfax, VA, USA
kdejong@gmu.edu

Abstract. Interest in co-evolutionary algorithms was triggered in part with Hillis 1991 paper describing his success in using one to evolve sorting networks. Since then there have been heightened expectations for using this nature-inspired technique to improve on the range and power of evolutionary algorithms for solving difficult computation problems. However, after more than two decades of exploring this promise, the results have been somewhat mixed.

In this talk I summarize the progress made and the lessons learned with a goal of understanding how they are best used and identify a variety of interesting open issues that need to be explored in order to make further progress in this area.

1 Introduction

In 1991 at the Artificial Life II meeting in Santa Fe Danny Hillis summarized his successful use of a co-evolutionary approach to evolve sorting networks, an approach inspired by host-parasite models from nature [6]. That early success has inspired several decades of interest in how our understanding of co-evolutionary systems in nature might be used to improve the problem-solving capabilities of existing evolutionary algorithms [1,7,13,14]. The results have been mixed in spite of a significant amount of both theoretical and empirical research.

The argument put forth here is that, in order to make further progress, we need first to sharpen our understanding of the biological phenomenon of co-evolution in order to better understand how it might inspire improved evolutionary algorithms, and second, we need to use that understanding to develop a more comprehensive and systematic framework for designing and analyzing co-evolutionary algorithms.

To that end, I first discuss biological notions of co-evolution, and then present a co-evolutionary framework intended to sharpen our algorithmic focus. The framework is then used to summarize our current understanding and identify important open issues.

2 What IS Co-Evolution?

When biologists talk about co-evolution it is in the context of an ecology with multiple species whose cross-species interactions in part determine the fitness of

© Springer International Publishing Switzerland 2015
M. Barros and Y. Labiche (Eds.): SSBSE 2015, LNCS 9275, pp. 3–11, 2015.
DOI: 10.1007/978-3-319-22183-0_1

individuals within a species. A classic example of a co-evolutionary prey-predator relationship is that of frogs evolving longer and stickier tongues for catching flies, and flies evolving better sensors and evasive tactics as their co-evolutionary response. Similarly, nature abounds with examples of co-evolutionary host-parasite relationships such as the bacteria in a host's digestive tract that are critical in breaking down ingested material into forms the host can make use of.

A key aspect is that the cross-species interactions are not one of cross-breeding, but rather an interaction that takes place on a shared fitness landscape. This has an immediate implication for co-evolutionary algorithm design. Our most common evolutionary algorithms (EAs) maintain a single population of interbreeding individuals, i.e., a single species from a biological perspective. If we are to remain faithful to the biological perspective, our co-evolutionary algorithms should either introduce speciation into single-population EAs or maintain multiple populations across which there is no interbreeding.

This is an important point because it is not uncommon for a discipline to import a concept from another area and then use in ways that are different than the original meaning, often resulting in misunderstandings and confusion. Here's an example of where that shows up in EC. Suppose I'm interested in evolving a chess playing program. If I adopt the standard EC perspective, I evaluate the fitness of an individual program via some procedure that is external to and independent of the current population. For example, have it play against one or more externally developed chess programs. But that leads to a classic chicken-egg problem in that one needs to have good chess programs in order to evolve good chess programs!

An alternative is to evaluate the fitness of an individual by playing other individuals in the current population resulting in a dynamically changing fitness landscape as the population of chess programs evolves over time. If we do this, what shall we call this EA? Shall we refer to it as co-evolutionary? A biologist would say no - this is much more in keeping with the biological notion of an evolutionary system in which the fitness of individuals is determined in part by the other members of the population. To be co-evolutionary one would have a population of, say, American chess programs and another population of Russian programs, each reproductively isolated but constantly assessing fitness by playing against each other.

Does it matter what we call co-evolutionary? I think the answer is yes for two reasons. First, since our inspirations come from natural systems, we can inadvertently limit future inspiration by drifting too far from the underlying biological concepts. More importantly, the two EA systems described above, one with a single population and internal fitness competitions and one with multiple populations and cross-population fitness competition have significantly different evolutionary dynamics. So, by calling them both co-evolutionary algorithms we make our understanding of co-evolutionary systems more complicated than it needs to be.

My suggestion: let's refer to the first case as EAs using some form of self-adaptive fitness evaluation, following the terminology and perspective taken by other forms of self-adaptation (e.g., self-adaptive mutation rates). Let's reserve the term co-evolution to those EAs that have multiple populations (or species) that share a coupled fitness landscape. That still leaves plenty of design decisions to be made and many open questions regarding these co-evolutionary algorithms (CoEAs). Here are some examples:

1. In what sense, if any, do CoEAs improve on our ability to solve optimization problems?
2. Are there other kinds of problems that CoEAs are particularly well-suited for?
3. How does one implement the notion of interlocking fitness landscapes in a computationally efficient and effective manner?
4. What are the differences between CoEAs and other multi-population models such as island models?
5. What aspects of our understanding and analysis of standard EAs can be usefully applied to CoEAs?
6. What aspects of our understanding and analysis of biological co-evolution can be usefully applied to CoEAs?

These are not new questions and in some cases there is a reasonable degree of understanding [3, 10]. The thesis presented here is that our understanding can be sharpened and extended if we adopt a common framework.

3 A CoEA Framework

We begin by laying out the framework for a 2-population/species CoEA, since most of the issues and ideas can be exposed with it, and since a large majority of existing CoEAs are in fact of this type.

First, each population/species has its own EA controlling its evolutionary trajectory. There is no *a priori* assumption that the two EAs share any common properties. For example, one could be a fairly traditional ES-like EA with a small population of real-valued vectors while the other could be a fairly traditional GP-like EA with a fairly large population of Lisp expressions.

A second aspect of the CoEA framework is that there is no *a priori* assumption as to how, if at all, the evolutionary clocks of the two EAs are synchronized. One might have completely unsynchronized clocks, or one might have a synchronized regime in which one EA is frozen while the other evolves for one or more generations.

A third aspect of the CoEA framework is the requirement for specifying how the fitness landscapes are to be coupled. This means specifying how individuals in one population interact with individuals in the other population in order to calculate their fitness.

Finally, one needs to specify what it means for a CoEA to produce a solution. That is, what do we extract from the running of a CoEA that represents a solution.

I refer to this as a CoEA framework in that each of its elements must be instantiated before it can be executed. The goal here is to use this framework to summarize and extend what we know about the implications of specific design choices and how that knowledge can be used to implement more effective CoEAs.

4   Understanding Co-Evolutionary Algorithms

The key difference between standard EAs and CoEAs is the dynamic interaction between populations with coupled fitness landscapes. Understanding that dynamic is a major step in the direction of understanding co-evolutionary systems. That observation suggests that viewing CoEAs as dynamical systems and applying dynamical systems analysis tools and techniques is a potentially useful line of research, and has in fact already provided a variety of useful insights [9,16].

If we look at a CoEA from the perspective of one of the evolving populations, we see that it faces the challenging task of responding to a time-varying fitness landscape. This suggests that our existing understanding of how to design/configure standard EAs for non-stationary landscapes might be potentially useful in how we configure the individual EAs in CoEA systems (see, for example, [8]).

A closely related issue is the manner in which, if at all, the evolutionary clocks of the individual EAs are synchronized. We know from time-varying landscape studies with standard EAs that rapidly changing fitness landscapes relative to an EA's evolutionary clock lead to poor results. This suggests that coordination of the EA clocks in a CoEA is an important (and mostly unexplored) area of research.

A computationally difficult as well semantically important isssue is the need to instantiate the notion of a coupled fitness landscape. The intuition is clear: one evaluates the fitness of an individual in population A via "interactions" with one or more individuals from population B. However, "the devil is in the details". Since, in general, a complete set of paired interactions is computationally infeasible, some sort of selection procedure must be used. If that procedure results in the selection of more than one interaction pairing, an additional decision is required to specify how the results of multiple interactions are combined to provide a single fitness value. This particular aspect of CoEA design has received a good deal of analysis and about which we have a reasonable measure of understanding (see, for example, [12,17]).

Finally, there is the surprisingly difficult issue of the sense in which CoEAs provide solutions to problems [2,11]. For example, if we show that certain CoEAs are dynamical systems that converge to a Nash equilibrium, and then apply the CoEA to optimization problems, what should we expect? If we attempt to use a CoEA to evolve a "world class" game playing program, what should we expect when the internal fitness assessment driving the evolutionary processes is only based on the current members of the populations? This is also an area that has received a good detail of attention, including being more precise about co-evolutionary "solution concepts" [5] and introducing additional non-evolutionary mechanisms such as "hall-of-fame" archival techniques [14].

Of course, just as is the case for standard EA design decisions, each of these additional CoEA design choices affect the observed behavior and performance of CoEAs in highly non-linear and complex ways. We explore this aspect in the following sections.

4.1   CoEAs as Dynamical Systems

Our initial understanding of CoEAs as dynamical systems came from Paul Wiegand's PhD thesis [16]. His approach was to leverage off the existing work in evolutionary game theory (EGT) as a means for understanding the dynamics of CoEAs. As a first-order fit, EGT seemed well suited in the sense that the evolutionary aspects of theoretical EGT models were nearly identical to our infinite population models of simple EAs with fitness proportional selection and no reproductive variation (i.e., just replicator dynamics). Under the mathematical assumption of "complete mixing" (all possible interactions), the EGT literature contains a rather impressive collection of theoretical results for two-population EGT models. The question Wiegand explored was the extent to which these EGT results might apply to CoEA systems involving finite populations with partial mixing and reproductive variation.

The results were instructive but somewhat disappointing. Like infinite population EGT models, finite population CoEAs with fitness-proportional replication and no reproductive variation were experimentally seen to converge to Nash equilibria. However, adding mutation and crossover to the mix produced dynamical trajectories that were difficult to understand and predict, and converged to non-Nash equilbria.

Wiegand explored these issues using simple multi-peaked fitness landscapes in which the peaks corresponded to Nash equilibria, allowing for additional insights regarding the use of these CoEAs for optimization. Again, the results were instructive but disappointing. With no reproductive variation, a CoEA converged to the Nash equilibrium point (local optimum) that exerted the strongest influence on the initial populations. Adding reproductive variation resulted in convergence to non-optimal points, and the traditional best-so-far curve analysis suggested little to be excited about with respect to global function optimization performance.

Elena Popovici added to our dynamical systems understanding of CoEAs by introducing the notion of "best response curves" generated by selecting the individual in population A with the best fitness to serve as the single point of interaction for evaluating the fitness of members of population B [9]. If we keep finite population A frozen for an indefinite number of evolutionary generations of population B, we identify in population B the best response to the current best individual in population A, and now repeat this process with the population roles reversed. The result is a time series of best responses which, when plotted provide considerable insight into the CoEA dynamics. In particular, Popovici was able to construct examples of simple synthetic landscapes on which CoEAs converged, cycled endlessly or went chaotic.

4.2 CoEAs and Dynamic Fitness Landscapes

There is a considerable amount of empirical evidence that the standard set of EAs used to solve static optimization problems perform poorly when the fitness landscape changes during the evolutionary search process. This has been addressed in a number of ways including making assumptions about the kind of changes a landscape will undergo (e.g., slowly drifting, cyclic, etc.). With CoEAs it is difficult to predict how a coupled landscape might change over time, although there are some tantalizing connections with the insights obtained from Popovici's synthetic landscapes referred to in the previous section.

What we do have is a clear sense of the importance of maintaining population diversity when dealing with dynamic landscapes. This is a relatively unexplored approach to improving CoEA performance in that we typically use our standard static-optimization-oriented EAs for evolving each of our CoEA populations. What remains unexplored is whether the simple changes to standard EAs to promote diversity produce a positive impact of CoEA performance.

The one notable exception is the use of spatially-structured EAs, the properties of which are fairly well understood (e.g., [15]), one of which is the ability to maintain diversity for a much longer period of time. Their use in CoEAs has proved initially to be quite beneficial [8,18], and deserves further exploration and understanding.

4.3 CoEA Time Clocks

One of the least explored areas of the CoEA framework is the way in which the evolutionary clocks of the individual populations are linked. There are at least 3 possibilities:

- The clocks are completely unlinked in the sense that asynchronous updates to either population can happen at any time.
- The clocks are linked in the sense that one population is frozen in time while the other population completes a generational cycle, and then the population roles are reversed.
- The same freeze/thaw linking as the previous case but now allow multiple evolutionary generations to occur while the other population is frozen.

Most of the CoEAs in use today are of type 2 and a few of type 3. At little reflection here should suggest an obvious relationship to the previous section and indicate some opportunities for further analysis. Case 1 is likely to result in landscapes changing dynamically at a rate that results in poor performance just as we see with standard EAs. Case 2 reduces that rate of change but is still potentially quite high. If we allow too many generations to pass in Case 3, we are likely to lose the diversity we need for dealing with dynamic landscapes. That suggests there may be a sweet spot in Case 3 where increasing the number of generations to a small number > 1 will result in performance improvements.

4.4   Coupling CoEA Fitness Landscapes

The manner in which the coupling of the fitness landscapes of the CoEA populations via interactions between members during fitness assessment is a well-studied aspect of CoEA design. Potter showed that for CoEAs involving co-operative interactions, evaluating the fitness of the individuals in one population using a single best representation from the other populations was algorithmically similar to familiar line search techniques and suffered the same limitations in dealing with function optimization problems involving coupled variables [12]. He showed that adding a second interaction with a randomly chosen individual improved performance without a significant increase in computational complexity.

Wiegand et al. were able to take this analysis a step further by showing that only certain kinds of epistatic interactions caused difficulty [17]. In addition, there were few observed additional benefits obtained by using more than two interactions per fitness assessment. Similar to results in using standard EAs to solve problems with noisy fitness landscapes, the additional fitness evaluations used to obtain a better estimate of an individual's fitness are generally more productively spent on additional evolutionary search.

The issue of evolutionary time clocks discussed in the previous section also has an impact here. Case 1 results in far too much instability in the coupling process, and is another reason why it is hard to find positive examples of this type.

4.5   CoEA Problem Solutions

From the very beginning there have been heated biological discussions about whether evolution is best understood as an optimization process. What is clear is that, inspired by evolutionary processes, we have developed powerful optimization algorithms. This is not the case, however, for our co-evolutionary algorithms. In general, they appear to be no more effective than our standard EAs and in some cases worse. One possible explanation is that we need to spend more time analyzing the design issues discussed in the previous section. Another explanation is that co-evolution is fundamentally not an optimization process and therefore not a particularly useful inspiration for developing optimization algorithms.

Discussions of this issue take several forms. One is to focus on the kind of fitness coupling involved: whether the interactions are competitive in nature (I win, you lose) or co-operative in nature (we win/lose together). As it turns out, problems that can be cast as co-operative interactions (e.g., a decomposition of a difficult optimization problem into subcomponents) can be effectively solved via CoEAs. By contrast, when CoEAs are applied to problems with competitive interactions (e.g., game playing), they are much more likely to produce uninteresting dynamics such as loss of gradients or endless mediocrity rather than continuous improvement via an arms race [18].

This has led to a discussion about problems other than standard optimization that might be a better fit for CoEAs, particularly problems with competitive interactions [4,5]. These discussions have adopted the notion of a "solution concept" as a way of describing the kinds of problems and solutions a CoEA might be applied to. An example: not knowing what opponent I might face in the near future, I would like to minimize the maximum negative impact he/she might have on me.

5   Conclusions

While there are examples of significant improvements in our ability to solve difficult optimization problems by using CoEAs, other examples exhibit either neutral or negative results. In part, this is a reflection of the need for a deeper understanding of the implications of the design decisions that one must make when implementing a CoEA. Another important aspect of this is the possibility that co-evolution is better understood as a sophisticated process of co-adaptation, and that the real power of CoEAs is in solving problems of this nature.

References

1. Angeline, P.J., Pollack, J.B.: Competitive environments evolve better solutions for complex tasks. In: Proceedings of the 5th International Conference on Genetic Algorithms, pp. 264–270. Morgan Kaufmann Publishers Inc., San Francisco (1993)
2. Bader-Natal, A., Pollack, J.B.: A population-differential method of monitoring success and failure in coevolution. In: Deb, K., Tari, Z. (eds.) GECCO 2004. LNCS, vol. 3102, pp. 585–586. Springer, Heidelberg (2004)
3. Bucci, A., Pollack, J.B.: A mathematical framework for the study of coevolution. In: Proceedings of the Seventh Workshop on Foundations of Genetic Algorithms, Torremolinos, Spain, pp. 221–236, 2–4 September 2002
4. de Jong, E.D., Pollack, J.B.: Ideal evaluation from coevolution. Evol. Comput. **12**(2), 159–192 (2004)
5. Ficici, S.G.: Solution Concepts in Coevolutionary Algorithms. Ph.D. thesis, Brandeis University, Waltham, MA, USA (2004). AAI3127125
6. Hillis, D.: SFI studies in the sciences of complexity co-evolving parasites improve simulated evolution as an optimization procedure. Artificial Life II **10**, 313–324 (1991)
7. Juille, H., Pollack, J.B.: Coevolving the "ideal" trainer: application to the discovery of cellular automata rules. In: University of Wisconsin, pp. 519–527. Morgan Kaufmann (1998)
8. Pagie, L., Mitchell, M.: A comparison of evolutionary and coevolutionary search. Int. J. Comput. Intell. Appl. **2**(1), 53–69 (2002)
9. Popovici, E.: An analysis of two-population coevolutionary computation. Ph.D. thesis, George Mason University, Fairfax, VA (2006)
10. Popovici, E., Bucci, A., Wiegand, R.P., de Jong, E.D.: Coevolutionary principles. In: Rozenberg, G., Bäck, T., Kok, J.N. (eds.) Handbook of Natural Computing, pp. 987–1033. Oxford University Press, Oxford (2012)
11. Popovici, E., De Jong, K.A.: Relationships between internal and external metrics in co-evolution. In: Proceedings of the IEEE Congress on Evolutionary Computation, CEC 2005, Edinburgh, UK, pp. 2800–2807, 2–4 September 2005

12. Potter, M.A., De Jong, K.A.: Cooperative coevolution: an architecture for evolving coadapted subcomponents. Evol. Comput. **8**(1), 1–29 (2000)
13. Potter, M.A., De Jong, K.A.: A cooperative coevolutionary approach to function optimization. In: Davidor, Y., Männer, R., Schwefel, H.-P. (eds.) PPSN 1994. LNCS, vol. 866. Springer, Heidelberg (1994)
14. Rosin, C., Belew, R.: New methods for competitive coevolution. Evol. Comput. **5**(1), 1–29 (1997)
15. Sarma, J.: An analysis of decentralized and spatially distributed genetic algorithms. Ph.D. thesis, George Mason University, Fairfax VA, USA (1998)
16. Wiegand, R.P.: An analysis of cooperative coevolutionary algorithms. Ph.D. thesis, George Mason University, Fairfax, VA (2004)
17. Wiegand, R.P., Liles, W., De Jong, K.: An empirical analysis of collaboration methods in cooperative coevolutionary algorithms. In: Proceedings of Genetic and Evolutionary Computation - GECCO 2001, pp. 1235–1242. Morgan Kaufmann (2001)
18. Wiegand, R.P., Sarma, J.: Spatial embedding and loss of gradient in cooperative coevolutionary algorithms. In: Yao, X., Burke, E.K., Lozano, J.A., Smith, J., Merelo-Guervós, J.J., Bullinaria, J.A., Rowe, J.E., Tiňo, P., Kabán, A., Schwefel, H.-P. (eds.) PPSN 2004. LNCS, vol. 3242, pp. 912–921. Springer, Heidelberg (2004)

Genetic Improvement of Software
for Multiple Objectives

William B. Langdon$^{(\boxtimes)}$

CREST, Department of Computer Science, University College London,
Gower Street, London WC1E 6BT, UK
w.langdon@cs.ucl.ac.uk
http://crest.cs.ucl.ac.uk/

Abstract. Genetic programming (GP) can increase computer program's functional and non-functional performance. It can automatically
port or refactor legacy code written by domain experts. Working with
programmers it can grow and graft (GGGP) new functionality into legacy
systems and parallel Bioinformatics GPGPU code. We review Genetic
Improvement (GI) and SBSE research on evolving software.

1 Introduction

Although the idea of using evolutionary computation to improve existing software has been in the air for a little while [1], the use of genetic programming (GP)
[2,3] to improve manually written code starts to take off in 2009 (see Fig. 2). First
with Wes Weimer et al.'s prize winning automatic bug fixing work [4–9] Sect. 3.1)
and also Orlov and Sipper's [10] use of GP to improve manually written code
by using it to seed the GP's population [11] (Sect. 2.3). The GISMO (http://
www.cs.ucl.ac.uk/staff/W.Langdon/gismo/) research project started four years
ago with the lofty aim of transforming the way we think about and produce
software. Now nearing its end, we can point to some successful applications
(Sects. 3.2 to 5.3) but perhaps the major impact has been the growth of "Genetic
Improvement" [12] and the increasing acceptance that search based optimisation
[13] can not only aid software engineers but also act upon their software directly.

We shall give an overview of Genetic Improvement (GI). This is based in
part on "Genetically Improved Software" [12] and work presented at the first
international event on GI (held in Madrid 12th July 2015 [14]). GI is the use of
optimisation techniques such as Genetic Algorithms and Genetic Programming
[2,3] to software itself. Although any optimisation technique might be used, so
far published work has concentrated upon using GP to improve human written
source code.

In the next section we start by briefly summarising research which evolved
complete software [15] and then move on to GI. Section 3 starts with automatically fixing real bugs in real C/C++ programs (Sect. 3.1). This is followed
by reviews of the GISMO project's work on gzip (Sect. 3.2), Bioinformatics

---

W.B. Langdon — http://www.cs.ucl.ac.uk/staff/W.Langdon/

© Springer International Publishing Switzerland 2015
M. Barros and Y. Labiche (Eds.): SSBSE 2015, LNCS 9275, pp. 12–28, 2015.
DOI: 10.1007/978-3-319-22183-0_2

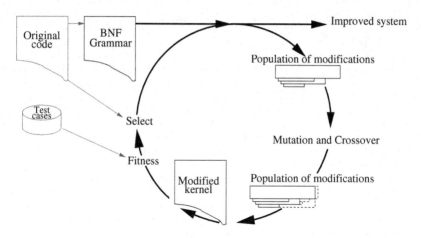

Fig. 1. Genetic Improvement of Program Source Code.

(Sect. 3.3) and parallel computing (Sects. 3.4 to 3.6). Section 4 describes evolving a human competitive version of MiniSAT from multiple existing programs. Whilst Sect. 5 describes three examples of GP and programmers working together including obtaining a 10 000 fold speedup. The last sections (Sects. 6 and 7) conclude with the project's main lessons.

2 Evolving Useful Programs from Primordial Ooze

2.1 Hashes, Caches and Garbage Collection

Three early examples of real software being evolved using genetic programming are: hashing, caching and garbage collection. Each has the advantages of being small, potentially of high value and difficult to do either by hand or by theoretically universal principles. These include examples where GP generate code exceeded the state-of-the art human written code. Whilst this is not to say a human could not do better. Indeed they may take inspiration, or even code, from the evolved solution. It is that to do so, requires a programmer skilled in the art, for each new circumstance. Whereas, at least in principle, the GP can be re-run for each new use case and so automatically generate an implementation specific to that user.

Starting with Hussain and Malliaris [16] several teams have evolved good hashing algorithms [17–19].

Paterson showed GP can create problem specific caching code [20]. O'Neill and Ryan [21] used their Grammatical Evolution approach also to create cache code. Whilst Branke et al. [22] looked at a slightly different problem: deciding which documents to retain to avoid fetching them again across the Internet.

Many computer languages provide a dynamic memory manager, which frees the programmer of the tedium of deciding exactly which memory is in use and provides some form of garbage collection whereby memory that is no longer in use

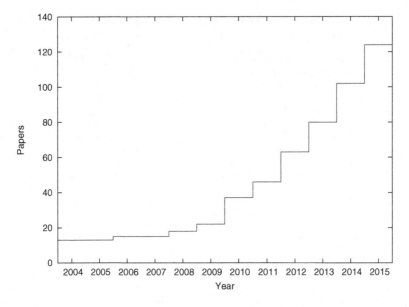

Fig. 2. Recent growth in number of entries in the genetic programming bibliography applying GP to generate or improve software (May 2015).

can be freed for re-use. Even with modern huge memories, memory management can impose a significant overhead. Risco-Martin et al. [23] showed the GP can generate an optimised garbage collector for the C language [24].

2.2 Mashups, Hyper-Heuristics and Multiplicity Computing

The idea behind web services is that useful services should be easily constructed from services across the Internet. Such hacked together systems are known as web mashups. A classic example is a travel service which invokes web servers from a number of airlines and hotel booking and car hire services, and is thus able to provide a composite package without enormous coding effort in itself. Since web services must operate within a defined framework ideally with rigid interfaces, they would seem to be ideal building blocks with which genetic programming might construct high level programs. Starting with Rodriguez-Mier, several authors have reported progress with genetic programming evolving composite web services [25–27].

There are many difficult optimisation problems which in practise are efficiently solved using heuristic search techniques, such as genetic algorithms. However typically the GA needs to be tweaked to get the best for each problem. This has lead to the generation of hyper-heuristics [28], in which the GA or other basic solver is tweaked automatically. Typically genetic programming is used. Indeed some solvers have been evolved by GP combining a number of basic techniques as well as tuning parameters or even re-coding GA components, such as mutation operators [29].

A nice software engineering example of heuristics is compiler code generation. Typically compilers are expected not only to create correct machine code but also that it should be in some sense be "good". Typically this means the code should be fast or small. Mahajan and Ali [30] used GP to give better code generation heuristics in Harvard's MachineSUIF compiler.

Multiplicity computing [31] seeks to over turn the current software monoculture where one particular operating system, web browser, software company, etc., achieves total dominance of the software market. Not only are such monopolies dangerous from a commercial point of view but they have allowed widespread problems of malicious software (especially computer viruses) to prosper. Excluding specialist areas, such as mutation testing [32,33], so far there has been only a little work in the evolution of massive numbers of software variants [34]. Only software automation (perhaps by using genetic programming) appears a credible approach to N-version programming (with N much more than 3). N-version programming has also been proposed as a way of improving predictive performance by voting between three or more classifiers [35,36] or using other non-linear combinations to yield a higher performing multi-classifier [37,38].

Other applications of GP include: creating optimisation benchmarks which demonstrate the relative strengths and weaknesses of optimisers [39] and first steps towards the use of GP on mobile telephones [40], connections to software product lines [41], security [42,43] and adaptability [44].

2.3   Genetic Programming and Non-Function Requirements

Andrea Arcuri was in at the start of inspirational work on GP showing it can create real code from scratch. Although the programs remain small, David White, he and John Clark [45] also evolved programs to accomplish real tasks such as creating pseudo random numbers for ultra tiny computers where they showed a trade off between "randomness" and energy consumption.

The Virginia University group (see next section) also showed GP evolving Pareto optimal trade offs between speed and fidelity for a graphics hardware display program [46]. Evolution seems to be particularly suitable for exploring such trade-offs [47,48] but (except for the work described later in this chapter) there has been little research in this area.

Orlov and Sipper [10] describe a very nice system, Finch, for evolving Java byte code. Effectively the GP population instead of starting randomly [49] is seeded [11] with byte code created by compiling the initial program. The Finch crossover operator acts on Java byte code to ensure the offspring program are also valid java byte code.

Archanjo and Von Zuben [50] present a GP system for evolving small business systems. They present an example of a database system for supporting a library of books.

Ryan [51] and Katz and Peled [52] provide interesting alternative visions. In genetic improvement the performance, particularly the quality of the mutated program's output, is assessed by running the program. Instead they suggest each mutation be provably correct and thus the new program is functionally the same as the original but in some way it is improved, e.g. by running in parallel. Katz and Peled [52] suggests combining GP with model checking to ensure correctness.

Cody-Kenny et al. [53] showed on a dozen Java examples (mostly different implementations of various types of sort from rosettacode.org) that GP was able to reduce the number of Java byte code instructions executed.

Schulte et al. [54] describes a system which can further optimise the low level Intel X86 code generated by optimising compilers. They show evolution can reduce energy consumption of non-trivial programs. (Their largest application contains 141 012 lines of code.) Mrazek et al. [55] showed it was possible to evolve an important function (the median) in a variety of machine codes.

3   Improvement of Substantial Human Written Code

3.1   Automatic Bug Fixing

As described in the previous two sections, recently genetic programming has been applied to the production of programs itself, however so far relatively small programs have been evolved. Nonetheless GP has had some great successes when applied to existing programs. Perhaps the best known work is that on automatic bug fixing [56]. Particularly the Humie award winning[1] work of Westley Weimer (Virginia University) and Stephanie Forrest (New Mexico) [5]. This has received multiple awards and best paper prizes [4,6]. GP has been used repeatedly to automatically fix most (but not all) real bugs in real programs [57]. Weimer and Le Goues have now shown GP bug fixing to be effective on over a million lines of C++ code. Once GP had been used to *do the impossible* others tried [58–60] and it was improved [61] and also people felt brave enough to try other techniques, e.g. [62–64]. Indeed their colleague, Eric Schulte, has shown GP can operate below the source code level, e.g. [43]. In [8] he showed bugs can be fixed via mutating the assembler code generated by the compiler or even machine code [65]. After Weimer and co-workers showed that automatic bugfixing was not impossible, people studied the problem more openly. It turns out, for certain real bugs, with modern software engineering support tools, such as bug localisation (e.g. [66]), the problem may not even be hard [67].

Formal theoretical analysis [68] of evolving sizable software is still thin on the ground. Much of the work presented here is based on GP re-arranging lines of human written code. In a study of 420 million lines of open source software Gabel and Su [69] showed that excluding white space, comments and details of variable names, any human written line of code has probably been written before. In other words, given a sufficiently large feedstock of human written code, current programs could have been written by re-using and re-ordering existing source code. In many cases in this and the following sections, this is exactly what GP is doing. Schulte et al. [9] provides a solid empirical study which refutes the common assumption that software is fragile. (See also Fig. 3). While a single

---

[1] Human-competitive results presented at the annual GECCO conference http://www. genetic-programming.org/combined.php.

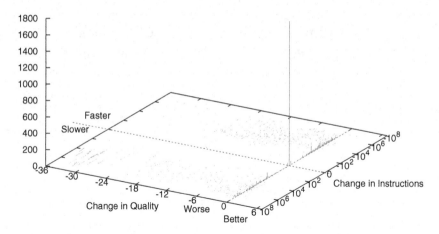

Fig. 3. Histogram of impact on speed and solution quality made by single mutations to Bowtie2 (Sect. 3.3). Many changes have no impact on quality, plotted along $x = 0$. Indeed a large number do not change its speed either (note spike at the origin). There are a few mutations which give *better* quality solutions. It is from these GP evolves a seventy fold speed up.

random change may totally break a program, mutation and crossover operations can be devised which yield populations of offspring programs in which some may be very bad but the population can also contains many reasonable programs and even a few slightly improved ones. Over time the Darwinian processes of fitness selection and inheritance [70] can amplify the good parts of the population, yielding greatly improved programs.

3.2 Auto Porting Functionality

The Unix compression utility gzip was written in C in the days of Digital Equipment Corp.'s mini-computers. It is largely unchanged. However there is one procedure (of about two pages of code) in it, which is so computationally intensive that it has been re-written in assembler for the Intel 86X architecture (i.e. Linux). The original C version is retained and is distributed as part of Software-artifact Infrastructure Repository http://sir.unl.edu [72]. We showed genetic programming could evolve a parallel implementation for an architecture not even dreamt of when the original program was written [71].

Whereas Le Goues and others use the original program's AST (abstract syntax tree) to ensure that many of the mutated programs produced by GP compile, we have used a BNF grammar (see Fig. 1). For CUDA gzip we created our grammar from generic code written by nVidia. The original function in gzip was instrumented to record its inputs and its outputs each time it was called (see Fig. 4). Essentially GP was told to create parallel code from the BNF grammar which when given a small number of example inputs (based on the instrumented code, Fig. 4) returned the same answers. The resulting parallel code is functionally the same as the old gzip code.

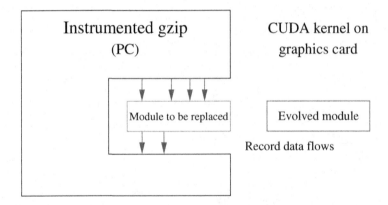

Fig. 4. Auto porting a program module to new hardware. The original code is instrumented to record the inputs (upper blue arrows) to the target function (red) and the result (lower blue arrows) it calculates. These become the test suite and fitness function when evolving the replacement code [71] (Color figure online).

3.3   Bowtie2^{GP} Improving 50 000 lines of C++

Finding the best match between strings is the life blood of Bioinformatics. Wikipedia lists more than 140 programs which do some form of Bioinformatics string matching. Modern NextGen sequencing machines generate billions of (albeit very noisy) DNA base-pair sequences.

The authors of all this software are in a bind. For their code to be useful they have to chose a tradeoff between speed, machine resources, quality of solution and functionality, which will: (1) be important to Bioinformatics and (2) not be immediately dominated by other programs. They have to choose a target point when they start, as once basic design choices (e.g. target data sources and type and size of computer) have been made, few research teams have the resources to discard what they have written and start again. Potentially genetic programming offers them a way of exploring this space of tradeoffs [47,48]. (Fig. 5 shows a two dimensional trade off between speed and quality.) GP can potentially produce many programs across a Pareto optimal front and so might say "here is a trade-off which you had not considered". This could be very useful even if the development team insist on coding a solution.

We have made a start by showing GP can transform human written DNA sequence matching code, moving it from one tradeoff point to another. In our example, the new program is specialised to a particular data source and sequence problem for which it is on average more than 70 times faster. Indeed on this particular problem, we were fortunate that not only is the variant faster but indeed it gives a slight quality improvement on average [75].

3.4   BarraCUDA

BarraCUDA [76] like Bowtie2^{GP} looks up DNA sequences. However BarraCUDA uses the computational power of nVidia graphics accelerators (GPUs) to process

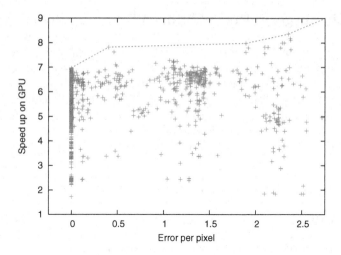

Fig. 5. Example of automatically generated Pareto tradeoff front [48]. Genetic programming used to improve 2D Stereo Camera code [73] for modern nVidia GPU [74]. Left (above 0) many programs are faster than the original code written by nVidia's image processing expert (human) and give exactly the same answers. Many other automatically generated programs are also faster but give different answers. Some (cf. dotted blue line) are faster than the best zero error program (Color figure online).

hundreds of thousands of short DNA sequences in parallel. Despite having been written by experts both on Bioinformatics and on GPUs, GP when targeted by a Human on a particular kernel was able to speed up that kernel by more than 100 times. Of course this kernel is only part of the whole program and overall speed up is more modest. Nevertheless on real examples the GI code [77] can be up to three times faster than the previous (100 % human) version Indeed with a top end K80 Tesla BarraCUDA can now be more than ten times faster than BWA on a 12 core CPU [78].

The GI version of BarraCUDA has been in use via SourceForge (http://sourceforge.net/projects/seqbarracuda/?source=typ_redirect) since 20 March 2015. In the first two months it was downloaded 230 times.

3.5 Genetically Improved GPU Based Stereo Vision

Originally the StereoCamera [73] system was specifically written by nVidia's image processing expert to show off their hardware. However in [74] we show GP is able to improve the code for hardware which had not even been designed when it was originally written. Indeed GP gave up to a seven fold speed up in the graphics kernel.

3.6 Genetically Improved GPU Based 3D Brain Imaging

GI can automatically tune an important CUDA kernel in the NiftyReg [79] medical imaging package for six very different graphics cards (see [80, Fig. 1]).

4 Plastic Surgery: Better MiniSAT from multiple Authors

Genetic Improvement has also been used to create an improved version of C++
code from multiple versions of a program written by different domain experts.
The Boolean satisfiability community has advanced rapidly since the turn of
the century. This is partly due to the "MiniSAT hack track", which encourages
people to make small changes to the MiniSAT code. Some of these variants were
evolved together to give a new MiniSAT tailored to solve interaction testing
problems [81]. It received a human competitive award (HUMIE) in 2014.

5 Creating and Incorporating New Functionality

5.1 Babel Pidgin: Adding Double Language Translation Feature

Jia et al. [82] describes another prize winning GI system. GP *including human
hints* was able to evolved new functionality externally and then search based
techniques [83] were used to graft the new code into an existing program (pidgin)
of more than 200 000 lines of C++.

5.2 Grow and Serve GP Citations

The GP grew code and grafted it into a Django web server to provide a citation
service based in Google Scholar. As an experiment, the GP bibliography used
this GP produced service. In the first 24 hours it was used 369 times from 29
countries [84].

5.3 $10^4\times$ Speedup on Folding RNA Molecules

GP was told approximately where to evolve new code within an existing parallel
program pknots [85]. It converted the original CUDA kernel, which processes
one Dynamic Programming matrix at a time, into one which processes multiple
matrices. Although only trained on five matrices, the evolved kernel can work
on up to 200 000 matrices, delivering speed ups of up ten thousand fold [86].

6 GISMO Key Findings

The idea of using existing code as its own specification is very valuable (see also
Fig. 4). Many existing specifications are informal and often incomplete. Whilst
the existing code may contain errors, the fact that it is in use shows it to be
near what is wanted and so can be used as a basis for new work. Also by using
existing test suites or automatic test case generation tools, the output of the
existing code under test can be used as its own test oracle and indeed the test
oracle for the new code. The number of tests available for validating the new code
is now only limited by machine (rather than human) resource limits. However
many of the GISMO examples given above show a very small number of tests,

perhaps just a handful (provided they are frequently changed), may be sufficient to guide the GI. With a much larger pool of tests or other validation techniques being available post evolution. Indeed when working at the source code level, GI generated software can potentially be validated by any of today's techniques, including manual inspection as well as intensive regression testing.

While human written code may be optimised for a particular objective, GI can optimise it for multiple objectives (Fig. 5). This may be particularly important if, whilst maintaining functionality of the existing code, GI can suggest unsuspected tradeoffs between speed, memory usage, energy consumption, network loading, etc. and quality.

Although code evolved from scratch tends to be small, grow and graft (GGGP) (Sect. 5) is a potential way around the problem. GGGP still evolves small new components but also uses GP to graft them into much bigger human written codes, thus creating large hybrid software.

The work on miniSAT (Sect. 4) shows GP can potentially scavenge not just code from the program it is improving but code from multiple programs by multiple authors. This GP plastic surgery [87] created in a few hours an award winning version of miniSAT tailored to solving an important software engineering problem. The automatically customised code was better at problems of this type than generic versions of miniSAT which has been optimised by leading SAT experts for years.

In software engineering there has always been a strong pressure to keep software as uniform as possible. To try and keep all the users running just a few versions. With the popularity of software product lines and possibility of multiplicity computing, we see an opposing trend. A desire to reduce the impact of malicious programmers by avoiding the current software monoculture and for more bespoke and adaptable systems. Already there is a little GI work in both avenues.

7   GISMO Impact

While the GI version of BarraCUDA (http://sourceforge.net/projects/seq barracuda/?source=typ_redirect) has been in use since March 2015, perhaps the biggest impact of the project has been to show automatic or even human assisted evolution of software can be feasible. Before 2009 automatic bug fixing was regarded as fantasy but following [4] this changed. The biggest impact of the project will be encouraging people to do what was previously considered impossible.

Sources and Datasets. The grammar based genetic programming systems and associated benchmarks are available via the GISMO (http://www.cs.ucl. ac.uk/staff/W.Langdon/gismo/#code) project web pages. Other authors have also made their systems available (e.g. Le Goues' genprog (http://genprog.cs. virginia.edu/)) or may be asked directly.

Acknowledgements. I am grateful for the assistance of Andrea Arcuri, Robert Feldt, Marc Schoenauer, Wes Weimer and Darrell Whitley. Tesla donated by nVidia (http://www.nvidia.com).

References

1. Ryan, C., Ivan, L.: Automatic parallelization of arbitrary programs. In: Langdon, W.B., Fogarty, T.C., Nordin, P., Poli, R. (eds.) EuroGP 1999. LNCS, vol. 1598, pp. 244–254. Springer, Heidelberg (1999). http://www.cs.bham.ac.uk/~ wbl/biblio/gp-html/ryan_1999_apap.html
2. Koza, J.R.: Genetic Programming: On the Programming of Computers by Natural Selection. MIT press (1992). http://www.cs.bham.ac.uk/~wbl/biblio/gp-html/koza_book.html
3. Poli, R., Langdon, W.B., McPhee, N.F.: A field guide to genetic programming (2008). Published via http://lulu.com and freely available at http://www.gp-field-guide.org.uk (With contributions by J.R. Koza). http://www.cs.bham.ac.uk/~wbl/biblio/gp-html/poli08_fieldguide.html
4. Weimer, W., Nguyen, T., Le Goues, C., Forrest, S.: Automatically finding patches using genetic programming. In: Fickas, S., (ed.) ICSE 2009, Vancouver, pp. 364–374 (2009). http://www.cs.bham.ac.uk/~wbl/biblio/gp-html/Weimer_2009_ICES.html
5. Forrest, S., Nguyen, T., Weimer, W., Le Goues, C.: A genetic programming approach to automated software repair. In: Raidl, G., et al. (eds.) GECCO 2009, pp. 947–954, ACM, Montreal (2009) (Best paper). http://www.cs.bham.ac.uk/~wbl/biblio/gp-html/DBLP_conf_gecco_ForrestNWG09.html
6. Weimer, W., Forrest, S., Le Goues, C., Nguyen, T.: Automatic program repair with evolutionary computation. Commun. ACM **53**(5), 109–116 (2010). http://www.cs.bham.ac.uk/~wbl/biblio/gp-html/Weimer_2010_ACM.html
7. Fast, E., Le Goues, C., Forrest, S., Weimer, W.: Designing better fitness functions for automated program repair. In: Branke, J., et al. (eds.) GECCO 2010, pp. 965–972. ACM (2010). http://www.cs.bham.ac.uk/~wbl/biblio/gp-html/Fast_2010_GECCO.html
8. Schulte, E., Forrest, S., Weimer, W.: Automated program repair through the evolution of assembly code. In: ASE 2010, pp. 313–316. ACM, Antwerp (2010). http://www.cs.bham.ac.uk/~wbl/biblio/gp-html/schulte10_autom_progr_repair_evolut_assem_code.html
9. Schulte, E., Fry, Z.P., Fast, E., Weimer, W., Forrest, S.: Software mutational robustness. Genet. Program Evolvable Mach. **15**(3), 281–312 (2014). http://www.cs.bham.ac.uk/~wbl/biblio/gp-html/schulte10_autom_progr_repair_evolut_assem_code.html
10. Orlov, M., Sipper, M.: Flight of the FINCH through the Java wilderness. IEEE Trans. EC **15**(2), 166–182 (2011). http://www.cs.bham.ac.uk/~wbl/biblio/gp-html/Orlov_2011_ieeeTEC.html
11. Langdon, W.B., Nordin, J.P.: Seeding genetic programming populations. In: Poli, R., Banzhaf, W., Langdon, W.B., Miller, J., Nordin, P., Fogarty, T.C. (eds.) EuroGP 2000. LNCS, vol. 1802, pp. 304–315. Springer, Heidelberg (2000). http://www.cs.bham.ac.uk/~wbl/biblio/gp-html/langdon_2000_seed.html
12. Langdon, W.B.: Genetically improved software. In: Gandomi, A.H., et al. (eds.) Handbook of Genetic Programming Applications. Springer (forthcoming). http://www.cs.bham.ac.uk/~wbl/biblio/gp-html/langdon_2015_hbgpa.html

13. Harman, M., Jones, B.F.: Search based software engineering. Inf. Softw. Technol. **43**(14), 833–839 (2001)
14. Langdon, W.B., Petke, J., White, D.R.: Genetic improvement 2015 chairs' welcome. In: GECCO 2015 Companion. ACM, Madrid (2015). http://www.cs.bham.ac.uk/~wbl/biblio/gp-html/langdon_2015_gi.html
15. Arcuri, A., Yao, X.: Co-evolutionary automatic programming for software development. Inf. Sci. **259**, 412–432 (2014). http://www.cs.bham.ac.uk/~wbl/biblio/gp-html/Arcuri2010.html
16. Hussain, D., Malliaris, S.: Evolutionary techniques applied to hashing: An efficient data retrieval method. In: Whitley, D., et al. (eds.) GECCO-2000, p. 760. Morgan Kaufmann, Las Vegas, Nevada, USA (2000). http://www.cs.bham.ac.uk/~wbl/biblio/gp-html/Hussain_2000_GECCO.html
17. Berarducci, P., Jordan, D., Martin, D., Seitzer, J.: GEVOSH: using grammatical evolution to generate hashing functions. In: Poli, R., et al. (eds.) GECCO 2004 Workshop Proceedings, Seattle, Washington, USA (2004). http://www.cs.bham.ac.uk/~wbl/biblio/gp-html/berarducci_2004_ugw_pber.html
18. Estebanez, C., Saez, Y., Recio, G., Isasi, P.: Automatic design of noncryptographic hash functions using genetic programming. Computational Intelligence (forthcoming). http://www.cs.bham.ac.uk/~wbl/biblio/gp-html/Estebanez_2014_CI.html
19. Karasek, J., Burget, R., Morsky, O.: Towards an automatic design of noncryptographic hash function. In: TSP 2011, pp. 19–23, Budapest (2011). http://www.cs.bham.ac.uk/~wbl/biblio/gp-html/Karasek_2011_TSP.html
20. Paterson, N., Livesey, M.: Evolving caching algorithms in C by genetic programming. In: Koza, J.R., et al. (eds.): Genetic Programming, pp. 262–267. Morgan Kaufmann, Stanford University, CA, USA (1997). http://www.cs.bham.ac.uk/~wbl/biblio/gp-html/Paterson_1997_ecacGP.html
21. O'Neill, M., Ryan, C.: Automatic generation of caching algorithms. In: Miettinen, K., et al. (eds.) Evolutionary Algorithms in Engineering and Computer Science, pp. 127-134, John Wiley and Sons, Jyväskylä, Finland (1999). http://www.cs.bham.ac.uk/~wbl/biblio/gp-html/oneill_1999_AGCA.html
22. Branke, J., Funes, P., Thiele, F.: Evolutionary design of en-route caching strategies. Appl. Soft Comput. **7**(3), 890–898 (2006). http://www.cs.bham.ac.uk/~wbl/biblio/gp-html/Branke_2006_ASC.html
23. Risco-Martin, J.L., Atienza, D., Colmenar, J.M., Garnica, O.: A parallel evolutionary algorithm to optimize dynamic memory managers in embedded systems. Parallel Comput. **36**(10–11), 572–590 (2010). http://www.cs.bham.ac.uk/~wbl/biblio/gp-html/RiscoMartin2010572.html
24. Wu, F., Weimer, W., Harman, M., Jia, Y., Krinke, J.: Deep parameter optimisation. In: GECCO 2015. ACM, Madrid (2015). http://www.cs.bham.ac.uk/~wbl/biblio/gp-html/Wu_2015_GECCO.html
25. Rodriguez-Mier, P., Mucientes, M., Lama, M., Couto, M.I.: Composition of web services through genetic programming. Evol. Intell. **3**(3–4), 171–186 (2010). http://www.cs.bham.ac.uk/~wbl/biblio/gp-html/Rodriguez-Mier_2010_EI.html
26. Fredericks, E.M., Cheng, B.H.C.: Exploring automated software composition with genetic programming. In: Blum, C., et al. (eds.) GECCO 2013 Companion, pp. 1733–1734. ACM, Amsterdam, The Netherlands (2013). http://www.cs.bham.ac.uk/~wbl/biblio/gp-html/Fredericks_2013_GECCOcomp.html
27. Xiao, L., Chang, C.K., Yang, H.-I., Lu, K.-S., Jiang, H.-Y.: Automated web service composition using genetic programming. In: COMPSACW 2012, pp. 7–12, Izmir (2012). http://www.cs.bham.ac.uk/~wbl/biblio/gp-html/Xiao_2012_COMPSACW.html

28. Burke, E.K., Gendreau, M., Hyde, M., Kendall, G., Ochoa, G., Ozcan, E., Qu, R.: Hyper-heuristics: a survey of the state of the art. JORS **64**(12), 1695–1724 (2013). http://www.cs.bham.ac.uk/~wbl/biblio/gp-html/Burke2013.html

29. Pappa, G.L., Ochoa, G., Hyde, M.R., Freitas, A.A., Woodward, J., Swan, J.: Contrasting meta-learning and hyper-heuristic research: the role of evolutionary algorithms. Genet. Program Evolvable Mach. **15**(1), 3–35 (2014). http://www.cs.bham.ac.uk/~wbl/biblio/gp-html/Pappa_2013_GPEM.html

30. Mahajan, A., Ali, M.S.: Superblock scheduling using genetic programming for embedded systems. In: ICCI 2008. IEEE, pp. 261–266 (2008). http://www.cs.bham.ac.uk/~wbl/biblio/gp-html/Mahajan_2008_ieeeICCI.html

31. Cadar, C., Pietzuch, P., Wolf, A.L.: Multiplicity computing: a vision of software engineering for next-generation computing platform applications. In Sullivan, K., ed.: FoSER 2010 FSE/SDP workshop, pp. 81-86. ACM, Santa Fe, New Mexico, USA (2010). http://dx.doi.org/10.1145/1882362.1882380

32. DeMillo, R.A., Offutt, A.J.: Constraint-based automatic test data generation. IEEE Trans. Software Eng. **17**(9), 900–910 (1991). http://dx.doi.org/10.1109/32.92910

33. Langdon, W.B., Harman, M., Jia, Y.: Efficient multi-objective higher order mutation testing with genetic programming. JSS **83**(12), 2416–2430 (2010). http://www.cs.bham.ac.uk/~wbl/biblio/gp-html/langdon_2010_jss.html

34. Feldt, R.: Generating diverse software versions with genetic programming: an experimental study. IEE Proceedings **145**(6), 228–236 (1998). http://www.cs.bham.ac.uk/~wbl/biblio/gp-html/feldt_1998_gdsvGPes.html

35. Imamura, K., Foster, J.A.: Fault-tolerant computing with N-version genetic programming. In Spector, L., et al. (eds.) GECCO-2001, p. 178, Morgan Kaufmann, San Francisco, California, USA (2001). http://www.cs.bham.ac.uk/~wbl/biblio/gp-html/imamura_2001_gecco.html

36. Imamura, K., Soule, T., Heckendorn, R.B., Foster, J.A.: Behavioral diversity and a probabilistically optimal GP ensemble. Genet. Program Evolvable Mach. **4**(3), 235–253 (2003). http://www.cs.bham.ac.uk/~wbl/biblio/gp-html/imamura_2003_GPEM.html

37. Langdon, W.B., Buxton, B.F.: Genetic programming for combining classifiers. In Spector, L., et al. (eds.) GECCO-2001, pp. 66–73. Morgan Kaufmann, San Francisco, California, USA (2001). http://www.cs.bham.ac.uk/~wbl/biblio/gp-html/langdon_2001_gROC.html

38. Buxton, B.F., Langdon, W.B., Barrett, S.J.: Data fusion by intelligent classifier combination. Meas. Contr. **34**(8), 229–234 (2001). http://www.cs.bham.ac.uk/~wbl/biblio/gp-html/imamura_2003_GPEM.html

39. Langdon, W.B., Poli, R.: Evolving problems to learn about particle swarm and other optimisers. In: Corne, D., et al. (eds.) CEC-2005, pp. 81–88. IEEE Press, Edinburgh, UK (2005). http://www.cs.bham.ac.uk/~wbl/biblio/gp-html/langdon_2005_CECb.html

40. Cotillon, A., Valencia, P., Jurdak, R.: Android genetic programming framework. In: Moraglio, A., Silva, S., Krawiec, K., Machado, P., Cotta, C. (eds.) EuroGP 2012. LNCS, vol. 7244, pp. 13–24. Springer, Heidelberg (2012). http://www.cs.bham.ac.uk/~wbl/biblio/gp-html/cotillon_2012_EuroGP.html

41. Lopez-Herrejon, R.E., Linsbauer, L.: Genetic improvement for software product lines: an overview and a roadmap. In: GECCO 2015 Companion. ACM, Madrid (2015). http://www.cs.bham.ac.uk/~wbl/biblio/gp-html/Lopez-Herrejon_2015_gi.html

42. Landsborough, J., Harding, S., Fugate, S.: Removing the kitchen sink from software. In GECCO 2015 Companion. ACM, Madrid (2015). http://www.cs.bham. ac.uk/~wbl/biblio/gp-html/Landsborough_2015_gi.html

43. Schulte, E., Weimer, W., Forrest, S.: Repairing COTS router firmware without access to source code or test suites: A case study in evolutionary software repair. In: GECCO 2015 Companion. ACM, Madrid (2015). http://www.cs.bham.ac.uk/ ~wbl/biblio/gp-html/Schulte_2015_gi.html

44. Yeboah-Antwi, K., Baudry, B.: Embedding adaptivity in software systems using the ECSELR framework. In: GECCO 2015 Companion. ACM, Madrid (2015). http://www.cs.bham.ac.uk/~wbl/biblio/gp-html/Yeboah-Antwi_2015_gi.html

45. White, D.R., Arcuri, A., Clark, J.A.: Evolutionary improvement of programs. IEEE Trans. EC **15**(4), 515–538 (2011). http://www.cs.bham.ac.uk/~wbl/ biblio/gp-html/White_2011_ieeeTEC.html

46. Sitthi-amorn, P., Modly, N., Weimer, W., Lawrence, J.: Genetic programming for shader simplification. ACM Trans. Graphics, **30**(6), article: 152 (2011). http://www.cs.bham.ac.uk/~wbl/biblio/gp-html/DBLP_journals_tog_Sitthi-amornMWL11.html

47. Feldt, R.: Genetic programming as an explorative tool in early software development phases. In: Ryan, C., Buckley, J. (eds.) Proceedings of the 1st International Workshop on Soft Computing Applied to Software Engineering, pp. 11–20. Limerick University Press, University of Limerick, Ireland (1999). http://www.cs.bham. ac.uk/~wbl/biblio/gp-html/feldt_1999_GPxtxsdp.html

48. Harman, M., Langdon, W.B., Jia, Y., White, D.R., Arcuri, A., Clark, J.A.: The GISMOE challenge: constructing the Pareto program surface using genetic programming to find better programs. In: ASE 2012, pp. 1–14. ACM, Essen, Germany (2012). http://www.cs.bham.ac.uk/~wbl/biblio/gp-html/Harman_2012_ASE.html

49. Lukschandl, E., Holmlund, M., Moden, E.: Automatic evolution of Java bytecode: first experience with the Java virtual machine. In: Poli, R., et al. (eds.) Late Breaking Papers at EuroGP 1998, Paris, France, CSRP-98-10, pp. 14–16, The University of Birmingham, UK (1998). http://www.cs.bham.ac.uk/~wbl/biblio/gp-html/lukschandl_1998_1java.html

50. Archanjo, G.A., Von Zuben, F.J.: Genetic programming for automating the development of data management algorithms in information technology systems. Advances in Software Engineering (2012). http://www.cs.bham.ac.uk/~wbl/biblio/gp-html/Archanjo_2012_ASE.html

51. Ryan, C.: Automatic Re-Engineering of Software using Genetic Programming. Kluwer Academic Publishers (1999). http://www.cs.bham.ac.uk/~wbl/biblio/gp-html/ryan_book.html

52. Katz, G., Peled, D.: Synthesizing, correcting and improving code, using model checking-based genetic programming. In: Bertacco, V., Legay, A. (eds.) HVC 2013. LNCS, vol. 8244, pp. 246–261. Springer, Heidelberg (2013). http://www.cs.bham.ac.uk/~wbl/biblio/gp-html/conf_hvc_KatzP13.html

53. Cody-Kenny, B., Lopez, E.G., Barrett, S.: locoGP: improving performance by genetic programming java source code. In: GECCO 2015 Companion. ACM, Madrid (2015). http://www.cs.bham.ac.uk/~wbl/biblio/gp-html/Cody-Kenny_2015_gi.html

54. Schulte, E., Dorn, J., Harding, S., Forrest, S., Weimer, W.: Post-compiler software optimization for reducing energy. In: ASPLOS 2014, pp. 639–652. ACM, Salt LakeCity, Utah, USA (2014). http://www.cs.bham.ac.uk/~wbl/biblio/gp-html/schulte2014optimization.html

55. Mrazek, V., Vasicek, Z., Sekanina, L.: Evolutionary approximation of software for embedded systems: median function. In: GECCO 2015 Companion. ACM, Madrid (2015). http://www.cs.bham.ac.uk/~wbl/biblio/gp-html/Mrazek_2015_gi.html

56. Arcuri, A., Yao, X.: A novel co-evolutionary approach to automatic software bug fixing. In: Wang, J., (ed.) WCCI 2008. IEEE, pp. 162–168 (2008). http://www.cs.bham.ac.uk/~wbl/biblio/gp-html/Arcuri_2008_cec.html

57. Le Goues, C., Dewey-Vogt, M., Forrest, S., Weimer, W.: A systematic study of automated program repair: Fixing 55 out of 105 bugs for 8 each. In: Glinz, M., (ed.) ICSE 2012, pp. 3–13 Zurich (2012). http://www.cs.bham.ac.uk/~wbl/biblio/gp-html/LeGoues_2012_ICSE.html

58. Wilkerson, J.L., Tauritz, D.: Coevolutionary automated software correction. In: Branke, J., et al. (eds.) GECCO 2010, pp. 1391-1392. ACM, Portland, Oregon, USA (2010). http://www.cs.bham.ac.uk/~wbl/biblio/gp-html/Wilkerson_2010_gecco.html

59. Bradbury, J.S., Jalbert, K.: Automatic repair of concurrency bugs. In: Di Penta, M., et al. (eds.) SSBSE 2010, Benevento, Italy (2010) (Fast abstract). http://www.cs.bham.ac.uk/~wbl/biblio/gp-html/BradburyJ10.html

60. Ackling, T., Alexander, B., Grunert, I.: Evolving patches for software repair. In: Krasnogor, N., et al. (eds.) GECCO 2011, pp. 1427-1434. ACM, Dublin, Ireland (2011). http://www.cs.bham.ac.uk/~wbl/biblio/gp-html/Ackling_2011_GECCO.html

61. Kessentini, M., Kessentini, W., Sahraoui, H., Boukadoum, M., Ouni, A.: Design defects detection and correction by example. In: ICPC 2011, pp. 81–90. IEEE, Kingston, Canada (2011). http://www.cs.bham.ac.uk/~wbl/biblio/gp-html/Kessentini_2011_ICPC.html

62. Nguyen, H.D.T., Qi, D., Roychoudhury, A., Chandra, S.: SemFix: program repair via semantic analysis. In: Cheng, B.H.C., Pohl, K., (eds.) ICSE 2013, pp. 772–781. IEEE, San Francisco, USA (2013). http://www.cs.bham.ac.uk/~wbl/biblio/gp-html/Nguyen_2013_ICSE.html

63. Kim, D., Nam, J., Song, J., Kim, S.: Automatic patch generation learned from human-written patches. In: ICSE 2013, pp. 802–811, San Francisco, USA (2013). http://www.cs.bham.ac.uk/~wbl/biblio/gp-html/Kim_2013_ICSE.html

64. Tan, S.H., Roychoudhury, A.: relifix: Automated Repair of Software Regressions. In: Canfora, G., et al. (eds.) ICSE 2015, pp. 471–482. IEEE, Florence Italy (2015)

65. Schulte, E., DiLorenzo, J., Weimer, W., Forrest, S.: Automated repair of binary and assembly programs for cooperating embedded devices. In: ASPLOS 2013, pp. 317–328. ACM, Houston, Texas, USA (2013). http://www.cs.bham.ac.uk/~wbl/biblio/gp-html/Schulte_2013_ARB_2451116_2451151.html

66. Yoo, S.: Evolving human competitive spectra-based fault localisation techniques. In: Fraser, G., Teixeira de Souza, J. (eds.) SSBSE 2012. LNCS, vol. 7515, pp. 244–258. Springer, Heidelberg (2012). http://www.cs.bham.ac.uk/~wbl/biblio/gp-html/Yoo_2012_SSBSE.html

67. Weimer, W.: advances in automated program repair and a call to arms. In: Ruhe, G., Zhang, Y. (eds.) SSBSE 2013. LNCS, vol. 8084, pp. 1–3. Springer, Heidelberg (2013). http://www.cs.bham.ac.uk/~wbl/biblio/gp-html/Weimer_2013_SSBSE.html

68. Cody-Kenny, B., Barrett, S.: The emergence of useful bias in self-focusing genetic programming for software optimisation. In: Ruhe, G., Zhang, Y. (eds.) SSBSE 2013. LNCS, vol. 8084, pp. 306–311. Springer, Heidelberg (2013). Graduate Student Track http://www.cs.bham.ac.uk/~wbl/biblio/gp-html/Cody-Kenny_2013_SSBSE.html

69. Gabel, M., Su, Z.: A study of the uniqueness of source code. In: FSE 2010, pp. 147–156. ACM (2010). http://www.cs.bham.ac.uk/~wbl/biblio/gp-html/Gabel_2010_FSE.html

70. Darwin, C.: The Origin of Species. Penguin classics, 1985 edn. John Murray (1859)

71. Langdon, W.B., Harman, M.: Evolving a CUDA kernel from an nVidia template. In: Sobrevilla, P., (ed.) WCCI 2010, pp. 2376-2383. IEEE, Barcelona (2010). http://www.cs.bham.ac.uk/~wbl/biblio/gp-html/langdon_2010_cigpu.html

72. Hutchins, M., Foster, H., Goradia, T., Ostrand, T.: Experiments on the effectiveness of dataflow- and control-flow-based test adequacy criteria. In: ICSE 1994, pp. 191–200 (1994). urlhttp://dx.doi.org/10.1109/ICSE.1994.296778

73. Stam, J.: Stereo imaging with CUDA. Technical report, nVidia (2008)

74. Langdon, W.B., Harman, M.: Genetically improved CUDA C++ software. In: Nicolau, M., Krawiec, K., Heywood, M.I., Castelli, M., García-Sánchez, P., Merelo, J.J., Rivas Santos, V.M., Sim, K. (eds.) EuroGP 2014. LNCS, vol. 8599, pp. 87–99. Springer, Heidelberg (2014). http://www.cs.bham.ac.uk/~wbl/biblio/gp-html/langdon_2014_EuroGP.html

75. Langdon, W.B., Harman, M.: Optimising existing software with genetic programming. IEEE Trans. EC **19**(1), 118–135 (2015). http://www.cs.bham.ac.uk/~wbl/biblio/gp-html/Langdon_2013_ieeeTEC.html

76. Klus, P., Lam, S., Lyberg, D., Cheung, M.S., Pullan, G., McFarlane, I., Yeo, G.S.H., Lam, B.Y.H.: BarraCUDA - a fast short read sequence aligner using graphics processing units. BMC Research Notes **5**(1), 27 (2012).http://dx.doi.org/10.1186/1756-0500-5-27

77. Langdon, W.B., Lam, B.Y.H., Petke, J., Harman, M.: Improving CUDA DNA analysis software with genetic programming. In: GECCO 2015. ACM, Madrid (2015). http://www.cs.bham.ac.uk/~wbl/biblio/gp-html/Langdon_2015_GECCO.html

78. Langdon, W.B., Lam, B.Y.H.: Genetically improved barraCUDA. Research Note RN/15/03, Department of Computer Science, University College London (2015). http://arxiv.org/abs/arXiv:1505.07855

79. Modat, M., Ridgway, G.R., Taylor, Z.A., Lehmann, M., Barnes, J., Hawkes, D.J., Fox, N.C., Ourselin, S.: Fast free-form deformation using graphics processing units. Comput. Methods Programs Biomed. **98**(3), 278–284 (2010). http://dx.doi.org/10.1016/j.cmpb.2009.09.002

80. Langdon, W.B., Modat, M., Petke, J., Harman, M.: Improving 3D medical image registration CUDA software with genetic programming. In: Igel, C., et al. (eds.) GECCO 2014, pp. 951-958. ACM, Vancouver, BC, Canada (2014). http://arxiv.org/abs/arXiv:1505.07855

81. Petke, J., Harman, M., Langdon, W.B., Weimer, W.: Using genetic improvement and code transplants to specialise a C++ program to a problem class. In: Nicolau, M., Krawiec, K., Heywood, M.I., Castelli, M., García-Sánchez, P., Merelo, J.J., Rivas Santos, V.M., Sim, K. (eds.) EuroGP 2014. LNCS, vol. 8599, pp. 137–149. Springer, Heidelberg (2014). http://www.cs.bham.ac.uk/~wbl/biblio/gp-html/Petke_2014_EuroGP.html

82. Harman, M., Jia, Y., Langdon, W.B.: Babel Pidgin: SBSE can grow and graft entirely new functionality into a real world system. In: Le Goues, C., Yoo, S. (eds.) SSBSE 2014. LNCS, vol. 8636, pp. 247–252. Springer, Heidelberg (2014). http://www.cs.bham.ac.uk/~wbl/biblio/gp-html/Harman_2014_Babel.html

83. Harman, M.: Software engineering meets evolutionary computation. Comput. **44**(10), 31–39 (2011). Cover feature http://www.cs.bham.ac.uk/~wbl/biblio/gp-html/Harman_2011_ieeeC.html

84. Jia, Y., Harman, M., Langdon, W.B., Marginean, A.: Grow and serve: Growing Django citation services using SBSE. In: Yoo, S., Minku, L. (eds.) SSBSE 2015. Challenge Track, Bergamo, Italy (2015). http://www.cs.bham.ac.uk/~wbl/biblio/gp-html/jia_2015_gsgp.html

85. Reeder, J., Steffen, P., Giegerich, R.: pknotsRG: RNA pseudoknot folding including near-optimal structures and sliding windows. Nucleic Acids Res. **35**(Suppl. 2), W320–W324 (2007). http://dx.doi.org/10.1093/nar/gkm258

86. Langdon, W.B., Harman, M.: Grow and graft a better CUDA pknotsRG for RNA pseudoknot free energy calculation. In: GECCO 2015 Companion. ACM, Madrid (2015). http://www.cs.bham.ac.uk/~wbl/biblio/gp-html/langdon_2015_gi_pknots.html

87. Barr, E.T., Brun, Y., Devanbu, P., Harman, M., Sarro, F.: The plastic surgery hypothesis. In: Orso, A., et al. (eds.) FSE 2014. ACM, Hong Kong (2014). http://earlbarr.com/publications/psh.pdf

Research Papers

Amortised Optimisation of Non-functional Properties in Production Environments

Shin Yoo[(✉)]

Korea Advanced Institute of Science and Technology,
291 Daehak-ro, Yuseong-gu, Daejeon 305-338, Republic of Korea
shin.yoo@cs.kaist.ac.kr

Abstract. Search Based Software Engineering has high potential for optimising non-functional properties such as execution time or power consumption. However, many non-functional properties are dependent not only on the software system under consideration but also the environment that surrounds the system. This necessitates a support for online, in situ optimisation. This paper introduces the novel concept of amortised optimisation which allows such online optimisation. The paper also presents two case studies: one that seeks to optimise JIT compilation, and another to optimise a hardware dependent algorithm. The results show that, by using the open source libraries we provide, developers can improve the speed of their Python script by up to 8.6 % with virtually no extra effort, and adapt a hardware dependent algorithm automatically for unseen CPUs.

1 Introduction

Non-functional properties have increasingly been the focus of Search Based Software Engineering (SBSE) work [2]. The inherent dynamic nature of SBSE, i.e. measuring the fitness from actual executions of the subject of optimisation, makes it a powerful tool to deal with non-functional properties. Testing of temporal behaviours have received a considerable amount of interest [4,8,16,18]; other properties like Quality of Service [6,14] and security [5,9,10] are emerging fields of research.

Most existing literature on non-functional properties concerns what can be called *offline* optimisation: we define an optimisation problem to improve a specific non-functional property, and consequently obtain one or more solutions by using meta-heuristic optimisation algorithms, which are then deployed. This approach overlooks an important and challenging element of non-functional properties: environmental dependency. Non-functional behaviours of software systems are hard to predict precisely because they are heavily affected by the various environmental factors ranging from operational profiles of input data to the hardware that runs the system. By performing the optimisation offline, we detach the subjects from their environments and tailor our solution to the specific environment in which we optimise.

M. Barros and Y. Labiche (Eds.): SSBSE 2015, LNCS 9275, pp. 31–46, 2015.
DOI: 10.1007/978-3-319-22183-0_3

This offline approach raises two issues about the quality of the resulting solutions. First, it is difficult to avoid sampling bias. Recreating the production environment precisely can be difficult, because certain factors are either highly variable (e.g. hardware components), or hard to emulate (e.g. realistic user load for web applications). Consequently, offline optimisation can introduce bias that favours the often limited optimisation environment. Second, even when the offline optimisation is satisfactory, the production environment may change in such a way that degrades the behaviour of the deployed system (e.g. upgraded hardware with different performance profiles). This necessitates that the system is taken offline and re-optimised, which may be difficult in industrial settings.

One way to overcome these problems is to provide built-in adaptivity in the deployed software, so that the optimisation can take place in the production environment after deployment. Since we will be optimising in the real environment, there cannot be any sampling bias. Because the adaptivity is built-in, there is no need to take the system offline to optimise for the changed environment; the system will continue to adapt to changes. Naturally, the focus is on how to perform the optimisation without damaging the performance of the system in the production environment.

We introduce a novel concept called amortised optimisation. Executions of any metaheuristic optimisation can be amortised across multiple fitness evaluations. Normally, optimisation algorithms perform fitness evaluations either one by one (if it is a local search) or as a group (a population-based algorithm). With amortised optimisation, it is the fitness evaluation that drives the optimisation algorithm. Whenever the System Under Metaheuristic Optimisation (SUMO) is executed, we measure one fitness value out of it, and drive the optimisation forward by a single step. One iteration of the optimisation – either the evaluation of neighbours and the move to a better neighbour (a local search), or the evaluation of an entire population and the move to the next generation (a population-based algorithm) – will consist of multiple executions of SUMO.

The paper investigates this novel approach to optimisation of non-functional properties through two case studies. The first concerns adapting to different software: we apply the amortised optimisation to improve Just-In-Time (JIT) compilation parameters in a state-of-the-art Python runtime, pypy [3], and measure the impact on speed using benchmarks. For the pypy runtime, this can be seen as adapting to Python scripts it has not executed before. The second study focuses on hardware differences: we apply amortised optimisation to improve blocked matrix multiplication [7], whose performance depends on the combination of block size parameter and the size of the L1 cache in the CPU that executes the blocked algorithm. From the point of the algorithm, this can be seen as adapting to a CPU that it has not been executed on before. Both studies are supported by open source implementations of amortised optimisation techniques. The results show that amortised optimisation can improve non-functional properties of SUMO without knowing the details of the production environment in advance.

The contributions of this paper are as follows:

- **Amortised Optimisation:** we introduce the concept of amortised optimisation, which takes place over multiple executions of SUMO in order to reduce the optimisation overhead with each execution. We make open source libraries for Java and pypy JIT optimisation available.
- **Empirical Evaluation:** we present two exploratory case studies of the application of amortised optimisation, focusing on software and hardware differences respectively. The first study seeks to optimise JIT compilation parameters of a Python runtime, without knowing which scripts will be executed in advance. The second study aims to optimise the block size in blocked matrix multiplication, without knowing which CPU the algorithm will be executed on in advance.

The rest of the paper is organised as follows. Section 2 introduces the concept of amortised optimisation. Section 3 presents the case study on JIT compilation parameters, while Sect. 4 presents the case study on blocked matrix multiplication. Section 5 discusses the related work, and Sect. 6 concludes.

2   Amortised Optimisation

Many of non-functional properties of software depend on the exact context and environment it is being used in. Consequently, the best way to adapt to different contexts and environments is to optimise these properties *in situ*. However, meta-heuristic optimisation often relies on a non-trivial number of fitness evaluations, which, in the context of Search-Based Software Engineering, may contain other software, model, or even hardware in the loop [12]. The inhibitive cost effectively prevents software to be optimised in the production environment.

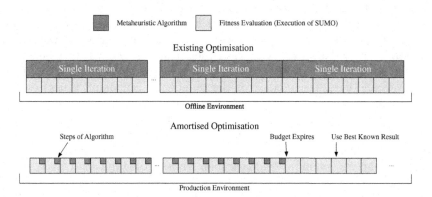

Fig. 1. Amortised optimisation interleaves executions of SUMO, from which the fitness is measured, with partial executions of metaheuristic algorithms. Each normal use of SUMO doubles as a single fitness evaluation, driving the optimisation by small steps. When the initial budget for optimisation expires, SUMO simply continues to run with the best known result.

We posit that the cost of in situ optimisation can be amortised. Figure 1 presents the conceptual overview of the amortised optimisation approach. With existing optimisation techniques (depicted at the top), algorithms perform multiple iterations, each of which, in turn, executes the SUMO to measure the fitness. This process is performed in the offline environment, and the result is deployed. With amortised optimisation (depicted at the bottom), a single iteration of a metaheuristic algorithm is broken down into several smaller steps to be executed as part of each execution of SUMO. Essentially, we seek to pause and resume the metaheuristic algorithms with persistence support. By keeping each step smaller, we minimise the computational overhead to the normal operation of SUMO. Gradually, SUMO will find better solutions: when the budget for optimisation runs out, SUMO can continue to use the best known result.

Any metaheuristic algorithm can be amortised in the proposed way, because there is little dependency between the algorithm itself and the execution of SUMO for fitness evaluation. A more limiting factor would be the nature of the optimisation problem: since we are to explore the search space with the actual uses of SUMO, we cannot afford to functionally sabotage any execution. For example, a suboptimal candidate solution may be allowed to slow the software a little bit, or use more memory than usual. However, it cannot affect the functionality of SUMO so that it produces incorrect output. Consequently, amortised optimisation is more easily applicable to tuning performance-related parameters than to perform Genetic Improvement that may crash the SUMO [13]. For the latter, parallel execution of two instances of SUMO may provide a solution: such parallel execution has been previously studied to recover from regression faults while the system is running online [11].

2.1 State-Based Steps: A Hill Climbing Example

Let us present a high-level model of amortised hill climbing algorithm, which is shown in Fig. 2 in a state-based model format. Vertices represent the state the algorithm can be in; edges represent potential control flows between algorithm states. Edge labels are written in the format of X/Y, where X denotes a transition trigger and Y denotes the set of actions performed during the transition. Variable eval keeps track of the number of remaining fitness evaluations available to the algorithm. N is a set of neighbouring solutions: NEXT(N) iterates over neighbours, while HASNEXT(N) checks whether the iteration is over. ISLOCALOPTIMA() checks whether the current candidate solution is a local optimum. Finally, RETURN(x) returns x as a candidate solution for the SUMO to use. Note that we assume a feedback loop from the SUMO back to x, which provides the fitness value: this is not depicted in Fig. 2.

Whenever the SUMO is executed, it asks for a candidate solution x from the amortised optimisation. The amortised hill climbing algorithm first retrieves its current status from the persistence layer, then executes transitions until it makes a RETURN(x) call. For example, when the SUMO with the amortised hill climbing algorithm is executed for the first time, it will start in the initial node ("Random Solution"): since $eval > 0$ at the beginning, a transition is triggered,

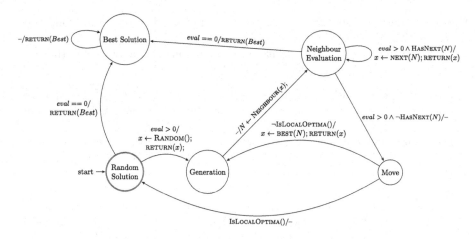

Fig. 2. State-based model of amortised hill climbing algorithm: $return(x)$ decreases the remaining number of fitness evaluations, $eval$, by 1.

and the algorithm returns the randomly generated x. Finally, it records the current state ("Generate") to the persistence layer and pauses. The next time the SUMO is executed, the algorithm resumes itself from the stored status, and the next transition (to "Evaluate Neighbours") is immediately triggered, while generating neighbours of the current x. This time, the algorithm only pauses when the second transition is triggered and the call RETURN(x) is made (which returns the first solution in N).

3 Case Study: Optimising the JIT Parameters for Pypy

3.1 JIT Parameter Optimisation

Pypy is a Python runtime implementation with a strong focus on Just In Time (JIT) compilation [3]. The JIT compilation mechanism used by pypy is the meta-tracing JIT. Tracing JIT starts by profiling the code to identify frequently executed, or *hot*, loops. In the next stage, the runtime records the history of all operations executed during a single iteration of a hot loop. These are then translated into the native machine code. What is unique with pypy is that the tracing JIT is not applied to the user script, but rather to the interpreter that runs the user script (hence the name, *meta*-tracing).

How aggressively pypy tries to JIT compile the user script depends on a set of parameters that control the behaviour of the tracing JIT. While JIT compilation in general can make Python, which is interpreted, significantly faster with pypy, it is not always the case that JIT compiling more of the user script results in shorter execution time. The more aggressive pypy tries to JIT compile, the higher the cost of tracing becomes. If the gain in JIT compilation does not exceed the cost, compiling more of the user script can actually slow pypy down. This trade off is unique to each user script and the environment pypy runs in. Therefore, finding the desirable set of JIT parameters for pypy can be an ideal application for the in situ, amortised optimisation.

Among the parameters that control the behaviour of the pypy JIT, the case study in this paper focuses on the following three:

- **Function threshold:** This parameter determines the number of times a function has to be executed before it is traced from the beginning. Default value in pypy is 1619.
- **Loop threshold:** This parameter determines the number of times a loop has to be executed before it is identified as a hot loop. Default value in pypy is 1039.
- **Trace eagerness:** To ensure correctness, pypy inserts *guards* in the translated code. When guards fail (an unpredicted branching direction can be a potential cause), tracing JIT falls back to interpreting the loop. If guard failure happens above certain threshold, tracing JIT attempts to translate the sub-path from the point of guard failure to the end of the loop (this is called a *bridge*). This parameter determines the number of times a guard has to fail before pypy compiles the bridge. Default value in pypy is 200.

These parameters have been chosen after consulting the developers of pypy. We have also been advised to set the loop threshold to be smaller than the function threshold. Consequently, the implementation of amortised optimisation of JIT for pypy replaces the loop threshold parameter with a threshold ratio parameter, whose value is within $(0, 1)$. The actual loop threshold parameter is set to [function threshold] · [threshold ratio]. For function threshold, we use the range of $[10, 4900]$; for trace eagerness, we use the range of $[1, 1000]$.

3.2   Experimental Setup

Benchmarks. We chose 8 benchmark scripts from the standard benchmark suite with which the speed of pypy is evaluated [17]. Table 1 describes the user script studied in this paper.

Each benchmark script contains a main test function that performs the operation described in Table 1. The scripts have been slightly modified to repeat their main test functions 50 times with each execution: this is to overcome the inherent randomness in measuring execution times. The execution time is measured using the system clock, starting from the invocation of the test function, and ending when it returns. It does not include any time used by the amortised optimisation itself. The rationale is twofold: the overhead for a single execution of the user script is very light, and when the amortised optimisation finishes (i.e. runs out of the allocated fitness evaluations), it becomes virtually zero.

Implementation. The amortised optimisation for JIT parameters is implemented into a Python package called piacin[1]. Since the JIT parameters only

---

[1] Piacin is made available as open source software at https://bitbucket.org/ntrolls/piacin.

Table 1. Benchmark user scripts used for the JIT optimisation case study

Script	Description
bm_call_method.py	Repeated method calls in Python
bm_django.py	Use django to generate 100 by 100 tables
bm_nbody.py	Predict n-body planetary movements[a]
bm_nqueens.py	Solve the 8 queens problem
bm_regex_compile.py	Forced recompliations of regular expressions
bm_regex_v8.py	Regular expression matching benchmark adopted from V8[b]
bm_spambayes.py	Apply a Bayesian spam filter[c] to a stored mailbox
bm_spitfire.py	Generate HTML tables using spitfire[d] library

[a]Adopted from http://shootout.alioth.debian.org/u64q/benchmark.php?test= nbody&lang=python&id=4.
[b]Google's Javascript Runtime: https://code.google.com/p/v8/.
[c]http://spambayes.sourceforge.net
[d]A template compiler library: https://code.google.com/p/spitfire/

need to be set once during the execution of a single user script, piacin similarly only needs to be called twice: when the user script starts (to configure pypy with the current parameters), and when it finishes (to record the fitness value associate with the current parameters). The first hook is implemented by implementing piacin as a Python package, and placing the JIT configuration code as part of the package initialisation. The second hook is implemented by using the atexit hook provided by Python by default. The benefits of this package-based design is that the user only needs to include piacin package (i.e. to have import piacin at the beginning of the user script) to benefit from it.

The amortised optimisation algorithm in piacin is steepest ascent hill climbing. Neighbourhood solutions are generated by adding and subtracting predefined step values to each of the parameters: 20 for function threshold, 10 for trace eagerness, and 0.05 for threshold ratio. When the newly generated candidate solution has any parameter outside the predefined range, the parameter value is wrapped around the range.

We use the default parameters of pypy as the starting point of the hill climbing. Since these parameters are the result of careful benchmarking, it would be wasteful to discard them without consideration. However, when the hill climbing reaches local optima, we fall back to the random restart mechanism.

Control vs. Treatment Group. The control group consists of 20 un-optimised runs of user benchmark scripts. Each control group run contains 20 un-optimised pypy executions of the corresponding scripts. The treatment group consists of 20 optimised runs of user benchmark scripts. Each treatment group run contains 100 optimised pypy executions of the corresponding scripts: 80 executions at the beginning are used for optimisation, the best solution from which is used by the remaining 20 executions. Both groups have been executed with pypy version

2.4.0 on Mac OS X 10.10.2, using Intel Xeon 3.3 Hz CPU with 6 cores and 16 GB
of RAM. All the user scripts are single threaded and were executed one by one.

3.3   Results

Figures 3 and 4 show the boxplots of 20 runs of both control and treatment
groups. The x-axis shows the sequence of repeated executions of user scripts in
each run; the y-axis shows the execution time in seconds. Visual observation
reveals that, for some user scripts, the execution time after the amortised optimisation can be indeed shorter than before: optimisation for bm_regex_v8.py
shows a very clear trajectory with improving fitness (i.e. decreasing execution time), while bm_nbody.py, bm_nqueens.py, bm_regex_compile.py, and
bm_spambayes.py settle down with shorter execution times after exploring the
search space during the optimisation.

With some user scripts, such as bm_nbody.py and bm_nqueens.py, the very
first execution of the user script during amortised optimisation already shows
shorter execution time. This appears to be counter-intuitive, as the parameters
are the same as the default ones when the amortised optimisation runs begin.

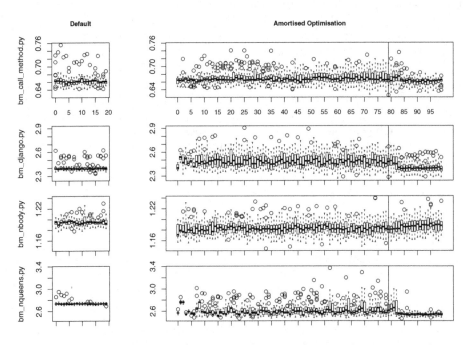

Fig. 3. Boxplots of execution times of user scripts with and without amortised optimisation applied to pypy. Plots on the left shows the execution times of benchmark
scripts from 20 separate runs, each of which repeats the script 20 times. Plots on the
right shows 20 runs, each of which repeats the script 100 times. The first 80 executions
are used for the amortised optimisation; the remaining 20 executions show the results
of the optimised JIT parameters.

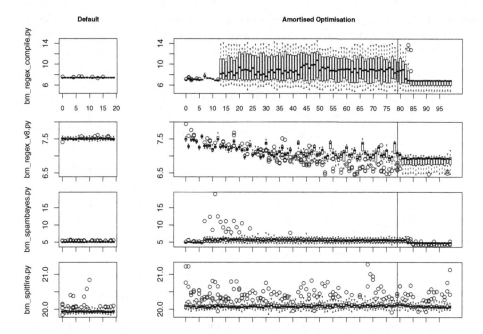

Fig. 4. Boxplots of execution times of user scripts with and without amortised optimisation applied to pypy. Plots on the left shows the execution times of benchmark scripts from 20 separate runs, each of which repeats the script 20 times. Plots on the right shows 20 runs, each of which repeats the script 100 times. The first 80 executions are used for the amortised optimisation; the remaining 20 executions show the results of the optimised JIT parameters.

This is explained by the fact that, when piacin is applied, pypy does execute a little bit more Python code (that belongs to piacin) before the benchmark test function is invoked. Since the tracing JIT in pypy is applied to the interpreter of Python rather than the user script, this extra Python code will inevitably make certain parts of Python interpreter within pypy *hotter* than when the user script is executed without piacin.

Table 2 contains both the descriptive statistics and the results of the hypothesis testing. Execution times of both the default and optimised runs passed the Shapiro-Wilk normality test; consequently, we use mean and standard deviation as descriptive statistics and t-test to test the alternative hypothesis that the execution times from the optimised runs are shorter than those from the default ($\alpha = 0.05$). The results of the hypothesis tests confirm the visual observation, as five user scripts show shorter execution time that are statistically significant. In case of bm_regex_v8.py, the optimised runs are faster by 8.6 %.

Table 2. Descriptive statistics of the execution time (in seconds) and the p-values of the hypothesis testing from the `pypy` case study. The user script `bm_regex_v8.py` becomes 8.6 % faster after the amortised optimisation.

Subject	Default		Optimised		p-value
	Mean	Std. Dev.	Mean	Std. Dev.	
`bm_call_method.py`	0.6631	0.0150	0.6630	0.0130	0.4478
`bm_django.py`	2.4018	0.0397	2.4161	0.0753	0.9996
`bm_nbody.py`	1.1948	0.0071	1.1871	0.0136	<1e-4
`bm_nqueens.py`	2.7367	0.0237	2.5595	0.0743	<1e-4
`bm_regex_v8.py`	7.5045	0.0347	6.8580	0.1583	<1e-4
`bm_regex_compile.py`	7.4155	0.0471	6.8786	1.5073	<1e-4
`bm_spambayes.py`	5.0654	0.1654	4.9346	0.3851	<1e-4
`bm_spitfire.py`	19.9485	0.0861	20.1045	0.1228	1.0000

4   Case Study: Optimising Algorithms to Hardware

The second case study concerns the optimisation of performance critical parameter against different hardware components. The subject algorithm is the Blocked Matrix Multiplication (BMM).

Algorithm 1. BMM

Input: Size of matrices, n, n-by-n matrices A and B

Output: matrix C, which equals to $A \cdot B$

(1) $n\_blocks \leftarrow \lceil \frac{n}{BS} \rceil$
(2)   **for** $b_i = 0$ **to** $b_i < n\_blocks$
(3) $i \leftarrow b_i * BS$
(4)   **for** $b_j = 0$ **to** $b_j < n\_blocks$
(5) $j \leftarrow b_j * BS$
(6)   **for** $b_k = 0$ **to** $b_k < n\_blocks$
(7) $k \leftarrow b_k * BS$
(8)   BLOCK(n, A, B, C, i, j, k)

Algorithm 2. BLOCK

Input: Matrix size, n, matrices A, B, and C,
indices i, j, and k

Output: Updates matrix C

(1) $\_M \leftarrow (i + BS > n?n - i : BS)$
(2) $\_N \leftarrow (j + BS > n?n - j : BS)$
(3) $\_K \leftarrow (k + BS > n?n - k : BS)$
(4)   **for** $\_i = 0$ **to** $\_i < \_M$
(5)   **for** $\_j = 0$ **to** $\_j < \_N$
(6) $\_cij \leftarrow C[j + i * n +_j +_i * n]$
(7)   **for** $\_k = 0$ **to** $\_k < \_K$
(8) $\_cij+ = A[i \cdot n + k + \_i \cdot n + \_k] \cdot$
(9) $B[j + k \cdot n + \_j + \_k \cdot n]$
(10) $C[j+i\cdot n+\_j+\_i\cdot n] = \_cij$

4.1   Blocked Matrix Multiplication (BMM)

Algorithms 1 and 2 collectively present the Blocked Matrix Multiplication for square matrices. Algorithm 1 breaks down the matrices into smaller blocks of size BS (Block Size), and invokes Algorithm 2 for each of them. The introduction of additional loops may appear harmful to performance. However, having nested loops around a smaller region of memory allows BMM to exploit better CPU pipelining and higher cache hit rate, resulting in faster overall computation.

The key to the increased performance is the size of the block. However, choosing the ideal size depends on details of the hardware environment, such as the size of the L1 cache. Hard-coding a fixed block size into BMM may produce desirable performance on one machine, but if the code is deployed to and executed on another machine with a different CPU, there is no guarantee that the same performance will be retained. This provides a compelling use case for amortised optimisation.

4.2   Experimental Setup

Implementation. We use a Java implementation of the BMM algorithm for matrices of double type. The amortised optimisation framework, called NIA^{3}CIN (Non-Invasive Amortised and Automated Adaptivity Code Injection), is based on the hill climbing algorithm and is also implemented in Java[2]. To be as unintrusive as possible, NIA^{3}CIN uses a publish-subscribe style event bus to establish communication between the SUMO and the optimisation. Parameters to be optimised (in the case study, the block size), as well as the measure of the fitness (in the case study, the number of floating point multiplications performed per millisecond), need to be marked with annotation. Before the parameter is to be used, the SUMO needs to call NIA^{3}CIN so that the parameter variable is updated with the current solution; after the parameter has been used, the SUMO needs to call NIA^{3}CIN so that the fitness is fed back to the optimisation.

The range of block size was set to $[1, 512]$. NIA^{3}CIN generates neighbouring solutions by adding and subtracting 1 to the current block size. When moving through consecutive block sizes, certain sizes will be evaluated twice: first as the current solution, and second as a neighbour. Since the non-functional fitness measure is expected to be noisy, the redundant behaviour was left in NIA^{3}CIN deliberately, providing opportunities to evaluate the same solution more than once (and, therefore, getting clearer measures of fitness).

Environment. Table 3 shows three different CPUs for which the BMM algorithm was optimised in this study. Intel Xeon is a 6 code desktop CPU with 32 KB instruction and data cache; the Core-i7 used for this study is a mobile (laptop) version, which has the same cache provision as the Xeon CPU. Finally, to investigate how well the amortised optimisation can adapt to an environment

---

[2] NIA^{3}CIN is made available as open source software at https://bitbucket.org/ntrolls/ niacin.

Table 3. Information about CPUs for which BMM was optimised

CPU	Clock frequency	L1 instruction cache	L1 data cache
Intel Xeon W3680[a]	3.33 GHz	32 KB	32 KB
Intel Core-i7 3820QM[a]	2.7 GHz	32 KB	32 KB
ARM1176 (BCM2835 SoC)[b]	250 MHz	16 KB	16 KB

[a]These Intel CPUs share data and instruction caches between two processor threads.
[b]Raspberry Pi Model B, first edition.

with very limited resources, we use the ARM1176 core on a Broadcom BCM2835 System-on-Chip, which is found in Raspberry Pi version 1 model B. Both Intel CPUs ran OS X 10.10.2 and Java SE Runtime (build 1.8.0_25-b17) with the HotSpot 64-Bit Server VM (build 25.25-b02); Raspberry Pi ran Linux 3.18.8 and Java SE Runtime (build 1.8.0-b132, mixed mode) with the HotSpot Client VM (build 25.0-b70, mixed mode).

Data Collection. For this study, to have a control group without the amortised optimisation would mean to execute the BMM algorithm with a fixed arbitrary block size, which would contribute little to investigating how the optimisation can help. Instead, we fixed the starting block size to 2 and repeated matrix multiplications for 100 times on different CPUs: 80 multiplications have been used by the amortised optimisation to search for the best block size, while the remaining 20 multiplications used the known best block size. This process was repeated for 20 times per CPU to cater for the inherent randomness in the algorithm. On Intel CPUs, we used matrices of size 1,000 by 1,000; on the Raspberry Pi, we used matrices of size 500 by 500. The fitness value is measured by the number of floating point operations per millisecond, using the system clock.

4.3   Results

Figure 5 shows the results of the amortised optimisation of the BMM algorithm for different CPUs. The boxplots on the left show how the fitness value (the number of floating point operations per millisecond) across the 20 different runs (x-axis represents the number of times the BMM is executed). The boxplots on the right show which block size was tried: although the hill climbing algorithm relies on the random restart at different points in different runs, these boxplots still reveal interesting trends in the optimisation of the block size. The vertical lines depict the point at which the optimisation stops and the BMM starts using the best known solution.

Both Xeon and Core-i7 benefit from larger block size, up to around 30, which can be observed from the relatively smooth shapes formed of individual boxplots and the straight, consistent increase in the block size in executions 1 to 30. Block sizes from ARM1176 show a much wider exploration of the search space, which did not necessarily result in increased fitness value. For all three CPUs, both

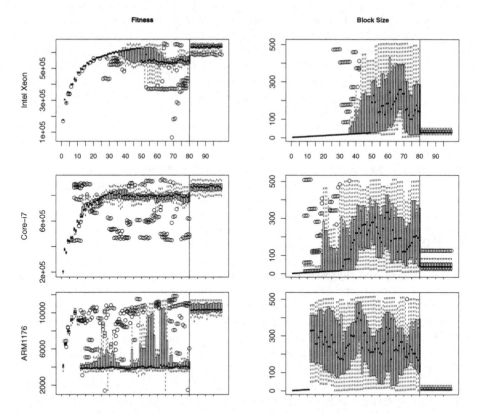

Fig. 5. Changes in the fitness (i.e. number of floating point operations per millisecond) and the block size from 20 runs of BMM for different CPUs. BMM on both Xeon and Core-i7 benefits from increasing block sizes up to around 30. BMM on ARM1176 performs better with much a smaller block size.

the fitness values and the block sizes show relatively small dispersion, suggesting that the optimisations did converge.

Table 4 shows the descriptive statistics of the BMM algorithm, before (i.e. of the first executions of each of the 20 runs) and after the amortised optimisation (i.e. of the last 20 executions of each of the 20 runs). Both the fitness values and the block sizes passed Shapiro-Wilk normality test. For all CPUs, the amortised optimisation can significantly increase the performance of the BMM. An interesting observation is the comparison of Xeon and Core-i7. Despite the higher clock frequency, Xeon performs fewer floating point operations per millisecond. While seemingly counter-intuitive, this shows that NIA^{3}CIN exploits the capabilities of each CPU appropriately. The Xeon W3680 is an older model than the Core-i7 3820QM, and the Core-i7 has been shown to outperform the Xeon in a single core benchmark [1].

Note that this optimisation has been performed automatically and *while* the BMM was operating correctly, using 80 executions. More importantly, if the

Table 4. Descriptive statistics of the BMM algorithm

CPU	Block size = 2		Optimised			
	Mean fitness	Std. Dev.	Mean fitness	Std. Dev.	Mean block size	Std. Dev.
Xeon	305189.00	1118.35	634510.13	17254.99	32.25	10.52
Core-i7	377196.74	6360.66	863878.91	34566.63	44.05	26.85
ARM1176	6531.64	124.07	10486.23	574.29	12.90	8.97

algorithm is deployed onto a different CPU, the optimisation can start again simply by assigning more budget for fitness evaluations. This can be a significant reduction in effort compared to manual trial and error approach.

5   Related Work

Existing SBSE work that seek to improve non-functional properties almost exclusively uses offline optimisation. Langdon and Harman improved a non-functional property of a non-trivial C++ program using Genetic Programming (GP) [13]. The GP modified several lines in the source code of the original program, making it 70 times faster on average while being as good as the original semantically. The GP-based improvement is much more profound than changing the value of a variable, as it actually patches the source code. However, it also required a significant amount of computation time for off-line optimisation. GP has also been applied to specialise the MiniSAT solver for specific problem instances [15]. Wu et al. optimised the behaviour of the dynamic memory allocation in C programs by revealing and optimising hidden parameters [19]. While the aspect of parameter optimisation bears similarity to this paper, Wu et al. also optimised the SUMO in an offline environment. As far as we know, this is the first work that injects the optimisation into the SUMO so that the non-functional properties can be optimised in situ.

6   Conclusion

This paper introduces the concept of amortised optimisation and presented two case studies: optimisation of JIT compilation parameters of pypy Python runtime, and optimisation of the block size of Blocked Matrix Multiplication (BMM) algorithm. In both cases, the optimisation gradually takes place while the Software Under Metaheuristic Optimisation (SUMO) operates normally. Both implementations are available as ready-to-use open source libraries. Using these libraries, developers can inject online adaptivity into their software system, allowing users to gain performance simply by using the software repeatedly. The JIT optimisation can result in up to 8.6 % improvement in speed; the BMM optimisation can adapt to new hardware platform by finding an effective block size automatically.

Acknowledgement. We would like to thank Carl Friedrich Bolz and Laurence Tratt for the informative discussion about the technical details of pypy.

References

1. CPUBoss: a benchmark comparison between Xeon W3680 and Core-i7 3820QM. http://cpuboss.com/cpus/Intel-Xeon-W3680-vs-Intel-Core-i7-3820QM
2. Afzal, W., Torkar, R., Feldt, R.: A systematic review of search-based testing for non-functional system properties. Inf. Softw. Technol. **51**(6), 957–976 (2009)
3. Bolz, C.F., Cuni, A., Fijalkowski, M., Rigo, A.: Tracing the meta-level: Pypy's tracing JIT compiler. In: Proceedings of the 4th Workshop on the Implementation, Compilation, Optimization of Object-Oriented Languages and Programming Systems, ICOOOLPS 2009, pp. 18–25. ACM, New York (2009)
4. Briand, L.C., Labiche, Y., Shousha, M.: Stress testing real-time systems with genetic algorithms. In: Proceedings of the Genetic and Evolutionary Computation Conference, GECCO 2005, pp. 1021–1028 (2005)
5. Budynek, J., Bonabeau, E., Shargel, B.: Evolving computer intrusion scripts for vulnerability assessment and log analysis. In: Proceedings of the Genetic and Evolutionary Computation Conference, GECCO 2005, pp. 1905–1912 (2005)
6. Canfora, G., Penta, M.D., Esposito, R., Villani, M.L.: An approach for QoS-aware service composition based on genetic algorithms. In: Proceedings of the 2005 Conference on Genetic and Evolutionary Computation (GECCO 2005), pp. 1069–1075. ACM, Washington, D.C., 25–29 June 2005
7. Eves, H.: Elementary Matrix Theory. Dover Publication, New York (1980)
8. Groß, H.G.: An evaluation of dynamic, optimisation-based worst-case execution time analysis. In: ITPC 2003: Proceedings of the International Conference on Information Technology: Prospects and Challenges in the 21st Century, Kathmandu, pp. 8–14 (2003)
9. Grosso, C.D., Antoniol, G., Penta, M.D., Galinier, P., Merlo, E.: Improving network applications security: a new heuristic to generate stress testing data. In: Proceedings of the 2005 Conference on Genetic and Evolutionary Computation (GECCO 2005), pp. 1037–1043. ACM, Washington, D.C., 25–29 June 2005
10. Grosso, C.D., Antoniol, G., Merlo, E., Galinier, P.: Detecting buffer overflow via automatic test input data generation. Comput. Oper. Res. **35**(10), 3125–3143 (2008)
11. Hosek, P., Cadar, C.: Safe software updates via multi-version execution. In: Proceedings of the 2013 International Conference on Software Engineering, ICSE 2013, pp. 612–621. IEEE Press, Piscataway (2013)
12. Kruse, P.M., Wegener, J., Wappler, S.: A highly configurable test system for evolutionary black-box testing of embedded systems. In: Proceedings of the Genetic and Evolutionary Computation Conference, GECCO 2009, pp. 1545–1552 (2009)
13. Langdon, W., Harman, M.: Optimizing existing software with genetic programming. Trans. Evol. Comput. **19**(1), 118–135 (2015)
14. Penta, M.D., Canfora, G., Esposito, G., Mazza, V., Bruno, M.: Search-based testing of service level agreements. In: Proceedings of the Genetic and Evolutionary Computation, GECCO 2007, pp. 1090–1097 (2007)

15. Petke, J., Harman, M., Langdon, W.B., Weimer, W.: Using genetic improvement and code transplants to specialise a C++ program to a problem class. In: Nicolau, M., Krawiec, K., Heywood, M.I., Castelli, M., García-Sánchez, P., Merelo, J.J., Rivas Santos, V.M., Sim, K. (eds.) EuroGP 2014. LNCS, vol. 8599, pp. 137–149. Springer, Heidelberg (2014)
16. Pohlheim, H., Wegener, J.: Testing the temporal behavior of real-time software modules using extended evolutionary algorithms. In: Proceedings of the Genetic and Evolutionary Computation Conference, pp. 1795–1802, July 1999
17. Torres, M.: Pypy Speed Centre. http://speed.pypy.org/
18. Wegener, J., Grochtmann, M.: Verifying timing constraints of real-time systems by means of evolutionary testing. Real-Time Syst. 15(3), 275–298 (1998)
19. Wu, F., Weimer, W., Harman, M., Jia, Y., Krinke, J.: Deep parameter optimisation. In: Genetic and Evolutionary Computation Conference (2015, to appear)

Search-Based Refactoring:
Metrics Are Not Enough

Chris Simons[1]([✉]), Jeremy Singer[2], and David R. White[2]

[1] Department of Computer Science and Creative Technologies,
University of West England, Bristol BS16 1QY, UK
chris.simons@uwe.ac.uk
[2] School of Computing Science, University of Glasgow, Glasgow G12 8RZ, UK
{jeremy.singer,david.r.white}@glasgow.ac.uk

Abstract. Search-based Software Engineering (SBSE) techniques have been applied extensively to refactor software, often based on metrics that describe the object-oriented structure of an application. Recent work shows that in some cases applying popular SBSE tools to open-source software does not necessarily lead to an improved version of the software as assessed by some subjective criteria. Through a survey of professionals, we investigate the relationship between popular SBSE refactoring metrics and the subjective opinions of software engineers. We find little or no correlation between the two. Through qualitative analysis, we find that a simple static view of software is insufficient to assess software quality, and that software quality is dependent on factors that are not amenable to measurement via metrics. We recommend that future SBSE refactoring research should incorporate information about the dynamic behaviour of software, and conclude that a human-in-the-loop approach may be the only way to refactor software in a manner helpful to an engineer.

Keywords: Search-based software engineering · Metrics · Optimisation · Software quality

1 Motivation

Search-Based Software Engineering (SBSE) has been extensively applied to refactor object-oriented software based on metrics that quantify structural properties of an object-oriented design, such as measures of cohesion, coupling, the number of classes and the nature of the object hierarchy (e.g. [20,22,27,31]).

Recent work shows that applying SBSE refactoring using metrics to the open-source Apache Ant project [8] does not result in an improved design as assessed by an expert. Other work reveals that when refactoring is conducted using a number of cohesion metrics, there can be disagreement between the metrics [32].

This raises the question of whether metrics are a good guide to software quality, at least in the context of refactoring. If metrics indicate that a refactored design is improved, but an engineer does not perceive any improvement, how is the engineer judging the quality differently? That is, metrics are essentially a

© Springer International Publishing Switzerland 2015
M. Barros and Y. Labiche (Eds.): SSBSE 2015, LNCS 9275, pp. 47–61, 2015.
DOI: 10.1007/978-3-319-22183-0_4

proxy for something described as *software quality*, but what exactly is it that we are trying to find a proxy for? And if we can answer that question, is the correlation between the metrics we are using and the quality that we trying to optimise well-established?

In this paper, we try to answer these questions, by placing the ultimate judgement of software quality in the hands of expert industrial software engineers, by measuring the correlation between metrics used in SBSE and human judgement, and by examining the articulated justifications for those judgements.

2   Hypothesis

We formulate our hypotheses such that the null hypothesis makes no assumption of an effect:

- H_0: There is no correlation between software metric values and software engineer evaluation of quality for a given software design.
- H_1: There is a correlation between software metric values and software engineer evaluation of quality for a given software design.

3   Survey Design

The goal of our survey is to ask software engineers for their evaluation of a set of software designs in order to compare their impressions of design quality with scores derived from metrics. We chose to conduct a survey of software engineers by means of an online questionnaire. The selection of appropriate software designs, design qualities, metrics and engineers for the questionnaire requires careful consideration. Thus drawing upon best survey practice (e.g. [13,14,17,29]), each of these components is described as follows.

3.1   Selection of Software Designs

We included two problem domains to strengthen the generality of our findings. Examples needed to be large enough to be meaningful to an engineer whilst not imposing excessive cognitive load and hence fatigue. We sought industrial benchmark designs, but none were readily available, and therefore two standard examples were selected: the Automated Teller Machine [12] and a nautical cruise booking system [5]. To reduce cognitive load, we used the Unified Modelling Language (UML) [33], widely heralded as "the lingua franca" of object-oriented modelling [35]. We explored the idea of using refactoring tools (e.g. CodeImp [31]) to generate designs, but no available tool met our requirements. Thus we invited five experienced software engineers to produce class designs for the two problems. Minor adjustments were made to the ten designs to ensure both a consistent level of abstraction and a range of metric scores.

3.2   Selection of Design Qualities

There exist a variety of software design quality definitions, including those from the International Standards Organisation and International Electrotechnical Commission (ISO/IEC 25010:2011) [21]. We drew inspiration from studies relating design qualities to corresponding properties and metrics (e.g. [24]). Bansiya and Davis [7] propose a Quality Model for Object-Oriented Design (QMOOD) that is popular in the literature and offers a hierarchical model of qualities, properties and metrics together with mappings between them. QMOOD defines six qualities: reusability, flexibility, understandability, functionality, extendibility and effectiveness (see [7], Table 1). While such quality attributes are good candidates for use in our survey, we considered that evaluating six qualities would place an unreasonable cognitive load on respondents, and so we focused on the most problem-domain independent qualities i.e. the first three. The Bansiya and Davis definitions of reusability, flexibility and understandability are given in Table 1.

3.3   Selection of Metrics

In order to select suitable metrics for the experiment, we conducted a simple review of the SBSE literature. We drew upon previous metrics reviews [24,38] and guidelines for conducting systematic literature surveys [25,26].

We addressed the question: *what is the distribution of software metrics among the SBSE refactoring literature?* We chose to rely upon the SBSE Repository [39] and through a simple search query of "software metrics", extracted 57 papers. We narrowed this list, by examining their titles, abstracts, introductions and conclusions. Examples of excluded sources included papers on software defect prediction and effort estimation. This process yielded 23 papers.

Our analysis reveals 118 different metrics used in the 23 sources. The metrics relate mostly to structural integrity such as cohesion and coupling, but measures of design size, complexity and elegance are also present. Of the 118 metrics, only three individual metrics — Lack of Cohesion of Methods (LCOM) and its variants, Module Quality (MQ) and Evaluation Metric (EVM) — are reported in

Table 1. Bansiya, Davis [7] definitions of reusability, flexibility, understandability

Quality attribute	Definition
Reusability	Reflects the presence of object-oriented design characteristics that allow a design to be reapplied to a new problem without significant effort
Flexibility	Characteristics that allow the incorporation of changes in a design. The ability of a design to be adapted to provide functionally related capabilities
Understandability	The properties of a design that enable it to be easily learned and comprehended. This directly relates to the complexity of the design structure

Table 2. Metrics and papers reporting use

Metrics	Papers reporting use
MQ	Azar, 2009 [6], Glavas, 2011 [15], Glavas, 2011b [16], Harman, 2004 [18], Harman, 2005 [19]
EVM	Barros, 2013 [8], Harman, 2005 [19]
LCOM and variants	Azar, 2009 [6], Barros, 2013 [8], Ó Cinnéide, 2012 [32], Koc, 2012 [28]
QMOOD suite	Jensen, 2010 [22], O'Keeffe, 2007 [34]

more than one paper; the use of only one suite of metrics (QMOOD) is reported twice. These results are illustrated in Table 2.

In selecting the metrics to be evaluated, we considered that those found in multiple were a reflection of wider use in the field. We first considered LCOM, MQ and EVM. However, LCOM relies on knowledge of implementation dependencies e.g. what methods use which attributes in a class, while MQ and EVM are metrics for dependency-based module clustering. All typically require programming language source code for calculation. Alternatively, the QMOOD metrics suite is used in two studies, and the metrics may be mapped to design quality attributes [7], which is consistent with our chosen hypothesis.

Inspection of the 11 QMOOD metrics reveals that their straightforward computation makes them amenable to evaluation on both human-produced design models and programming language source code. Closer analysis reveals that 3 of the metrics i.e. Design Size in Classes (DSC), Direct Class Coupling (DCC) and Number of Methods (NOM) are readily applicable to the human-generated design models. Metrics relating to inheritance (Number Of Hierarchies, NOH, Average Number of Ancestors, ANA) are excluded as only six of the final designs show inheritance, with only one class hierarchy each.

Thus DSC, DCC and NOM have been selected from the QMOOD suite for use in the experiment. Two other metrics were selected: Numbers among classes (NAC) [37], and Numbers of Attributes and Methods (NOAM). NAC was chosen as it had been used previously by Barros and Farzat [8] to relate design improvements to understandability. The NOAM metric was introduced to cater for any influence of the number of attributes in a design, which was otherwise lacking. Both NAC and NOAM are readily calculated for human-generated designs.

3.4 Correlation Analysis

We use correlation analysis to compare the chosen metrics to the opinions of engineers. Whether our conclusions apply to the derivation of high-level properties from metrics in suites such as QMOOD depends greatly on how those suites use metric values. For example, in a weighted-sum method there may be a trade-off between two metrics in defining a high-level quality, and thus correlation analysis may be insufficient to validate such an approach. However, the weightings involved may be somewhat arbitrary — how can you compare an increase in design size against a reduction in cohesion? The range of metric values is also problem-specific, therefore it is likely that one metric will dominate another, and a simple correlation analysis will be sufficient in such cases. To fully evaluate QMOOD and similar approaches, it would be necessary to evaluate all of the metrics employed in any given suite, which is impractical in a survey of this type, and thus we must focus on the evaluation of individual metrics.

3.5   Target Population

In selecting the target population of software engineers, we concluded that industrial practitioners would provide the best audience given the aim of the survey. We considered that academics should not be targeted as their design experience might be confined to educational software design. The sampling frame of the target population was achieved by inviting members of the Association of C and C++ Users (ACCU) [1] and the British Computer Society (BCS) [10] — two organisations prominent in promoting professionalism and best practice in software design and development. We investigated the possibility of using Amazon Mechanical Turk (AMT) [4], but this required US residency.

4   Questionnaire Design

We wished to present a design of meaningful size and complexity without cognitively overloading the engineer. We chose two case studies and five solutions to each; the designs are online [36], together with their calculated metrics values (DSC, DCC, NOM, NAC and NOAM). Designs were presented at random to the participants, one model per participant. To capture their judgement of design qualities, we used a Likert Scale with seven levels: "strongly disagree", "disagree", "somewhat disagree", "neutral", "somewhat agree", "agree" and "strongly agree". We asked participants to provide rationale for their judgements, and analysed responses using thematic coding. We requested a participant's number of years of design and development experience, as well as their opinion of their own design expertise and confidence on the same Likert Scale.

Informed consent was obtained from participants prior to conducting the questionnaire and participant withdrawal was possible at any point. Any personal data recorded, e.g. email addresses, was entirely at the discretion of the participant. All survey information was strictly confidential and published survey information is reported either as aggregate data or is anonymised.

Full details of our questionnaire design are available [36]. Pretesting (see [13], Chap. 10) was conducted. Five experienced software engineers undertook the draft questionnaire and their response experiences evaluated with respect to:

- *Assimilation:* respondents reported being able to satisfactorily attend to and remember relevant questions and instructions.
- *Comprehension:* respondents also reported being able to understand the questions and definitions of the three design qualities.

- *Recall:* some respondents found difficulty in recalling a design when completing their evaluation. As a result, "back" buttons were made more explicit.
- *Reporting:* respondents reported that Likert scales and the free text response answers were clear and offered adequate opportunity for responses.

We used SurveyGizmo as our survey platform, as it supports sufficient logic to enable the randomisation of problem description and model assignments we required. As an incentive for participation, we also offered participants the opportunity to be entered into a prize draw.

5   The Survey Process

Our survey was open from 18 January to 28 February 2015, a total of 42 days. Invitations to participate were dispatched to approximately 900 ACCU [1] members and 200 members of the Bristol (UK) branch of the BCS [11]. An invitation to participate in the survey was also posted on a discussion forum via the BCS Members' Group on LinkedIn [30] to which approximately 11,000 BCS practitioners have access, although the number of regular contributors is much lower.

Some lively comments were posted to the LinkedIn forum. Despite piloting the questionnaire, a number of participants posted feedback stating that it was not realistic to form an impression of design qualities using a UML class model in isolation from other aspects of software development e.g. dynamic models of behaviour, requirements, test plan etc. (although this is exactly what search-based refactoring is doing). One forum contributor remarked to the authors of the survey: *"it seems your idea of what quality is and how to judge it is not the same as many of us in the industry,"* foreshadowing our survey results.

6   Results

A total of 50 responses was received, although we discarded one of these (see Sect. 8). We were pleased to receive 50 responses and we are grateful to those engineers who gave up the time to carefully examine the case studies.

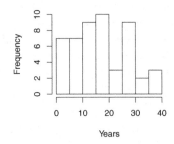

Fig. 1. Histogram of the programming experience of our respondents

The distribution of engineers' experience is given in Fig. 1, which illustrates that our respondents were on the whole very experienced. We asked them to rate their expertise in the area of software design, and their confidence in their own judgement — the results are shown in Fig. 2. We are very confident of the experience and expertise of our respondents.

We divide our results between responses to the quantitative questions, where we asked respondents to rate the qualities of software on a Likert scale, and the qualitative answers, where asked them to justify their quantitative responses.

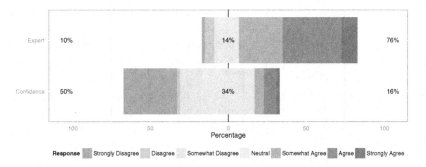

Fig. 2. Respondents' self-assessed significant expertise in software design and confidence in their ratings of the models

6.1   Quantitative Results

In order to test our hypothesis, we perform correlation analysis on the relationship between the responses of those surveyed and the selected metrics. Engineers were asked three questions: whether they agreed that the design was Understandable, Reusable, and Flexible. These questions required a Likert response on a seven-step scale from "strongly disagree" to "strongly agree". We plotted responses against the corresponding value of each software metric for that design.

Figure 3 gives correlation plots for each quality. A score of one corresponds to "strongly disagree". Table 3 gives the Spearman's Rank Coefficient for each correlation. We observe from these results that there is *almost no correlation between the perception of software engineers and the metrics*. We then performed a two-sided significance test against the Spearman's Rank coefficients, and the p-values are given in Table 4. No correlations were significant at the 0.05 level.

Thus, we are unable to refute our null hypothesis H_0. This is quite a significant result: if we assume that our experimental results are valid (see Sect. 8 for threats to validity) and that they generalise to other object designs, then the metrics we are examining are *not helpful in improving these software qualities*.

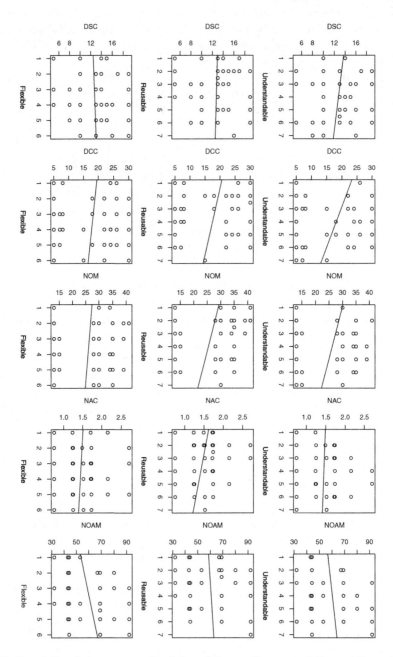

Fig. 3. Correlation between expert opinion of three software qualities and five software metrics

Table 3. Spearman's Rank coefficients for the correlation between our metrics and human judgement (to 3 s.f.)

Quality	DSC	DCC	NOM	NAC	NOAM
Understandable	−0.128	−0.271	−0.203	−0.0400	0.103
Reusable	−0.0280	−0.158	−0.195	−0.200	0.0572
Flexible	0.0386	−0.0806	−0.0677	−0.0613	0.202

Table 4. P-values for a two-sided test of the Spearman's Rank correlation coefficients in Table 3 (to 3 s.f.)

Quality	DSC	DCC	NOM	NAC	NOAM
Understandable	0.375	0.0571	0.156	0.783	0.478
Reusable	0.847	0.272	0.174	0.163	0.693
Flexible	0.790	0.578	0.640	0.672	0.160

6.2   Qualitative Results

We were intrigued as to why there was no correlation between the quality metrics and the judgement of software engineers. In particular, we wished to understand the thought processes of software engineers: what makes one design better than another? We asked the engineers to justify their judgements in prose.

We then coded their responses as per *grounded theory* ([14] Chap. 4, [29] Chap. 11), an inductive process where text responses are categorised in order to derive trends from textual responses. This process is somewhat subjective; two of the authors coded the data independently and then resolved their differences through comparison and discussion. We divide the coding results between the three questions, and the results are given in Tables 5, 6 and 7. The frequency column indicates the number of responses that fell into a given category; a single response may fall into multiple categories. We make the following observations:

Table 5. Classifications for rationale behind judgement of "Understandable"

Coding	Frequency
Needs something more (dynamics, context, reqts, rationale etc.)	22
Incorrect or unclear responsibility assignment	13
Clear traceability to problem domain	10
Clear breakdown of purpose	6
Clear element naming	5
Missing abstractions	4
No response or no explanation	3
Poor layout	1

Table 6. Classifications for rationale behind judgement of "Flexible"

Coding	Frequency
Parts of the design should be easy to modify	12
Problem specific	11
Needs something more (dynamics, context, reqts etc.)	8
Incorrect or missing abstractions	8
Class coupling	5
Incorrect/unclear responsibility assignment	2
Separation of concerns	2
Hard to test	1
Simplistic	1
No response/no clear explanation	8

Table 7. Classifications for rationale behind judgement of "Reusable"

Coding	Frequency
Problem specific	24
Parts of the design are reusable, others not	18
Class coupling	5
Needs something more (dynamics, context, reqts etc.)	5
Incorrect abstractions	3
Lack of object-oriented design	2
Separation of concerns	2
OO languages	1
Simplistic	1
No response	1

A Class Diagram is Not Enough. The responses reflect the conversation on the professional network LinkedIn (see Sect. 5). It is clear that our respondents are unable to assess the design of a system based solely on the class diagram; for example, one respondent commented on their ability to understand the system:

> "[A class diagram] offers no information about the interactions, procedures or validations and therefore is a really superficial view of the software design"

We agree with this comment, and we are unaware of any object-oriented SBSE refactoring that takes as input a description of the dynamic behaviour of a system design. How can we expect to imitate the judgement of a software engineer if we do not take into account the same information? The most commonly request was for information about system behaviour.

The Problem Domain Matters. Another trend was the relationship between the design and the problem domain: from fundamental decisions such as the names given to objects and associations, to the high-level mapping between requirements and the model, it is clear that judging the model in isolation from the problem domain is not meaningful to an engineer. Many comments referred to the problem domain, or the way in which the problem had been analysed.

Qualities Have Meaning only in a Given Context. When considering a given quality, there is a need for context. Many comments were along the lines of "Reusable for what purpose?" or "Reusability depends on context...". It is not enough to look at the high-level structure alone:

> "Reusability is about more than just a class diagram and function definition. It's about how the software is actually written and this can be good or bad".

> "Re-use only has meaning if it itself is defined/scoped, tested and managed as part of the project".

We may also consider parts of a model as representing distinct contexts: respondents pointed out that the qualities may vary across different parts of the model. It is perhaps naive to expect to holistically optimise a system.

Good Design is Intuitive. There was a clear difficulty amongst some respondents in articulating their thought processes, as if it involved some aesthetic judgement: for example, some replies included: "My guts says no", "Seems to fit together well", "intuitive". Such responses appear to resonate with the design patterns notion of *Quality Without a Name* [2], generally taken to mean that good quality is something that can be recognised, but difficult to describe in words: i.e. "you know it when you see it".

Our Standard Metrics Play a (Minor) Part. The aspects of the model that could be judged by our respondents do indeed overlap with the intentions of our chosen metrics. For example, engineers consider the object hierarchy, separation of concerns, cohesion, and division of responsibilities as important elements in judging design quality. However, these properties are given minor consideration in their responses compared to the central concerns mentioned above.

7 Related Work

Although examples of related empirical investigations are not abundant in the literature, Katmarksi and Koschke [23] conducted an empirical study to investigate whether complexity metrics agree with programmer opinion. They selected examples of Java source code for programmer complexity evaluation, and applied a variety of control-flow and data-flow complexity metrics. Among 200 participants, they report some matching of programmer ranking with complexity metrics, although participants were presented with small Java methods (12–51 lines of code) and object-oriented design aspects were ignored. Moreover, the 200 participants were drawn from a sample of students and academics, and Katmarksi and Koschke suggest that *"professional programmers might report differently"*.

Ó Cinnéide et al. [32] conducted a rigorous investigation into refactoring metrics — rather than refactoring source code, their goal was to assess the software metrics that guide the automated refactoring through repeated refactoring experiments. They investigated five cohesion metrics using eight real-world Java systems, involving 300,000 lines of code and over 3,000 refactorings. The authors report that the cohesion metrics disagreed with each other in 55 % of cases. It is also interesting to note the disagreement among metrics alongside the disagreement in software engineers' impressions of software qualities in this experiment.

Recent studies by Bavota et al. [9] investigate possible relationships between metrics, code smells and developer refactoring activities. They mined the evolution history of three Java open source projects to investigate whether refactoring activities occur on code components for which certain indicators such as quality metrics or the presence of smells as detected by tools suggest there might be need for refactoring operations. Their results indicate that, more often than not, quality metrics do not show a clear relationship with refactoring. In other words, refactoring operations are generally focused on code components for which quality metrics do not suggest there might be need for refactoring operations. Such findings do seem to resonate with the lack of correlation between quality metrics and software engineer impressions of software qualities found in this experiment.

8   Threats to Validity

The biggest weakness of the survey is that the class models are small educational examples. This was constrained by two factors: the screen space used to display designs, and the cognitive overhead on respondents to understand the requirements and design sufficiently to answer our questions. As a consequence, we excluded metrics that are only meaningful when considering larger models (for example, those measuring the inheritance hierarchy). We spent much time selecting and refining our case studies, after considering various approaches and problems, and decided upon those that we considered to be as large as the aforementioned restrictions would allow.

The qualities are often discussed informally within software engineering without attention to their precise meaning. To reduce the risk of ambiguity, we included definitions within the survey. Respondents were free to move between the survey pages, meaning they could return to the definitions as necessary, and indeed some respondents quoted our definitions within their rationale.

With any survey, there is a danger of bias in terms of the respondent population. We tried to avoid this by targeting a specific set of organisations directly relevant to the study, i.e. software engineers, through a set of professional institutions. One final lesson we learnt from the process is that we did not pilot the survey sufficiently. For example, it transpired that the survey did not work on all mobile devices, which may have skewed our sample.

9   Conclusions

9.1   Refactoring Metrics Are Not Correlated with Human Judgement

In Sect. 6.1, we were unable to refute the null hypothesis that there is no correlation between these standard SBSE refactoring metrics and software quality. Thus we are unable to support the conjecture that SBSE refactoring tools relying solely on these metrics will consistently propose useful refactored models to engineers. Whilst we dealt with only a subset of available metrics and two example problems, our qualitative results suggest that this statement will generalise to other metrics and problem domains, simply because metrics do not take into account the information required to make a sound judgement.

9.2   Wider Lessons Regarding Refactoring

We conclude from our qualitative analysis that metrics based on an object-oriented design are insufficient to optimise software quality. Furthermore, no simple metrics will be able to entirely capture the essential aspects of a software design used by human engineers when making judgements of software qualities.

Software is inextricably connected to a problem domain, and attempting to treat the design of a system in isolation disregards this connection. We note the recent advances in Machine Learning and automatic programming to address such concerns e.g. [3], and do not discount that such developments could one day solve the problem of machine judgement of software quality. However, without such advances we recommend that, although not novel, *human-in-the-loop* systems are the only viable method for automated refactoring tools that produce meaningful solutions.

Future work could include repeating the exercise but including some form of design concerning the dynamic behaviour of each system. The lack of a dynamic view (for example, a statechart) was the most common complaint amongst respondents, and it would be interesting to see how this affects their ability to discern the qualities of the software design, as well as the impact it may have on the articulation of their rationale. However, we suspect that such an experiment may be subject to very low response rates, and we recommend a smaller focus-group approach involving observed exercises and interviews.

Omitting information that could deanonymise a respondent, the data gathered and used to produce the figures in this paper are online [36].

Acknowledgements. We would like to thank our colleagues at UWE for their help in the design of the survey; Mel Ó Cinnéide and Iman Hemati Moghadam for generously sharing code; Per Runeson for his insightful advice; the professional organisations the ACCU and BCS for permitting mailshots to their members; and we are very especially grateful to all those who took the time to respond to the survey.

References

1. ACCU: Association of C and C++ Users. http://www.accu.org/. Accessed: 3 June 2015
2. Alexander, C.: The Timeless Way of Building, vol. 1. Oxford University Press, Oxford (1979)
3. Amal, B., Kessentini, M., Bechikh, S., Dea, J., Said, L.B.: On the use of machine learning and search-based software engineering for Ill-defined fitness function: a case study on software refactoring. In: Le Goues, C., Yoo, S. (eds.) SSBSE 2014. LNCS, vol. 8636, pp. 31–45. Springer, Heidelberg (2014)
4. AMT: Amazon Mechanical Turk. http://www.mturk.com/mturk/welcome/. Accessed: 3 June 2015
5. Apperly, H., Hofman, R., Latchem, S., Maybank, B., McGibbon, B., Piper, D., Simons, C.: Service- and Component-based Development. Addison-Wesley (2003)
6. Azar, D., Harmanani, H., Korkmaz, R.: A hybrid heuristic approach to optimize rule-based software quality estimation models. Inf. Softw. Technol. **51**(9), 1365–1376 (2009)
7. Bansiya, J., Davis, C.G.: A hierarchical model for object-oriented design quality assessment. IEEE Trans. Softw. Eng. **28**(1), 4–17 (2002)
8. de Oliveira Barros, M., de Almeida Farzat, F.: What can a big program teach us about optimization? In: Ruhe, G., Zhang, Y. (eds.) SSBSE 2013. LNCS, vol. 8084, pp. 275–281. Springer, Heidelberg (2013)
9. Bavota, G., De Lucia, A., Di Penta, M., Oliveto, R., Palomba, F.: An experimental investigation on the innate relationship between quality and refactoring. J. Syst. Softw. **107**, 1–14 (2015)
10. BCS: British Computer Society. http://www.bcs.org/. Accessed: 3 June 2015
11. BCS-BRISTOL: British Computer Society Bristol Branch. http://www.bristol.bcs.org.uk/. Accessed: 3 June 2015
12. Bjork, R.: ATM Simulation. http://www.math-cs.gordon.edu/courses/cs211/ATMExample/. Accessed: 3 June 2015
13. Blair, J., Czaja, R., Blair, E.: Designing Surveys: A Guide to Decisions and Procedures. Sage Publications, London (2014)
14. Gibbs, G.: Analysing Qualitative Data. Sage Publications, London (2007)
15. Glavas, G., Fertalj, K.: Metaheuristic approach to class responsibility assignment problem. In: Proceedings of the ITI 33rd International Conference on Information Technology Interfaces (ITI). IEEE (2011)
16. Glavaš, G., Fertalj, K.: Solving the class responsibility assignment problem using metaheuristic approach. J. Comput. Inf. Technol. **19**(4), 275–283 (2011)
17. Groves, R., Fowler, F., Couper, M., Lepkowski, J., Singer, E., Tourangeau, R.: Survey Methodology. Wiley, New York (2004)
18. Harman, M., Clark, J.: Metrics are fitness functions too. In: Proceedings of the 10th International Symposium on Software Metrics. IEEE (2004)
19. Harman, M., Swift, S., Mahdavi, K.: An empirical study of the robustness of two module clustering fitness functions. In: GECCO 2005. ACM (2005)
20. Harman, M., Tratt, L.: Pareto optimal search based refactoring at the design level. In: GECCO 2007. ACM (2007)
21. ISO/IEC: Standard 25010:2011. http://www.iso.org/iso/catalogue_detail.htm?csnumber=35733. Accessed: 3 June 2015
22. Jensen, A., Cheng, B.: On the use of genetic programming for automated refactoring and the introduction of design patterns. In: GECCO 2010. ACM (2010)

23. Katzmarski, B., Koschke, R.: Program complexity metrics and programmer opinions. In: Proceedings of the 20th International Conference on Program Comprehension (ICPC). IEEE (2012)
24. Khan, Y., Khararah, O.: A systematic review on the relationships between MOOD/QMOOD metrics and external software quality attributes. Technical report, Department of Information and Computer Science, King Fahd University of Petroleum and Minerals, Dhahran, Saudi Arabia (2014)
25. Kitchenham, B.: Guidelines for performing systematic literature reviews in software engineering. Technical report, EBSE-2007-01, School of Computer Science and Mathematics, Keele University, Keele, Staffs, ST5 5BG, United Kingdom (2007)
26. Kitchenham, B., Mendes, E., Travassos, G.: A systematic review of cross-vs. within-company cost estimation studies. In: Proceedings of the 10th International Conference on Evaluation and Assessment in Software Engineering. British Computer Society (2006)
27. Koc, E., Ersoy, N., Andac, A., Camlidere, Z., Cereci, I., Kilic, H.: An empirical study about search-based refactoring using alternative multiple and population-based search techniques. In: Gelenbe, E., Lent, R., Sakellari, G. (eds.) Computer and Information Sciences II, pp. 59–66. Springer, London (2012)
28. Koc, E., Ersoy, N., Camlidere, Z.S., Kilic, H.: A web-service for automated software refactoring using artificial bee colony optimization. In: Tan, Y., Shi, Y., Ji, Z. (eds.) ICSI 2012, Part I. LNCS, vol. 7331, pp. 318–325. Springer, Heidelberg (2012)
29. Lazar, J., Feng, J., Hochheiser, H.: Research Methods in Human-Computing Interaction. Wiley, New York (2010)
30. LinkedIn: LinkedIn Professional Network. https://uk.linkedin.com/. Accessed: 3 June 2015
31. Moghadam, I., Ó Cinnéide, M.: Code-Imp: a tool for automated search-based refactoring. In: Proceedings of the 4th Workshop on Refactoring Tools (WRT 2011). ACM Press (2011)
32. Ó Cinnéide, M., Tratt, L., Harman, M., Counsell, S., Moghadam, I.: Experimental assessment of software metrics using automated refactoring. In: Proceedings of the ACM-IEEE International Symposium on Empirical Software Engineering and Measurement. ACM (2012)
33. Object Management Group: Unified Modelling Language. http://www.uml.org/. Accessed: 3 June 2015
34. O'Keeffe, M., Ó Cinnéide, M.: Automated design improvement by example. In: Frontiers in Artificial Intelligence and Applications, vol. 161, p. 315 (2007)
35. Petre, M.: UML in practice. In: Proceedings of the International Conference on Software Engineering (ICSE). IEEE (2013)
36. Simons, C., Singer, J., White, D.R.: Survey Materials and Data. http://www.cems.uwe.ac.uk/~clsimons/MetricsAreNotEnough/. Accessed: 3 June 2015
37. Simons, C., Parmee, I.: Elegant object-oriented software design via interactive, evolutionary computation. IEEE Trans. Syst. Man Cybern. Part C: Appl. Rev. 42(6), 1797–1805 (2012)
38. Sjoberg, D., Anda, B., Mockus, A.: Questioning software maintenance metrics: a comparative case study. In: Proceedings of the ACM-IEEE International Symposium on Empirical Software Engineering and Measurement. ACM Press (2012)
39. Zhang, Y.: SBSE repository. http://crestweb.cs.ucl.ac.uk/resources/sbse_repository/. Accessed: 3 June 2015

Weaving Parallel Threads
Searching for Useful Parallelism in Functional Programs

José Manuel Calderón Trilla[1]([✉]), Simon Poulding[2], and Colin Runciman[1]

[1] University of York, York, UK
jmct@jmct.cc
[2] Blekinge Institute of Technology, Karlskrona, Sweden

Abstract. As the speed of processors is starting to plateau, chip man-
ufacturers are instead looking to multi-core architectures for increased
performance. The ubiquity of multi-core hardware has made parallelism
an important tool in writing performant programs. Unfortunately, parallel programming is still considered an advanced technique and most
programs are written as sequential programs.

We propose that we lift this burden from the programmer and allow
the compiler to automatically determine which parts of a program can
be executed in parallel. Historically, most attempts at auto-parallelism
depended on static analysis alone. While static analysis is often able to
find *safe* parallelism, it is difficult to determine *worthwhile* parallelism.
This is known as the *granularity problem*. Our work shows that we can
use static analysis *in conjunction with* search techniques by having the
compiler execute the program and then alter the amount of parallelism
based on execution speed. We do this by annotating the program with
parallel annotations and using search to determine which annotations to
enable.

This allows the static analysis to find the safe parallelism and shift
the burden of finding worthwhile parallelism to search. Our results show
that by searching over the possible parallel settings we can achieve better
performance than static analysis alone.

1 Introduction

Moore's law has often provided a 'free lunch' for those looking to run faster
programs without the programmer expending any engineering effort. Throughout the 1990s in particular, an effective way of having a faster x86 program
was to wait for Intel[TM] to release its new line of processors and run the program on your new CPU. Unfortunately, clock speeds have reached a plateau
and we no longer get speedups for free [23]. Increased performance now comes
from including additional processor cores on modern CPUs. This means that
programmers have been forced to write parallel and concurrent programs when
looking for improved wall-clock performance. Unfortunately, writing parallel and
concurrent programs involves managing complexity that is not present in single-
threaded programs. The goal of the work outlined in this paper is to convince

M. Barros and Y. Labiche (Eds.): SSBSE 2015, LNCS 9275, pp. 62–76, 2015.
DOI: 10.1007/978-3-319-22183-0_5

the reader that not all hope is lost. By looking for the *implicit parallelism* in programs that are written as single-threaded programs we can achieve performance gains without programmer effort.

Our work focuses on F-Lite: a pure, non-strict functional language that is suitable as a core language of a compiler for a higher-level language like Haskell [17]. We have chosen to use a non-strict language because of the lack of arbitrary side-effects [11], and many years of work in the area of implicit parallelism [6,10,13] however we feel that many of our techniques would transfer well to other language paradigms.

The primary contribution of this paper is to demonstrate that using search based on dynamic execution of the parallelised program is a robust way to help diminish the *granularity* problem that is difficult for static analysis alone. We show that for some programs, the combination of search and static analysis can achieve speed-ups that are nearly linear with respect to the number of cores.

The rest of this paper describes our technique in more detail. Section 2 discuss the main background to this work: implicit parallelism in functional languages. Section 3 provides a worked example to illustrate the static analysis we perform to determine potential parallelism. We describe our empirical method and results in Sect. 4. Lastly, we offer our conclusions and discuss related work in Sect. 6.

2   Implicit Parallelism in Functional Languages

In this section we will motivate and discuss the benefits and drawbacks of implicit parallelism in a lazy purely functional language. We will also give a high-level overview of *strictness analysis* which allows us to find safe parallelism in lazy languages.

2.1   Background

Research into parallelism in lazy purely functional languages has a long history that dates back to the early work on lazy functional languages [1,12,19,20][1]. Non-strictness makes it difficult to reason about when expressions are evaluated. This forces the programmer to avoid the use of arbitrary side-effects. The resulting purity means that functions in pure functional languages are *referentially transparent*, or the result of a function depends only on the values of its arguments (i.e. there is no global state that could effect the result of the function or be manipulated by the function).

Purity alone is of huge benefit when dealing with parallelism. Because functions do not rely on anything but their arguments the only communication between threads necessary is the result of the thread's computation, which is shared via the program's graph using the same mechanism used to implement laziness [19].

Laziness, while forcing the programmer to be pure (which is a boon to parallelism), is an inherently sequential evaluation strategy. Lazy evaluation only

---

[1] For a comprehensive review we suggest [7].

evaluates expressions when they are *needed*. This is what allows for the use of infinite data structures, only what is needed will be computed.

The two reductions of *sqr* in Fig. 1 illustrate the key differences between lazy evaluation and eager, or strict, evaluation.

Eager Evaluation	Lazy Evaluation
$sqr\ (5 * 5)$	$sqr\ (5 * 5)$
$= sqr\ 25$	$= let\ x\ =\ 5 * 5\ in\ x * x$
$= let\ x\ =\ 25\ in\ x * x$	$= let\ x\ =\ 25\ in\ x * x$
$= 25 * 25$	$= 25 * 25$
$= 625$	$= 625$

Fig. 1. Eager and Lazy evaluation order for squaring a value.

In the case of eager evaluation the argument to *sqr* is evaluated *before* entering the function body. For lazy evaluation the argument is passed as a suspended computation that is only *forced* when the value is needed (in this case when x is needed in order to multiply $x * x$). Notice that under lazy evaluation $5 * 5$ is only evaluated once, even though it is used twice in the function. This is due to the *sharing* of the result. This is why laziness is often described as call-by-need *with sharing* [7].

In the case of *sqr* in Fig. 1, both eager and lazy evaluation required the same number of *reductions* to compute the final result. This is not always the case; take the following function definitions

$$bot\ ::\ Int\ \rightarrow\ Int$$
$$bot\ x\ =\ x + bot$$

$$const\ ::\ a\ \rightarrow\ b\ \rightarrow\ a$$
$$const\ x\ y\ =\ x$$

In an eager language the expression *const* 5 *bot* will never terminate, while it would return 5 in a lazy language as only the first argument to *const* is actually *needed* in its body.

This tension between the call-by-need convention of laziness with parallelism's desire to evaluate expressions *before* they are needed is well known [24]. The most successful method of combating this tension is through the use of *strictness analysis* [9,16,27].

2.2   Strictness, Demand Context, and Strategies

Here we will describe the method by which we identify the *safe* parallelism in F-Lite programs and arrange for the evaluation of these expressions in parallel.

The *strictness* properties of a function determine which arguments are definitely needed for the function to terminate, whereas the *demand* on an argument tells us *how much* of the argument's structure is needed. *Strategies* are functions that evaluate their argument's structure to a specific depth. By analysing the program for strictness and demand information, we can then generate strategies for the strict arguments to a function and evaluate the strategies in parallel to the body of the function. The strategies we generate will only evaluate the arguments to the depth determined by the demand analysis.

Strictness. Because we are working in a lazy language it is not always safe to evaluate the arguments to a function before we enter the body of a function. However, if a function uses the value of an argument within its body it is safe to evaluate that argument before, or in parallel to, the execution of the body of the function. In order to determine which arguments can be evaluated in this way modern compilers use *strictness analysis* [16]. More formally, a function f of n arguments

$$f\ x_1 \dots\ x_i\ \dots x_n = \dots$$

is strict in its ith argument if and only if

$$f\ x_1 \dots\ \bot\ \dots x_n = \bot$$

What this states is that f is only strict in its ith argument if f becomes non-terminating[2] by passing a non-terminating value as its ith argument.

Knowing the strictness information of a function is the first step in automatic parallelisation. This is because if f is strict in its ith argument we do not risk introducing non-termination (which would not otherwise be present) by evaluating the ith argument in parallel. In other words, evaluating x_i in parallel would only introduce non-termination to the program if evaluating f with x_i would have resulted in f's non-termination anyway.

F-Lite has two primitives for taking advantage of strictness information: *par* and *seq*.

$$
\begin{array}{ll}
seq\ ::\ a \to b \to b & \qquad par\ ::\ a \to b \to b \\
seq\ x\ y = y & \qquad par\ x\ y = y
\end{array}
$$

Fig. 2. Semantics of seq and par.

Both functions return the value of their second argument. The difference is in their *side-effects*. *seq* returns its second argument only *after* the evaluation of its first argument. *par* forks the evaluation of its first argument in a new parallel

---

[2] In this paper we use the convention that $\bot$ represents erroneous or non-terminating expressions.

thread and then returns its second argument; this is known as *sparking* a parallel task [4].

Strictness analysis was a very active research area in the 1980's and the development of analyses that provide the type of strictness information outlined above is a well understood problem [2,5,16]. However, as outlined above, strictness analysis does not provide satisfactory information about complex data-structures [26]. This can be remedied by the use of *projections* to represent *demand*.

Demand. So far our discussion of strictness has only involved two levels of 'definedness': a defined value, or $\perp$. This is the whole story when dealing with *flat* data-structures such as Integers, Booleans or Enumerations. However, in lazy languages nested data-structures have *degrees* of definedness.

Take the following example function and value definitions in F-Lite

```
length []     = 0                sum []     = 0
length (x:xs) = 1 + length xs    sum (x:xs) = x + sum xs

definedList = [1,2,3,4]          infiniteList = [1,2,3...

partialList = [1,2,bot,4]        loop = loop
```

Both `length` and `sum` are functions on lists, but they use lists differently. `length` does not use the elements of its argument list. Therefore `length` would accept `definedList` and `partialList` (which has a non-terminating element) as arguments and still return the correct value. On the other hand `sum` *needs* the elements of the list, otherwise it would not be able to compute the sum. For this reason, `sum` only terminates if it is passed a fully defined list and would result in non-termination if passed `partialList`. Neither function would terminate if passed `infiniteList`, since even `length` requires the list to have a finite length (some functions do not require a finite list, such as `head`, the function that returns the first element in a list). With these examples we say that `length` *demands* a finite list, whereas `sum` *demands* a fully-defined list.

This additional information about a data-structure is extremely useful when trying to parallelise programs. If we can determine *how much* of a structure is needed we can then evaluate the structure to that depth in parallel.

The work that introduced this representation of demands was by Wadler and Hughes [27] using the idea of *projections* from domain theory. The technique we use in our compiler is a projection-based strictness analysis based on the work in Hinze's dissertation [9]. Hinze's dissertation is also a good resource for learning the theory of projection-based strictness analysis.

Strategies. With the more sophisticated information provided by projection-based analysis, we require more than simply *par* and *seq*. To this end we use the popular technique of *strategies* for parallel evaluation [15,25]. Strategies are designed to evaluate structures up to a certain depth in parallel to the use of those structures. Normally, strategies are written by the programmer for use in hand-parallelised code. In order to facilitate auto-parallelisation we have developed a method to *derive* an appropriate strategy from the information provided to us by projection-based strictness analysis. The rules for the derivation are presented as a denotational semantics and can be found in our earlier work [3].

2.3   The Granularity Problem

We have now discussed how we find the parallelism that is implicit in our program, but none of the analysis we provide determines whether the safe parallelism is *worthwhile*. Often static analysis will determine that a certain structure is *safe* to compute in parallel, but it is very difficult to know when it is actually of any benefit. Parallelism has overheads that require the parallel tasks to be substantial enough to make up for the cost. A *fine-grained* task is unlikely to require more computation than the cost of sparking and managing the thread, let alone the potential to interrupt productive threads [7, 10].

One of the central arguments in our work is that static analysis *alone* is insufficient at finding both the implicit parallelism and determining whether the introduced parallelism is substantial enough to warrant the overheads.

Our proposal is that the compiler should *run* the program and use the information gained from running it (even if it only looks at overall execution time) to *remove* the parallelism that is too fine-grained. By doing this we shift the burden of the granularity problem away from our static analysis and onto our search techniques. This way our static analysis is only used to determine the safe parallel expressions, and not the granularity of the expressions.

3   Overview

In this section we will present a high-level overview of our technique. This will provide the context for our discussion in the subsequent sections.

The program listed in Fig. 3 is the Tak program benchmark, often used for testing the performance of recursion in interpreters and code generated by compilers [14].

```
tak :: Int -> Int -> Int -> Int
tak x y z = case x <= y of
               True  -> z
               False -> tak (tak (x - 1) y z)
                            (tak (y - 1) z x)
                            (tak (z - 1) x y)

main = tak 24 16 8
```

Fig. 3. Source listing for Tak

After we perform our projection-based strictness analysis, and introduce the safe **par** annotations, we transform the program into a parallelised version. The result of this transformation on Tak is listed in Fig. 4.

```
tak x y z = case x <= y of
                True  -> z
                False -> let x' = tak ((x - 1)) y z
                             y' = tak ((y - 1)) z x
                             z' = tak ((z - 1)) x y
                         in (par x'
                                 (par y'
                                      (seq z'
                                           (tak x' y' z')))))


main  = tak 24 16 8
```

Fig. 4. Source listing for Tak after analysis, transformation, and **par** placement

Each strict argument is given a name via a **let** binding. This is so that any parallel, or **seq**ed, evaluation can be shared between threads. When there are multiple strict arguments (as is the case for **tak**) we spark the arguments in left-to-right order except for the last strict argument, which we **seq**. This is a common technique that is used to avoid potential collisions [25]. Collisions occur when a thread requires the result of another thread before the result has been evaluated. By ensuring that one of the arguments is evaluated in the current thread (by using **seq**) we give the parallel threads more time to evaluate their arguments, lessening the frequency of collisions.

While static analysis has determined that x' and y' can be evaluated in parallel *safely*, it does not determine whether parallel evaluation of those expressions is *worthwhile*. In order to address this issue we take advantage of two key properties of our **par** annotations:

1. Each introduced **par** sparks off a unique subexpression in the program's source
2. The semantics of **par** (as shown in Fig. 2) allow us to return its second argument, ignoring the first, without changing the semantics of the program as a whole.

These two properties allow us to represent the **par**s placed by static analysis and transformation as a bit string. Each bit represents a specific **par** in the program AST. When a **par**'s bit is 'on' the **par** behaves as normal, sparking off its first argument to be evaluated in parallel and return its second argument. When the bit is 'off' the **par** returns its second argument, ignoring the first.

This allows us to change the *operational* behavior of the program without altering any of the program's semantics.

4   Experimental Setup and Results

In this section we evaluate the use of search in finding an effective enabling of pars that achieves a worthwhile speed-up when the parellelised program is run in a multi-core architecture. As a reminder, the starting point for our proposed technique is a program that was originally written to be run sequentially on a single core; static analysis identifies potential sites at which par functions *could* be applied; and then search is used to determine the subset of sites at which the par is actually applied.

4.1   Research Questions

Our hypothesis is that enabling a subset of the pars will often be preferable to enabling them all, hence the first research question:

RQ1. What speed-up is achieved by using search to enable a subset of pars compared to the enabling all the pars found by static analysis?

Since the overall goal is to speed-up a sequential program by parallelising it to use multiple cores, the second question is:

RQ2. What speed-up is achieved by parallelisation using search compared to the original software-under-test (SUT) executed as a sequential program?

In this empirical work, we consider two algorithms: a simple hill-climbing algorithm and a greedy algorithm:

RQ3. Which search algorithm achieves the larger speed-ups, and how quickly do these algorithms achieve these speed-ups?

Since some pars can only have an effect when one or more other pars are also enabled, there is an argument that a sensible starting point for both algorithms is to have all pars enabled. An alternative is to start with a random subset of the pars enabled. This motivates the final research question:

RQ4. Which form of initialisation enables the algorithm to find the best speed-ups: all pars enabled (we refer to this as *'all-on'* initialisation), or a random subset enabled (*'random'* initialisation)?

4.2   Algorithms

Representation. We represent the choice of enabled pars as a bit string where a 1 indicates that the par is applied at a site, and 0 that it is not. The length of the bit string is the number of potential pars annotations found by the static analysis.

Fitness. To facilitate experimentation, the SUTs are executed using a simulator which records the number of reductions made by each thread. A parameter to the simulator controls the number of cores available to the SUT, and thus the maximum number of threads that may be run in parallel. We choose the number of reductions made by the main thread as the fitness metric. The main thread cannot complete until all the other threads it has started have completed, and so this number of reductions is an indication of the SUT's runtime. The simulator includes a realistic overhead of 250 reductions for handling each additional thread.

Hill-Climbing Algorithm. We utilise a simple hill-climbing algorithm in which the neighbours of the current bitstring are those formed by flipping a single bit. At each iteration, these neighbours of the current bitstring are considered in a random order, and the fitness evaluated for each in turn. The first neighbour that has a better fitness, i.e. fewer reductions are made by the main thread, than the current bitstring becomes the current bitstring in the next iteration. The algorithm terminates when no neighbour of the current bitstring has a better fitness.

Greedy Algorithm. The greedy algorithm considers the bits in representation in a random order. As each bit is considered, the bit is flipped from its current setting and the resulting bit string evaluated; the setting of the bit—current or flipped—with the better fitness is retained. The algorithm terminates once all the bits have been evaluated.

4.3   Software-Under-Test

SumEuler. SumEuler is a common parallel functional programming benchmark first introduced with the work on the $\langle \nu, G \rangle$-Machine in 1989 [1]. This program is often used a parallel compiler benchmark making it a 'sanity-check' for our work. We expect to see consistent speed-ups in this program when parallelised (9 par sites).

Queens + Queens2. We benchmark two versions of the nQueens program. Queens2 is a purely symbolic version that represents the board as a list of lists and does not perform numeric computation (10 par sites for Queens and 24 for Queens2). The fact that Queens2 has more than double the number of par sites for the same problem shows that writing in a more symbolic style provides more opportunity for *safe* parallelism.

SodaCount. Solves a word search problem for a given grid of letters and a list of keywords. Introduced by Runciman and Wakeling, this program was chosen because it exhibits a standard search problem and because Runciman and Wakeling hand-tuned and profiled a parallel version, demonstrating that impressive speed-ups are possible with this program [21] (15 par sites).

Tak. Small recursive numeric computation that calculates a Takeuchi number. Knuth describes the properties of Tak in [14] (2 par sites).

Taut. Determines whether a given predicate expression is a tautology. This program was chosen because the algorithm used is *inherently sequential*. We feel that it was important to demonstrate that not all programs have implicit parallelism within them, sometimes the only way to achieve parallel speed-ups is to rework the algorithm (15 par sites).

MatMul. List of list matrix multiplication. Matrix multiplication is an inherently parallel operation, we expect this program to demonstrate speed-ups when parallelised (7 `par` sites).

4.4 Method

The following four algorithm configurations were evaluated:

- hill-climbing with all-on initialisation
- greedy with all-on initialisation
- hill-climbing with random initialisation
- greedy with random initialisation.

Each algorithm configuration was evaluated for four settings of the number cores: 4, 8, 16 and 24 cores. Each algorithm/core count combination was evaluated against each of the seven SUTs described above.

Since both search algorithms are stochastic, multiple runs were made for each algorithm/core count/SUT combination, each using 30 different seeds to the pseudo-random number generator. For all runs, after each fitness evaluation, the best bit string found and its fitness (the number of reductions made by the main thread), was recorded.

In addition, the fitness (number of reductions) was evaluated for a bit string where all bits are set to 1: this equivalent to using the static analysis without optimisation using search. This evaluation was made for each combination of core count and SUT. Finally, the fitness was evaluated for the sequential version of each SUT.

4.5 Results

The results are summarised in Table 1. This table compares the speed-up, calculated as the ratio of the medians of the reduction counts, of hill-climbing with all-on initialisation compared to (a) the parallelisation that would result from the static analysis without optimisation; (b) the sequential version of the program; (c) the greedy algorithm with all-on initialisation; and (d) the hill-climbing algorithm with random initialisation. The speed-up is calculated as the factor by which the number of reductions is reduced, and so values greater than 1 indicate that the SUT parallelised using hill-climbing with all-on initialisation would be faster in the multi-core environment. Values in bold in the table indicate that differences between the algorithms used to calculate the speed-up are statistically significant at the 5 % level using a one- or two-sample Wilcoxon test as appropriate[3].

---

[3] Since in the following we discuss the results for each SUT, or combination of SUT and number of cores, individually as well as for the entire set of results as a family, we do not apply a Bonferroni or similar correction to the significance level. Nevertheless we note here that most of the currently significant differences would remain significant if such a correction were applied.

Table 1. The speed-up, calculated as the ratio of the medians of the reduction counts, achieved by the hill-climbing algorithm using all-on initialisation compared to the default parallelisation from static analysis (static parallel), a sequential implementation of the SUT (sequential), the greedy algorithm (greedy), and hill climbing using random initialisation (random init). Speed-ups are rounded to 4 significant figures. Values in bold font are significant at the 5 % level.

| SUT | Cores | Hill-climbing speed-up compared to: | | | |
		Static parallel	Sequential	Greedy	Random init
MatMul	4	**4.903**	**1.021**	1	1
MatMul	8	**4.625**	**1.021**	1	1
MatMul	16	**4.485**	**1.021**	1	1
MatMul	24	**4.439**	**1.021**	1	1
Queens	4	**1.080**	**1.294**	1	1
Queens	8	**1.043**	**1.369**	1	1
Queens	16	**1.017**	**1.401**	1	1
Queens	24	**1.003**	**1.401**	1.000	1
Queens2	4	**6.479**	**3.843**	1	1
Queens2	8	**6.421**	**7.607**	1	1
Queens2	16	**6.263**	**14.79**	1	1
Queens2	24	**6.101**	**21.54**	1	1
SodaCount	4	**4.237**	**3.773**	1.000	1.055
SodaCount	8	**3.544**	**6.207**	**1.007**	**1.071**
SodaCount	16	**3.110**	**10.40**	**1.081**	**1.072**
SodaCount	24	**2.810**	**13.26**	**1.004**	1
SumEuler	4	**1.494**	**3.948**	1	1
SumEuler	8	**1.486**	**7.773**	1	1
SumEuler	16	**1.460**	**14.77**	1	1
SumEuler	24	**1.432**	**20.69**	1	1
Tak	4	**1.609**	**1.560**	1	1
Tak	8	**1.609**	**3.118**	1	1
Tak	16	**1.608**	**6.230**	1	1
Tak	24	**1.608**	**9.330**	1	1
Taut	4	**1.000**	**1.000**	**1.000**	1
Taut	8	**1.000**	**1.000**	**1.000**	1.000
Taut	16	**1.000**	**1.000**	**1.000**	1
Taut	24	**1.000**	**1.000**	**1.000**	1

4.6   Discussion

RQ1. For most of SUTs there is a relatively large speed-up of the hill-climbing algorithm compared to the default parallelisation where all `pars` are enabled. The largest speed-ups are for Queens2 where we might expect a wall-clock run time that is more than 6 times better than the default parallelisation. For Queens and Taut the speed-ups are closer to 1, but are in all cases statistically significant.

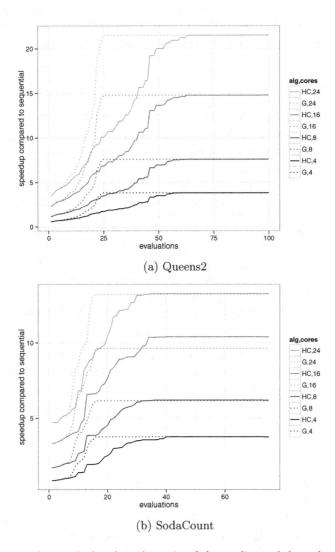

(a) Queens2

(b) SodaCount

Fig. 5. The speed-up, calculated as the ratio of the medians of the reduction counts, obtained so far by the algorithm plotted against the number of fitness evaluations. HC and G indicate the hill-climbing and greedy algorithm respectively, both using all-on initialisation. The numbers following the algorithm abbreviation indicate the number of cores (Color figure online).

We conclude that the hill-climbing algorithm can improve parallel performance across a range of SUTs and across a range of core counts.

RQ2. For Queens2 and SumEuler, the speed-up compared the sequential version of these SUTs is almost linear: it approaches the number of cores available. For example, for SumEuler on 4 cores, the speed-up compared to the sequential version is 3.95. A linear speed-up is the best that can be achieved, and so these results are indicative that our proposed technique could be very effective in practice. Meanwhile, for other SUTs such as MathMaul and Taut, there is little speed-up over the sequential version of the SUT.

RQ3. The results show that for most SUTs, there is little difference in the speed-up achieved by the hill-climbing and greedy algorithm. (For clarity, the table shows the comparison only between the two algorithms using all-on initialisation, but similar results are obtained when initialisation is random.) Only for SodaCount is there a non-trivial and statistically significant difference between the hill climber and greedy algorithm for all core sizes. Figure 5 performs a further analysis for this research question: for two of the SUTs, it plots the best speed-up (compared to sequential) obtained so far by the algorithm against the number of fitness evaluations. For Queens2 at all core counts, the greedy algorithm finds the same best speed-up as the hill-climbing, but finds it in fewer fitness evaluations, i.e. the search is faster. For SodaCount, the greedy algorithm finds its best speed-up in relatively few evaluations. The hill-climber takes longer but finds a better speed-up at all cores counts; the difference is most noticeable in the results for 16 cores. For frequently-used SUTs that account for a significant part of a system's performance, the additional effort required to find the best parallelisation using hill-climbing may be justified, but will depend on context.

RQ4. For most SUTs there is no statistically significant difference between all-on and random initialisation. For SodaCount, the all-on initialisation is slightly better for core counts of 4, 8, and 16. This result provides evidence that all-on initialisation may be beneficial, but requires further investigation to confirm the generality.

5   Related Work

Research into parallel *functional* programming has been an active research area since the early 1980s. Before research into implicit parallelism fell out of favor, much of the work focused on the use of static analysis alone in parallelising programs [7,10]. Harris and Singh used runtime feedback to *find* parallelism in functional programs without the use of static analysis [8]. Our approach can be seen as reversal of their approach, *introduce* parallelism at compile-time and *remove* parallelism using runtime feedback.

A number of researchers in the late 1990s applied metaheuristic search to transform serial *imperative* programs into parallel ones. Both Nisbet [18] and

Williams [28] independently targeted FORTRAN programs using metaheuristics to find an appropriate sequence of code transformation to enable the program to take advantage of a target parallel architecture. The Paragen framework described by Ryan and his collaborators applies genetic programming to optimise a tree-like representation of parallelising transformations that are applied to blocks of code, and a linear representation of transformations that are applied to loops in the program [22]. The fitness used by Paragen is a combination of the speed-up obtained and the equivalence of the serial and parallel versions of the program based on a post hoc analysis of data dependencies. The two key differences from the work described in this paper are that: (a) here the search does not derive a sequence of transformations, but instead determines which potential transformations, found by prior static analysis, are enabled; and, (b) any transformed parallel program is guaranteed to be equivalent to the original serial program by construction. We believe that these differences may facilitate scalability in our approach.

6 Conclusions

We have shown in this paper that the combination of static analysis and search can parallelise programs. For some programs we are able to achieve close to linear speed-ups which is as performant as can expected. As future work we will investigate more sophisticated algorithms, including genetic algorithms and estimation of distribution algorithms; and confirm the scalability of our approach.

References

1. Augustsson, L., Johnsson, T.: Parallel graph reduction with the $\langle v, G \rangle$-machine. In: Proceedings of the Fourth International Conference on Functional Programming Languages and Computer Architecture. FPCA 1989, pp. 202–213. ACM, New York (1989)
2. Burn, G.L., Hankin, C., Abramsky, S.: Strictness analysis for higher-order functions. Sci. Comput. program. **7**, 249–278 (1986)
3. Calderón Trilla, J.M., Runciman, C.: Improving implicit parallelism. In: Proceedings of the ACM SIGPLAN Symposium on Haskell. Haskell 2015 (2015). Under submission
4. Clack, C., Peyton Jones, S.: The four-stroke reduction engine. In: Proceedings of the 1986 ACM Conference on LISP and Functional Programming, pp. 220–232. ACM (1986)
5. Clack, C., Peyton Jones, S.L.: Strictness analysis-a practical approach. In: Jouannaud, J.-P. (ed.) Functional Programming Languages and Computer Architecture. LNCS, vol. 201, pp. 35–49. Springer, Heidelberg (1985)
6. Hammond, K.: Parallel functional programming: an introduction (1994). http://www-fp.dcs.st-and.ac.uk/~kh/papers/pasco94/pasco94.html
7. Hammond, K., Michelson, G.: Research Directions in Parallel Functional Programming. Springer-Verlag (2000)
8. Harris, T., Singh, S.: Feedback directed implicit parallelism. SIGPLAN Not. **42**(9), 251–264 (2007). http://doi.acm.org/10.1145/1291220.1291192

9. Hinze, R.: Projection-based strictness analysis: theoretical and practical aspects. Inaugural dissertation, University of Bonn (1995)
10. Hogen, G., Kindler, A., Loogen, R.: Automatic parallelization of lazy functional programs. In: Krieg-Brückner, B. (ed.) ESOP 1992. LNCS, vol. 582, pp. 254–268. Springer, Heidelberg (1992)
11. Hughes, J.: Why functional programming matters. Comput. J. **32**(2), 98–107 (1989)
12. Hughes, R.J.M.: The design and implementation of programming languages. Ph.D. thesis, Programming Research Group, Oxford University, July 1983
13. Jones, M., Hudak, P.: Implicit and explicit parallel programming in haskell (1993). Distributed via FTP at http://nebula.systemsz.cs.yale.edu/pub/yale-fp/reports/RR-982.ps.Z. Accessed July 1999
14. Knuth, D.E.: Textbook examples of recursion. In: Lifschitz, V. (ed.) Artificial Intelligence and Theory of Computation, pp. 207–229. Academic Press, Boston (1991)
15. Marlow, S., Maier, P., Loidl, H., Aswad, M., Trinder, P.: Seq no more: better strategies for parallel haskell. In: Proceedings of the Third ACM Haskell Symposium on Haskell, pp. 91–102. ACM (2010)
16. Mycroft, A.: The theory and practice of transforming call-by-need into call-by-value. In: Robinet, B. (ed.) International Symposium on Programming. LNCS, vol. 83, pp. 269–281. Springer, Heidelberg (1980)
17. Naylor, M., Runciman, C.: The reduceron reconfigured. ACM Sigplan Not. **45**(9), 75–86 (2010)
18. Nisbet, A.: GAPS: A compiler framework for genetic algorithm (GA) optimised parallelisation. In: Proceedings of the International Conference and Exhibition on High-Performance Computing and Networking, pp. 987–989. HPCN Europe 1998 (1998)
19. Peyton Jones, S.L.: Parallel implementations of functional programming languages. Comput. J. **32**(2), 175–186 (1989)
20. Plasmeijer, R., Eekelen, M.V.: Functional Programming and Parallel Graph Rewriting, 1st edn. Addison-Wesley Longman Publishing Co., Inc., Boston (1993)
21. Runciman, C., Wakeling, D. (eds.): Applications of Functional Programming. UCL Press Ltd., London (1996)
22. Ryan, C., Ivan, L.: Automatic parallelization of arbitrary programs. In: Langdon, W.B., Fogarty, T.C., Nordin, P., Poli, R. (eds.) EuroGP 1999. LNCS, vol. 1598, pp. 244–254. Springer, Heidelberg (1999)
23. Sutter, H.: The free lunch is over: a fundamental turn toward concurrency in software. Dr. Dobbs J. **30**(3), 202–210 (2005)
24. Tremblay, G., Gao, G.R.: The impact of laziness on parallelism and the limits of strictness analysis. In: Proceedings High Performance Functional Computing, pp. 119–133. Citeseer (1995)
25. Trinder, P.W., Hammond, K., Loidl, H.W., Peyton Jones, S.L.: Algorithm + strategy = parallelism. J. Funct. Program. **8**(1), 23–60 (1998)
26. Wadler, P.: Strictness analysis on non-flat domains. In: Abramsky, S., Hankin, C.L. (eds.) Abstract Interpretation of Declarative Languages, pp. 266–275. Ellis Horwood, Chichester (1987)
27. Wadler, P., Hughes, R.J.M.: Projections for strictness analysis. In: Kahn, G. (ed.) FPCA 1987. LNCS, vol. 274, pp. 385–407. Springer, Heidelberg (1987)
28. Williams, K.P.: Evolutionary algorithms for automatic parallelization. Ph.D. thesis, Department of Computer Science, University of Reading, December 1998

An Improved Beam-Search for the Test Case Generation for Formal Verification Systems

Mahmoud A. Bokhari[1,2], Thorsten Bormer[3], and Markus Wagner[4]([✉])

[1] Computer Science School, University of Adelaide, Adelaide, Australia
[2] Computer Science Department, Taibah University,
Medina, Kingdom of Saudi Arabia
[3] Institute for Theoretical Informatics, Karlsruhe Institute of Technology,
Karlsruhe, Germany
[4] Optimisation and Logistics, University of Adelaide, Adelaide, Australia
markus.wagner@adelaide.edu.au

Abstract. The correctness of software verification systems is vital, since they are used to confirm that safety and security critical software systems satisfy their requirements. Modern verification systems need to understand their target software, which can be done by using an axiomatization base. It captures the semantics of the programming language used for writing the target software. To ensure their correctness, it is necessary to validate both parts: the implementation and the axiomatization base. As a result, it is essential to increase the axiom coverage in order to verify its correctness. However, creating test cases manually is a time consuming and difficult task even for verification engineers. We present a beam search approach to automatically generate test cases by modifying existing test cases as well as a comparison between axiomatization and code coverage. Our results show that the overall coverage of the existing test suite can be improved by more than 20 %. In addition, our approach explores the search space more efficiently than existing ones.

Keywords: Beam search · Formal verification · System testing

1 Introduction

Formal verification is the act of proving or disproving that an algorithm or its implementation is correct with respect to its formal specification. The formal mathematical approaches include, amongst others, model checking, deductive verification, and program derivation [4,7,12].

The correctness of the program verification systems themselves is imperative if they are to be used in practice. In principle, instead of or in addition to testing, parts of verification tools (in particular the axiomatization and the calculus) can be formally verified. For example, the Mobius project [2], the LOOP project [15], and the Bali project [18], all aimed at the development of fully verified verification systems. One may employ formal methods to prove a system or

M. Barros and Y. Labiche (Eds.): SSBSE 2015, LNCS 9275, pp. 77–92, 2015.
DOI: 10.1007/978-3-319-22183-0_6

its calculus to be correct. But—as for any other type of software system—testing and cross-validation are of great importance [3,10].

In our situation of testing formal verification systems, all tests have to be programs (along with their formal specifications) that can be verified successfully, whether it is with or without human interaction. Due to their inherent complexity, creating such test cases by hand is already a challenging problem for experienced verification engineers. Currently, it is unknown how tests can be generated automatically from scratch using existing methods.

A verification system consists of many testable components (e.g., parsers, the user interface, proof procedures), and the so-called *axiomatization* is one of them. It carries the formal definitions of the target program language, which makes it a core component of the systems. The correctness of this component is of outmost importance, *especially* when safety- and security-critical programs are to be verified.

To ensure the correctness of program verification tools, it is necessary to validate both parts: the implementation, as well as the axiomatization. Only testing the implementation is not sufficient, even if a high code coverage is achieved. For example, it was noted in [6] that there is a certain amount of "core code" exercised by all tests, while there is only a small number of "core axioms" used by many tests. Some logical defects stay hidden within the axiomatization unless it is fully exercised. The work in [6] discovered two bugs in the axiomatization as a result of the coverage maximization research.

Our goal is to increase the proportion of the axiomatization that is actively used in successful verification attempts [6]. As a consequence, new bugs ("regressions") are more likely to be found in regression testing, when the implementation of the verification system (and its axiomatization) is changed. The problem is challenging for iterative search approaches due to the large number of axioms (typically 100's) and due to the time consuming verification process (sometimes minutes), which also makes it unsuitable for population-based evolutionary algorithms or ant-colony optimization as they require many evaluations [1,13]. Besides the time-consuming evaluation process, the vast number of infeasible ways of creating test cases renders the problem inappropriate for disruptive approaches, such as simulated annealing and even the simple (1+1) evolutionary algorithms. In [19] a collection of various breadth-first and depth-first approaches with randomized components to this problem was investigated. These approaches were not problem-specific in the sense that the search for the next test case was completely uninformed. In contrast to this, we are using in this article a beam search approach [8,9] that is informed by previous runs. We do this in order to achieve two goals: (1) reduction of the likelihood to generate infeasible solutions, and (2) increase of the likelihood to cover previously uncovered axioms.

First, we outline the specific problem in Sect. 2, and in Sect. 3 we formulate it as an optimization problem. In the subsequent Sect. 4, we describe our informed approach. We analyze our results and compare them with existing approaches in Sect. 5. The paper concludes in Sect. 6 with a summary of key findings and a description of potential future research.

2   Target of Optimization: Program Verification Systems

In this article, we concentrate on modern verification systems that allow for *auto-active verification*. In auto-active verification, the requirement specification together with all relevant information to find a proof (e.g., loop invariants) is given to the verification tool right from the start of the verification process—interaction hereafter is not possible. While some tools such as VCC [11] and Caduceus [14] allow only this type of interaction, other such as the KeY tool [4], offer in addition an interactive mode for the proof construction.

Program verification tools have to capture the program language semantics of the programs to be verified. In some tools (e.g., as with logical frameworks like Isabelle/HOL [17]) these semantics are mostly stored as one huge axiomatization or a set of calculus rules and separate from the actual proof system. At this end of the spectrum of program verification systems, (at least) one rule is defined per program language construct (e.g., control flow statements or evaluation of arithmetic expressions) in order to conduct proofs about program correctness. The task of the actual implementation part of the verification tool is then mostly to apply these rules, respectively axioms.

We consider in this article system tests, i.e., the verification tool is tested as a whole. Though the correctness of a tool, of course, depends on the correctness of its components and it makes sense to also test these components independently, not all components are easy to test individually. For example, it is possible (and useful) to unit-test an SMT solver that is used by a tool. But the verification condition generator is hard to test separately as it is very difficult to specify its correct behaviour. In the following, we concentrate on functional tests that can be executed automatically, i.e., user-interface properties are not considered.

As is typical for verification tools following the auto-active verification paradigm, we assume that a verification problem consists of a program to be verified and a requirement specification that is added in form of annotations to the program. Typical annotations are, e.g., invariants, pre-/postcondition pairs, and assertions of various kinds. If P is a program and A is a set of annotations, then we call the pair $P+A$. Besides the requirement specification, a verification problem usually contains additional auxiliary annotations that help the system in finding a proof. We assume that all auxiliary input (e.g., loop invariants) are made part of the testing input, such that the test can be executed automatically.

Possible outcomes of running a verification tool on a test $P+(REQ \cup AUX)$ (a verification problem consisting of a program P, a requirement specification REQ, and auxiliary annotations AUX) are:

Proved: A proof has been found showing that the program P satisfies $REQ \cup AUX$.

Not provable: There is no proof (either P does not satisfy REQ or AUX is not sufficient); the system may provide additional information on why no proof exists, e.g., by a counter example or by showing the current proof state.

Timeout: No proof could be found given the allotted resources (time and space).

In the following, we are only considering test cases for which the intended outcome is that KeY finds a proof given the allocated computational resources.

3 Problem Formulation

In this section, we present how we determine the amount of testing done, and how we intend to improve it.

3.1 Axiomatization Coverage

Measuring code coverage is an important method in software testing to judge the quality of a test suite. This is also true for testing verification tools. However, code coverage is not an indicator for how well the declarative logical axioms and definitions—that define the semantics of programs and specifications and that make up an important part of the system—are tested.

To solve this problem, we use the notion of axiomatization coverage [6]. It measures the extent to which a test suite exercises the axioms (that capture the program language semantics) used in a verification system. The idea is to compute the percentage of axioms that are actually used in the proofs for the verification problems that make up a test suite. The higher the coverage of a test suite is, the more likely it is that a bug that is introduced in a new version of the verification system is discovered.

We use the following version of axiomatization coverage: the percentage of axioms needed to successfully verify correct programs. An axiom is defined to be *needed* to verify a program, if it is an element of a *minimal axiom subset*, using which the verification system is able to find a proof. That is, if the axiom is removed from this subset, the tool is not able anymore to prove the correctness of the program.

Definition 1 ([6]). *A test case $P+(REQ \cup AUX)$ covers the axioms in a set Th if $Th \vdash P+(REQ \cup AUX)$ but $Th' \nvdash P+(REQ \cup AUX)$ for all $Th' \subsetneq Th$.*

Note that, in general, the minimal set of axioms covered by a given verification problem is not unique.

To compute an approximation of the axiom coverage for a test case $P+(REQ \cup AUX)$, the procedure is as follows. In a first step, we verify the test case with the verification tool using the complete axiom base available. Besides gathering information on resource consumption of this proof attempt, information on which axioms are actually used in the proof are recorded as set T.[1] Then, the iterative reduction phase starts. In a reduction step, we start from the empty set C of *covered* axioms. For each axiom t in the set of initially used axioms T, an attempt to prove the test case using axioms $C \cup (T \setminus \{t\})$ is made. If the proof does not succeed, we consider t to be necessary and we add t to the set C. Then, we remove axiom t from T and start the next proof iteration until

---

[1] "Used" does not imply that the application of the axiom was necessary.

$T = \varnothing$. After a single iteration of this computation, we repeat these operations but this time on C, until no more axiom removal is possible without affecting the ability to find a proof. As a result, this fixed-point algorithm finds a true minimal set of axioms to construct the proof.

3.2   Maximizing Axiomatization Coverage

We increase the amount of testing done by generating additional tests from existing ones. We achieve this by preventing the verification system to use certain parts of the axiomatization. Thus, we force the system to find alternative ways of constructing a correctness proof for a given test case $P+(REQ \cup AUX)$, while using only a subset of the total set of axioms. We will refer to this subset of allowed axioms as the whitelist WL. Now, the notion of what a test case constitutes actually changes: it becomes a tuple of $\langle P+(REQ \cup AUX), WL\rangle$, of a program P with a requirement specification REQ and auxiliary annotations AUX, and a whitelist WL.

The introduction of the whitelists allows us to reuse existing test cases, by modifying the WL for each program and its specification. This is a big advantage over writing new test cases, which is a very time consuming process even for experienced verification engineers. On the other hand, our approach cannot fully replace the need to extend test suites through additional test cases. For example, take axioms for bitwise XOR-operations or for certain simplifications of inequalities. Even though many parts of the axiomatization will be reused over and over, it may not be possible to cover these, if the corresponding characteristics are never found in any of the existing test cases.

4   Metaheuristic Approach

In the following, we describe the verification system that is the subject of our study. Subsequently, we present our heuristic approaches to the problem. Note that our approaches can be applied to the testing of further verification systems, if these can provide information on which axioms were used during the construction of the proof; for example, this is the case for Microsoft's VCC [11].

4.1   The KeY System

As the target for our case study we have chosen the KeY tool [4], a verification system for sequential Java Card programs. In KeY, the Java Modeling Language (JML) is used to specify properties about Java programs with the common specification constructs like pre- and postconditions for methods and object invariants. Like in other deductive verification tools, the verification task is modularized by proving one Java method at a time.

In the following, we will briefly describe the workflow of the KeY system. Let us assume the user has chosen one method to be verified against a single pre-/postcondition pair. First, the relevant parts of the Java program, together with its JML annotations are translated to a sequent in Java Dynamic Logic, a multimodal predicate logic. Validity of this sequent implies that the program is correct with respect to its specification. Proving the validity is done using automatic proof strategies within KeY, which apply sequent calculus rules implemented as so-called *taclets*. For an in-depth introduction, we refer the interested reader to [4]. The set of taclets provided with KeY captures the semantics of Java. Additionally, it contains taclets that deal with first order logic formulas. The development version of KeY as of 16 August 2012, contains 1520 taclets and rules; we will call these *axioms* in the remainder of this article to facilitate reading. Note that not all axioms are always available when performing a proof, as some exist in several versions, depending on proof options chosen.

4.2   Algorithms

As stated above, we are aiming at maximizing the axiomatization coverage through the creation of test cases $\langle P+(REQ \cup AUX), WL \rangle$. The test suite that we will consider already contains pairs $P+(REQ \cup AUX)$, such that we can focus on the search for whitelists. This process can be very time consuming (several hours) due to the reduction phases. Furthermore, it is very often the case that infeasible whitelists are created, as they miss elements that are crucial for the construction of the eventual proof. Even a very "careful" random generation of whitelists is rarely successful. Therefore, we use an informed conservative approach in which we attempt to use the knowledge gained so far.

Guidance Table. To efficiently navigate the search space, we propose a new approach that uses a guidance table GT to guide and inform the search. This GT consists of the following: each found axiom encountered in any minimal sets, its replacement sets if it is successfully replaced, the total number of successful uses for each replacement set, the total number of all successful replacements, and the total number of unsuccessful replacements. All data is recorded for each axiom. Table 1 illustrates an example of the guidance table: it shows that *ax3* was replaced successfully four times; once by {*ax5*, *ax6*} and three times by {*ax7*}. It also shows that it was not possible to replace {*ax3*}.

Table 1. Guidance Table example

Axiom	Replacement Set	Successful Times	Total Successful Times	Unsuccessful Times
ax1	{ax4}	1	1	0
ax2		0	0	1
ax3	{ax5, ax6}	1	4	1
	{ax7}	3		0

The major purpose of using the guidance table is to find equivalences between axioms.[2] In other words, it lists equivalent sets of axioms for each axiom or axiom sets. For example, Table 1 depicts that *ax3* has two equivalent sets of axioms which are {*ax5*, *ax6*} and {*ax7*}. It is worth mentioning that these two sets are only equivalent to that axiom in four cases in total. However, as they are not completely equal to *ax3*, the first set could not replace *ax3* in one instance.

In addition, discovering relationships between axioms enables the proposed technique to find axioms that have a relatively large number of equivalent sets to guide the search. Since our proposed method is based on the beam search technique, which requires information regarding the search space, it is essential to construct such a table that can be used to inform and guide it towards promising nodes. Moreover, the guidance table can identify irreplaceable axioms that have not been replaced successfully. Avoiding these axioms improves the performance of the search process and the framework.

BeamSearch Approach. Algorithm 1 illustrates our informed beam search. As can be seen at the first stage, the GT is initialised and sorted by the values of the total successful replacement times. Then, the initial set of used axioms T for proving the test case TC—in the form of $\langle P+(REQ \cup AUX), WL \rangle$—is obtained by running the verification tool on TC. If no proof can be constructed, the method terminates. If a proof can be constructed, then we reduce the set T to a minimal set M.

In the next stage, the GT is used to fill the promising node list that is used for selecting the best nodes to explore. It includes all axioms that are found in M as well as in GT, however, in some cases an axiom may not found in the GT which means it is a newly covered axiom. Furthermore, these axioms must have relatively high successfully replacement rates. Lastly, axioms that have not been replaced are stored in the discarded list to be avoided in the search process.

In the subsequent stage, where the axioms are not found in the GT, the method adds them to the promising node list. This step is considered to guarantee that all new axioms have to be dropped from the WL. As a result, new equivalent axioms may get covered, which increases the chances of maximising the overall axiomatization coverage.

In the final stage, the promising list is sorted by each axiom's successful replacements in a descending order, then the method starts exploring the promising axioms. We do this by dropping one at a time from the axiomatization base WL and then re-running the proving procedure using the shorter WL (Step 1). As a consequence a new test case might be generated, but this time an axiom which has several logically equivalent sets of axioms has been removed from it, which increases the chances of forcing the verification tool to use different axioms.

BEAMSERCH^{FastMinSet}. In order to reduce the computation time, we use some additional information obtained by the GT tool from the previous test runs.

---

[2] "Equivalence" is not strictly logical here, but regarding the tool's capability to find a proof in a different way.

Algorithm 1. BeamSearch

Data: GT: guidance table (sorted by successful replacements)
Data: TC: test case $\langle P+(REQ \cup AUX), WL \rangle$
Data: T: initially used set of axioms during the proof
Data: M: minimal set of axioms needed for finding the proof
Data: WL: axiomatization base used by the verification tool
Data: PromisingNodeList: list containing the most promising nodes
Data: DiscardedList: list containing discarded nodes
Result: union of all minimal lists

```
 1  T = Run(TC) ;                                    /* run the verification tool */
 2  if TC is not Proved OR Timeout then
 3  |   Stop;
 4  else
 5  |   M = Reduce(T);
 6  |   Add M to result;                             /* add the newest minimal list */
 7  |   foreach axiom in M do
 8  |   |   if GT contains axiom then
 9  |   |   |   if axiom in GT has total successful time greater than 0 then
10  |   |   |   |   Add axiom to PromisingNodeList;
11  |   |   |   else
12  |   |   |   |   Add axiom to DiscardedList;
13  |   |   |   end
14  |   |   else
15  |   |   |   Add axiom to PromisingNodeList;      /* adding new axiom, since it has not
                                                         been in the GT so far */
16  |   |   end
17  |   end
18  |   sort(PromisingNodeList);                     /* by total replacements (descending) */
19  |   foreach axiom in PromisingNodeList do
20  |   |   Drop axiom from current WL;
21  |   |   Repeat from Step 1;
22  |   end
23  end
24  return result;
```

For each test case TC, the GT tool collects and stores all of the initially used axiom sets T and their reduced minimal sets of axioms M. In addition, it arranges these sets to speed up the whole testing process. This can be done by mapping each TC and T to a set of M. As a result, the tool generates a hash table where the keys are pairs of $\langle TC, T \rangle$ and the values are sets of M.

The approach BeamSearch[FastMinSet] has two main parts: (1) it effectively tries to quickly re-discover the previously found minimal sets M, and (2) constructs the promising list to inform the search. Algorithm 2 illustrates only the first part, as the second part (i.e., building the promising list) is already discussed in BeamSearch Approach in Sect. 4.2. As can be seen, the set T of axioms used in proofs is obtained by running the verification tool on the test case TC using the whole white list WL. Additionally, the approach looks for the corresponding minimal set M from the hash table HT.

In the next stage, when M is found, the BeamSearch[FastMinSet] reruns the tool again, but this time the WL is replaced by the corresponding M (which was a successful reduction at least once before), to ensure the validity of M. It is worth mentioning that we add this step, since the verification tool may undergo some modifications that affect the proof procedure. Then the BeamSearch[FastMinSet] uses the valid M for building the promising list. However, in case the HT does

---

Algorithm 2. BEAMSEARCH^{FastMinSet}

Data: HT: hash table ((TC, T), M)
Data: TC: test case $\langle P+(REQ \cup AUX), WL\rangle$
Data: T: initially used set of axioms during the proof
Data: M: minimal set of axioms needed for finding the proof
Data: WL: axiomatization base used by the verification tool
Result: union of all minimal lists

```
 1  T = Run(TC) ;                              /* run the verification tool on TC */
 2  if TC is not proved OR Timeout then
 3  │   Stop;
 4  else
 5  │   if HT contains ⟨TC,T⟩ then
 6  │   │   M = Get M from HT by ⟨TC,T⟩;
 7  │   │   WL = M;
 8  │   │   T = Run(TC) ;                           /* rerun to ensure M is valid */
 9  │   │   if TC is proved then
10  │   │   │   Add M to result;                    /* add the newest minimal list */
    │   │   │   /* construct promising and discarded lists as in BEAMSEARCH       */
11  │   │   else
    │   │   │                                       // TC is not proved, run BEAMSEARCH
12  │   │   end
13  │   else
    │   │                                           // HT does not contain ⟨TC,T⟩, run BEAMSEARCH
14  │   end
15  end
16  return result;
```

---

not contain such T (i.e., it is new, or M is not valid), the BEAMSEARCH^{FastMinSet} continues its job as BEAMSEARCH, by reducing T to a new minimal set M and then constructs the promising list.

As can be noted, using BEAMSEARCH^{FastMinSet} significantly reduces the testing time by eliminating the time needed for reducing T to M. Although BEAM-SEARCH^{FastMinSet} runs the verification tool twice, still it is considerably faster than the complete reduction of T to the minimal set M, since the later can require dozens or even hundreds of verification attempts.

5   Experimental Investigations

In this section, we will first describe the experimental setup. We will briefly look into the information that our beam search uses, before presenting and analyzing the coverage results.

5.1   Experimental Setup

Our testing framework automatically executes the 319 test cases mentioned above and measures the axiomatization coverage[3]. We also use Emma tool version 2.0 to measure the code coverage[4]. It worth mentioning that we run 2 separated experiments, one for each coverage criterion. For code coverage the

---

[3] The full code and the logfiles are available online http://cs.adelaide.edu.au/~optlog/research/software.php.

[4] www.emma.sourceforge.net (last accessed: 5 April 2015).

reduction phase is disabled during the test, and therefore the number of covered axioms is slightly different to those in the axiomatization experiment.

This test and all subsequent runs are performed on Intel Xeon E5430 CPUs (2.66 GHz), on Debian GNU/Linux 5.0.8, with Java SE RE 1.7.0. The internal resource constraints are set to twice the amount of resources needed for the first proof run recorded initially. This allows for calculating axiom coverage in reasonable time and ensures comparability of coverage measures between computers of different processing power. Still, the computation of a single fix-point takes typically minutes, and in a few cases even hours. Therefore, we limit the computation time for each of the 319 test cases to 24 h for each approach, which means an investment of 0.87 CPU years per approach. We compare our informed beam-search approach to the different variant of uninformed breadth-first and depth-first approaches reported in [19]. We observed in preliminary testing that even the approaches with random selectivity produced the same results in independent runs with negligible deviations (±1 covered axiom), which is why (in addition to the computational cost) we limit our investigations to only one run per approach.

Before our experiments, we build the guidance table for our beam search based on re-runs of the APPROACHES 1–5 in [19]. This guidance table contains, amongst others, the following interesting information. This step is mandatory, as otherwise our approach default to a simple breadth-first search.

First, let us look at individual axioms. In Fig. 1, we show for all covered axioms the number of times that they have been successfully and unsuccessfully replaced. The use of this data is not straight-forward, since there is no specific pattern. For instance, one of these axioms has 188 unsuccessful replacements, while it is successfully replaced 36 times. Such axioms have to be moved towards the end the promising list, as they appear to be dead ends more often than not. On the end of the spectrum, one axiom is successfully replaced 143 times, while it is unsuccessfully replaced only three times. This makes it a good candidate for the beam search.

Once an axiom is replaced, we can often see that it is replaced by a set of two axioms or by even larger sets. Figure 2 shows how many different single axioms

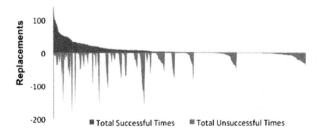

Fig. 1. Number of successful vs. unsuccessful replacements for each single axiom, shown as positive and negative values. The axioms (along the x-axis) are sorted in a decreasing order according to the number of successful replacements.

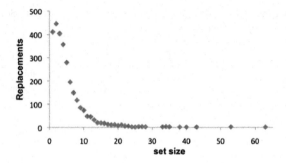

Fig. 2. Replacement set's sizes and number of replacements for single axioms BEAM-SEARCH^{FastMinSet}

are replaced by a set of axioms. For example, 446 pairs of axioms successfully replace a single axiom, and there is one case where one axiom is replaced by an enormous set of 63 axioms. In the future, we can study such cases in order to identify equivalent sets of axioms. Moreover, they can help us to improve the framework by restricting the number of times that we replace that one axiom in the future, since it may increase the execution time for the proof procedure.

5.2 Code Coverage Results

Achieving high code coverage in software testing is of great importance to judge the test suite. Nevertheless, in verifying deductive verification systems, our results show axiomatization coverage is essential. This is because although in 295 test cases the lines of code (LOC) coverage is more than 34 %, the axiomatization coverage is less than 10 %; moreover, 41 test cases have less than 1 % of axiom coverage. Table 2 shows a summary of the coverage details for the test cases.

As can be seen, the average LOC coverage is 37 %, in contrast, it is only 4.43 % for the axiomatization coverage. Most of test cases exercised nearly the same proportion of the code as the standard deviation for LOC is 2.5 %. On the other hand, there are fluctuations in the amount of covered axioms by the test suite. This is due to the logical properties within each test case.

In addition, some test cases managed to exercise 89 % and 44 % of the class and LOC coverage respectively, which is the maximum LOC coverage; nonetheless, they could not cover even 17 % of the axioms individually. In short, there is no clear correlation between the exercised code and the used axioms.

The overall axiomatization coverage—as it is expected—is low with only 45 %. Additionally, the LOC coverage is only 51 %, which is significantly less than the 85 % recommended by the software testing (see e.g. [20]). Though the class coverage reached 90 %, after we analyzed the EMMA outputs, we find that many classes are only partially covered. This includes classes that appear to be crucial for the proof procedure: the LOC coverage there ranges from 62 % down to even 0 % (see Table 3 for some examples).

Table 2. Code Coverage vs. Axiomatization Coverage (excerpt). Sorted by axiom percentage in descending fashion.

Test Cases	Code Coverage		Axiomatization Coverage	
	Class Coverage	Line Coverage	Number of Axioms	Axiom Percent
standard_key-java_dl-arrayUpdateSimp .... 182 test cases	87 %	35 %	3	0.20 %
heap-SmansEtAl-Iterator_list ... 134 test cases	83 %	40 %	62	4.08 %
heap-list-ArrayList_concatenate	85 %	44 %	255	16.78 %
min/max	81 %/89 %	34 %/44 %	3/255	0.2 %/17 %
mean$_{\text{standard deviation}}$	85 %$_{1.9\%}$	37 %$_{2.5\%}$	67$_{52}$	4.43 %$_{3.4\%}$
union	90 %	51 %	691	45 %

Table 3. Some classes within KeY tool.

Class	Method Coverage	Line Coverage
Taclet	66 %	62 %
TacletBuilder	61 %	47 %
Proof	54 %	50 %
CompoundProof	0 %	0 %

5.3 Axiomatization Coverage Results

The coverage statistics of the different approaches are listed in Table 4. The number 611 represents the result of the naive approach, where the full set of 1520 axioms is used and no alternatives are sought. This is our base value.

We start with some general observations. First, each of the individual approaches improves the total coverage over the first minimal sets by about 12–15 % each. The highest individual improvements are made by our BEAM-SEARCH^{FastMinSet}.

When considering all approaches together, then the initial coverage of about 611 axioms increases to a total of 755 axioms through the use of whitelists. This means that all approaches together improve the achievable coverage autonomously by about 24 %, and that is without requiring a verification engineer to write a single new test case.

It is an interesting coincidence that our BEAMSEARCH^{FastMinSet} achieves a total coverage of 722 axioms, which is identical to the coverage achieved by APPROACHES 1–5 together. As we can see via the 755 axioms that are covered by the union of all seven approaches, our beam search does not only cover most of what APPROACHES 1–5 do, but it also covers additional 33 axioms. It appears that the combination of guidance table and the fast reduction (when available) allows it to search more effectively than the previous approaches.

Table 4. Coverage statistics. The *first minimal sets* refer to those found first by the approaches, which initially use all 1520 axioms. The results for APPROACHES 1–5 are based on reruns from [5].

axioms covered in ...	DEPTH-FIRST SEARCH	RANDOM DEPTH-FIRST SEARCH	GREEDY	BREADTH-FIRST SEARCH	RANDOM BREADTH-FIRST SEARCH	Union APPROACHES 1–5	BEAMSEARCH	BEAMSEARCH^{FastMinSet}	Union of all seven approaches
... the first minimal sets	611 (40%)	611 (40%)	610 (40%)	613 (40%)	609 (40%)	615 (40%)	611 (40%)	612 (40%)	638 (42%)
... all minimal sets	701 (46%)	699 (46%)	688 (45%)	687 (45%)	684 (45%)	722 (48%)	692 (46%)	722 (48%)	755 (50%)

Table 5. Successful vs. unsuccessful replacements: unique single axioms.

	Successfully replaced single axioms	Unsuccessfully replaced single axioms	Total	Successfully replaced axioms
DEPTH-FIRST SEARCH	29	230	259	11%
RANDOM DEPTH-FIRST SEARCH	26	235	261	10%
GREEDY	21	218	239	9%
BREADTH-FIRST SEARCH	181	259	440	41%
RANDOM BREADTH-FIRST SEARCH	193	267	460	42%
BEAMSEARCH	211	97	308	69%
BEAMSEARCH^{FastMinSet}	231	90	321	72%

Table 6. Analysis: equivalent sets found by each approach.

	Equivalent sets	Total	% of equivalent sets
DEPTH-FIRST SEARCH	7,544	132,735	6%
RANDOM DEPTH-FIRST SEARCH	3,880	40,446	10%
GREEDY	2,458	80,886	3%
BREADTH-FIRST SEARCH	9,037	26,733	34%
RANDOM BREADTH-FIRST SEARCH	10,784	28,842	37%
BEAMSEARCH	33,178	75,180	44%
BEAMSEARCH^{FastMinSet}	54,821	258,319	21%

Let us now investigate the differences between the approaches. First, by using our GT tool, we obtain the number of times that a single axiom is successfully replaced. The results are shown in Table 5, and they clearly show the structural differences between the approaches. For example, the depth-first APPROACHES 1–3 have the smallest number of replacements of single axioms, which is expected given their nature: they will explore shorter and shorter white lists first. The breadth-first APPROACHES 4/5 on the other hand achieve significantly higher single replacements, since they explore the replacement of single axioms first. Our beam search achieves the highest number of replacements here, since it prefers the replacements of single axioms, and it also considers single axioms when it comes across new ones in the search. This has the big advantage for the use of the guidance table that shorter keys are more likely to be existent, and therefore of help. We will see this in the following.

Next, we obtain the number of equivalent sets found by each approach. Table 6 presents the total *attempts*, as well as the amount of equivalent sets and their percentages. As we can see, the success rate is in favor of BEAM-SEARCH with 44 %. On the other hand, among all BEAMSEARCH^{FastMinSet} is the fourth with 21 %, it comes after the RANDOM BREADTH-FIRST SEARCH and BREADTH-FIRST SEARCH with 37 % and 34 %, respectively. This is because BEAMSEARCH^{FastMinSet} eliminates the reduction time for finding the minimal sets M, which in turn enables it to spend more time exploring the search space. In addition, it is worth mentioning that the numbers of the total attempts represent the sizes of each approach's generated guidance table, which shows that a large amount of information for the beam search is extracted.

In contrast to this, the number of equivalent sets for BEAMSEARCH^{FastMinSet} is the largest amongst the algorithms. Moreover, there is a significant difference between our beam search approaches and the breadth-first approaches RANDOM BREADTH-FIRST SEARCH and BREADTH-FIRST SEARCH, that achieve the fourth and fifth highest number of equivalent sets. In total, all 74,219 unique test cases created by all approaches are stored and are ready to be used for regression testing, currently achieving a coverage that is 24 % higher than that achieved by the 319 original test cases.

Summarizing the results of this section, we make the following conclusions:

1. Through the use of the guidance table, BEAMSEARCH^{FastMinSet} and BEAM-SEARCH search more efficiently. This also allows us to identify more logical relationships among the axioms to improve our framework for future runs.
2. Moreover, our results clearly show that even though BEAMSEARCH^{FastMinSet} is using heuristic information and it has the ability to decrease the reduction time, the problem of finding potential candidates within such a difficult search space makes it increasingly hard to cover further axioms. Therefore we conjecture that we are getting increasingly close to the local optimum that we can achieve with our current approach.

6   Conclusions and Future Work

In this article, we present a beam search approach for increasing the axiomatization coverage in deductive verification systems, where a set of axioms—logical rules that capture the semantics of a programming language—is used to find a proof that a program satisfies its formal specifications. Our approach automatically creates test cases by preventing the verification tool from using previously covered axiom. Therefore, the system tries to find alternative axioms to prove the program. A test case consists of the verifiable program, its requirements, and the allowed set of axioms.

Our heuristic approach involves a learning process where the beam search method uses a guidance table that contains special historical data from previous runs. As a result, It explores the search space more effectively than previous approaches that use uninformed breadth-first and depth-first variants. Whilst successful in increasing the coverage of our tested verification system, these uninformed techniques often generated infeasible solutions during their search, and they are not much directed towards an actual increase of the coverage.

The experiments reveal several interesting insights. First, our approach achieves a coverage comparable to that of the union of five previous approaches, when given the same computation budget. Furthermore, the overall coverage has been improved over the starting point by 24 %. Second, the high number of unsuccessful replacement attempts by our fast approach strongly indicates that we are getting increasingly close to the local optimum of "maximum coverage" that we can reach with our test case reuse. Finally, we found there is no correlation between code and axiomatization coverage and therefore it is essential to focus on maximizing the axiom coverage to uncover hidden defects.

We will continue our research in the following areas:

1. We plan to investigate the reasons why some axioms are not covered, amongst others, using the help of developers of the verification systems. We will systematically write specific test cases aimed to increase the axiomatization coverage for specific axioms.
2. Once we will have reached a satisfactory axiomatization coverage, we will need to focus on combinations of axioms. Failures in a variety of domains are often caused by combinations of several conditions (see studies like [16]). We plan to combine combinatorial testing with combinatorial search techniques. Then, combinations of language features and axioms will be used to form complex test cases. The knowledge gained from the work presented here will help us to focus our efforts in comprehensive testing.

References

1. Back, T., Fogel, D.B., Michalewicz, Z.: Handbook of evolutionary computation. IOP Publishing Ltd., (1997)
2. Barthe, G., et al.: MOBIUS: mobility, ubiquity, security. In: Montanari, U., Sannella, D., Bruni, R. (eds.) TGC 2006. LNCS, vol. 4661, pp. 10–29. Springer, Heidelberg (2007)

3. Beckert, B., Klebanov, V.: Must program verification systems and calculi be verified? In: Verification Workshop (VERIFY), Workshop at Federated Logic Conferences (FLoC), pp. 34–41 (2006)
4. Beckert, B., Hähnle, R., Schmitt, P.H. (eds.): Verification of Object-Oriented Software. The KeY Approach. LNCS, vol. 4334. Springer, Heidelberg (2007)
5. Beckert, B., Bormer, T., Wagner, M.: Heuristically creating test cases for program verification systems. In: Metaheuristics International Conference (MIC) (2013)
6. Beckert, B., Bormer, T., Wagner, M.: A metric for testing program verification systems. In: Veanes, M., Viganò, L. (eds.) TAP 2013. LNCS, vol. 7942, pp. 56–75. Springer, Heidelberg (2013)
7. Bérard, B., Bidoit, B., Finkel, M., Laroussinie, F., Petit, A., Petrucci, L., Schnoebelen, P.: Systems and Software Verification: Model-checking Techniques and Tools. Springer, Heidelberg (2010)
8. Blum, C., Blesa, M.J.: Probabilistic beam search for the longest common subsequence problem. In: Stützle, T., Birattari, M., H. Hoos, H. (eds.) SLS 2007. LNCS, vol. 4638, pp. 150–161. Springer, Heidelberg (2007)
9. Bokhari, M., Wagner, M.: Improving test coverage of formal verification systems via beam search. In: Companion of the 2015 Conference on Genetic and Evolutionary Computation, GECCO 2015. ACM (2015) (to be published)
10. Bormer, T., Wagner, M.: Towards testing a verifying compiler. In: International Conference on Formal Verification of Object-Oriented Software (FoVeOOS) Pre-Proceedings, pp. 98–112. Karlsruhe Institute of Technology (2010)
11. Cohen, E., Dahlweid, M., Hillebrand, M., Leinenbach, D., Moskal, M., Santen, T., Schulte, W., Tobies, S.: VCC: a practical system for verifying concurrent C. In: Berghofer, S., Nipkow, T., Urban, C., Wenzel, M. (eds.) TPHOLs 2009. LNCS, vol. 5674, pp. 23–42. Springer, Heidelberg (2009)
12. Dijkstra, E.W.: Guarded commands, nondeterminacy and formal derivation of programs. Commun. ACM **18**, 453–457 (1975)
13. Dorigo, M., Birattari, M., Stutzle, T.: Ant colony optimization. IEEE Comput. Intell. Mag. **1**, 28–39 (2006)
14. Filliâtre, J.-C., Marché, C.: Multi-prover verification of C programs. In: Davies, J., Schulte, W., Barnett, M. (eds.) ICFEM 2004. LNCS, vol. 3308, pp. 15–29. Springer, Heidelberg (2004)
15. Jacobs, B., Poll, E.: Java program verification at nijmegen: developments and perspective. In: Futatsugi, K., Mizoguchi, F., Yonezaki, N. (eds.) ISSS 2003. LNCS, vol. 3233, pp. 134–153. Springer, Heidelberg (2004)
16. Kuhn, D.R., Wallace, D.R., Gallo, A.M.: Software fault interactions and implications for software testing. IEEE Trans. Softw. Eng. **30**, 418–421 (2004)
17. Nipkow, T., Paulson, L.C., Wenzel, M. (eds.): Isabelle/HOL. LNCS, vol. 2283. Springer, Heidelberg (2002)
18. von Oheimb, D.: Hoare logic for Java in Isabelle/HOL. Concurrency Comput. Pract. Experience **13**, 1173–1214 (2001)
19. Wagner, M.: Maximising axiomatization coverage and minimizing regression testing time. In: IEEE Congress on Evolutionary Computation (CEC), pp. 2885–2892 (2014)
20. Zhu, H., Hall, P.A.V., May, J.H.R.: Software unit test coverage and adequacy. ACM Comput. Surv. **29**, 366–427 (1997)

Combining Multiple Coverage Criteria in Search-Based Unit Test Generation

José Miguel Rojas[1], José Campos[1(✉)], Mattia Vivanti[2], Gordon Fraser[1], and Andrea Arcuri[3,4]

[1] Department of Computer Science, The University of Sheffield, Sheffield, UK
{j.rojas,jose.campos,gordon.fraser}@sheffield.ac.uk
[2] Università Della Svizzera Italiana (USI), Lugano, Switzerland
mattia.vivanti@usi.ch
[3] Scienta, Oslo, Norway
arcuri82@gmail.com
[4] University of Luxembourg, Luxembourg City, Luxembourg

Abstract. Automated test generation techniques typically aim at maximising coverage of well-established structural criteria such as statement or branch coverage. In practice, generating tests only for one specific criterion may not be sufficient when testing object oriented classes, as standard structural coverage criteria do not fully capture the properties developers may desire of their unit test suites. For example, covering a large number of statements could be easily achieved by just calling the `main` method of a class; yet, a good unit test suite would consist of smaller unit tests invoking individual methods, and checking return values and states with test assertions. There are several different properties that test suites should exhibit, and a search-based test generator could easily be extended with additional fitness functions to capture these properties. However, does search-based testing scale to combinations of multiple criteria, and what is the effect on the size and coverage of the resulting test suites? To answer these questions, we extended the EvoSuite unit test generation tool to support combinations of multiple test criteria, defined and implemented several different criteria, and applied combinations of criteria to a sample of 650 open source Java classes. Our experiments suggest that optimising for several criteria at the same time is feasible without increasing computational costs: When combining nine different criteria, we observed an average decrease of only 0.4 % for the constituent coverage criteria, while the test suites may grow up to 70 %.

1 Introduction

To support developers in creating unit test suites for object-oriented classes, automated tools can produce small and effective sets of unit tests. Test generation is typically guided by structural coverage criteria; for example, the search-based unit test generation tool EvoSuite by default generates test suites optimised for branch coverage [4], and these tests can achieve higher code coverage than manually written ones [8]. However, although manual testers often *check*

© Springer International Publishing Switzerland 2015
M. Barros and Y. Labiche (Eds.): SSBSE 2015, LNCS 9275, pp. 93–108, 2015.
DOI: 10.1007/978-3-319-22183-0_7

the coverage of their unit tests, they are usually not *guided* by it in creating their test suites. In contrast, automated tools are only guided by code coverage, and do not take into account *how* this coverage is achieved. As a result, automatically generated unit tests are fundamentally different to manually written ones, and may not satisfy the expectations of developers, regardless of coverage benefit.

```
public class ArrayIntList
        extends RandomAccessIntList
        implements IntList, Serializable {
  public int set(int index, int element) {
    checkRange(index);
    incrModCount();
    int oldval = _data[index];
    _data[index] = element;
    return oldval;
  }
}
```

```
@Test
public void test9() throws Throwable {
  ArrayIntList arrayIntList0 = new ArrayIntList();
  // Undeclared exception!
  try {
    int int0 = arrayIntList0.set(200, 200);
    fail("Expecting IndexOutOfBoundsException");
  } catch(IndexOutOfBoundsException e) {
    // Should be at least 0 and less than 0, found 200
  }
}
```

(a) Source code excerpt.   (b) Test case generated by EvoSuite.

Fig. 1. This example shows how EvoSuite covers method `set` of the class `ArrayIntList`: the method is called, but statement coverage is not achieved.

For example, consider the excerpt of class `ArrayIntList` from the Apache Commons Primitives project in Fig. 1a. Applying EvoSuite results in a test suite including the test case in Fig. 1b: The test calls `set`, but with parameters that do not pass the input validation by `checkRange`, such that an exception is thrown. Nevertheless, EvoSuite believes `set` is covered with this test, and adds no further tests, thus not even satisfying statement coverage in the method. The reason is that EvoSuite follows common practice in bytecode-based coverage analysis, and only checks if branching statements evaluated to true and false [13].

```
public class Complex {
  public Complex log() {
    if (isNaN) {
      return NaN;
    }
    return createComplex(FastMath.log(abs()),
            FastMath.atan2(imaginary, real));
  }

  public Complex pow(double x) {
    return this.log().multiply(x).exp();
  }
  ...
}
```

```
@Test
public void test1() throws Throwable {
  Complex complex0 = new Complex(Double.NaN);
  Complex complex1 = complex0.pow(Double.NaN);
  assertEquals(Double.NaN, complex1.getArgument(),0.01D);
}

@Test
public void test2() throws Throwable {
  Complex complex0 = Complex.ZERO;
  Complex complex1 = complex0.pow(complex0);
  assertFalse(complex1.isInfinite());
  assertTrue(complex1.isNaN());
}
```

(a) Source code excerpt.   (b) Test cases generated by EvoSuite.

Fig. 2. This example shows how EvoSuite covers method `log`, even though there is no test that directly calls the method.

To cover method `set` fully, one would also need to aim at covering all instructions. However, when optimising test suites to cover branches *and* instructions, automated techniques may find undesired ways to satisfy the target criteria. For example, consider the excerpt of class `Complex` from the Apache Commons Math project shown in Fig. 2a: EvoSuite succeeds to cover method `log`, but because `log` is called by `pow`, in the end often only tests calling `pow` (see Fig. 2(b) are retained, which makes it hard to check the behaviour of `log` independently (e.g., with test assertions on the return value of `log`), or to debug problems caused by faults in `log`. Thus, a good test suite has different properties, which cannot easily be captured by any individual structural coverage criterion.

In this paper, we define different criteria and their fitness functions to guide search-based test suite generation, and investigate the effects of combining these during test generation. Such a combination of multiple optimisation criteria raises concerns about the effects on the size of resulting test sets, as well as on the effectiveness of the test generators used for this optimisation. To investigate these concerns, we performed a set of experiments on a sample of 650 open source classes. In detail, the contributions of this paper are as follows:

- Identification of additional criteria to guide unit test suite generation.
- Implementation of these criteria as fitness functions for a search-based test suite optimisation.
- An empirical study of the effects of multiple-criterion optimisation on effectiveness, convergence, and test suite size.

Our experiments suggest that optimising for several criteria at the same time is feasible without increasing computational costs, or sacrificing coverage of the constituent criteria. The increase in size depends on the combined criteria; for example, optimising for line and branch coverage instead of just line coverage increases test suites by only 10 % in size., while optimising for nine different criteria leads to an increase of 70 % in size. The effects of the combination of criteria on the coverage of the constituent criteria are minor; for criteria with fine-grained fitness functions the overall coverage may be reduced slightly (0.4 % in our experiments), while criteria with coarse fitness functions (e.g. method coverage) may benefit from the combination with other criteria.

2   Whole Test Suite Generation for Multiple Criteria

In principle, the combination of multiple criteria is independent of the underlying test generation approach. For example, dynamic symbolic execution can generate test suites for any coverage criteria as by-product of the path exploration [10]. However, our initial usage scenario lies in unit testing for object oriented classes, an area where search-based approaches have been shown to perform well. In search-based testing, the test generation problem is cast as a search problem, such that efficient meta-heuristic search algorithms can be applied to create tests.

2.1   Whole Test Suite Generation

Whole test suite generation refers to the generation of test suites, which has been shown to be more effective than iteratively generating individual test cases [5].

When applying search-based testing for this task, a common technique is to use a genetic algorithm, which starts with a population of random test suites, and then evolves these using standard evolutionary operators [5]. The evolution is guided by a *fitness function* that estimates how close a candidate solution is to the optimal solution; i.e., 100 % coverage in coverage-oriented test generation.

A *test suite* is a collection of *unit tests* for a target Class Under Test (CUT). The CUT comprises a set of methods, each of which consists of a list of statements. Each statement can be a conditional statement (e.g., `if`), a method call or a regular statement. A conditional statement results in two branches depending on the evaluation of its predicate. A *unit test* is an executable function which sets up a test scenario, calls some methods in the CUT, and checks that the observed behaviour matches the expected one. For simplicity, a unit test can be regarded as a sequence of calls to methods of the CUT. Executing a unit test yields an *execution trace*, i.e., a sequence of executed statements which can either end normally with a regular statement, or with an uncaught exception.

2.2 Fitness Functions

In search-based test suite generation, a fitness function measures how good a test suite is with respect to the search optimisation objective, which is usually defined according to a test coverage criterion. Importantly, a fitness function usually also provides additional search guidance leading to satisfaction of the goals. For example, just checking in the fitness function whether a coverage target is achieved would not give any guidance to help covering it.

Method Coverage. Method Coverage is the most basic criterion for classes and requires that all methods in the CUT are executed by a test suite at least once, either via a direct call from a unit test or via indirect calls.

Top-Level Method Coverage. For regression test suites it is important that each method is also invoked directly (cf. Fig. 2). Top-Level Method Coverage requires that all methods are covered by a test suite such that a call to the method appears as a statement in a test case.

No-Exception Top-Level Method Coverage. In practice, classes often consist of many short methods with simple control flow. Often, a generated test suite achieves high levels of coverage by calling these simple methods in an invalid state or with invalid parameters (cf. Fig. 1). To avoid this, No-exception Top-level Method Coverage requires that all methods are covered by a test suite via direct invocations from the tests and considering only normal-terminating executions (i.e., no exception).

The fitness functions for Method Coverage, Top-Level Method Coverage and No-exception Top-level Method Coverage are *discrete* and thus have no possible guidance. Fitness values are simply calculated by counting the methods that have been covered by a test suite. Let *TotalMethods* be the set of all public methods in the CUT and *CoveredMethods* be the set of methods covered by the test suite, then:

$$f_{crit}(Suite) = |\ TotalMethods\ | - |\ CoveredMethods_{crit}\ |$$

Line Coverage. A basic criterion in procedural code is statement coverage, which requires all statements to be executed. Modern test generation tools for Java or C# often use the bytecode representation for test generation, and bytecode instructions may not directly map to source code statements. Therefore, a more common alternative in coverage analysis tools, and the de-facto standard for most Java bytecode-based coverage tools, is to consider coverage of *lines* of code. Each statement in a class has a defined line, which represents the statement's location in the source code of the class. The source code of a class consists of non-comment lines, and lines that contain no code (e.g., whitespace or comments). A unit test suite satisfies the Line Coverage criterion only if it covers each non-comment source code line of the CUT with at least one of its tests. Line Coverage is very easy to visualise, interpret, and to implement in an analysis tool; all these reasons probably contribute to its popularity.

To cover each line of source code, we need to ensure that each basic code block is reached. In traditional search-based testing, this reachability would be expressed by a combination of approach-level and branch distance [14]. The approach-level measures how far an individual execution and the target statement are in terms of the control dependencies (i.e., distance between point of diversion and target statement in control dependence graph). The branch distance estimates how far a predicate is from evaluating to a desired target outcome. For example, given a predicate x == 5 and an execution with value 3, the branch distance to the predicate evaluating to true would be $|3 - 5| = 2$, whereas an execution with value 4 is closer to being true with a branch distance of $|4 - 5| = 1$. Branch distances can be calculated by applying a set of standard rules [12,14].

In contrast to test case generation, if we optimise a test suite to execute all statements then the approach level is not necessary, as all statements will be executed by the same test suite. Thus, we only need to consider the branch distance of all branches that are control dependencies of any of the statements in the CUT. That is, for each conditional statement that is a control dependency for some other statement in the code, we require that the branch of the statement leading to the dependent code is executed. Thus, the Line Coverage fitness value of a test suite can be calculated by executing all its tests, calculating for each executed statement the minimum branch distances $d_{min}(b, Suite)$ among all observed executions to every branch b in the set of control dependent branches B_{CD}, i.e., the distances to all the branches which need to be executed in order to reach such a statement. The Line Coverage fitness function is thus defined as:

$$f_{LC}(Suite) = \nu(|\ NCLs\ | - |\ CoveredLines\ |) + \sum_{b \in B_{CD}} \nu(d_{min}(b, Suite))$$

where *NCLs* is the set of all non-comment lines of code in the CUT, *CoveredLines* is the total set of lines covered by the execution traces of every test in the suite, and $\nu(x)$ is a normalising function in $[0, 1]$ (e.g., $\nu(x) = x/(x+1)$) [2].

Branch Coverage. The concept of covering branches is also well understood in practice and implemented in popular tools, even though the practical definition of branch coverage may not always match the more theoretical definition of covering all edges of a program's control flow. Branch coverage is often interpreted as maximising the number of branches of conditional statements that are covered by a test suite. Hence, a unit test suite is said to satisfy the Branch Coverage criterion if and only if for every branch statement in the CUT, it contains at least one unit test whose execution evaluates the branch predicate to *true*, and at least one unit test whose execution evaluates the branch predicate to *false*.

The fitness function for the Branch Coverage criterion estimates how close a test suite is to covering all branches of the CUT. The fitness value of a test suite is measured by executing all its tests, keeping track of the branch distances $d(b, Suite)$ for each branch in the CUT. Then:

$$f_{BC}(Suite) = \sum_{b \in B} v(d(b, Suite))$$

Here, $d(b, Suite)$ for branch $b \in B$ (where B is the set of all branches in the CUT) on the test suite is defined as follows:

$$d(b, Suite) = \begin{cases} 0 & \text{if the branch has been covered,} \\ \nu(d_{min}(b, Suite)) & \text{if the predicate has been} \\ & \text{executed at least twice,} \\ 1 & \text{otherwise.} \end{cases}$$

Note that a predicate must be executed at least twice, because we need to cover the true and false evaluation of the predicate; if the predicate were only executed once, then the search could theoretically oscillate between true and false.

Direct Branch Coverage. When a test case covers a branch in a public method indirectly, i.e., without directly invoking the method that contains the branch, it is more difficult to understand how the test relates to the branch it covers (cf. Fig. 2). Anecdotal evidence, from previous work with EVOSUITE, also indicates that developers dislike tests that cover branches indirectly, because they are harder to understand and to extend with assertions [8]. Direct Branch Coverage requires each branch in a public method of the CUT to be covered by a direct call from a unit test, but makes no restriction on branches in private methods. The fitness function is the same as the Branch Coverage fitness function, but only methods directly invoked by the test cases are considered for the fitness and coverage computation of branches in public methods.

Output Coverage. Class `ArrayIntList` from Fig. 1 has a method `size` that simply returns the value of a member variable capturing the size of the internal array; class `Complex` from Fig. 2 has methods `isNaN` or `isInfinite` returning boolean member values. Such methods are known as *observers* or *inspectors*, and method, line, or branch coverage are all identical for such methods. Developers in this case sometimes write unit tests to cover not only in the input values of methods, but also in the output (return) values they produce; indeed output diversity can help improve the fault detection capability [1].

To account for output uniqueness and diversity, the following function maps method return types to abstract values that serve as output coverage goals:

$$output(Type) = \begin{cases} \{true, false\} & if\ Type \equiv Boolean \\ \{-, 0, +\} & if\ Type \equiv Number \\ \{alphabetical, digit, *\} & if\ Type \equiv Char \\ \{null, \neq null\} & otherwise \end{cases}$$

A unit test suite satisfies the Output Coverage criterion only if for each public method M in the CUT and for each $V_{abst} \in output(type(M))$, there is at least one unit test whose execution contains a call to method M for which the concrete return value is characterised by the abstract value V_{abst}.

The fitness function for the Output Coverage criterion is then defined as:

$$f_{OC}(Suite) = \sum_{g \in G} \nu(d_o(g, Suite))$$

where G is the total set of output goals for the CUT and $d_o(g, Suite)$ is an output distance function that takes as input a goal $g = \langle M, V_{abst} \rangle$:

$$d_o(g, Suite) = \begin{cases} 0 & if\ g\ is\ covered\ by\ at\ least\ one\ test, \\ \nu(d_{num}(g, Suite)) & if\ type(M) \equiv Number\ and\ g\ is\ not\ covered, \\ 1 & otherwise. \end{cases}$$

In the case of methods declaring numeric return types, the search algorithm is guided with normalised numeric distances (d_{num}). For example, if a call to a method m with integer return type is observed in an execution trace and its return value is 5 (positive integer), the goal $\langle m, + \rangle$ has been covered, and the distances 5 and 6 are computed for goals $\langle m, 0 \rangle$ and $\langle m, - \rangle$, respectively.

Weak Mutation. Test generation tools typically include values generated to satisfy constraints or conditions, rather than values developers may prefer; in particular, anecdotal evidence suggests developers like boundary cases. Test generation can be forced to produce such values using weak mutation testing, which applies small code modifications to the CUT, and then checks if there exists a test that can distinguish between the original and the *mutant*. In weak mutation, a mutant is considered to be covered ("killed") if the execution of a test on the mutant leads to a different state than the execution on the CUT. A unit test suite hence satisfies the Weak Mutation criterion if and only if for each mutant for the CUT at least one its tests reaches state infection.

The fitness function for the Weak Mutation criterion guides the search using infection distances with respect to a set of mutation operators [7]. We assume a minimal infection distance function $d_{min}(\mu, Suite)$ exists and define:

$$d_w(\mu, Suite) = \begin{cases} 1 & \text{if mutant } \mu \text{ was not reached,} \\ \nu(d_{min}(\mu, Suite)) & \text{if mutant } \mu \text{ was reached.} \end{cases}$$

This results in the following fitness function for weak mutation testing:

$$f_{WM}(Suite) = \sum_{\mu \in \mathcal{M}_C} d_w(\mu, Suite)$$

where $\mathcal{M}_C$ is the set of all mutants generated for the CUT.

Exception Coverage. One of the most interesting aspects of test suites not captured by standard coverage criteria is the occurrence of actual faults. If exceptions are directly thrown in the CUTs with a `throw` statement, those will be retained in the final test suites if for example we optimise for line coverage. However, this might not be the case if exceptions are unintended (e.g., a null-pointer exception when calling a method on a null instance) or if thrown in the body of external methods called by the CUT. Unfortunately, it is not possible to know ahead of time the total number of feasible undeclared exceptions (e.g., null-pointer exceptions), in particular as the CUT could use custom exceptions that extend the ones in the Java API.

As coverage criterion, we consider all possible exceptions in each method of the CUT. However, in contrast to the other criteria, it cannot be defined with a percentage (e.g., we cannot say a test suite covers 42 % of the possible exceptions). We rather use the sum of all unique exceptions found per CUT method as metric to maximise. The fitness function for Exception Coverage is thus also discrete, and is calculated in terms of the number of exceptions N_E, explicit and implicit, that have been raised in the execution of all the tests in the suite:

$$f_{EC}(Suite) = \frac{1}{1 + N_E}$$

2.3 Combining Fitness Functions

All criteria considered in this paper are non-conflicting: we can always add new tests to an existing suite to increase the coverage of a criterion without decreasing the coverage of the others. However, with limited time it may be necessary to balance the criteria, e.g., by prioritising weaker ones to avoid over-fitting for just some of the criteria involved. Thus, multi-objective optimisation algorithms based on Pareto dominance are less suitable than a linear combination of the different objectives, and we can define a combined fitness function for a set of n non-conflicting individual fitness functions $f_1 \ldots f_n$ as: $f_{comp} = \sum_{i=1}^{n} w_i \times f_i$, where $w_1 \ldots w_n$ are weights assigned to each individual function which allow for prioritisation of the fitness functions involved in the composition. Given enough time, a combined fitness search is expected to have the same result for each involved non-conflicting fitness function as if they were optimised for individually.

For some of the above-defined fitness functions, a natural partial order exists. For instance, Method Coverage subsumes Top-level Method Coverage. The intuition is that we first want to cover all methods, independently of whether they are invoked directly from a test case statement or not. In turn, Top-level Method Coverage subsumes No-Exception Top-level Method Coverage, that is, covering all methods with direct calls from test cases is more general than covering all methods with direct calls from test cases which do not raise any exception. However, there is no natural order between other functions like for instance Output Coverage and Weak Mutation. In this paper, we arbitrarily assign $w_i = 1$ for all i and leave the question of what are optimal w_i values for future work.

3   Experimental Evaluation

In order to better understand the effects of combining multiple coverage criteria, we empirically aim to answer the following research questions:

RQ1. What are the effects of adding a second coverage criterion on test suite size and coverage?

RQ2. How does combining of multiple coverage influence the test suite size?

RQ3. Does combining multiple coverage criteria lead to worse performance of the constituent criteria?

RQ4. How does coverage vary with increasing search budget?

3.1   Experimental Setup

Unit Test Generation Tool. We have implemented the discussed criteria in the EVOSUITE [4] tool for automatic unit test suite generation. EVOSUITE uses a genetic algorithm where each individual is a test suite [5]. Once a test suite has been generated, EVOSUITE applies *minimisation* in order to optimise the size of the resulting test suite both in terms of total number of lines of code and in number of unit tests. For each coverage goal defined by the selected criterion, a test that covers this goal is selected from the test suite. Then, on a copy of that test, all statements that do not contribute to satisfaction of the goal are successively removed. When minimising for multiple criteria, the order in which each criterion is evaluated may influence the resulting minimised test suite. In particular, if criterion C_1 subsumes criterion C_2, then minimising for criterion C_2 first and then for C_1 may lead to tests being added during minimisation for C_2, but made redundant later, by tests added during minimisation for C_1. EVOSUITE counters this problem with a second minimisation pass where a final minimised test suite with no redundant tests is produced.

Subject Selection. We used the SF110 corpus [6] of Java classes for our experimental evaluation. SF110 consists of more than 20,000 classes in 110 projects;
running experiments on all classes would require an infeasibly large amount of
resources. Hence, we decided to select a stratified random sample of 650 classes.
That is, we constructed the sample iteratively such that in each iteration we
first selected a project at random, and then from that project we selected a class
and added it to the sample. As a result, the sample contains classes from all 110
projects, totalling 63,191 lines of code.

Experiment Procedure. For each selected class, we ran EVOSUITE with ten different configurations: (1) All fitness functions combined; (2) Only Line Coverage
(baseline); 3-10) For each fitness function f defined in Sect. 2.2 (except Line Coverage) a fitness function combining f and Line Coverage. Combining the other
criteria with Line Coverage instead of using each of them in isolation allows a
more objective evaluation, since not all the fitness functions for these other criteria can provide guidance to the search on their own. Each configuration was
run using two time values for the search: 2 and 10 min. To take the randomness
of the genetic algorithm into account, we repeated the two minutes experiments
40 times, and the 10 min experiments five times.

Experiment Analysis. We used coverage as the main measurement of effectiveness, for all the test criteria under study. Furthermore, we also analysed the
size of the resulting test suites; as the number of unit tests could be misleading,
we analysed the size of a test suite in terms of its total number of statements.
Statistical analysis follows the guidelines discussed in [3]: We use the Wilcoxon-
Mann-Whitney statistical symmetry test to assess the performance of different experiments. Furthermore, we use the Vargha-Delaney $\hat{A}_{ab}$ to evaluate if a
particular configuration a used on experiments performed better than another
configuration b. E.g, a $\hat{A}_{ab}$ value of 0.5 means equal performance between configurations; when $\hat{A}_{ab}$ is less than 0.5, the first configuration (a) is worse; and
when $\hat{A}_{ab}$ is more than 0.5, the second configuration (b) is worse.

3.2 Results and Discussion

*RQ1: What are the effects of adding a second coverage criterion on test suite
size and coverage?* Table 1 shows the results of the experiments when using a
two minute timeout for the search. Considering line coverage as baseline, adding
a further coverage criterion does not increase test suite size by a large amount.
For example, adding branch coverage only increases average test suite size from
22.25 statements to 24.92 (a relative $\frac{24.92-22.25}{22.25} = 12\%$ increase). The largest
increase is for the Exception Coverage testing criterion, which adds a further
$28.00 - 22.25 = 5.75$ statements on average to the test suites.

Regarding coverage of the criteria, already a basic criterion like line coverage can achieve reasonable results. For example, targeting also branch coverage explicitly only increases it by 3 % (from 73 % to 77 %). For other criteria,
improvements are higher. For example, we obtain a $88 - 71 = 17\%$ coverage

Table 1. Coverage results for each configuration, average of all runs for all CUTs. Size is measured in number of statements in the final minimised test suites.

Criteria	Lines	Branches	D. Branches	Methods	Top Methods	M. No Exc.	Exceptions	Mutation	Output	Size
ALL	0.78	0.75	0.75	0.87	0.90	0.88	1.35	0.75	0.64	38.01
Lines	0.78	0.73	0.22	0.81	0.74	0.71	0.45	0.69	0.27	22.25
L. & Branches	0.78	0.77	0.24	0.81	0.74	0.72	0.47	0.70	0.27	24.92
L. & D. Branches	0.78	0.76	0.76	0.87	0.85	0.82	0.48	0.70	0.27	26.73
L. & Methods	0.79	0.73	0.22	0.87	0.80	0.77	0.46	0.70	0.27	22.33
L. & Top Methods	0.78	0.73	0.22	0.87	0.89	0.86	0.48	0.70	0.27	24.89
L. & M. No Exc.	0.78	0.73	0.23	0.87	0.89	0.88	0.40	0.69	0.27	25.26
L. & Exceptions	0.78	0.72	0.22	0.81	0.78	0.70	1.93	0.70	0.27	28.00
L. & Mutation	0.79	0.75	0.23	0.81	0.75	0.72	0.50	0.76	0.27	27.45
L. & Output	0.77	0.71	0.21	0.80	0.77	0.75	0.36	0.69	0.64	23.98

improvement of No-exception Top-level Method Coverage, although with the need of $25.26 - 22.25 = 3.01$ more statements. Of particular interest is the case of Output coverage, where a $64 - 27 = 37\%$ increase is achieved with only slightly larger test suites (less than two statements). The Direct Branch Coverage criterion shows the largest increase ($76 - 22 = 54\%$), which confirms that in the traditional approach code is often covered through indirect calls; this increase comes at the cost of $26.73 - 22.25 = 4.48$ statements on average.

> **RQ1:** *In our experiments, adding a second criterion increased test suites size by 14%, and coverage by 20% over line coverage test suites.*

RQ2: How does combining of multiple coverage influence the test suite size? When combining all criteria together, test suite sizes increase substantially, from 22.25 to 38.01 statements. However, we argue that the resulting test suites could still be manageable for developers: Their size is still less than twice the size of the average baseline test suite. Interestingly, this increase of 15.76 ($38.01 - 22.25$) is also less than the sum of the increases observed for each criterion in isolation (25.56). This shows that the criteria are related and lead to coincidental coverage, where tests covering one particular goal may lead to coverage of other goals.

> **RQ2:** *In our experiments, combining all nine criteria increased test suites size by 70%.*

RQ3: Does combining multiple coverage criteria lead to worse performance of the constituent criteria? When combining different criteria together, the test generation becomes more complicated. Given the same amount of time, it could even happen that for some criteria we would get lower coverage compared to just targeting those criteria in isolation. For example, the class `Auswahlfeld` in the SF110 project `nutzenportfolio` consists of 29 methods, each consisting of only a single line. There are only 15 mutants, and when optimising for line coverage and weak mutation all mutations are easily covered within two minutes. However, when using all criteria, then the number of additional test goals based

Table 2. For each criterion, we compare the "All" configuration for that criterion with the configuration for that criterion and line coverage. Averaged effect sizes are reported with p-values of the statistical tests of symmetry around 0.5.

Criterion	All	Just Line & Criterion	Avg. $\hat{A}_{12}$	p-value
Line	0.78	0.78	0.47	≤ 0.001
Branch	0.75	0.77	0.47	≤ 0.001
Direct Branch	0.75	0.76	0.47	≤ 0.001
Exception	1.35	1.93	0.43	≤ 0.001
Method	0.87	0.87	0.50	0.015
Top Method	0.90	0.89	0.50	0.025
Method No Exc.	0.88	0.88	0.51	≤ 0.001
Mutation	0.75	0.76	0.46	≤ 0.001
Output	0.64	0.64	0.51	≤ 0.001

on the many methods (many of which return primitive types) means that on average after two minutes of test generation only seven mutations are covered.

On the other hand, it is conceivable that coverage criteria can "help each other", in the sense that they might smooth the search landscape. For example, the `NewPassEventAction` class from the `jhandballmoves` project in SF110 has two complex methods with nested branches, and the `if` statements have complex expressions with up to four conditions. When optimising method calls without exceptions, after two minutes the constructor is the only method covered without exceptions, as the search problem is a needle-in-the-haystack type search problem. However, if optimising for all criteria, then branch coverage helps reaching test cases where both methods are called without exceptions.

Table 2 shows the comparison of the "All" configuration on each criterion with the configuration that optimises line coverage and each particular criterion. For each class, we calculated the Vargha-Delaney $\hat{A}_{12}$ effect size [3]. For each configuration comparison, we calculated the average $\hat{A}_{12}$ and ran a Wilcoxon-Mann-Whitney symmetry test on 0.5, to see if a configuration leads to better or worse results on a statistically higher number of classes.

There is strong statistical difference in all the comparisons except Method Coverage and Top-Level Method Coverage, which seem to consist of methods that are either trivially covered by all criteria, or never covered. For No-exception Top-level Method Coverage and Output Coverage there is a small increase in coverage; this is likely because these criteria provide little guidance and benefit from the combination with criteria with better guidance. For Exception Coverage targeting all criteria decreases the average number of exceptions substantially from 1.35 to 1.93, which may be caused by the search focusing more on valid executions related to branches and mutants, whereas without that the search becomes more random. For all other criteria there is a decrease in coverage, although very small ($\leq 2\%$).

RQ3: *Combining multiple criteria leads to a 0.4 % coverage decrease on average; criteria with coarse fitness functions can benefit more from the combination than criteria with finer grained guidance.*

RQ4: How does coverage vary with increasing search budget? Fig. 3 compares the performance of the "All" configuration with the ones of Line Coverage combined with each further criterion. Performance is measured with different coverage criteria in each subplot based on the type of comparison. For example, Branch Coverage is used as performance metric when "All" is compared with "Line &Branch" configuration, whereas Method Coverage is used as performance metric when

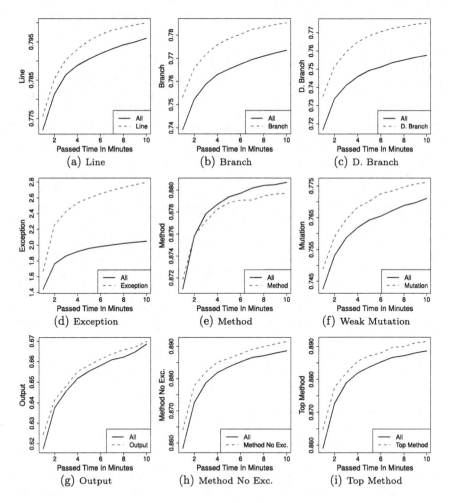

Fig. 3. Time analysis, per minute, for each criterion for the "All" configuration compared with just optimising Line Coverage together with each of those criteria, one at a time.

"All" is compared with "Line & Method". Performance is reported through time, from one minute to ten. The vertical y axes are scaled between the minimum and maximum value each metric obtained.

Given enough time, the performance between each compared configuration should converge to the same value. In other words, given enough time, one could expect that the performance of "All" in each metric would become maximised and equal to just generating data for that criterion alone. Figure 3 shows that for the majority of criteria the performance of the "All" configuration remains slightly below the more focused search, and for Exception Coverage the more focused search even improves over time. For Output Coverage both configurations seem to converge around ten minutes and for Method Coverage the "All" configuration even takes a small lead. Overall, these results suggest that 10 min might not be a long enough time interval to see convergence for all criteria; possibly there might also be side-effects between the combination of criteria in the "All" configuration that generate fitness plateaus in the search landscape. Another possible conjecture is that, because the search in EVOSUITE minimises size as a secondary objective, over time the amount of exploration in the search space will be reduced, making it more difficult to hit additional targets that are not closely related to what is already covered. This could in principle be overcome by keeping an archive of already covered goals and matching tests, and letting the fitness function focus on uncovered goals.

> **RQ4:** *The influence of combining criteria is not limited to early phases of the search but persists over longer time, and the combination does not catch up with focused search within ten minutes.*

Threats to Validity. To counter internal validity, we have carefully tested our framework, and we repeated each experiment several times and followed rigorous statistical procedures in the analysis. To cope with possible threats to external validity, the SF110 corpus was employed as case study, which is a collection of 100 Java projects randomly selected from SourceForge and the top 10 most popular projects [6]. We used only EVOSUITE for experiments and did not compare with other tools; however, at least in terms of the generated tests EVOSUITE is similar to other unit test generation tools. Threats to construct validity might result from our focus on coverage; for example, this does not take into account how difficult it will be to manually evaluate the test cases for writing assert statements (i.e., checking the correctness of the outputs).

4 Related Work

Coverage criteria are well established to estimate the quality of test sets [18], and combinations of criteria have been considered in the context of regression testing [15]. For example, using multiple criteria can improve the fault detection ability after minimisation [11], and Yoo and Harman [16,17] combined coverage criteria with non-functional aspects such as execution time during minimisation.

Non-functional aspects have also been considered during test generation; for example, Harman et al. [9] generated tests optimised for branch coverage and memory consumption. In contrast to this approach, we combine different non-conflicting functional criteria, and thus do not require specialised multi-objective optimisation algorithms. In fact, some of the criteria previously implemented in EVOSUITE were already combinations of constituent criteria included in this paper. For example, the default branch coverage configuration [5] in EVOSUITE combines method and branch coverage. Mutation coverage [7] combines branch coverage with the infection distances used in this paper.

5   Conclusions

Although structural coverage criteria are well established in order to evaluate existing test cases, they may be less suitable in order to guide test generation. As with any optimisation problem, an imprecise formulation of the optimisation goal will lead to unexpected results: For example, although it is generally desirable that a reasonable test suite covers all statements of a Class Under Test (CUT), the reverse may not hold—not every test suite that executes all statements is reasonable. Indeed the desirable properties of a test suite are multi-faceted.

In this paper, we have tried to identify standard criteria used in practice as well as functional aspects that are not captured by standard structural coverage criteria, but are still common practice in object oriented unit testing. We have implemented a search-based approach to generate test suites optimised for combinations of these criteria. Experiments with a sample of open source Java classes have shown that such a combination does neither mean that the test suite sizes become unreasonable, nor that the test generation performance suffers. In fact some aspects can even benefit from the combination, for example when search guidance in the case of search-based test generation is only coarse. An important question that remains to be answered in future work is which selection of criteria matches the expectations of practitioners; for this, we plan to perform controlled experiments with real programmers.

Besides the criteria used in our experiments, the same approach could also be applied in order to enhance test generation with other structural criteria, such as dataflow criteria. On the other hand, there are also non-functional properties of unit test suites that test generation will have to consider in future research, such as the readability of the generated unit tests. However, unlike combinations of functional criteria the inclusion of non-functional aspects may require dedicated multi-objective optimisation algorithms, as functional and non-functional goals may be conflicting (e.g., coverage vs. size).

Acknowledgments. Supported by the National Research Fund, Luxembourg (FNR/P10/03) and the EPSRC project "EXOGEN" (EP/K030353/1).

References

1. Alshahwan, N., Harman, M.: Coverage and fault detection of the output-uniqueness test selection criteria. In: Proceedings of ISSTA 2014, pp. 181–192. ACM (2014)
2. Arcuri, A.: It really does matter how you normalize the branch distance in search-based software testing. Softw. Test. Verif. Reliab. **23**(2), 119–147 (2013)
3. Arcuri, A., Briand, L.: A Hitchhiker's guide to statistical tests for assessing randomized algorithms in software engineering. Softw. Test. Verif. Reliab. **24**(3), 219–250 (2014)
4. Fraser, G., Arcuri, A.: EvoSuite: automatic test suite generation for object-oriented software. In: Proceedings of FSE 2011, pp. 416–419. ACM (2011)
5. Fraser, G., Arcuri, A.: Whole test suite generation. IEEE Trans. Softw. Eng. **39**(2), 276–291 (2013)
6. Fraser, G., Arcuri, A.: A large scale evaluation of automated unit test generation using evosuite. ACM Trans. Softw. Eng. Methodol. **24**(2), 8:1–8:42 (2014)
7. Fraser, G., Arcuri, A.: Achieving scalable mutation-based generation of whole test suites. Empirical Softw. Eng. **20**(3), 1–30 (2014)
8. Fraser, G., Staats, M., McMinn, P., Arcuri, A., Padberg, F.: Does automated whitebox test generation really help software testers? In: Proceedings of ISSTA 2013, pp. 291–301. ACM (2013)
9. Harman, M., Lakhotia, K., McMinn, P.: A multi-objective approach to search-based test data generation. In: Proceedings of GECCO 2007, pp. 1098–1105. ACM (2007)
10. Jamrozik, K., Fraser, G., Tillman, N., de Halleux, J.: Generating test suites with augmented dynamic symbolic execution. In: Veanes, M., Viganò, L. (eds.) TAP 2013. LNCS, vol. 7942, pp. 152–167. Springer, Heidelberg (2013)
11. Jeffrey, D., Gupta, N.: Improving fault detection capability by selectively retaining test cases during test suite reduction. IEEE Trans. Softw. Eng. **33**(2), 108–123 (2007)
12. Korel, B.: Automated software test data generation. IEEE Trans. Softw. Eng. **16**(8), 870–879 (1990)
13. Li, N., Meng, X., Offutt, J., Deng, L.: Is bytecode instrumentation as good as source code instrumentation: an empirical study with industrial tools (experience report). In: Proceedings of ISSRE 2013, pp. 380–389. IEEE (2013)
14. McMinn, P.: Search-based software test data generation: a survey. Softw. Test. Verif. Reliab. **14**(2), 105–156 (2004)
15. Sampath, S., Bryce, R., Memon, A.: A uniform representation of hybrid criteria for regression testing. IEEE Trans. Softw. Eng. **39**(10), 1326–1344 (2013)
16. Yoo, S., Harman, M.: Pareto efficient multi-objective test case selection. In: Proceedings of ISSTA 2007, pp. 140–150. ACM (2007)
17. Yoo, S., Harman, M.: Using hybrid algorithm for pareto efficient multi-objective test suite minimisation. J. Syst. Softw. **83**(4), 689–701 (2010)
18. Zhu, H., Hall, P.A.V., May, J.H.R.: Software unit test coverage and adequacy. ACM Comput. Surv. **29**(4), 366–427 (1997)

Epistatic Genetic Algorithm for Test Case Prioritization

Fang Yuan, Yi Bian, Zheng Li$^{(\boxtimes)}$, and Ruilian Zhao

Department of Computer Science, Beijing University of Chemical Technology,
Beijing 100029, People's Republic of China
yuanfang_cs@163.com, arven_0@126.com, z.li@ieee.org,
rlzhao@mail.buct.edu.cn

Abstract. Search based technologies have been widely used in regression test suite optimization, including test case prioritization, test case selection and test suite minimization, to improve the efficiency and reduce the cost of testing. Unlike test case selection and test suite minimization, the evaluation of test case prioritization is based on the test case execution sequence, in which genetic algorithm is one of the most popular algorithms employed. When permutation encoding is used to represent the execution sequence, the execution of previous test cases can affect the presence of the following test cases, namely epistatic effect. In this paper, the application of epistatic domains theory in genetic algorithms for test case prioritization is analyzed, where Epistatic Test Case Segment is defined. Two associated crossover operators are proposed based on epistasis. The empirical studies show that the proposed two-point crossover operator, E-Ord, outperform the crossover PMX, and can produce higher fitness with a faster convergence.

Keywords: Test case prioritization · Epistasis · Genetic algorithm

1 Introduction

Test Case Prioritization (TCP) is an important branch in regression testing. The other technologies are Test Suite Minimization (TSM) and Test Case Selection (TCS) [1], in which a subset of test suite is obtained to fulfill a certain testing criterion. It has been shown that some important test cases may be missed in TSM and TCS, which leads the software in a high risk of containing undetected errors [2]. TCP works on all test cases in a test suite and aims to identify the best test case execution sequence to meet a certain testing criterion, which can lower the risk of undetected errors [3].

In order to find the best test case execution sequence in TCP, all possible permutations of a test suite should be investigated as candidates, thus TCP is an NP-hard problem [3]. In practice, many test criteria are introduced to TCP which leads TCP in multi-objective optimization. Heuristic optimization algorithms have been employed to solve TCP, such as Non-dominated Sorting

© Springer International Publishing Switzerland 2015
M. Barros and Y. Labiche (Eds.): SSBSE 2015, LNCS 9275, pp. 109–124, 2015.
DOI: 10.1007/978-3-319-22183-0_8

Genetic Algorithm (NSGA-II) [4], Ant Colony Optimization [5] and Particle Swarm Optimization [6], where a challenge comes from the chromosome representation, i.e., the binary encoding, which is used in test case selection and test suite minimization, cannot be used in test case prioritization. Instead permutation encoding is employed in TCP, on which the fitness functions are defined.

In the permutation encoding, a former test case may significantly affect the presence of the latter test cases, namely epistasis. Epistatic domains theory is introduced to analyze the different genes with the interaction of other genes in practical problems, such as two-dimensional bin-packing and graph coloring problems [7], where the presence of a gene of a chromosome depends on genes elsewhere in terms of fitness function value.

The effectiveness and efficiency are always the keys considered in the optimization of search algorithms. GA has been used to solve TCP, TCS and TSM. It is obvious that the evaluation of TCP is sequence related, while TCS and TSM are not. Epistasis has been proven to have a high impact on GA for certain problems, but not considered yet in the GA for TCP.

In this paper, we first analyze the interactions between genes in GA for TCP, and then define Epistatic Test Case Segment (ETS) that is a gene segment with the deterministic impact on fitness. Two refined crossover operators are proposed with the application of epistasis in TCP and the empirical study shows a higher fitness with a faster convergence.

The primary contributions of this paper are as follows:

1. This paper is the first of analyzing epistasis on TCP, where Epistatic Test case Segment is defined to gain insight of problem domains.
2. Two proposed crossover operators are introduced based on epistasis for TCP.
3. Empirical study is conducted with respect to programs from Software-artifact Infrastructure Repository (SIR) and a large scale open source V8 JavaScript Engine from Google. The results suggest that GA with proposed adaptive crossover strategies can better solve TCP.

The rest of the paper is organized as follows: Sect. 2 presents TCP and epistasis. Section 3 presents the proposed crossover operators. Section 4 elaborates the experimental setup and results analysis. The related work is reviewed in Sect. 6. Finally, Sect. 7 gives conclusions and future work.

2   Background

2.1   Search Based Test Case Prioritization

The purpose of TCP aims to find the optimal test case execution sequences that can fulfill a set of testing objects as fast as possible. In order to identify the best sequence in vast amount of possible permutations of test cases, search-based technologies [8] have been employed to search for the optimal or near optimal solutions. Genetic Algorithms (GA) is one of the most widely used algorithms, in which the permutation encoding is used to represent test case

Table 1. An example of 5 statements covered by 4 test cases

Test case	Statement				
	1	2	3	4	5
A		X		X	
B		X	X		X
C	X			X	
D	X		X		

execution sequence. Table 1 presents a simple example of program fraction with 5 statements and 4 test cases. The execution sequence of B-D-C-A represents that the test case B is executed first, then D and C, and test case A is the last.

In general, a variety of coverage criteria, such as statement coverage, branch coverage and block coverage [9], are used as test objects in TCP. In this study reported in the paper, we focus on GA and only statement coverage is considered in the experiments. In practice, all the other types of criteria can be applied to the algorithm. Consequently, Average Percentage of Statement Coverage (APSC) [3] is used as the fitness function to evaluate a test case execution sequence. For a program with M statements and N test cases, the APSC is defined as follows [3]:

$$APSC = 1 - \frac{TS_1 + TS_2 + \cdots + TS_M}{NM} + \frac{1}{2N} \tag{1}$$

where TS_i denotes the id of the test case that first covers the statement i in the execution sequence. Also for the example shown in Table 1, for the sequence of B-D-C-A, $TS_1 = 2$ means the statement 1 is first covered by the second test case D since the first test case B doesn't cover the statement 1 and the second test case D does in the sequence of B-D-C-A. Based on the formula 1, APSC is 82.5 %.

2.2   The Epistasis in Genetic Algorithms

The epistasis is defined by geneticists to represent the influence between genes [10]. In GA, a gene is said to be epistatic when its presence suppresses the effect of a gene at another locus [11]. It has been applied in the two-dimensional bin-packing problem and an adaptive algorithm based on the epistatic domains theory is proposed that can quickly converge on the best solution. It has been also reported that a representation of GA should be constructed in a manner incorporating mild epistasis (neither too high nor too large) [12]. Recently, an analysis of genetic algorithms is presented, in which epistasis plays an important role [13].

Epistatic domains were mostly studied in GA with binary encoding or real number encoding [14]. Seo and Moon [15] proposed an improved encoding/crossover scheme for Travelling Salesman Problem (TSP), in which the distance between two genes were explicitly defined by corresponding epistasis. Permutation encoding has been widely used in GA for TCP. In this paper, we analyze GA with permutation encoding based on the epistatic domains theory and hope to gain insights into the epistatic effects in TCP.

3   TCP with Epistasis

In this section, Epistatic Test case Segment is first defined for TCP, and then two refined crossover operators are introduced based on the epistatic domains theory.

3.1   Epistatic Test Case Segment

In GA of TCP, permutation encoding is commonly used, in which a gene is the id of a test case, and a chromosome is a permutation of all test cases in a test suite. As TCP aims to seek a test cases execution sequence, the presence of current test case will be suppressed by the execution of previous test cases.

Consider the program fraction presented in Table 1 with two test cases sequences, $T1$: A-B-C-D, and $T2$: B-C-A-D. Figure 1 shows the percentages of statements coverage as a function of the fraction of the test suite, for the two permutations $T1$ and $T2$, respectively. The area under the curve represents APSC values, where the area filled with straight lines is the APSC for $T1$ and the area in grey shadow for $T2$.

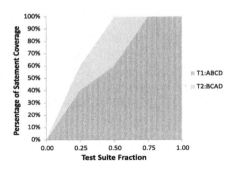

Fig. 1. The APSC for the example in Table 1

For the sequence $T1$: A-B-C-D, test case A is executed first and covers two statements that haven't been covered yet, accordingly the percentage statements coverage becomes 40 % as shown in Fig. 1. While in the sequence $T2$: B-C-A-D, test case A is executed after B and C, consequently A does not cover any more statements that haven't been covered, thus there is no change of APSC value. Further observation reveals that once the maximum statement coverage is reached (100 % in Fig. 1), the APSC value becomes constant.

Definition 1 Epistatic Test Case Segment (ETS). *Given a permutation of all test cases in a test suite, the epistatic test case segment is a test cases segment which starts from the first test case in the execution sequence and ends with the test case that first reaches the maximum value of the test object.*

For example, the segment A-B-C is the ETS for the sequence $T1$:A-B-C-D, as shown in Fig. 1. It can be observed that for a test cases execution sequence in TCP, the value of fitness function only depends on its ETS, and test cases following ETS will not further improve the fitness value (although these test cases are still ordered with the same criterion in general). Thus with the evolution of a execution sequence in GA, the fitness value becomes higher, and the length of ETS tends to become shorter.

In GA, the nature of crossover operators is to vary a chromosome or chromosomes to create next generation. Certainly the new generation should be different with the previous in terms of fitness. However in search-based TCP, if a variation to a chromosome doesn't occur within the ETS, the fitness value would be the same as the previous value. Thus for a chromosome with ETS, the crossover operators should vary the ETS rather than the whole chromosome. So, in this study, two widely used crossover operators are refined in order to make the crossover change occur within ETS.

3.2   One-point Crossover with Epistasis

One-point crossover, namely single-point crossover (SC), randomly selects a cut point k within a chromosome then interchanges the two parent chromosomes at this point to produce two new offsprings. When permutation encoding is used in GA, simply swapping genes segments may cause the repetition of genes that leads in a invalid offspring chromosome. Then in SC with permutation encoding, the first part of offspring chromosome comes from one parent and the rest is completed by genes from the other parent not used in offspring yet. Figure 2a provides an example to illustrate the SC process.

Considering the epistatic test case segment (ETS) when GA is applied to TCP, it's possible that the randomly selected position k is out of ETS. Thus the offspring has the same fitness with the parent. As discussed in Sect. 3.1, with more iterations in GA, the length of ETS tends to become shorter, accordingly the possibility that random k is outside of ETS becomes higher, which weakens the ability of SC to produce chromosomes with new fitness function values.

In order to make the change of crossover occur in ETS, Epistasis-based single-point crossover (E-SC) is proposed in this paper. Figure 2b illustrates the E-SC operator and the detailed steps are presented in Algorithm 1. The highlighted step 2 marks the difference between SC and E-SC: SC preserves the first k elements of p_1, while E-SC varies the first k elements of p_1.

Algorithm 1. Epistasis-based Single-point Crossover

---

1. Select a random position k between 1 and the chromosome length l.

2. Copy last $l - k$ genes from p_1 to o_1.

3. Copy all genes of p_2 to o_1 but excluding the duplicated genes copied from p_1 as the first k genes of $o1$.

4. Exchange p_1 and p_2 and re-execute step 1–3 to construct o_2.

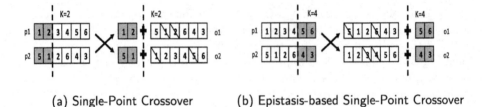

(a) Single-Point Crossover   (b) Epistasis-based Single-Point Crossover

Fig. 2. The illustrations of Single-point Crossover (SC) and Epistasis-based Single-point Crossover (E-SC), where the difference is different gene segments (highlighted in gray) of parents are selected to preserve.

3.3 Two-point Crossover with Epistasis

Two-point crossover, as its name implies, is a type of crossover that randomly selects two cut points and exchanges the genes between them to produce off-springs. Order crossover (Ord), one of two-point crossover operators, is first proposed for TSP and has been shown to preserve good gene segments from the parents effectively [16]. Figure 3a illustrates how an offspring is generated with Ord. It first randomly selects two positions within the chromosome where the gene segment between them (highlighted in gray) are copied to the offspring from one parent, then the rest are copied from the other parent with their original order. The arrow indicates the start position for the rest genes copied to the offspring.

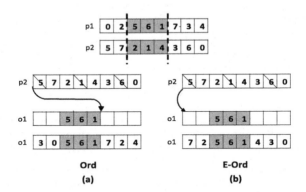

Fig. 3. The illustrations of Order Crossover and Epistasis-based Order Crossover. The only difference is the start position to generate offsprings.

Considering the epistatic test case segment (ETS), when GA with Ord is applied to TCP, the genes constructing ETS for offspring mostly come from the later genes of the parent, rather than from the ETS in parent. Consequently, the offspring is unlikely to inherit good gene segments within ETS from parent.

Epistasis-based Order Crossover (E-Ord) is introduced to address the issue. As shown in Fig. 3b, E-Ord only changes the arrow position, i.e., the start position for the rest genes copied from the second parent.

Algorithm 2 presents the detailed steps of the E-Ord. The highlighted line marks the difference between Ord and E-Ord. More specifically, in the step 3, E-Ord copies genes from the beginning of the parent to the beginning of the offspring, thus the ETS in offspring can inherit gene segment from the ETS in parent.

Algorithm 2. Epistasis-based Order Crossover

---

1. Select two random positions k_1, k_2 in the chromosome.
2. Copy elements in $[k_1, k_2]$ of p_1 to o_1.
3. From the beginning, copy p_2 as the rest elements of o_1 (excluding the elements copied from p_1.)
4. Exchange p_1 and p_2, execute step 1–3 again to construct o_2.

3.4 Discussion

GA starts with a randomly generated population. Then new chromosomes are reproduced from the parents and chromosomes with lower fitness values are replaced until the termination condition is met. In the process producing, good characteristics are spread throughout the population by favouring the mating of fitter chromosomes, as a result, the most promising areas of the search space are explored [17]. Although mutation also produces new chromosomes, it's generally agreed that crossover is the main force leading to a thorough search of the problem space.

In crossover, little variation in ETS will lead to the increasing chromosomes with the similar ETS. Crossover of chromosomes with almost identical ETS produces few chromosomes with new ETSes. When a ETS becomes predominant in the population, it is just as likely to become more predominant in the next generation as it is to become less predominant [17]. In the end, sustained increase of ETS in predominance over several successive generations will lead the ETSes of population to being stable. Then, crossover cannot produce chromosomes with new ETSes, which can be referred to as premature convergence of GA.

However, too large variation in ETS will cause the inheritance loss of good characteristic of ETS identified by fitness function. Little inheritance will make GA not produce offsprings from good ETSes and almost degenerate back to a random search. A pure random search is good at exploration, but does no exploitation. Then GA will lose its exploitation.

Above all, the qualitative scale of ETS's change is presented in Fig. 4. The coordinate axis shows the percentage scale of ETS's change, changing bigger from left to right. The proper variation scale of ETS should be near to the middle of the axis although accurate scale isn't given in this paper.

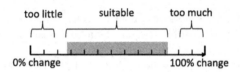

Fig. 4. The change scale of ETS

4   Empirical Study

This section describes the details of experiments and results. The following research questions motivate our experiments:

RQ1: Does the proposed crossover operators based on epistatic domains theory outperform the original crossovers in terms of effectiveness for TCP?
RQ2: Does the proposed crossovers based on epistatic domains theory outperform the original crossovers in terms of efficiency for TCP?
RQ3: Does the proposed crossovers based on epistatic domains theory outperform other two-point crossovers in terms of efficiency for TCP?

4.1   Experiment Setup

The study focuses on the impact of epistasis in GA for TCP, as three widely studied relatively large programs and one large open source are selected as subjects. *flex*, *space* and *bash* that from SIR Repository, have been used in previous studies on GA for TCP, and *v8* is an open source JavaScript engine employed in Google Chrome browser. Each subject program has 100 test suites which are produced by randomly selecting test cases from the test pool until the maximum statement coverage is achieved. The information of the subjects is presented in Table 2, including the subject size in term of source lines of code (SLOC) and associated test suites size.

Table 2. Subjects in the experiments

Subject	SLOC	Test suite size		
		Min	Max	Average
flex	3016	1047	1470	1350.17
space	3815	1208	3229	1894.29
bash	6181	764	1467	1063.17
v8	59412	2564	6159	3909.15

All experiments are run on a CentOS 6.0 server with 24 Intel Xeon (R) E5-2620 cores and 16 GB memory.

4.2 Experimental Design

Three groups of experiments are designed. The first two are the comparison between the consideration with epistasis and without, for single crossovers and two point crossovers, respectively. To further illustrate the effectiveness and efficiency the crossover, a widely used two-point crossover Partially-Mapped crossover operator (PMX) [16] is compared in the third group of experiments.

Two types of GA termination conditions are set for three groups of experiments, namely termination A and B. Termination A is to terminate GA while the fitness of APSC reaches a stable status, and the number of iterations is counted to measure the convergence of GA. Here a stable status is confirmed when the difference between two adjacent generations' best APSC values is less than 10^{-5} for continuous ten generations. Termination B fixes the number of iterations of 300 for GA execution, the highest fitness is recorded to measure the effectiveness of the algorithm. Table 3 summarizes three groups of the six experiments briefly.

Table 3. Three groups of experiments, SC vs E-SC, Ord vs E-Ord, E-Ord vs PMX.

Experiment	Setup
1A	SC vs E-SC with termination A
1B	SC vs E-SC with termination B
2A	Ord vs E-Ord with termination A
2B	Ord vs E-Ord with termination B
3A	E-Ord vs PMX with termination A
3B	E-Ord vs PMX with termination B

Each experiment is repeatedly executed 30 times as suggested in [18], except $v8$ with only 10 times executions due to the limit of time. The population sizes of all experiments are set 128.

4.3 Experimental Results

Experiments for SC and E-SC. To evaluate the effectiveness of GA with the epistasis-based crossover, we first conduct the experiments with SC and E-SC under termination conditions 1A and 1B, respectively. Figure 5 presents the number of iterations of GA using SC and E-SC under the condition 1A for all four subjects, where the X axis represents the sizes of 100 test suites, and Y axis shows the iterations plotted in monotonically increasing order on the X axis.

It is interesting to notice that the iterations of GA keep almost the same with either SC or E-SC along with increasing sizes of test suite, and the similar trend can be found in all four programs, as Fig. 5 shown. This observation reveals that when to solve TCP problem using GA with single-point crossover, there is no correlation between the numbers of iterations and the sizes of test suites. However, compared to GA with SC, GA with E-SC always takes more iterations to reach a stable fitness.

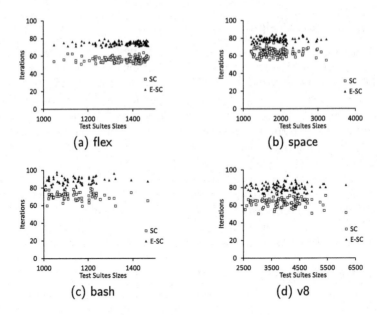

Fig. 5. The average number of iterations to reach a stable APSC for each test suite by GA with SC and E-SC, plotted in monotonically increasing order of the sizes of test suites on X axis, for all four subjects respectively.

It seems that the proposed E-SC results in higher costs, i.e., larger numbers of iterations for GA. However further investigations on quality of the fitness are presented in Table 4, including the average iterations and the average final APSC values for all 30 runs on each subject. The results show that the average APSC obtained by GA with E-SC is higher than that with SC for each subject.

Table 4. The average iterations and average final APSC on each subject

Subject	SC			E-SC		
	Avg iters	Avg APSC	Variation	Avg iters	Avg APSC	Variation
flex	56.12	0.9883	2.08E-06	74.28	0.9946	4.90E-07
space	63.52	0.9855	6.91E-07	78.42	0.9888	5.25E-07
bash	70.60	0.9590	6.23E-06	88.16	0.9686	3.69E-06
v8	62.26	0.9811	4.03E-06	79.98	0.9896	1.60E-06

From above experiments under the condition 1A, it can be concluded that GA can get better results with more iterations by using the proposed E-SC in test case prioritization.

Does the higher number of iterations mean the slower convergence of the GA? To answer this question, the experiment is conducted under the condition 1B, in which the maximal number of iterations is fixed at 300, and the best APSC values along with each generation are recorded. Figure 6 presents the results for all four programs, where the X axis is the number of iterations and Y axis corresponds to the highest fitness value among all individuals in the iterations. It can be seen that for any generation, GA with E-SC always achieves higher fitness value than that with SC. That is, E-SC has a faster convergence than SC does.

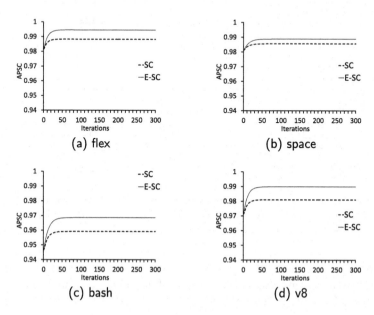

Fig. 6. The average APSC values with the increasing iterations in GA with SC and E-SC for four subjects respectively.

In conclusion, GA with E-SC gets significantly better APSC and achieves the best result with fewer iterations. The reason may be inspired from the discussion in Sect. 3.4, that is certain variation should be occurred within ETS. Too little change of ETS may lead in the premature of GA.

Experiments for Ord and E-Ord. To evaluate the effectiveness of GA with the proposed epistasis-based two-point crossover, the experiments are conducted with Ord and E-Ord under the conditions 2A and 2B. Figure 7 presents the iterations of GA with Ord and E-Ord for four subjects respectively. Similar with the trend showed under the condition 1A, the experiment under the condition 2A also confirms that there is no strong correlation between the numbers of iterations of GA and the sizes of test suites for both Ord and E-Ord. Further more, GA with E-Ord always takes more iterations in average to reach a stable fitness than GA with Ord.

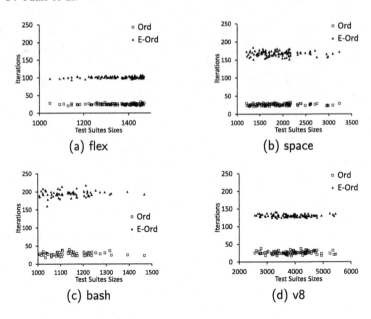

Fig. 7. The average number of iterations to reach a stable APSC for each test suite by GA with Ord and E-Ord, plotted in monotonically increasing order of the sizes of test suites on X axis, for all four subjects respectively.

Table 5 presents the further statistic results. The average iterations of Ord for different scales of programs are all around 25, while iterations of E-Ord are various in different programs, but all larger than that of Ord.

Table 5. The average iterations and average final APSC with Ord and E-Ord

Test Case	Ord			E-Ord		
	Avg iters	Avg APSC	Variation	Avg iters	Avg APSC	Variation
flex	24.93	0.9867	1.93E-06	101.08	0.9980	3.32E-08
space	26.29	0.9838	7.30E-07	167.78	0.9940	2.06E-07
bash	27.42	0.9553	7.10E-06	194.34	0.9836	1.34E-06
v8	25.98	0.9782	4.28E-06	130.64	0.9971	1.90E-07

As discussed in Sect. 3.4, too large variation in ETS will degenerate GA to random search in TCP and further reduce the efficiency of GA. This may seriously affect the speed of convergence in generation process.

Figure 8 presents the results of the experiment under the condition 2B, in which the maximal number of iterations is fixed at 300. It can be seen that E-Ord always has a higher fitness value than of Ord along with the increasing iterations.

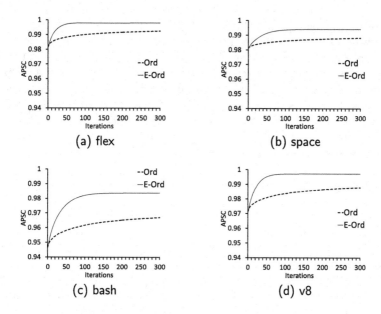

Fig. 8. The average APSC values with the increasing iterations in GA with Ord and E-Ord for four subjects respectively.

Experiments for E-Ord and PMX. To further illustrate the effectiveness and efficiency of E-Ord, a more advanced two point crossover, Partially-Mapped crossover operator(PMX) [16], is compared in the third group of experiments.

For the space limitation, we only report the results for 3A, i.e., the algorithms terminated when the APSC is stable. Table 6 presents the average iterations and the best APSC value achieved. It can be seen that both GAs achieved very high APSC value (although the average APSC obtained by GA with E-Ord is a little higher than that with PMX for all four subjects, and statistic analysis confirms that the difference is statistical significant), but the number of iterations for E-Ord is much fewer than that for PMX.

Table 6. The average iterations and average final APSC with PMX and E-Ord.

Test Case	PMX			E-Ord		
	Avg iters	Avg APSC	Variation	Avg iters	Avg APSC	Variation
flex	157.04	0.9967	1.93E-06	101.08	0.9980	3.32E-08
space	187.93	0.9929	3.67E-06	167.78	0.9940	2.06E-07
bash	229.54	0.9801	7.10E-06	194.34	0.9836	1.34E-06
v8	226.88	0.9964	4.08E-06	130.64	0.9971	1.90E-07

Discussion. In single-point crossover, the original crossover operator has little change within ETS, while in two-point crossover, the ordinal crossover is recognized to make much change within ETS. When GA is applied to TCP, too small change in ETS will narrow search space in generations and cause the premature convergence of GA, while too much variation will degenerate GA to random search. Thus the proposed two refined crossover operators are trying to fix these issues and the empirical results also provide the evidence to support our proposal. Further, the additional experiments prove that our E-Ord is better than another advanced two-point crossover PMX.

5   Threats to Validity

The external threat that might have affected the accuracy of experiments is the features of the subjects under test in this paper. Although there are three SIR programs and an industrial program $v8$, their features may hardly cover the most existing software. Thus, systematical analysis to ETS in TCP needs more different scales of programs. Simultaneously more experiments are demanded to further verify the effectiveness of ETS on GA in TCP. Another concern might be the evaluation object used in experiments. APSC is employed as the objective in the experiments to evaluate the different crossovers which directly affect the effectiveness of ETS on GA.

The internal threat which might have influenced the experimental results is that the repeated times of $v8$ is 10. There might exists some deviations in results of experiments about $v8$ when we measured the APSC values, but this may not strongly affect conclusions in this paper.

6   Related Work

TCP optimization is one of the most important activities in regression testing, where the efficiency of algorithms is a key issue. Li et al. [3] first empirically studied five algorithms to TCP with single objective. There are also other algorithms presented to TCP, including Ant Colony Optimization [19] and Particle Swarm Optimization [6]. Recently, multi-objective TCP optimization is introduced [20].

Considering the computational cost, GPU based parallel computing is adapted. Yoo et al. [21] used the GPGPU to accelerate the process of test cases selection and test suite minimization. Then Li et al. [4] proposed the fine-grain and coarse-grain GPU based parallel approaches for TCP where the crossover operators were executed on GPU. Epitropakis et al. [20] analyzed three different multi-objective algorithms in TCP using Coverage Compaction technology to reduce the scale of computations, thus the effectiveness can be increased in optimization process.

Improving algorithm operations is another direction to reduce the cost of TCP. Srinivas adapted the probabilities of crossover and mutation to improve GA [22] and some optimization to original algorithms were proposed [23]. This paper studied the epistatic domains theory in GA for TCP and proposed two adaptive crossover operators.

7   Conclusions and Future Works

The optimization of test case prioritization is a search problem and many heuristic algorithms have been applied, to which permutation encoding is used to represent a test case execution sequence. Considering the epistasis in GA, this paper defines the Epistatic Test Case Segment (ETS) for TCP, and proposes two refined crossover operators that focus on the change within ETS. The empirical studies based on four subjects provide the evidence that GA with the proposed crossover operators are better in terms of the effectiveness and the efficiency. Further analysis shows that the change caused by crossover operators in ETS should be mild (neither too small nor too large).

The discussion of ETS is macroscopic with empirical study. In the future, the interaction among the genes in ETS will be analysed theoretically, and multi-objective ETS for TCP is also considered in next step.

Acknowledgments. The work described in this paper is supported by the National Natural Science Foundation of China under Grant No. 61170082 and 61472025, the Program for New Century Excellent Talents in University (NCET-12-0757) and SRF for ROCS, SEM (LXJJ201303).

References

1. Yoo, S., Harman, M.: Regression testing minimization, selection and prioritization: a survey. Softw. Test. Verif. Reliab. **22**(2), 67–120 (2012)
2. Wong, W.E., Horgan, J.R., London, S., Mathur, A.P.: Effect of test set minimization on fault detection effectiveness. In: 17th International Conference on Software Engineering, ICSE 1995, p. 41. IEEE (1995)
3. Li, Z., Harman, M., Hierons, R.M.: Search algorithms for regression test case prioritization. IEEE Trans. Softw. Eng. **33**(4), 225–237 (2007)
4. Li, Z., Bian, Y., Zhao, R., Cheng, J.: A fine-grained parallel multi-objective test case prioritization on GPU. In: Ruhe, G., Zhang, Y. (eds.) SSBSE 2013. LNCS, vol. 8084, pp. 111–125. Springer, Heidelberg (2013)
5. Singh, Y., Kaur, A., Suri, B.: Test case prioritization using ant colony optimization. ACM SIGSOFT Software Eng. Notes **35**(4), 1–7 (2010)
6. Hla, K.H.S., Choi, Y., Park, J.S.: Applying particle swarm optimization to prioritizing test cases for embedded real time software. In: Proceedings of the 2008 IEEE 8th International Conference on Computer and Information Technology Workshops, Sydney, Australia, pp. 527–532. IEEE, 8–11 July 2008
7. Davis, L.: Applying adaptive algorithms to epistatic domains. In: IJCAI, vol. 85, pp. 162–164 (1985)
8. Harman, M., Jones, B.F.: Search-based software engineering. Inf. Softw. Technol. **43**(14), 833–839 (2001)
9. Rothermel, G., Untch, R.H., Chu, C., Harrold, M.J.: Prioritizing test cases for regression testing. IEEE Trans. Softw. Eng. **27**(10), 929–948 (2001)
10. Smith, J.M., et al.: Evolutionary Genetics. Oxford University Press, Oxford (1989)
11. Beaslev, D., Bull, D.R., Martin, R.R.: An overview of genetic algorithms: Part 2, research topics. Univ. Comput. **15**(4), 170–181 (1993)

12. Davidor, Y.: Epistasis variance: suitability of a representation to genetic algorithms. Complex Syst. **4**(4), 369–383 (1990)
13. Paixão, T., Barton, N.: A variance decomposition approach to the analysis of genetic algorithms. In: Proceeding of the Fifteenth Annual Conference on Genetic and Evolutionary Computation Conference, pp. 845–852. ACM (2013)
14. Rochet, S., Slimane, M., Venturini, G.: Epistasis for real encoding in genetic algorithms. In: Australian and New Zealand Conference on Intelligent Information Systems, pp. 268–271. IEEE (1996)
15. Seo, D.I., Moon, B.R.: Voronoi quantizied crossover for traveling salesman problem. In: GECCO, pp. 544–552 (2002)
16. Larrañaga, P., Kuijpers, C.M.H., Murga, R.H., Inza, I., Dizdarevic, S.: Genetic algorithms for the travelling salesman problem: a review of representations and operators. Artif. Intell. Rev. **13**(2), 129–170 (1999)
17. Beasley, D., Martin, R., Bull, D.: An overview of genetic algorithms: Part 1. fundamentals. Univ. Comput. **15**, 58 (1993)
18. Arcuri, A., Briand, L.: A practical guide for using statistical tests to assess randomized algorithms in software engineering. In: 2011 33rd International Conference on Software Engineering (ICSE), pp. 1–10. IEEE (2011)
19. Singh, Y., Kaur, A., Suri, B.: Test case prioritization using ant colony optimization. ACM SIGSOFT Softw. Eng. Notes **35**(4), 1–7 (2010)
20. Epitropakis, M.G., Yoo, S., Harman, M., Burke, E.K.: Pareto efficient multiobjective regression test suite prioritisation. Techreport **14**(01), 01 (2014)
21. Yoo, S., Harman, M., Ur, S.: Highly scalable multi objective test suite minimisation using graphics cards. In: Cohen, M.B., Ó Cinnéide, M. (eds.) SSBSE 2011. LNCS, vol. 6956, pp. 219–236. Springer, Heidelberg (2011)
22. Srinivas, M., Patnaik, L.M.: Adaptive probabilities of crossover and mutation in genetic algorithms. IEEE Trans. Syst. Man Cybern. **24**(4), 656–667 (1994)
23. Deb, K., Agrawal, S., Pratap, A., Meyarivan, T.: A fast elitist non-dominated sorting genetic algorithm for multi-objective optimization: NSGA-II. In: Deb, K., Rudolph, G., Lutton, E., Merelo, J.J., Schoenauer, M., Schwefel, H.-P., Yao, X. (eds.) PPSN 2000. LNCS, vol. 1917, pp. 849–858. Springer, Heidelberg (2000)

Haiku - a Scala Combinator Toolkit for Semi-automated Composition of Metaheuristics

Zoltan A. Kocsis[1]([✉]), Alexander E.I. Brownlee[1], Jerry Swan[2], and Richard Senington[3]

[1] Computing Science and Mathematics, University of Stirling, Stirling FK9 4LA, UK
{zak,sbr}@cs.stir.ac.uk
[2] Computing Science, University of York, York YO10 5GW, UK
dr.jerry.swan@gmail.com
[3] Data Ductus AB, Skellefteå, Sweden
richard.senington@dataductus.se

Abstract. There is an emerging trend towards the automated design of metaheuristics at the software component level. In principle, metaheuristics have a relatively clean decomposition, where well-known frameworks such as ILS and EA are parametrised by variant components for acceptance, perturbation etc. Automated generation of these frameworks is not so simple in practice, since the coupling between components may be implementation specific. Compositionality is the ability to freely express a space of designs 'bottom up' in terms of elementary components: previous work in this area has used combinators, a modular and functional approach to componentisation arising from foundational Computer Science. In this article, we describe HAIKU, a combinator tool-kit written in the Scala language, which builds upon previous work to further automate the process by automatically composing the external dependencies of components. We provide examples of use and give a case study in which a programatically-generated heuristic is applied to the Travelling Salesman Problem within an Evolutionary Strategies framework.

1 Introduction

Early work in Search Based Software Engineering (SBSE) only needed to outperform manual approaches and in many cases random search and hill-climbing were sufficient for this. Now that the field is maturing and we wish to use SBSE to tackle more difficult problems, there is a need to employ more sophisticated search strategies. The difficulty facing the SBSE practitioner is the wealth of different metaheuristics available: e.g. can a software problem most usefully be solved with iterated local search, genetic algorithms, particle swarm or some hybridization of these techniques or their component parts?

A metaheuristic is instantiated for a particular problem domain via three domain-specific items, viz. a data structure for the representation of candidate solutions (e.g. bit-string, permutation etc.); the ability to efficiently compare

© Springer International Publishing Switzerland 2015
M. Barros and Y. Labiche (Eds.): SSBSE 2015, LNCS 9275, pp. 125–140, 2015.
DOI: 10.1007/978-3-319-22183-0_9

solution quality in order to guide the search process and lastly a collection of methods for transforming solutions. While metaheuristics can provide good results, operating at this level of abstraction offers no silver bullet. Rather, the family of techniques is ideally used as a toolbox, from which a practitioner can pick components and determine their effectiveness on a particular problem. Consequently, considerable development effort is focused on operator and parameter tuning for each new application (although it is encouraging to see increasing automation in this area [19]). It has also long been the norm to combine or *hybridise* methods, for example using several in parallel, attempting to introduce the strengths of one method to others. As a concrete example of 'composition by hand', previous work [6] has applied Tabu search [14] and simulated annealing [16] at different points in a multi-stage local search algorithm. The desire for greater automation has led to approaches such as hyper-heuristics [3], which are the application of search to the problem of finding good heuristics ('heuristics for searching the space of heuristics'). Of particular interest for the automated design of algorithms are generative hyper-heuristics [5], which assemble basic components into more complex search algorithms. It is also worth mentioning algorithm portfolios [38], which use a group (portfolio) of different algorithms at the same time to solve a difficult problem. Fortunately for SBSE researchers, it is possible to express the problem of creating search strategies as one of software component assembly, thereby jointly incorporating knowledge from the domains of software engineering and metaheuristics. This paper introduces HAIKU, a toolkit written in the Scala[1] language that facilitates the composition of metaheuristic components via combinators, extending previous work in the pure functional language Haskell [36].

Combinators are pure functions that depend exclusively on their input parameters. They are often higher-order functions, i.e. they can take other functions as parameters and (significantly) can return new functions, created dynamically from their inputs. A well-known example is function composition:

$$f \circ g = x \mapsto f(g(x))$$

The function $\circ$ takes two parameters, functions f and g, and returns a new function expressed in terms of these parameters. Functional programmers are in the habit of building reusable libraries using such functions because they encourage the expression of problems in terms of small building blocks. These building blocks can be combined and extended in a vast number of ways, with permissible combinations being enforced by the type system of the host programming language. Metaheuristics are a good fit for this pattern: individual metaheuristics can take functions (e.g. to provide an ordering of solutions or define acceptance criteria) as parameters but are themselves functions which can be passed to other metaheuristics (e.g. using an iterative improver as one component of a memetic algorithm [26]).

Recent work [34] on the use of combinators to build search heuristics notes that they have the look-and-feel of a Domain-Specific programming Language

---

[1] for an introduction, see http://www.artima.com/scalazine/articles/steps.html.

(DSL). Their modular nature allows new search algorithms to be developed for a specific application with reduced effort [25]. Further, their pure functional nature greatly simplifies the automated assembly of new search algorithms. In this context, the basic principles of modularity and re-use (well-established practices in software engineering) are fundamental to algorithm implementation. DSLs have already found uses in parameter control for evolutionary algorithms [18].

Modularity means that components are self-contained and can be developed independently, communicating only through clearly-defined interfaces. If the interfaces are sufficiently general, parts can be *re-used* and recombined in new ways. However, there is often a high degree of interdependence between algorithm components, reducing modularity and inhibiting re-use. This is known as *content coupling*, where the implementation of one component requires deep knowledge of (and in many cases, access to) the internal mechanisms and implementation details of another. This is a hindrance to the combination of different components and their substitutability within metaheuristic frameworks. The HAIKU tool-kit presented in this article is structured in such a way that modularity and re-usability are inherent in the component implementations.

The remainder of the paper is structured as follows: Sect. 2 summarises related work. Section 3 introduces combinators in more detail and Sects. 4 and 5 describe the design and implementation of HAIKU. A simple example of HAIKU's use is provided in Sects. 6 and 7, composing combinators for Tabu search and simulated annealing and applying all three to the Travelling Salesman Problem. Finally, Sect. 8 provides conclusions and future work.

2   Related Work

There is a body of work applying combinators in the field of constraint programming. Perron [30] describes a compositional approach in which search heuristics are termed 'goals'. This does not seem intended to support additional combinators, and specifically targets depth-first search. The Comet system [39] features 'fully-programmable' search: in contrast to the composition approach of combinators, a search controller is used to determine the behaviour of the search heuristic [40]. Choi et al. [7] describe a compositional framework for search that relies on composing search engines and Desouter [8] describes a Scala framework using combinators to build custom heuristics for constraint satisfaction problems. 'Monadic constraint programming' was introduced by Schrijvers et al. [33], describing 'stackable search transformers'. While these only provide a limited and low-level form of search control, the concept is extended by Schrijvers [34], who introduces the concept of search combinators. This bridges the gap between a high-level modelling language for search and its efficient implementation. The user is able to define application-specific search strategies by combining a small set of primitives, effectively providing a Domain-Specific Language (DSL). This also serves as the foundation of the work in [32], where a search algorithm is used to automate the composition process.

McGillicuddy et al. [24] achieve rapid prototyping of combinatorial optimisation algorithms via functional implementation of DSLs, as applied to dynamic programming problems (unbounded knapsack and longest common substring). Senington [36] argues for a specific function signature as forming a good basis for building metaheuristics from combinators: metaheuristics are regarded as stream transformations (i.e. functions that take a stream of solutions and return an updated stream) which are composed into more complex search algorithms. The paper presents a toolkit for expressing metaheuristics in the pure functional language Haskell. Building on this toolkit, [35] describes the use of combinators to move between perturbation, recombination and neighbourhood methods in metaheuristics, demonstrated for the Travelling Salesman Problem (TSP).

Marmion et al. [22,23] propose a generic structure for stochastic local search (SLS) algorithms, represented in a text-based grammar. The productions of the grammar represent local search hybrids. In this structure, each SLS algorithm has a definition of perturbation, optional subsidiary SLS, and acceptance criterion. Hybridisation is possible by assembling algorithms via the subsidiary local search. In common with this article, most of the human effort required is in devising problem-specific components for neighbourhoods, perturbations and heuristics. There are also some major differences with our work: HAIKU defines a search using program code rather than via a grammar, with the attendant programmatic flexibility, compile-time checking and IDE support that this provides. HAIKU's automated mechanism for composing 'environmental' state (described in more detail subsequently) is both less onerous and less error prone that the requirement to manually embed information such as search trajectory within the algorithm itself.

In order to automate metaheuristic construction, we need to be able to unambiguously determine the contribution of a component. This is clearly essential for learning schemes involving reinforcement and/or credit assignment: if component state is hidden, then we cannot determine which changes contribute to the sucess of a metaheuristic. Popular metaheuristic frameworks such as ECJ or JMetal [11,21] etc. do not prevent components from making arbitrary changes to non-local state. In contrast, the various works on combinators due to Schrijvers and Senington (above) allow unambiguous component substitution because of their pure functional nature. Recall that the aspects of modularity that concern us include decomposability of the different components as well as their *recombinability*: the metaheuristic components such as acceptance, perturbation should all be equipped with suitable composition operations (compositors). This latter aspect of modularity is absolute (rather than quantitative). Existing metaheuristic frameworks don't achieve the level of modularity that is sufficient for recombination purposes. The essential contribution of this work is to address this outstanding issue, as described in the following sections.

3   Combinators

Formally speaking, a combinator is a 'pure' function (i.e. referentially transparent and without side-effects) with no free variables (i.e. they are self-contained, with no reference to external state). This modularity means that they can provide useful building blocks for describing a particular domain. Through the use of higher-order functions, combinators can combine their function parameters to provide more sophisticated control flow. Combinator libraries have been successfully employed in functional languages to provide clean and extensible capabilities for a diverse range of problems including real-time systems control [42] and expressing parser logic [15,17]. These libraries capture patterns across diverse operations; provide mechanisms for combining these building blocks and allow extensibility via the provision of new constructs and control structures as different end-uses become apparent.

Parsers provide a good example of the power and mechanism of combinators since there is an obvious need to provide for many control structures, e.g. matching a pattern *many* times in sequence; matching a single character or matching one pattern separated by another pattern. These can all be expressed as higher-order functions. In particular, most of this functionality can be defined so that parsers tend to act on other parsers, hence anything which is a parser can be passed to the library. This provides the high degree of customisability and extensibility that we desire from combinators. What follows is an example of a CSV parser written using parser combinators (this example is adapted from [28]), illustrating the creation of several user defined blocks of code (such as *cell*) built from library combinators and then reused.

```scala
val eol = Scanners.isChar('\n') // end of line
val cell = Scanners.notAmong(",\n").many()
// a cell is anything until , or \n
val line = cell.sepBy(Scanners.isChar(','))
// a line is a series of separated cells
val csvFile = line.endBy(eol);
// a csvfile is lines each ended by
```

The library of possible combinators can also be easily extended with user code, e.g. an operator that matches an identical symbol on either side of a given term. This could be coded by a user in the following manner and used in any expression which takes a parser as a parameter:

```scala
def surroundedBy( b : Parser, a : Parser ) : Parser = a.followedBy(b).endBy(a)
```

As discussed above, combinator libraries are essentially embedded DSLs and hence (unlike 'configuration-file' based approaches) can make use of the full power of the host language, as well as being customisable via the problem-specific code used to parametrise the system. In devising an appropriate meta-heuristic, we have a toolbox of common patterns ('iterate until local optima', 'accept unimproved moves in inverse proportion to the number of iterations' etc.) and a desire to automatically combine different elements of this toolbox. Metaheuristics therefore share with combinators the essential notion of functionally parametrised and (recursively) composable control structures. The use of combinators is a natural fit for a generic metaheuristic library, allowing the problem-specific elements to be coded in the host language without limitations.

```scala
def iteratedPerturbation[Sol](incumbent : Sol,
  perturb : Sol => Sol,
  accept : (Sol,Sol) => Sol,
  isFinished : Sol => Boolean ) : Sol = {
    while( !isFinished(incumbent) ) {
      val incoming = perturb(incumbent)
      incumbent = accept(incumbent, incoming)
    }
    // the return keyword is implicit in Scala:
    incumbent
}
```

Listing 1.1. Iterated perturbation framework using polymorphic components

4   The Design of Haiku

There are many popular metaheuristic software libraries (e.g. [9,11,12,20,21, 41]), several of which abstract out common components such as acceptance, perturbation, recombination et c. It is typically the case that well-known meta-heuristics such as iterated local search, evolutionary and swarm algorithms etc. then act as instances of the 'Template Method' design pattern [44], i.e. providing a pre-defined invocation sequence for the concrete instantiations of the abstract components with which they are (manually or automatically) configured. For example, a framework for iterated perturbation which is parametrised by the components for perturbation, acceptance and termination condition is given in Listing 1.1.

It is therefore desirable to be able to combinatorially configure such frameworks with different combinations of components. It is also known that different components can perform well at different points in the search (see e.g. [37]), which is particularly important in the case of dynamic environments [27]. One method of composition for components is to use the 'Composite' Design Pattern [13], i.e. to create a new component as a (perhaps dynamically-generated) function of existing components. As described by Woodward et al. [43], ensembles are a popular example of this approach. An elementary example would be to define a composite fitness function c as an aggregate of the fitness of a collection of surrogate functions $\{f_1, \ldots, f_k\}$, e.g. with c being given as a weighted sum of surrogates:

$$c : Sol \to \mathbb{R}$$
$$c : x \mapsto c_1 * f_1(x) + c_2 * f_2(x) + \ldots + c_k * f_k(x)$$

In order to ensure that our composite function can be plugged into the target framework, it needs to have the same signature as the abstract component that it instantiates. For the elementary generation of composites (e.g. weighted sum of fitness values, as above) this is straightforward: i.e. (in the case of a single-objective) the surrogates and the composite can all be defined in terms of functions from $\mathbb{R} \to \mathbb{R}$.

Unfortunately, the composition of many popular metaheuristic components is intrinsically not so straightforward. As a motivating example, consider an attempt to compose the well-known methods of Exponential Monte Carlo (EMC) [16] and Tabu acceptance [14]. EMC employs an *annealing schedule*, which tends to decrease the probability of accepting unimproved solutions as the search progresses. The Tabu scheme uses a *Tabu list* to prohibit the acceptance of recently-encountered solutions or operators. When attempting to automatically compose these components, a problem therefore arises because they depend on different notions of *component state*: e.g. EMC acceptance depends on the current state of the annealing schedule, while Tabu Acceptance (TA) depends on the Tabu list. Define acceptance to have signature:

$$State \times State \to State$$

where *State* is a generic type representing some combination of solution state *Sol* and component state. For solution state *Sol*, this means that EMC has signature:

$$emc : (Sol, Schedule) \times (Sol, Schedule) \to (Sol, Schedule)$$

and TA has:

$$ta : (Sol, TabuList) \times (Sol, TabuList) \to (Sol, TabuList)$$

An attempt to build a combinator that composes EMC with TA requires boilerplate to propagate component state information for *both* acceptance criteria:

$$\begin{aligned} hybrid : &(Sol, (Schedule, TabuList)) \times \\ &(Sol, (Schedule, TabuList)) \to \\ &(Sol, (Schedule, TabuList)) \end{aligned}$$

This exemplifies a general issue: a composite combinator needs to be parametrised by the Cartesian product of the component states. This situation is particularly onerous for the metaheuristic designer since boilerplate code needs to be written for each specific combination of component states. What is therefore required is an automated means of dealing with Cartesian products of component states by 'lifting' pre-existing operations so that they correctly apply to the product state. The means by which HAIKU provides this functionality is described in more detail in the following section.

5 Haiku - Implementation

Tabu(diff, size=3)
transforms plainOldEMC
yielding hybridSearch

Actual HAIKU code

HAIKU is implemented in the Scala programming language. Scala was chosen because it has previously been used to implement combinator libraries [28], and its type system facilitates creating objects that behave like functions (e.g. fitness below). Scala runs on the Java Virtual Machine (JVM) and can call (and be called from) Java libraries and programs.

All HAIKU components are parametrised by the type Dec[Sol], where Sol is the type of solutions (as above) and Dec[Sol] (short for 'decorable') is a data type containing the solution along with the environment, i.e. the aggregated state of all composed components. The composition of components in HAIKU is simply illustrated in the context of the Evolutionary Strategy (ES) metaheuristic [2]. ES is a population-based metaheuristic that has been applied across a wide range of problem domains. In the general framework of ES, each iteration a set of one or more solutions ('parents') is selected from the population according to their fitness. λ new solutions ('children') are generated from these by duplication, recombination and mutation. The children become members of the population, and the population is reduced back to its original size μ. EA approaches are classified into $(\mu + \lambda)$ and (μ, λ), according to the strategy used for reducing the population back to μ solutions (generational succession). With $(\mu + \lambda)$, the combined population of children and parents is ranked according to fitness, and the μ highest-ranking solutions are retained. Children only replace parents if they represent improvements. In (μ, λ) ES only the highest ranking μ children remain in the population. Parents are deleted, even if the children represent a decrease in fitness.

A single step of ES can be abstractly described by the composition of three operations neighbourhood, bias and select, with signatures as follows:

$$neighbourhood[Sol] = \qquad\qquad Dec[Sol] \rightarrow List[Dec[Sol]]$$
$$bias[Sol] = \qquad\qquad List[Dec[Sol]] \rightarrow List[Double]$$
$$select[Sol] = \qquad List[(Dec[Sol], Double)] \rightarrow Dec[Sol]$$

For some solution state s, the output of the neighbourhood function is defined to consist of s together with its λ children. As explained in a subsequent section, this formulation makes it easy to generalise the 'plus' and 'comma' strategies described above for generational succession. The actual Scala code for a single-step of ES is given in Listing 1.2 and is depicted diagrammatically in Fig. 1.

```scala
case class ES[ Sol ] {
    type State = Dec[Sol]
    def update( currentState : State ) : State =
        select(neighbourhood(currentState) zip bias(neighbourhood(currentState)))
    // the zip function creates a list of pairs from the two list
}
```

Listing 1.2. Evolutionary Strategies update

It is important to remember that different neighbourhood, bias and select functions may in fact have different associated component states. Therefore, the requirement to form the Cartesian products of states is, as explained above, unavoidable if one wishes to compose components. HAIKU, uniquely among metaheuristic frameworks, frees the end-user of the burden of having to do this

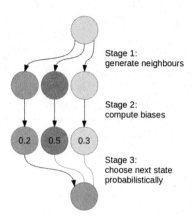

Stage 1:
generate neighbours

Stage 2:
compute biases

Stage 3:
choose next state
probabilistically

Fig. 1. A single step of ES described by the composition of the neighbourhood, bias and select operations

manually. In implementation terms, this is achieved by storing the relevant environments as entries in a map. To ensure that access to this map is type-checked and documented in the component declarations, the public interface requires that callers implement the Uses[Env] marker trait.

Storing the aggregate component state in this manner has several benefits. In particular, alternative approaches to aggregate state (e.g. monad transformer stacks [33]) keep the ordering of the combinators explicit, so reordering combinators requires writing boilerplate (involving the infamous $lift$ function). In contrast, the map-based approach requires no boilerplate for reordering combinators. The only drawback of this approach is that the presence of a decoration can no longer be ensured at run-time: the combinators have to check for, and handle the "missing decorations" case.

The Scala definition of Dec can be seen in Listing 1.3[2].

```scala
trait Uses[Env] { } // marker interface
case class Dec[A]( extract : A, private val decor : Map[Uses[_],Any] ) {
  def get[Env](c : Uses[Env]) : Option[Env] =
    decor.get(c).map(_.asInstanceOf[Env])
  def set[Env](c : Uses[Env], value : Env) : Dec[A] =
    Dec(extract, decor.updated(c,value)))
}
```

Listing 1.3. The Dec class

---

[2] We would like to consider $Dec[A]$ to be a subtype of A. This is not expressible in Scala or any other mainstream language. Instead, we rely on Scala's implicit conversions to ensure that Dec[A] can be substituted for A.

6   Case Study: TSP

In this section, we use HAIKU to create a hybrid metaheuristic for solving the well-known Travelling Salesman Problem (TSP) [1]. The techniques used in HAIKU are not specific to the TSP, but it is a suitable problem for illustration. First, an appropriate solution representation needs to be chosen. This example uses the simplest possible one: a Tour is a permutation, implemented as a list of nodes in the order they were visited.

```
type Node = Int
type Tour = Dec[List[Node]]
```

As described above, HAIKU uses a *bias function* to measure solution quality. This allows us to compose measures of solution quality in various ways (as described in more detail below), thereby facilitating the creation of surrogate fitness measures. A fitness function is a deterministic bias function, mapping the solution to an ordered set. The search algorithm then operates to minimise or to maximise its value accordingly. In the case of the TSP, the goal is to optimise the tour length associated with the solution. The following code defines the corresponding bias function.

```
def length : FitnessFunction[Tour,Double] =
  Minimise { x =>
    val xnext = x.tail ++ List( x.head )
    // the .zipped method turns a pair of lists into a list of pairs,
    // and map invokes the tsp.dist function on each resulting pair.
    val distances = ( x, xnext ).zipped map ( tsp.dist )
    distances.sum
  }
```

The search requires an initial state: the following code creates a random tour:

```
val seed : Tour = RNG.shuffle { (0 until tsp.size).toList }
```

The RNG singleton provides the sole point of access to HAIKU's random number generator. Since the combinator implementation is stateless, results are reproducible from a given random seed. The HAIKU ES implementation uses a neighbourhood function to move around the search space. The neighbourhood function takes the current state of the search, and returns a list consisting of the current state and its offspring. In the example below, *lambda* children are created by reversing a random segment of the parent.

```
def transition = NeighbourhoodFunction { (x : Tour, lambda : Int) =>
  val children = for( i ← 0 until lambda ) yield {
    val a = RNG.nextInt( tsp.size )
    val b = a + RNG.nextInt( tsp.size − a )
    val reversed = x.drop( a ).take( b ).reverse
    x.take( a ) ++ reversed ++ x.drop( a ).drop( b )
  }
  List( x ) ++ children
}
```

Search objects encapsulate the information required for running a search, viz. the neighbourhood function, the bias function, and the environmental variables (if any). The following code creates a search object and executes 1000 iterations of the search:

```
val search : Search[Tour] = ES( seed, transition, length ) (†)
val result = search.run(1000)
```

6.1   Semi-automated Composition of Metaheuristics

We can use the combinator-decorator mechanisms of HAIKU to create a acceptance criterion as a composite of Tabu search and simulated annealing. A previous comprehensive study [29] indicates that acceptance criteria can have a strong effect on the cross-domain generalisability of a hyper-heuristic, so the ability to create such hybrids is likely to have general utility. In HAIKU, a combinator is an object with a transforms method, of signature $transforms : Search[A] \rightarrow Search[B]$. The following code sets up EMC acceptance using the simulated annealing combinator SA:

```
val emcSearch = SA.EMCAccept( 100, t => 0.95*t, length ) transforms search (†)
```

The first two arguments determine the annealing schedule. The last argument is the fitness function to be optimised. Naturally, simulated annealing requires a real-valued fitness function. Tabu Search additionally requires a *difference function*, which yields the changes in the solution state from iteration to iteration. The following code defines such a function:

```
def changes(x : Tour, y : Tour) : List[Node] = {
    val diff = (x,y).zipped filter ((x,y) => x != y)
    diff._2
}
```

Using this difference function, the Tabu combinator can be invoked:

```
val hybridSearch = Tabu( changes, size = 2 ) transforms emcSearch (†)
```

Note that the change in environment (first from an empty environment to an environment with temperature, then to an environment with a temperature and a Tabu list) is handled without the end-user having to write any additional boilerplate. Since bias functions are List[Double]-valued, it is possible to define custom distributions over the neighbourhood. This can be seen as a generalisation of the standard ES generational succession strategy: as mentioned above, a neighbourhood consists of the current state and its offspring, so if we always assign a bias of 0 to the current state, we can obtain a $(1, \lambda)$-ES otherwise we obtain a generalisation of $(1 + \lambda)$-ES in which the incumbent succeeds to the next generation with some probability. The composition mechanism also allows for fine-grained control over how the hybridisation occurs. For example, the default compositor for Tabu is 'intersection' (i.e. takes the smaller of the two acceptance probabilities, which can be seen in Fig. 2). The Compositor object provides several built-in compositors, as can be seen in the following:

```
Tabu( changes, size = 2, Compositor.union ).transforms(emcSearch) (†)
```

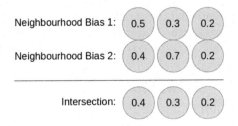

Fig. 2. The intersection composition operation

We used the Tabu and SA combinators to create the hybrid. Other elementary combinators provided by HAIKU for decorating a search via the 'transform' method include:

1. Threshold: Adds threshold acceptance capabilities to a search object.
2. Inspector: Allows observation of the search object while the search is in progress. Strict typing ensures that the search trajectory remains unchanged.

Notice that defining each hybrid (listings marked with †) for solving the TSP requires only a single line of code.

7   Experiments

As an illustration of the utility of the composition mechanism, we demonstrate that it is possible to find superior hybrids. We achieve this by performing a hyper-heuristic search in the space of composed bias functions. Recall from Sect. 5 that a bias function is given a neighbourhood and yields a *bias*, i.e. a list of corresponding non-negative values. A bias compositor (such as union, intersection etc. as described above) takes a pair of biases and returns a new bias. A simple bias compositor that returns a list containing the weighted average of the corresponding input values is defined below. It contains a weight value $0.0 \leq m \leq 1.0$ as the sole hyper-heuristic parameter. This value essentially acts as an 'interpolator' between the contribution of the two input biases:

def weightedAverageCompositor(x: Bias, y: Bias): Bias = x*m + y*(1−m)

In order to show that the composition mechanism can yield useful hybrids, we performed a hyper-heuristic search for suitable m. Note that this search is over $[0, 1] \in \mathbb{R}$, despite the underlying space being permutation-based. The parameter values were as shown in Table 1, with input biases as given for the Tabu and EMC searches defined above. The heuristics were evaluated on 5 TSP instances from TSPLib [31] having less than 100 cities (att48,eil51,eil76,pr76,st70). In all of these instances, EMC significantly outperformed Tabu search (according to the Mann-Whitney U/Wilcox signed rank test with $p = 0.05$).

The top-level hyper-heuristic search was performed using the real-valued optimization method CMAES[3], an extension of ES which maintains a numerical

---

[3] the default implementation in the Apache Commons Math 3.3 library.

Table 1. Parameter values

Parameter	Value
Tabu List Size	3
Max MH ((1{plus,comma}1)-ES) iter	500
Num MH runs per HH iter	21
Max HH (CMAES) iter	1000

approximation of the search gradient. The fitness value for the hyper-heuristic search was determined from an average of 21 runs of the $(1\{comma, plus\}1) - ES$ metaheuristic. In each case, CMAES converged quickly, taking resp. 117, 65, 57, 41 and 33 iterations [4].

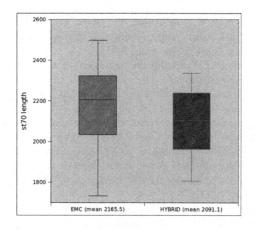

Fig. 3. Comparison of the tours found by EMC and Hybrid searches on instance st70

In one of the five cases (st70), the hyper-heuristic search found a hybrid (the weight $m = 0.091$) that was significantly better (according to the Mann-Whitney U/Wilcox signed rank test with $p = 0.05$) than EMC search. Figure 3 is box plot comparing the tour lengths found by the two algorithms.

8   Conclusion

We described HAIKU, a combinator tool-kit written in Scala, for semi-automated hybridisation of metaheuristics. HAIKU addresses an intrinsic issue in the automated assembly of metaheuristic components, viz. the composition of component state. Experiments on instances of the Travelling Salesman Problem reveal that

---

[4] execution time: 117.7s, 162.7s, 80.8s, 57.8s and 59.4 s on an Intel Xeon 2.13 GHz with 4 GB RAM.

such hybridisation can indeed be useful: we implemented a real-valued hyper-heuristic which interpolates between a pair of acceptance criteria and used this to demonstrate the existence of a Tabu-annealing hybrid which significantly out-performs both its base components.

As discussed in Sect. 5, an important limitation of the library is the necessity of additional run-time tests due to the lack of compile-time checking for missing decorations. Hopefully, the type-level programming techniques of Scala will alleviate this issue in a future version of the library.

Future work should also widen the variety of available hybrids. Expanding the palette of components (e.g. with Great Deluge [10] and Late Acceptance [4] criteria) will allow a larger number of hybridisations to be explored inside the HAIKU framework.

References

1. Applegate, D.L., Bixby, R.E., Chvatal, V., Cook, W.J.: The Traveling Salesman Problem: A Computational Study (Princeton Series in Applied Mathematics). Princeton University Press, Princeton (2007)
2. Beyer, H.G., Schwefel, H.P.: Evolution strategies - a comprehensive introduction. Nat. Comput. 1(1), 3–52 (2002)
3. Burke, E.K., Gendreau, M., et al.: Hyper-heuristics: a survey of the state of the art. J. Oper. Res. Soc. 64, 1695–1724 (2013)
4. Burke, E.K., Bykov, Y.: A late acceptance strategy in hill-climbing for examination timetabling problems. In: Proceedings PATAT (2008)
5. Burke, E.K., Hyde, M.R., Kendall, G., Ochoa, G., Ozcan, E., Woodward, J.R.: Exploring hyper-heuristic methodologies with genetic programming. In: Mumford, C.L., Jain, L.C. (eds.) Computational Intelligence. ISRL, vol. 1, pp. 177–201. Springer, Heidelberg (2009)
6. Cambazard, H., Hebrard, E., OŚullivan, B., Papadopoulos, A.: Local search and constraint programming for the post enrolment-based course timetabling problem. Ann. Oper. Res. 194, 111–135 (2012)
7. Choi, C.W., Henz, M., Ng, K.B.: A compositional framework for search. In: Pontelli, E. (ed.) Proceeding CICLOPS: Colloquium on Implementation of Constraint and LOgic Programming Systems, appeared as Technical report TR-CS-003/2001, New Mexico State University. Paphos, November 2001
8. Desouter, B.: Modular search heuristics in Scala. Master's thesis, Ghent University, Belgium (2012). http://bdsouter.github.io/thesis/thesis.pdf
9. Gaspero, L., Schaerf, A.: Easylocal++: an object-oriented framework for the flexible design of local-search algorithms. Softw. Pract. Exp. 33(8), 733–765 (2003)
10. Dueck, G.: New optimization heuristics: the great deluge algorithm and the record-to-record travel. J. Comput. Phys. 104, 86–92 (1993)
11. Durillo, J.J., Nebro, A.J.: jMetal: a Java framework for multi-objective optimization. Adv. Eng. Softw. 42, 760–771 (2011)
12. Fink, A., Voß, S.: Hotframe: a heuristic optimization framework. In: Voß, S., Woodruff, D. (eds.) Optimization Software Class Libraries, pp. 81–154. OR/CS Interfaces Series, Kluwer Academic, Boston (2002)
13. Gamma, E., Helm, R., Johnson, R., Vlissides, J.: Design Patterns: Elements of Reusable Object-Oriented Software. Addison-Wesley Longman Publishing Co., Inc., Boston (1995)

14. Glover, F., Laguna, M.: Tabu Search. Kluwer Academic, Norwell (1997)
15. Hutton, G., Meijer, E.: Monadic parsing in haskell. J. Funct. Program. **8**(4), 437–444 (1998)
16. Kirkpatrick, S., Gelatt, C.D., Vecchi, M.P.: Optimization by simulated annealing. Sci. **220**(4598), 671–680 (1983)
17. Leijen, D., Meijer, E.: Parsec: direct style monadic parser combinators for the real world. Technical reports UU-CS-2001-27, Dep. of Comp. Sc., Univ. Utrecht (2001)
18. Liu, S., Bryant, B., Mernik, M., Črepinšek, M., Zubair, M.: PPCea: A Domain-Specific Language for Programmable Parameter Control in Evolutionary Algorithms. INTECH Open Access (2011)
19. López-Ibáñez, M., Dubois-Lacoste, J., Stützle, T., Birattari, M.: The irace package, Iterated Race for Automatic Algorithm Configuration. Technical report TR/IRIDIA/2011-004, IRIDIA, Université Libre de Bruxelles, Belgium (2011)
20. Lukasiewycz, M., Glaß, M., Reimann, F., Teich, J.: Opt4J - A Modular Framework for Meta-heuristic Optimization. In: Proceedings of the GECCO, pp. 1723–1730. Dublin (2011)
21. Luke, S.: The ECJ Owner's Manual (Oct 2010)
22. Marmion, M.-E., Mascia, F., López-Ibáñez, M., Stützle, T.: Automatic design of hybrid stochastic local search algorithms. In: Blesa, M.J., Blum, C., Festa, P., Roli, A., Sampels, M. (eds.) HM 2013. LNCS, vol. 7919, pp. 144–158. Springer, Heidelberg (2013)
23. Marmion, M.É., Mascia, F., López-Ibáñez, M., Stützle, T.: Towards the automatic design of metaheuristics. In: Lau, H.C., Raidl, G., Hentenryck, P.V. (eds.) MIC 2013, Singapore, Aug 2013
24. McGillicuddy, D., Parkes, A.J., Nilsson, H.: An investigation into the use of Haskell for dynamic programming. Proceedings of the PATAT (2014)
25. Mernik, M., Heering, J., Sloane, A.M.: When and how to develop domain-specific languages. ACM Comput. Surv. **37**(4), 316–344 (2005)
26. Moscato, P.: Memetic algorithms: a short introduction. In: New Ideas in Optimization, pp. 219–234. McGraw-Hill Ltd., Maidenhead (1999)
27. Nguyen, T.T., Yao, X.: Continuous dynamic constrained optimization: the challenges. IEEE T Evol. Comput. **16**(6), 769–786 (2012)
28. O'Sullivan, B., Goerzen, J., Stewart, D.: Real World Haskell. O'Reilly, North Sebastopol (2008)
29. Özcan, E., Bilgin, B., Korkmaz, E.E.: A comprehensive analysis of hyper-heuristics. Intell. Data Anal. **12**(1), 3–23 (2008)
30. Perron, L.: Search procedures and parallelism in constraint programming. In: Jaffar, J. (ed.) Principles and Practice of Constraint Programming. LNCS, vol. 1713, pp. 346–360. Springer, Berlin Heidelberg (1999)
31. Reinelt, G.: TSPLIB - A T.S.P. library. Technical reports 250, Universität Augsburg, Institut für Mathematik, Augsburg (1990)
32. Samulowitz, H., Sabharwal, A., Schrijvers, T., Tack, G., Stuckey, P.: Automated design of search with composability (2013), 27th AAAI Conference on Artificial Intelligence
33. Schrijvers, T., Stuckey, P., Wadler, P.: Monadic constraint programming. J. Funct. Program. **19**, 663–697 (2009)
34. Schrijvers, T., Tack, G., Wuille, P., Samulowitz, H., Stuckey, P.: Search combinators. Constraints **18**(2), 269–305 (2013)
35. Senington, R., Duke, D.: Decomposing metaheuristic operations. In: Hinze, R. (ed.) IFL 2012. LNCS, vol. 8241, pp. 224–239. Springer, Heidelberg (2013)

36. Senington, R.J.: Hybrid meta-heuristic frameworks: a functional approach. Ph.D. thesis, University of Leeds (2013)
37. Soria-Alcaraz, J.A., Ochoa, G., Swan, J., Carpio, M., Puga, H., Burke, E.K.: Effective learning hyper-heuristics for the course timetabling problem. Euro. J. Oper. Res. **238**(1), 77–86 (2014)
38. Tang, K., Peng, F., Chen, G., Yao, X.: Population-based algorithm portfolios with automated constituent algorithms selection. Inform. Sci. **279**, 94–104 (2014)
39. Van Hentenryck, P., Michel, L.: Constraint-Based Local Search. MIT Press, Cambridge (2005)
40. Van Hentenryck, P., Michel, L.: Nondeterministic control for hybrid search. Constraints **11**(4), 353–373 (2006)
41. Wagner, S., Kronberger, G.: Algorithm and experiment design with heuristic lab: an open source optimization environment for research and education. In: Proceeding GECCO Companion, pp. 1287–1316. ACM, New York (2012)
42. Wan, Z.: Functional Reactive Programming for Real-Time Reactive Systems. Ph.D. thesis, Department of Computer Science, Yale University, December 2002
43. Woodward, J., Swan, J., Martin, S.: The 'Composite' design pattern in metaheuristics. In: Proceedings of the GECCO Companion pp. 1439–1444. ACM, New York (2014)
44. Woodward, J.R., Swan, J.: Template method hyper-heuristics. In: Proceedings of the GECCO Companion, pp. 1437–1438. ACM (2014)

Parameter Control in Search-Based Generation of Unit Test Suites

David Paterson, Jonathan Turner, Thomas White, and Gordon Fraser$^{(\boxtimes)}$

Department of Computer Science, The University of Sheffield, Sheffield, UK
Gordon.Fraser@sheffield.ac.uk

Abstract. Search-based testing supports developers by automatically generating test suites with high coverage, but the effectiveness of a search-based test generator depends on numerous parameters. It is unreasonable to expect developers to understand search algorithms well enough to find the optimal parameter settings for a problem at hand, and even if they did, a static value for a parameter can be suboptimal at any given point during the search. To counter this problem, *parameter control* methods have been devised to automatically determine and adapt parameter values throughout the search. To investigate whether parameter control methods can also improve search-based generation of test suites, we have implemented and evaluated different methods to control the crossover and mutation rate in the EvoSuite unit test generation tool. Evaluation on a selection of open source Java classes reveals that while parameter control improves the values of mutation and crossover rate successfully during runtime, the positive effects of this improvement are often countered by increased costs of fitness evaluation.

1 Introduction

Search-based testing has been successfully applied to generate software tests in various domains, such as unit tests for object-oriented classes [9,15]. Test generation tools implement efficient algorithms such as genetic algorithms (GAs), which have many parameters that influence the effectiveness of the search, for example mutation and crossover rates. A globally optimal setting of these parameters through *tuning* is difficult, as the best parameters depend on the specific problem at hand. However, it is unlikely that a software developer wanting to apply a search-based test generation tool knows enough about a genetic algorithm to set these to an optimal value. Even if they did, the optimal values are most likely to change during runtime [1]; for example, initially a higher mutation rate may be more beneficial to foster exploration, whereas a lower mutation rate for better exploitation may be preferrable in later parts of the search.

To overcome this problem, research has been carried out with the purpose of automatically adapting these parameters throughout the search. This process is referred to as *Parameter Control* (PC) [5]. Implementation of parameter control has been positive in many application areas, which suggests that parameter control could also be applied to search-based test generation. To determine whether

© Springer International Publishing Switzerland 2015
M. Barros and Y. Labiche (Eds.): SSBSE 2015, LNCS 9275, pp. 141–156, 2015.
DOI: 10.1007/978-3-319-22183-0_10

that is the case, we have implemented multiple different methods of parameter control into the EVOSUITE unit test generation tool [7]. Specifically, we implemented a *deterministic* control method that depends only on the progress of the search, an *adaptive* control method that changes values based on the overall search performance, and *self-adaptive* control methods, which adapt parameters based on individual fitness values. We applied these methods to control the mutation and crossover rates in EVOSUITE, and performed experiments to determine if parameter control also provides a performance increase in search-based test generation for object-oriented classes.

The experiments show that controlling parameters can have a major influence throughout the evolutionary search, but when optimising for unit test suites there is the problem that more frequent mutation increases the costs of fitness evaluation, which counters some of the beneficial effects of the control methods. We found that a deterministic control method nevertheless leads to coverage increase in seven out of ten classes, and self-adaptive control methods are particularly effective when controlling crossover rather than mutation, as the crossover rate does not have an effect on the costs of fitness evaluation. However, adapting the mutation and crossover rates per iteration has been shown to have negative effects, with eight out of 10 classes achieving lower overall branch coverage.

This paper is organised as follows: Sect. 2 describes the search problem addressed and introduces parameter control. Section 3 describes how different control methods can be applied in the context of unit test generation, and Sect. 4 contains the results of an empirical evaluation of these techniques.

2   Background

This section describes search-based unit testing, parameter tuning and control and the different categories of parameter control.

2.1   Search-Based Unit Test Generation

Search-based test generation is the application of meta-heuristic search algorithms to create test cases [12]. Test cases are usually generated with the objective to build test suites that maximise code coverage criteria (e.g., statement or branch coverage). The coverage criterion is encoded as a fitness function, which can guide search algorithms like genetic algorithms to producing these test suites. In the context of testing object-oriented classes, a test case is a *unit test*, i.e., a small piece of code (e.g., a method consisting of a sequence of statements) that checks whether the class under test is behaving as expected. The use of search-based testing to generate unit tests was first proposed by Tonella [15], and this approach as well as follow-up work (e.g., [3,9]) is based on genetic algorithms.

A genetic algorithm applies Darwin's theory of evolution over a possibly infinite search space. In unit test generation, the search space consists of all possible unit tests for a *class under test* (CUT). Fraser and Arcuri [9] extended this to a search space of unit test *suites* rather than unit tests, which is more efficient than generating individual tests iteratively [2]. Thus, the representation we consider in this paper is a unit test suite, which consists of a set of unit tests, each of which is a sequence of statements (e.g., method calls, constructor calls, etc.). Much of the evolution process in a genetic algorithm can be compared with a biological ecosystem, with a chromosome's genes changing through *mutation* and *crossover*, with the fittest members of each population surviving.

Mutation of test suites consists of mutation of the constituent unit tests, or insertion of new unit tests into the test suite (deletion happens when a test case has length 0 [9]). Each constituent unit test in a suite of size n is mutated with probability $1/n$, and the mutation of a unit test consists of deletion, insertion, and modification of statements, which is performed with probabiliy $1/3$. Statements in a unit test of length l are deleted or modified with probability $1/l$, and insertion uses a probability ρ, such that a new random statement is inserted at a random position in the test with probability ρ, then another one is inserted with probability ρ^2, and so on until no statement is inserted.

Crossover treats the test suites like sequences and is typically implemented as single point crossover. However, in order to avoid an undesired growth of the test suite sizes (bloat), a relative position crossover [8] is preferable. Here, a random value α is chosen from $[0, 1]$, and then the first offspring contains the first $\alpha|P_1|$ test cases from the first parent P_1, and the last $(1 - \alpha)|P_2|$ test cases from the second parent P_2; the second offspring consists of the first $\alpha|P_2|$ test cases from the second parent, followed by the last $(1 - \alpha)|P_1|$ test cases from the first.

Fitness calculation requires the execution of tests in a test suite, in order to produce execution traces on which to calculate metrics related to the targeted coverage objective (e.g., branch distances [10] when optimising for branch coverage). Because the computational costs of executing tests are typically high compared to the calculation of the actual fitness values from the execution traces, these traces can be saved together with the individuals. Then, re-execution of tests is only necessary when a test was changed through mutation; crossover does not require re-execution of any tests [7].

2.2 Parameter Tuning and Control

In any genetic algorithm implementation, there are a number of parameters that control the runtime operation of the method. These include *mutation rate* and *crossover rate*, i.e., the probability with which these search operators are applied on a new offspring. In many implementations, these values are set at the start of the generation and never change.

The process of determining a good assignment of values to these parameters is known as *parameter tuning*, and it can be beneficial to a genetic algorithm [6]. The process of tuning involves experimentation of the problem area with many different combinations of parameter values and on large sets of different example problems with the hope of finding a set of values that performs better than any other set. Arcuri and Fraser [1] investigated the possibility of tuning the parameters of a genetic algorithm in the context of unit test generation, but found that default values suggested in the literature produced better results than

144 D. Paterson et al.

parameters tuned on any specific sample of classes. Indeed, since the problem of search-based unit test generation is so varied, it seems unlikely to find parameter tuning methods that perform consistently better than default.

In some cases, however, using a static value cannot lead to optimal results. In mutation, for example, there are two ways a genetic algorithm can behave: *exploration*, using a high mutation rate to explore a larger section of the search space by changing each individual by an increased amount, and *exploitation*, using a low mutation rate to make very minor adjustments to the individuals when there is a relatively high overall fitness and exploration would result in too much change. Bäck and Schütz [4] propose the idea that the mutation should initially be exploring the search space, then further into the generations it should look to exploit the population to home in on a solution. Controlling and adapting the parameter values during the search is known as *parameter control*. Eiben et al. [5] categorise parameter control methods into three classes:

Deterministic: Deterministic parameter control methods, such as the one described by Bäck and Schütz [4], rely on the time or iteration progress of algorithm to determine the mutation rate, therefore providing a function of t. Deterministic methods by their nature, do not receive any feedback from the genetic algorithm. These methods can be implemented when a mathematical model of how a parameter should change over a period of time can be produced, for example a $1/x$ curve. This is useful if, for instance, the algorithm should explore the population at the start of generated (high quantity of mutations) and exploit the population later in generation (low quantity of mutations, high quantity of crossovers). Using deterministic parameter control, the rates of all parameters at any given point t can be calculated.

Adaptive: An adaptive parameter control method may look at which parameters are causing the most positive/negative impact on the best or average fitness of a population, and reward the parameters that are having positive impact. For example, the method described by Lin et al. [11] controls both mutation rate and crossover rate, seeing whether mutation or crossover is providing more positive impact before increasing one and decreasing the other by a small amount.

Self Adaptive: Self Adaptive parameter control uses the inherent properties of genetic algorithms to its advantage, by adding parameters to the individuals that are going to be mutated, and allowing evolution to occur not only on the individual but the parameters as well. The individual's parameters can then be used instead of the algorithms global parameters. This theoretically provides a way of calculating the 'best' mutation rates, because the better mutation rates will provide fitter individuals.

3 Parameter Control in Unit Test Generation

In this section, we describe how existing parameter control methods can be adapted to apply to search-based unit test suite generation. For each of the three categories of parameter control we have chosen a representative technique based on the literature.

3.1   Mutation Strength in Mutating Unit Test Suites

As described in Sect. 2.1, the mutation of test suites is typically done using probabilities based on the size of an individual, rather than fixed probabilities. The intuition behind this choice is that with a mutation probability of $1/n$ for a test suite of n tests, on average one test gets mutated. In order to apply parameter control to mutations, this operator needs to be changed; however, a variable mutation rate is not immediately applicable as the interpretation of such a rate would be highly dependent on the size of an individual. Therefore, we use a *mutation strength* [13], where the mutation parameter determines how often the regular mutation operator is applied. The value of the mutation rate is in the range $[0, 1]$ and is interpreted as the percentage of individuals that should be mutated on average. Thus, for a given test suite T and mutation rate M, the mutation rate for that individual is calculated as $m = M \times |T|$, and then we apply a mutation with probability m, then another one with probability $m - 1$, another one with probability $m - 2$, etc., until $m \leq 0$.

3.2   Deterministic Parameter Control

The deterministic parameter control described by Bäck and Schütz [4] follows the reasoning that mutation rate should decrease over time. The $1/x$ curve that is generated by the following equation, which drastically reduces mutation rate from a high initial point:

$$ P_m(t) = \left(2 + \frac{n-2}{T-1} \cdot t \right)^{-1} $$

where $p_0 = \frac{1}{2}$ and $p_{T-1} = \frac{1}{n}$, T is the maximum possible number of generations, t is the current generation number and n is the size of the individual. The initial high values for mutation makes it possible for mass exploration during early iterations. Early exploration allows the population to spread across the problem domain and provides a greater chance of being able to converge on a fitter individual at a later point. If this did not happen then the solution range would only contain the genes of the random initial population. As the algorithm progresses and mutation rate becomes closer to 0, mutation becomes less likely to occur. This allows for crossover to exploit individuals in the current population. This exploitation would hopefully allow for convergence towards the fittest individual. When applying this in the context of unit test generation, there are two difficulties: First, there is no fixed size n of the individuals — test suites can have variable numbers of tests, and therefore due to the incorrect value of the numerator in the equation, the generated curve tends to converge on 0 much quicker than intended. This early convergence is detrimental to the algorithm, and its effectiveness at mutating the initial population of test suites. Second, in addition to variable sizes, the execution costs of different tests may vary greatly. As a software developer applying a search-based test generation tool may not want to wait for an undetermined amount of time but rather a fixed duration (e.g., 1 min), the exact number of generations that will be executed in that time cannot be known beforehand. We have therefore experimentally determined the following function that approximates the Bäck and Schütz function, but is neither dependent on the number of generations nor on the size of individuals:

$$P_m(t) = (P_m max - P_m min) \cdot (2 + \frac{15t}{T-1})^{-1} + P_m min$$

where $P_m max$ and $P_m min$ are the maximum and minimum possible values for mutation (for EVOSUITE these values are set at 1 and 0 respectively, however this is dependent on the search problem). T is the total time the algorithm can run for and t is the current time since the algorithm began. By adding 2 to the value before ordering to the power of 1, the equation starts directly in the middle of the maximum and minimum possible mutation values. Changing the value 15 to a higher value makes the curve steeper, whilst decreasing it makes the curve more shallow. These values were chosen by experimentation in order to create an optimal curve, changing these values would affect the rate of change and initial value for mutation rate. Similarly to the original function, this function allows for the early stages of the algorithm to have high values for mutation, allowing for early exploration and later exploitation.

3.3   Adaptive Parameter Control

Lin et al. [11] described an adaptive control method that controls both mutation and crossover rate. The algorithm, known as the Progressive Rate Genetic Algorithm (PGRA), adapts the mutation rate and crossover rate during the run of the genetic algorithm. By calculating the average increase in fitness provided by both mutation and crossover, it is possible to find which function provides the greatest contribution to the fitness of the general population. This can be described simply by the following:

$$p_c = p_c + \theta_1 \text{ if } \widetilde{CP} > \widetilde{MP},$$
$$p_c = p_c - \theta_1 \text{ if } \widetilde{CP} < \widetilde{MP},$$
$$\text{and}$$
$$p_m = p_m + \theta_2 \text{ if } \widetilde{CP} < \widetilde{MP},$$
$$p_m = p_m - \theta_2 \text{ if } \widetilde{CP} > \widetilde{MP},$$

where p_m and p_c are mutation rate and crossover rate respectively. θ_1 and θ_2 are predefined constants, with the literature suggesting values of 0.01 to be most optimal. $\widetilde{MP}$ and $\widetilde{CP}$ are the average mutation and crossover performance. $\widetilde{MP}$ and $\widetilde{CP}$ are calculated by adding the increase in performance (e.g., increase in fitness for a search problem where the fitness function should be maximised, or decrease in fitness for a search problem where the fitness function should be minimised) in all individuals after mutation and crossover respectively, and dividing this number by the amount of mutations and crossovers that have occured. For example, if after five crossover operations the fitness values increase in total by 2.0, then the Crossover Performance (CP) would be $2.0/5 = 0.4$

For the above implementation of the PRGA, the literature suggests that initial values of 0.5 for both mutation rate and crossover rate will provide the most suitable solution. Despite this, we determined a value of 0.8 for crossover rate and 0.1 for mutation rate through experiments to achieve the best fitness values. These values may be specific for search-based test generation but it is worthy of note.

3.4 Self-Adaptive Parameter Control

The final parameter control approach is a derivative of many other self-adaptive approaches. By providing each individual with its own mutation and crossover rate, this value is mutated once per iteration if the individual is mutated. The mutation of these rates is carried out using Gaussian perturbation with a small standard deviation, e.g., 0.05. When deciding to apply mutation to an individual, the mutation rate defined by that individual is used rather than a global parameter. When applying crossover to two individuals, the average value of their two crossover rates is used as common crossover rate. In doing this, individuals which have a more suitable mutation and crossover rate for the current iteration are more likely to result in fitter offspring than others that do not, and are therefore more likely to survive.

Since unlike the method devised by Lin et al., this method does not perform a comparison between the benefit of mutation and crossover, it can be used to control either or both parameters. In doing so it may be possible to find if controlling one rate is beneficial over controlling another, or if controlling both rates produces fitter individuals.

4 Empirical Evaluation

In order to determine how well these parameter control techniques work in the context of unit test suite generation, we performed a set of experiments on a set of open source classes. In this section, we summarise our findings for each of the three types of control methods.

4.1 Experiment Set-Up

The parameter control techniques described in this paper were implemented into the EvoSuite test generation tool [7], and the mutation operator was adapted as described in Sect. 3.1 to allow for variation in the mutation strength. The default value of mutation rate is set to 0.1, which was empirically determined to perform similar to EvoSuite's default mutation.

To study the behaviour of the different control techniques, 10 classes were manually selected from the Apache Commons libraries [14]. The classes were selected based on them being non-trivial in terms of the number of branches, as a class with too few branches would lead to a solution being found too quickly regardless of whether or not parameter control was used. Furthermore, classes

Table 1. Table showing the classes selected, the line numbers they have and the amount of branches that EVOSUITE uses as goals.

Project	Class	Lines of Code (LOC)	Coverable branches
org.apache.commons.cli	CommandLine	152	49
	GnuParser	62	21
	HelpFormatter	416	143
	Option	227	98
	Options	106	33
	Parser	206	75
org.apache.commons.collections4	ListUtils	248	89
	CSVFormat	424	190
org.apache.commons.csv	CSVParser	209	69
	Lexer	245	141

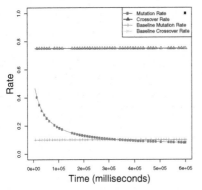 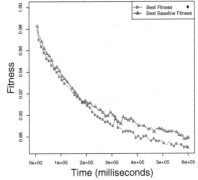

(a) Mutation rate over time for class CSVFormat.

(b) Fitness over time for class CSVFormat.

Fig. 1. Deterministic parameter control applied in time to the CSVFormat class of the org.apache.commons.csv package.

which required data from external sources (e.g., a database) were avoided, since these classes pose specific problems and this study was to be done using the default application scenario. See Table 1 for more information on the classes chosen. EVOSUITE ran on each of these 10 classes, with a maximum runtime of 10 min (allowing for all searches to converge), with each parameter control method being used independently. To ensure statistical correctness this process was repeated 50 times per class and parameter control combination.

Other experiments were also done in an attempt to tune the parameters used by the actual parameter control techniques. One such experiment ran to determine the optimal start position for mutation and crossover rate for self adaptive parameter control. The values of 0.1 for mutation rate and 0.8 for crossover rate were found to provide the most benefit.

Table 2. Average branch coverage and $\hat{A}_{12}$ effect size statistics after 10 min. Significant differences at $p < 0.05$ are shown in bold. $\hat{A}_{12} > 0.5$ means the control method is better than the baseline, $\hat{A}_{12} < 0.5$ means it is worse.

Class	Base	Deterministic		Adaptive		SA/Xover		SA/Mut.		Self-Adaptive	
		Cov.	$\hat{A}_{12}$	Cov.	$\hat{A}_{12}$	Cov.	$\hat{A}_{12}$	Cov.	$\hat{A}_{12}$	Cov.	$\hat{A}_{12}$
CSVFormat	0.95	0.95	0.65	**0.91**	**0.01**	0.96	**0.76**	0.95	0.49	0.94	0.52
CSVParser	0.74	0.72	0.32	**0.69**	**0.12**	0.72	0.33	**0.72**	**0.30**	0.72	0.33
CommandLine	0.97	0.98	0.59	0.98	0.65	0.98	0.56	**0.98**	**0.56**	0.98	0.56
GnuParser	0.94	**0.97**	**0.73**	0.94	0.52	**0.97**	**0.75**	0.95	0.60	**0.96**	**0.71**
HelpFormatter	0.87	0.88	0.63	0.86	0.44	0.88	0.63	0.87	0.55	0.86	0.43
Lexer	0.78	0.76	0.44	**0.66**	**0.05**	0.80	0.66	0.73	0.31	**0.72**	**0.27**
ListUtils	0.91	0.91	0.66	**0.89**	**0.27**	0.91	0.65	0.90	0.41	0.90	0.43
Option	1.00	1.00	0.51	**0.98**	**0.21**	1.00	0.51	1.00	0.49	1.00	0.45
Options	1.00	1.00	0.50	1.00	0.47	0.99	0.45	0.99	0.42	0.99	0.45
Parser	0.75	0.80	0.65	**0.62**	**0.17**	**0.85**	**0.76**	0.81	0.66	**0.84**	**0.74**

4.2   Results

Table 2 summarises the branch coverage achieved after 10 min for each of the classes and techniques. The default fitness function in EVOSUITE is branch coverage, therefore this can be used as the main metric on whether to judge if a parameter control method performs better than baseline. Deterministic parameter control leads to a significant improvement on the GnuParser class, and a non-significant increase on six other classes. For CSVParser and Lexer there is a non-significant decrease in coverage, and for class Option both techniques achieve full coverage in the 10 min. Adaptive parameter control is slightly, but non-significantly, better on CommandLine and GnuParser, but significantly worse on six other classes. Self-adaptive control of the crossover rate leads to an improvement on eight classes (three significant), and a non-significant decrease on Options and CSVParser. Using self-adaptive control for the mutation rate leads to an increase in four classes (significant for CommandLine, but worse coverage on six classes (significant for CSVParser). The combination of both parameters leads to a significant increase on GnuParser and Parser, and a non-significant increase on two; and decrease on six classes (significant for Lexer). For all classes, the differences in coverage are small, which is likely due to 10 min being ample time for EVOSUITE to achieve coverage with most reasonable parameter settings. Therefore, in the remainder of this section we take a closer look at how the parameters and fitness evolved throughout the search.

4.3 Deterministic Parameter Control

Figure 1a shows how the mutation rate starts at 0.5 as suggested by Bäck and Schütz [4], and then quickly drops down to lower values. The high mutation rate at the beginning achieves quick growth of the individuals, and in the early phases of the search this leads to an improvement in fitness. All 10 classes show an improvement in fitness after 400 generations, in particular Option, from the org.apache.commons.cli package, where there was a 25 % increase in fitness when using parameter control. The Option class (shown in Fig. 2a) had the lowest fitness value out of all 10 tested classes, bringing forward the hypothesis that deterministic parameter control performs better on classes that the baseline performs well on. By contrast, the CSVParser class shows almost no difference from the baseline.

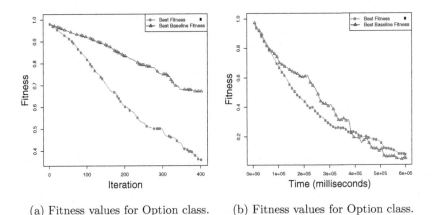

(a) Fitness values for Option class.   (b) Fitness values for Option class.

Fig. 2. Fitness values when using deterministic parameter control on the Option class of the org.apache.commons.cli package.

The improvement in fitness is less pronounced when viewing the evolution over time. In particular, for the Option class, 100 % coverage is achieved after 10 min with and without control, but it seems that the mutation rate drops *too low* to be useful (i.e., for there to be enough mutations to advance the population). In Fig. 2b, the baseline surpasses parameter control around 400 seconds (4e + 05 milliseconds). A possible reason for this is that using deterministic parameter control, once a mutation rate reaches such a low value that few mutations are occurring, it is impossible to recover from local optima, since the function is based on time alone.

4.4 Adaptive Parameter Control

The adaptive method devised by Lin et al. [11] changes the mutation and crossover rates at the end of every generation, depending on the performance of the operators while generating a new population. On the whole, the self-adaptive

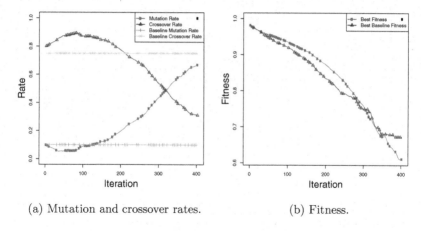

(a) Mutation and crossover rates.   (b) Fitness.

Fig. 3. Adaptive parameter control applied in iterations to the `Option` class of the `org.apache.commons.cli` package.

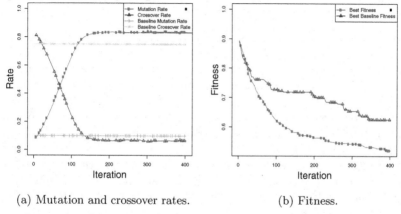

(a) Mutation and crossover rates.   (b) Fitness.

Fig. 4. Adaptive parameter control applied in iterations to the `GnuParser` class.

control method improves the fitness at 400 generations in 7 out of the 10 classes, with 5 of them being a significant improvement.

Figure 3a shows an example where the mutation and crossover rate for class `Option` initially stay close to the default values, with an improvement over the baseline fitness. The constant adaptation of crossover and mutation rates may allow the method to escape local minima to find a more optimal solution. For instance, if stuck in a local minimum, crossover would be expected to provide no increase in fitness, whereas mutation may increase the fitness by a larger margin, but with less probability. In this case mutation would be rewarded and therefore would be more influential in further iterations. Interestingly, after some time mutation seems to become more influential than crossover, which leads to an increase in mutation and a decrease in crossover probability. Eventually, the mutation rate even overtakes the crossover rate. This behaviour can be observed in all examples, and sometimes occurs even quicker, for example see

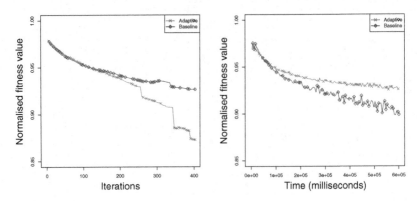

(a) Plot of average fitness across 10 classes in terms of iterations.

(b) Plot of average fitness across 10 classes in terms of time.

Fig. 5. Iteration and Time comparison of fitness for Adaptive Parameter Control vs Baseline.

class GnuParser shown in Fig. 4a. It is likely that in the initial phases of the search different test suites cover different parts of the class, such that crossover is particularly beneficial; later on in the search all test suites will cover the same branches, and the remaining branches often provide little or no guidance (e.g., boolean flags, reference comparisons, etc.). In these cases, there is less benefit from using crossover, whereas mutation will lead to coverage of new branches. Overall, this setting of parameters is justified in terms of the achieved improvement in fitness (Fig. 4b).

By design, the method devised by Lin et al. [11] performs very well when viewed in terms of iterations. Figure 5a shows that after approximately 200 iterations the method begins to drastically improve over baseline. However, higher mutation rates increase the costs of fitness evaluations: Test cases are only executed when mutated, so a higher mutation rate will lead to more test executions. Thus, when viewing the effect of adaptive control over *time* the result looks different: It is clear that when viewing best individual fitness in terms of time there is no improvement over baseline as shown by Fig. 5. The probable cause for this is that in 7 out of 10 classes the mutation rate reaches a level that will severely increase the iteration time of the algorithm due to the high cost of mutation. It is clear that maintaining a low iteration time, and therefore increasing the amount of iterations that can occur is essential in achieving optimal efficiency in the genetic algorithm.

4.5 Self-Adaptive Parameter Control

Unlike the adaptive parameter control used, self-adaptive control can be applied to parameters independently. We therefore consider controlling mutation and crossover rate individually and in combination. The results in Fig. 6(a), (b) and (c) show the self adaptive parameter control method working for 10 min of the genetic algorithm. Figure 6(a) is of both crossover and mutation rate being controlled and shows that the average fitness of the best individual across 10 classes was consistently better than the baseline through the entire run. An identical result can be seen in Fig. 6(b) which shows only mutation rate being controlled. However, Fig. 6(c) shows that controlling only crossover was substantially better in regards to time than the other two.

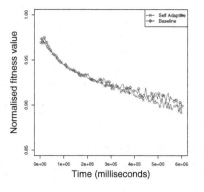

(a) Average Fitness of Best Individual of Self Adaptive PC controlling both rates vs. baseline.

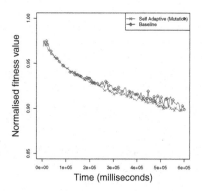

(b) Average Fitness of Best Individual of Self Adaptive PC controlling mutation rate vs. baseline.

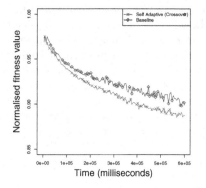

(c) Average Fitness of Best Individual of Self Adaptive PC controlling crossover rate vs. baseline.

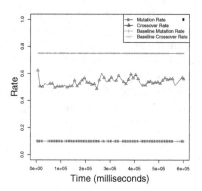

(d) Parameter Rates of Self Adaptive PC controlling only crossover on class `Option`.

Fig. 6. Self adaptive parameter control applied to EvoSuite.

The average mutation rate of self adaptive changed dramatically depending on what problem the genetic algorithm was facing. When testing some classes, the mutation rate would increase above the default mutation rate extremely and stay there, whereas with others the mutation rate would only slightly fluctuate around the default value. One example class which causes mutation rate to

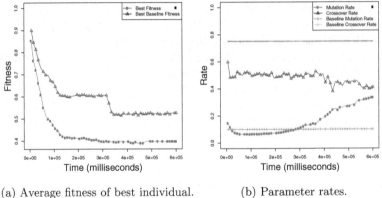

(a) Average fitness of best individual.   (b) Parameter rates.

Fig. 7. Self adaptive parameter control applied to the mutation and crossover rate on `CommandLine` class.

increase is `CommandLine` from the `org.apache.commons.cli` package. The fitness of the `CommandLine` class levels out before the 1 min mark (Fig. 7(a)). This could happen because the mutation rate has fallen low when being controlled and the local search has been diminished, or could be a local optimum. When this happens, the mutation rate starts to rise (Fig. 7(b)). The reason for this is that as no individual is getting fitter, the mutation rate cannot evolve so will diversify through the population. As the limits for mutation rate are 0.01 and 1, the value shown, which is the average mutation rate of the entire population, will tend to the half way value between these limits. This also has the positive effect of increasing the mutation rate which may help bypass a local optimum.

The self adaptive method that controls only mutation performed similar to controlling both parameters. This had the same trends for mutation rate that controlling both did (for example, in the `CommandLine` class, the fitness straightened and mutation rate started to increase to half way within the range). This also shows that the mutation operator is dominant in EVOSUITE and will affect the fitness of an individual more than crossover. This will be discussed in more detail below.

Finally, the method which only controlled crossover outperformed both other methods. A plausible explanation as to why this outperformed the other two methods could be that this method managed to do more iterations than the other methods that controlled mutation, as mutation never increased, and so fewer tests had to be revalidated, and subsequently the population of the genetic algorithm evolved more. This meant that more individuals were eliminated and a better fitness could be found. However, Fig. 6(d) shows the average crossover rate over time and shows that the crossover rate never stabilised when being controlled alone. That fact that mutation did find points that seemed *stable* shows that mutation influences an individual's fitness more than crossover.

Due to the behaviour of crossover rate and the values it changes to, it appears that some parameters are less closely linked to the fitness of an individual. This means that these parameters could be controlled but will never settle on the *correct* rate. If this is the case, it is likely that there is a range of rates that will perform similarly and the value will fluctuate in this range.

5 Conclusions

Parameter control has been successfully applied in different application areas of meta-heuristic search. In this paper, we investigated whether parameter control also leads to an improvement in the context of search-based generation of unit test suites. We implemented a deterministic, an adaptive, and a self-adaptive control method in the EvoSuite unit test generation tool, and used these to control the mutation and crossover rates in the underlying genetic algorithm.

Our experiments showed that controlling the mutation rate in EvoSuite usually has advantages when comparing the behaviour in terms of iterations of the genetic algorithm. However, a typical application scenario of EvoSuite would use time as a stopping condition rather than iterations, and in this case the influence of the mutation rate on the costs of fitness evaluations dramatically increase iteration times, which can lead to less evolution in the same time. Despite this, parameter control generally increases the fitness of the best individual in search-based software testing when using deterministic or self adaptive methods, and adaptive methods do not increase the fitness frequently due to the rapidly increasing iteration time that a high mutation rate can have.

Our findings suggest future work to refine existing control methods to take the costs of fitness evaluations into account. Furthermore, rather than controlling the rate of mutations, in the case of unit test generation it may be more beneficial to control and adapt the details of the mutation operator (e.g., whether to insert or delete statements), rather than its strength.

Acknowledgments. This work was supported by the EPSRC project "EXOGEN" (EP/K030353/1).

References

1. Arcuri, A., Fraser, G.: Parameter tuning or default values? An empirical investigation in search-based software engineering. Empir. Softw. Eng. **18**(3), 594–623 (2013). http://dx.doi.org/10.1007/s10664-013-9249-9
2. Arcuri, A., Fraser, G.: On the effectiveness of whole test suite generation. In: Le Goues, C., Yoo, S. (eds.) SSBSE 2014. LNCS, vol. 8636, pp. 1–15. Springer, Heidelberg (2014)
3. Baresi, L., Lanzi, P.L., Miraz, M.: Testful: an evolutionary test approach for java. In: IEEE International Conference on Software Testing, Verification and Validation (ICST), pp. 185–194 (2010)
4. Bäck, T., Schütz, M.: Intelligent mutation rate control in canonical genetic algorithms. In: Michalewicz, M., Raś, Z.W. (eds.) ISMIS 1996. LNCS, vol. 1079, pp. 158–167. Springer, Heidelberg (1996). http://dx.doi.org/10.1007/3-540-61286-6_141

5. Eiben, A., Hinterding, R., Michalewicz, Z.: Parameter control in evolutionary algorithms. IEEE Trans. Evol. Comput. **3**(2), 124–141 (1999)
6. Eiben, A., Smit, S.: Evolutionary algorithm parameters and methods to tune them. In: Hamadi, Y., Monfroy, E., Saubion, F. (eds.) Autonomous Search, pp. 15–36. Springer, Berlin Heidelberg (2012)
7. Fraser, G., Arcuri, A.: EvoSuite: automatic test suite generation for object-oriented software. In: ACM Symposium on the Foundations of Software Engineering (FSE), pp. 416–419 (2011)
8. Fraser, G., Arcuri, A.: Handling test length bloat. Softw. Test. Verif. Reliab. **23**(7), 553–582 (2013)
9. Fraser, G., Arcuri, A.: Whole test suite generation. IEEE Trans. Softw. Eng. (TSE) **39**(2), 276–291 (2013)
10. Korel, B.: Automated software test data generation. IEEE Trans. Softw. Eng. **16**, 870–879 (1990)
11. Lin, W.Y., Lee, W.Y., Hong, T.P.: Adapting crossover and mutation rates in genetic algorithms. J. Inf. Sci. Eng. **19**(5), 889–903 (2003)
12. McMinn, P.: Search-based software test data generation: a survey: research articles. Softw. Test. Verif. Reliab. **14**(2), 105–156 (2004)
13. Stoean, C., Stoean, R.: Support Vector Machines and Evolutionary Algorithms for Classification. Springer, Switzerland (2014)
14. The Apache Software Foundation: Apache commons released components (2015). http://commons.apache.org/components.html
15. Tonella, P.: Evolutionary testing of classes. In: ACM International Symposium on Software Testing and Analysis (ISSTA), pp. 119–128 (2004)

Hypervolume-Based Search for Test Case Prioritization

Dario Di Nucci[1]([✉]), Annibale Panichella[2], Andy Zaidman[2],
and Andrea De Lucia[1]

[1] University of Salerno, Salerno, Italy
{ddinucci,adelucia}@unisa.it
[2] Delft University of Technology, Delft, The Netherlands
{a.panichella,a.e.zaidman}@tudelft.nl

Abstract. Test case prioritization (TCP) is aimed at finding an ideal ordering for executing the available test cases to reveal faults earlier. To solve this problem greedy algorithms and meta-heuristics have been widely investigated, but in most cases there is no statistically significant difference between them in terms of effectiveness. The fitness function used to guide meta-heuristics condenses the cumulative coverage scores achieved by a test case ordering using the Area Under Curve (AUC) metric. In this paper we notice that the AUC metric represents a simplified version of the hypervolume metric used in many objective optimization and we propose HGA, a Hypervolume-based Genetic Algorithm, to solve the TCP problem when using multiple test criteria. The results shows that HGA is more cost-effective than the additional greedy algorithm on large systems and on average requires 36 % of the execution time required by the additional greedy algorithm.

Keywords: Test case prioritization · Genetic algorithm · Hypervolume

1 Introduction

Regression testing is aimed at verifying that software changes do not affect the unchanged parts compromising their behaviours. Many approaches have been proposed in literature for reducing the effort of regression testing [22,29], which remains a particular expensive maintenance activity. One of these approaches is *test case prioritization* (TCP) [11,25]. TCP is aimed at finding an ordering for executing the available test cases, with the goal of executing those test cases that are more likely to reveal faults earlier [12]. Most of the proposed techniques for TCP are based on a coverage criterion [29], such as branch coverage [25], used as a surrogate to prioritize test case with the idea that test cases having higher code coverage also have a higher probability to reveal faults. Once a coverage criterion is chosen, search algorithms can be applied for finding the ordering maximizing the selected criterion.

© Springer International Publishing Switzerland 2015
M. Barros and Y. Labiche (Eds.): SSBSE 2015, LNCS 9275, pp. 157–172, 2015.
DOI: 10.1007/978-3-319-22183-0_11

Greedy Algorithms have been widely investigated in literature for test case prioritization, such as simple greedy algorithms [29], additional greedy algorithms [25], 2-optimal greedy algorithms [22], or hybrid greedy algorithms [15]. Other than greedy algorithms, meta-heuristics have been applied as alternative search algorithms to test case prioritization. To allow the application of meta-heuristics, proper fitness functions have been developed [22], such as the Average Percentage Block Coverage (APBC), or the Average Percentage Statement Coverage (APSC). Each fitness function condenses the cumulative coverage scores achieved by a test case ordering using the Area Under Curve (AUC) metric. As such, multiple points are condensed in a single scalar value that can be used as a fitness function of meta-heuristics such as single-objective genetic algorithms. Later work on search-based TCP also employed multi-objective genetic algorithms considering different AUC-based metrics as different objectives to optimize [20,21]. Previous work shows that in most cases there is no statistically significant difference between genetic algorithms and additional greedy approaches in terms of effectiveness, i.e., in terms of the capability of the generated orderings to reveal regression faults earlier [22].

In this paper we notice that the AUC metrics used in the related literature for TCP represents a simplified version of the *hypervolume* metric [2], which is a widely know metric in many-objective optimization. Indeed, in many-objective optimization the problem of condensing multiple criteria has already been investigated by using the more general concept of *hypervolume under manifold* [2], which represents a generalization for the higher dimensional objective space of the AUC-based metrics used in previous TCP studies. Indeed, we show that the *hypervolume* metric allows to condense not only a single cumulative code coverage (as done by previous AUC metrics used in TCP literature) but also multiple testing criteria, such as the test case execution cost or further coverage criteria, in only one scalar value. Therefore, in this paper we propose HGA, a Hypervolume-based Genetic Algorithm to solve the TCP problem when using multiple criteria. To show the applicability of the proposed algorithm, we conducted an empirical study involving six real world open-source programs. The results achieved shows that HGA is more cost-effective than the additional greedy algorithm on large systems and on average requires 36 % of the execution time required by the additional greedy algorithm. As a further contribution, we also show that for TCP the computation of the hypervolume metric is polynomial with respect to the number of the testing criteria, while in general for traditional optimization problems it is exponential.

2   Background and Related Work

Test Case Prioritization (TCP) has been widely investigated in literature. The most investigated direction regards the choice of a proper testing criterion to use for generating a test case ordering aimed at maximizing the real fault detection rate. Since the fault capability can not be known to the tester in advance until the test cases are executed according to the chosen ordering, researchers have proposed to use surrogate metrics which are in some way correlated with the fault detection rate [29]. Code coverage is one of the most widely used prioritization criterion, such as branch coverage [25], statement coverage [11], block coverage [8], and function or method coverage [13]. Other prioritization criteria were also used instead of structural coverage, such as interaction [3], clustering-based [5], and requirement coverage [27].

In all the aforementioned works, once a prioritization criterion is chosen, a greedy algorithm is used to order the test cases according to the chosen criterion. Two main greedy strategies can be applied [15,32]: the *total* strategy selects test cases according to the number of code elements they cover, whereas the *additional* strategy iteratively selects a next test case that yields the maximal coverage of code elements not yet covered by previously selected test cases. Recently, Hao *et al.* [15] and Zhang *et al.* [32] proposed a hybrid approach that combines *total* and *additional* coverage criteria showing that their combination can be more effective than the individual components. Greedy algorithms have also been used to combine multiple testing criteria such as code coverage and cost. For example, Elbaum *et al.* [10] and Malishevsky *et al.* [23] considered code coverage and execution cost, where the additional greedy algorithm was customized to condense the two objectives in only one function (coverage per unit cost) to maximize. Three-objective greedy algorithms have been also used to combine statement coverage, history faults coverage and execution cost [24,29].

Other than greedy algorithms, meta-heuristics have been investigated as alternative search algorithms to test case prioritization. Li *et al.* [22] compared additional greedy algorithm, 2-optimal greedy, hill climbing and genetic algorithms for code coverage based TCP. To allow the application of meta-heuristics they developed proper fitness functions: APBC (Average Percentage Block Coverage), APDC (Average Percentage Decision Coverage) or APSC (Average Percentage Statement Coverage). Each of these metrics condenses the cumulative coverage scores (e.g., branch coverage) achieved when considering the test cases in the given order sequentially [22] using the Area Under Curve (AUC) metric. This area is delimited by the cumulative points whose y-coordinates are the cumulative coverage scores (e.g., statement coverage) achieved when varying the number of executed test cases (x-coordinates) according to a specified ordering [22]. Since this metric allows to condense multiple cumulative points in only one scalar value, single-objective genetic algorithms can be applied to find an ordering maximizing the AUC. According to the empirical results in [22], in most cases the difference between the effectiveness of permutation-based genetic algorithms and additional greedy approaches is not significant.

Later works highlighted that given the multi-objective nature of the TCP problem, permutation-based genetic algorithms should consider more than one testing criterion. For example, in a further paper Li *et al.* [21] proposed a two-objective permutation-based genetic algorithm to optimize APSC and execution cost required to reach the maximum statement coverage (cumulative cost). They use a multi-objective genetic algorithm, namely NSGA-II, to find a set of Pareto optimal test case orderings representing optimal compromises between the two corresponding AUC-based criteria. Similarly, Islam *et al.* [20] used NSGA-II to find Pareto optimal test case orderings representing trade-offs between three different AUC-based criteria: (i) cumulative code coverage, (ii) cumulative requirement coverage, and (iii) cumulative execution cost. Both these two multi-objective approaches to test case prioritization [20,21] have important drawbacks. Firstly, they can provide hundreds of orderings representing trade-offs between AUC metrics and not between the selected testing criteria. Furthermore, no guidelines are given to guide the decision maker in selecting the ordering to use. Another important limitation of these classical multi-objective approaches is that they lose their effectiveness as the problem dimensionality increases, as demonstrated by previous work in numerical optimization [18]. Therefore, other non classical many-objective solvers must be investigated in order to deal with multiple (many) testing criteria. Finally, in [20–22] there is no empirical evidence of the effectiveness of NSGA-II with respect to simple heuristics, such as greedy algorithms, in terms of cost-effectiveness.

In this paper we notice that the most natural way to deal with the multi-objective TCP problem is represented by the *hypervolume*-based solvers since the AUC metrics used in the related literature for TCP represent a specific simplified version of the *hypervolume* metric [2]. Indeed, in many-objective optimization the *hypervolume* metrics is widely used to condense points from a higher dimensional objective space in only one scalar value. Instead of using the Area Under Curve to condense multiple points, the hypervolume metric uses the more general concept of *hypervolume under manifold* for this aim [2]. For these reasons, in this paper we propose to use an hypervolume metric to solve the multi-objective TCP problem. Moreover, we determine that because of the *monotonicity* properties of the coverage criteria, the computation of the hypervolume for TCP requires polynomial time versus the exponential time required for traditional many-objective problems.

3   Hypervolume Indicator for TCP

In many-objective optimization there is a growing trend to solve many-objective problems using *quality scalar indicators* to condense multiple objectives into a single objective [2]. Therefore, instead of optimizing the objective functions directly, indicator-based algorithms are aimed at finding a set of solutions that maximizes the underlying quality indicator [2]. One of the most popular indicators is the *hypervolume*, which measures the quality of a set of solutions as the total size of the objective space that is dominated by one (or more) of such solutions (combinatorial union [2]). For two-objective problems, the *hypervolume* corresponds to the area under curve, i.e., the proportion of the area that is dominated by a given set of candidate solutions.

To illustrate intuitively the proposed hypervolume metric, let us consider for simplicity only two testing criteria: (i) maximizing the statement coverage and (ii) minimizing the execution cost of a test suite. When considering the test cases in a specific order, the cumulative coverage and the cumulative execution cost reached by each test case draw a set of points within the objective space. For example, consider the test suite $T = \{t_1, t_2, \ldots, t_n\}$ with the following statement coverage $Cov = \{cov_S(t_1), cov_S(t_2), \ldots, cov_S(t_n)\}$ and execution cost $Cost = \{cost(t_1), cost(t_2), \ldots, cost(t_n)\}$. As depicted in Fig. 1(a), if we consider the ordering $\tau = \langle t_1, t_2, \ldots, t_n \rangle$ we can measure the cumulative scores as follows: the first test case t_1 covers a specific set of code statements $cov_S(t_1)$ with cost equal to $cost(t_1)$ (first cumulative point p_1); the second test case in the ordering t_2 reaches a new cumulative statement coverage $cov_S(t_1, t_2)$ $= cov_S(t_1) \cup cov_S(t_2)$ with $cost(t_1, t_2) = cost(t_1) + cost(t_2)$ (second cumulative point p_2); and so on. Thus, each test case prioritization corresponds to a set of points in the two-objective space denoted by the two testing criteria, i.e., statement coverage and execution cost in our example (see Fig. 1(a)). These points are of *weakly monotonically increasing* since both cumulative coverage and cumulative cost increase when adding a new test case from the ordering, i.e., $cov_S(t_1) \leqslant cov_S(t_1, t_2)$ and $cost(t_1) \leqslant cost(t_1, t_2)$.

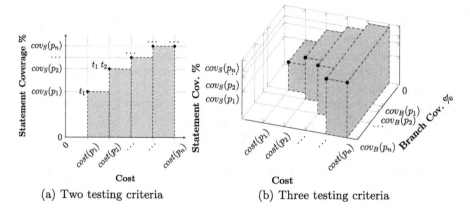

(a) Two testing criteria   (b) Three testing criteria

Fig. 1. Cumulative points in two- and three-objective test case prioritization. The gray area (or volume) denotes the portion of objective space dominated by the cumulative points $P(\tau)$.

Given this set of points we can measure how quickly the given ordering τ optimizes the two objectives by measuring the proportion of the *area* dominated by the corresponding cumulative points $P(\tau)$, denoted by the gray area in Fig. 1(a). The *dominated area* is represented by all points in the objective space that are worse than the cumulative points according to the concept of *dominance* in the multi-objective paradigm:

Definition 1. *We say that a point X dominates another point Y (also written $X >_p Y$) if and only if the values of the objective functions satisfy:*

$$cost(X) \leqslant cost(Y) \ \ and \ \ cov_S(X) > cov_S(Y)$$
$$or \tag{1}$$
$$cost(X) < cost(Y) \ \ and \ \ cov_S(X) \geqslant cov_S(Y)$$

Two different orderings correspond to two different cumulative points and then two different dominated areas. Therefore, we can compare the corresponding fraction of dominated areas to decide whether one candidate test case ordering is better or not than another one (fitness function): larger dominated areas imply faster statement coverage rate. In this two-objective space the dominated area can easily be computed as the sum of the rectangles of width $[cost(p_{i+1}) - cost(p_i)]$ and height $cov_S(p_i)$ as reported in Fig. 1(a). Similarly, if we consider a third testing criteria (such as branch coverage $cov_B(p_i)$) each candidate prioritization corresponds to a set of points in a three-dimensional space and, in this case, the dominated proportion of the objective space is represented by a volume instead of an area, as depicted in Fig. 1(b). Since even in this three-objective space the cumulative points are always *weakly monotonically increasing*, the dominated volume can be computed as the sum of the parallelepipeds of width $[cost(p_{i+1}) - cost(p_i)]$, height $cov_S(p_i)$ and depth $cov_B(p_i)$. For more than three testing criteria the objective space dominated by a set of cumulative points is called a *hypervolume* and represents a generalization of the *area* for a higher dimensional space.

Without loss of generality, let $T = \{t_1, t_2, t_3, \ldots, t_n\}$ be a test suite of size n and $F = \{cost, f_1, \ldots, f_m\}$ a set of testing criteria used to prioritize the test case in T, where $cost$ denotes the execution cost of each test case while $f_1, \ldots, f_m$ are the remaining m testing criteria to maximize. Given a permutation τ of test case in T we can compute the corresponding set of cumulative points $P(\tau) = \{p_1, \ldots, p_n\}$ obtained by cumulating the scores $cost, f_1, \ldots, f_m$ achieved by each test case in the order τ.

Definition 2. *The hypervolume dominated by a permutation $P(\tau)$ of test cases can be computed as follows:*

$$I_H(\tau) = \sum_{i=1}^{(n-1)} [cost(p_{i+1}) - cost(p_i)] \times f_1(p_i) \times \cdots \times f_m(p_i) \tag{2}$$

where $[cost(p_i) - cost(p_{i+1})] \times f_1(p_i) \times \cdots \times f_m(p_i)$ measure the hypervolume dominated by a generic cumulative point p_i but non-dominated by the next point p_{i+1} in the ordering τ. Since in test case prioritization the maximum values of all the testing criteria are known (e.g., the maximum execution cost or the maximum statement coverage are already known), we can express the hypervolume as a fraction of the whole objective space as follows:

Definition 3. *The fraction of the hypervolume dominated by a permutation* $P(\tau)$ *of test cases is:*

$$I_{HP}(\tau) = \frac{\sum_{i=1}^{(n-1)} [cost(p_{i+1}) - cost(p_i)] \times f_1(p_i) \times \cdots \times f_m(p_i)}{cost(p_n) \times f_1^{max} \times \ldots f_m^{max}} \qquad (3)$$

where $cost(p_n)$ is the execution cost of the whole test suite T. Such a metric ranges in the interval $[0; 1]$. It is equal to $+1$ in the ideal case where the test case ordering allows to reach the maximum test criteria scores independently from the execution cost value $cost(p_i)$. A higher $I_{HP}(\tau)$ mirrors a higher ability of the prioritization τ in maximizing the testing criteria with lower cost. In this paper we consider the $I_{HP}(\tau)$ metric as suitable fitness function to guide search algorithms, such as genetic algorithm, in finding the optimal ordering τ in multi-objective test case prioritization. As such, we propose a new genetic algorithm named HGA (Hypervolume-based Genetic Algorithm).

Since in TCP a candidate test case ordering corresponds to a set of *monotonically* increasing cumulative scores (as described in the previous section) we can use the Eq. 3 for computing the dominated hypervolume instead of the more expensive algorithm used in traditional many-objective optimization [2]. Specifically, the $I_{HP}(\tau)$ metric sums up the slices of dominated hypervolume delimited by two subsequent cumulative points. Thus, let m be the number of the testing criteria and let n be the number of cumulative points (corresponding to the size of the test suite), the $I_{HP}(\tau)$ requires to sum the n hypervolume slices, each one computed as the multiplication of m test criteria scores. Thus, the overall computational time is $O(n \times m)$. Conversely, in traditional many-objective optimization the points delimiting the non-dominated hypervolume are non-monotonically increasing and thus, the computation of hypervolume metric requires a more complex algorithm which is exponential with respect to the number of objectives m [2], or testing criteria for TCP.

The $I_{HP}(\tau)$ metric proposed in this paper can be viewed as a generalization of the cumulative scores used in previous work on search-based test case prioritization. For example, the APSC metric measures the average cumulative fraction of statements coverage as the Area Under Curve delimited by the test case ordering with respect to the cumulative statement coverage scores [22]. Under the light of the proposed hypervolume metric, APSC can be viewed as a simplified version of $I_{HP}(\tau)$ where all test cases have execution cost equal to one and only the statement coverage is considered as testing criterion. A similar consideration can be performed for all the other cumulative fitness functions used in previous work on search-based test case prioritization [20–22].

4   Empirical Evaluation

The *goal* of this study is to evaluate the Hypevolume-based GA, with the *purpose* of solving the test case prioritization problem. The *quality focus* of the study is represented in terms of three—possibly conflicting—testing criteria which are pursued when performing test case prioritization, namely execution cost (to minimize), statement coverage (to maximize), and past fault coverage (to maximize). The *context* of our study consists of six open-source and industrial programs available from the Software-artifact Infrastructure Repository (SIR) [19]: four GNU open-source programs `bash`, `flex`, `grep`, and `sed`; and two programs of the Siemens suite, namely `printtokens`, and `printtokens2`. Their main characteristics are summarized in Table 1. We selected these programs since they have been used in previous work on regression testing [4,7,22,30,31], hence, allowing us—wherever possible—to compare results. For two programs extracted from the Siemens suite, SIR provides a large number of test suites but with a limited number of test cases. Therefore, in the context of our study we considered all the available test cases.

Table 1. Programs used in the study.

Program	LOC	# of Test Cases	Description
bash	59,846	1,200	Shell language interpreter
flex	10,459	567	Fast lexical analyser
grep	10,068	808	Regular expression utility
printtokens	726	4,130	Lexical analyzer
printtokens2	520	4,115	Lexical analyzer
sed	14,427	360	Non-interactive text editor

The empirical evaluation is steered by the following research questions:

RQ$_1$: *What is the cost-effectiveness of HGA, compared to cost-aware additional greedy algorithms?* This research question aims at evaluating to what extent faults (*effectiveness*) can be detected earlier (lower execution *cost*) using the test cases ordering obtained by HGA, in comparison with a baseline technique namely two-and three-objective additional greedy algorithms. This reflects the software engineer's needs to obtain the maximum advantage from testing even if it is prematurely stopped at some point.

RQ$_2$: *What is the efficiency of HGA, compared to cost-aware additional greedy algorithms?* With this second research question we are interested in comparing the running time (*efficiency*) required by HGA to find an optimal ordering, in comparison with two- and three-objective additional greedy algorithms.

Testing Criteria. To answer our research questions we consider three objectives widely used in previous test case prioritization work [17,22]:

– *Statement coverage criterion.* We measure statement coverage achieved by each test case using the `gcov` tool part of the GNU C compiler (`gcc`).

- *Execution cost criterion.* In this paper we approximate the execution cost by counting the number of executed instructions in the code, instead of measuring the actual execution time, similarly as done in previous work [24, 29]. To this aim we use the gcov tool to measure the execution frequency of each source code instruction.
- *Past fault coverage criterion.* As for the past fault coverage criterion, we consider the versions of the programs with seeded faults available in the SIR repository [19]. SIR also specifies whether or not each test case is able to reveal these faults. Such information can be used to assign a past fault coverage value to each test case subset, computed as the number of known past faults that this subset is able to reveal in the previous version.

Problem Formulation. Using the three test case prioritization criteria described above, we examine two and three-objective formulations of TCP problem. The *two-objective TCP problem* is aimed at finding an optimal ordering of test cases which (i) minimizes the execution cost and (ii) maximizes the statement coverage. In this case the $I_{HP}(\tau)$ metric corresponds to the area under curve delimited by the two criteria. For the *three-objective TCP problem* we consider the past faults coverage as third criteria to be maximized. Thus, in this second case the $I_{HP}(\tau)$ metric corresponds to the volume under manifolds delimited by the three criteria. We note that it is possible to formulate other criteria by just providing a clear mapping between tests and criterion-based requirements. The formulations are used to illustrate how the Hypervolume-based metric introduced in this paper can be applied to any number and kind of testing criteria to be satisfied, where further criteria just represent additional axes to be considered when computing the fitness function $I_{HP}(\tau)$.

Evaluated Algorithms. For the two-objective formulation of the test case prioritization problem, we compare HGA instantiated with two criteria and the *additional greedy* algorithm used by Yoo and Harman [30] and by Rothermel *et al.* [25], which considers at the same time coverage and cost by maximizing the coverage per unit of time of the selected test cases (cost cognizant additional greedy). Note that, after reaching the maximum coverage with the additional greedy, there are possible remaining un-prioritized test cases that cannot add additional coverage. These remaining test cases could be ordered using any algorithm; in this work we re-apply *additional greedy* algorithm as done in previous work [22]. Similarly, for what concerns the three-objective formulation of the test case prioritization problem, we compare HGA instantiated for three criteria with the *additional greedy* algorithm used by Yoo and Harman [30], which conflates code coverage, execution cost and past coverage in one objective function to be minimized. Also in this case the *additional greedy* is re-applied multiple times in order to have a complete test cases ordering.

Implementation. All the algorithms have been implemented using *JMetal* [9], a Java-based framework for multi-objective optimization with metaheuristics. In details, we use the *Parallel Genetic Algorithm* which evaluates the individuals in parallel using multiple threads, thus reducing the execution time. We use a population of 100 individuals that are initially randomly generated within the solution space. At each generation, *offsprings* are generated by combining pairs of fittest individuals with probability $p_c = 0.90$ by using the *PMX-Crossover*, which swaps the permutation elements at a given crossover point. As mutation operator we use the *SWAP-Mutation*, which randomly swaps two chosen permutation elements within each offspring. The fittest individuals are selected using the *tournament selection* with *tournament size* equal to 10. The algorithm ends when reaching 250 generations. To account for the inherent randomness nature of GAs [1], we performed 20 independents runs for each program under study and for each TCP problem.

Evaluation Metrics. To address RQ_1 we use the *cost-cognizant average fault detection percentage* metric ($APFD_c$) proposed by Elbaum *et al.* [10]. This metric measures the effectiveness of a given test cases ordering by summing up the costs of the first test cases that are able to reveal the faults [10]. The higher the $AFDP_c$ value, the lower the average cost needed to detect the same number of faults. Since we performed 20 independent runs, we reports the mean and the standard deviation of the $APFD_c$ scores achieved for each program under study and for each TCP problem. We statistically analyze the obtained results, to check whether the differences between the $APFD_c$ scores produced by the compared algorithms over different independent runs are statistically significant or not. To this aim we use the *Welch's t test* [6] with a p-value threshold of 0.05 for both the TCP problems. Welch's t-test is generally used to test two groups with unequal variance, e.g., in our case the variance of the $APFD_c$ produced by the additional greedy and HGA is different[1]. Significant p-values indicate that the corresponding null hypothesis can be rejected in favour of the alternative ones. Other than testing the null hypothesis, we use the Vargha-Delaney ($\hat{A}_{12}$) statistical test [28] to measure the effect size, i.e., the magnitude of the difference between the $APFD_c$ achieved with different algorithms. To address RQ_2 we compare the average running time required by each algorithm for each software program used in the empirical study. The execution time was measured using a machine with Intel Core i7 processor running at 2.40GHz with 12GB RAM.

5   Empirical Results

Table 2 reports the $AFDP_c$ values for the two-objective and three-objective test case prioritization problem obtained by (i) the additional greedy algorithm, and (ii) HGA. Specifically, the table reports mean size and standard deviation over 20 independent runs of the algorithms. In both problem formulations, HGA is more cost-effective than the additional greedy algorithm for 4 out of 6 programs since the mean $AFDP_c$ is higher. In particular, for the two-objective formulation there is an improvement in terms of $AFDP_c$ ranging between 5 % and 11 %,

---

[1] Since the additional greedy is a deterministic algorithm, the variance over 20 independent runs is zero. Conversely, because of the random inheritance of GAs, HGA does not reach a zero variance.

Table 2. Test case prioritization problem: $AFDP_c$ achieved by HGA and additional greedy in two and three objective formulations. The best result for each program is highlighted in bold face.

Program	2-Objective			3-Objective		
	Add. Greedy	HGA		Add. Greedy	HGA	
		Mean	St. Dev.		Mean	St. Dev.
bash	0.658	**0.705**	0.046	0.658	**0.743**	0.053
flex	0.604	**0.677**	0.116	0.507	**0.578**	0.100
grep	0.793	**0.815**	0.023	0.793	**0.816**	0.039
printtokens	**0.588**	0.287	0.091	**0.496**	0.203	0.052
printtokens2	**0.733**	0.462	0.326	**0.312**	0.275	0.253
sed	0.787	**0.831**	0.081	0.688	**0.744**	0.103

while in the three-objective formulation the improvement ranges between 3 % and 12 %. This has practical implications from the tester's perspective since the test cases orderings obtained by HGA detect more faults at the same (or lower) execution cost. Conversely, the additional greedy algorithm has better performance on `printtokens` and `printtokens2` for both two- and three-objective TCP problems. Indeed, for these programs we can observe that the $AFDP_c$ values obtained by the additional greedy are substantially higher than the mean $AFDP_c$ values achieved by HGA (+27 % for two-objective problem and +3.27 % for the three-objective one on `printtokens2`). For these two programs we can also observe that HGA has a higher variability when compared with the other programs as demonstrated by the higher standard deviations: for example the standard deviation for `printtokens` is larger than 25 % for both two- and three-objective TCP while for `bash` it is less than 6 %. This high variability can be due to the fact that `printtokens` and `printtokens2` are two very small programs with less than 1,000 lines of code while their test suites are very large because they contain more than 4,000 test cases. Hence, for these programs reaching the maximum statement coverage and past faults coverage requires the execution of only 30 test cases on average, i.e., less than 1 % of the whole test suites. For the two considered coverage criteria the majority of test cases are equivalent (i.e., they have the same code and past fault coverage) but only few of them are really able to detect new faults. the obtained ordering. Thus, HGA might select other test cases that are equivalent in terms of code (or past fault) coverage but that have different fault detection capabilities. For the additional greedy algorithm this is not the case since it always generates the same test case ordering. This analysis highlights that the poor performance of HGA for `printtokens` and `printtokens2` can be due to the used testing criteria more than the algorithm itself.

To provide statistical support to our preliminary analysis, Table 3 reports the results of the Welch's t-test and the Vargha-Delaney ($\hat{A}_{12}$) statistic, obtained by

Table 3. Welch's t-test p-values of the hypothesis HGA > Additional Greedy for the two and three objective test case prioritization problem. $p-values$ that are statistically significant (i.e., $p - value < 0.05$) are reported in bold face. $\hat{A}_{12} > 0.5$ means HGA is better than Additional Greedy; $\hat{A}_{12} < 0.5$ means Additional Greedy is better than HGA, and $\hat{A}_{12} = 0.5$ means they are equal.

Program	2-Objective			3-Objective		
	p-value	$\hat{A}_{12}$	Magnitude	p-value	$\hat{A}_{12}$	Magnitude
bash	**< 0.01**	0.88	Large	**< 0.01**	0.95	Large
flex	**< 0.01**	0.70	Medium	**< 0.01**	0.75	Large
grep	**< 0.01**	0.85	Large	**< 0.01**	0.85	Large
printtokens	1	0.10	Large	1	0.10	Large
printtokens2	1	0.30	Large	0.73	0.40	Small
sed	**0.01**	0.85	Large	**0.01**	0.80	Large

comparing (across the 20 GA runs) the $AFDP_c$ value yielded by the algorithms under investigation. As expected, HGA is statistically better than the additional greedy in 4 cases out of 6 for both two- or three-objective TCP problems. For these cases the effect size ($\hat{A}_{12}$) is always *large* with the only exception of `flex` where for the two-objective TCP problem the effect size is *medium*. For `printtokens` we can observe that HGA is statistically worse than the additional greedy algorithm for both two- and three-objective TCP problems and the magnitude of the difference is also *large* according to the $\hat{A}_{12}$ statistic. For `printtokens2` there is no statistically significant difference between HGA and the greedy algorithm for the three-objective TCP problem while for the two-objective problem there is a statistically significant difference in favour of the additional greedy.

Table 4. Average Execution Time for Algorithms

Program	2-Objective		3-Objective	
	Add. Greedy	HGA	Add. Greedy	HGA
bash	2h 21 min 57s	**3 min 1s**	2h 46 min 40s	**11 min 13s**
flex	2 min 19s	**43s**	2 min 46s	**51s**
grep	9 min 41s	**2 min 19s**	11 min 21s	**2 min**
printtokens	2 min 47s	**2s**	3 min 19s	**11s**
printtokens2	3 min 11s	**1s**	6 min 51s	**5s**
sed	25s	**12s**	30s	**16s**

To answer our RQ_2, Table 4 reports the mean execution time required by each algorithm for each software program used in the empirical study. For both two- and tree-objective formulation, we can note that HGA requires less execution time for its convergence with respect to the additional greedy algorithm. Specifically, HGA on average takes 36 % of the execution time required by the additional greedy for the same software system. This is an important improvement if we also consider that HGA is not only much faster than the additional greedy algorithm, but it also provides orderings that are able to reveal more faults ($\mathbf{RQ_1}$).

It is important to highlight that the running times of the additional greedy algorithms reported in this paper are substantially higher than the running times reported in previous studies for test case selection using the same additional greedy algorithms and for the same software systems [24,31]. For example in [31] the average running time of the two-objective additional greedy algorithm for grep is 20 seconds against 11 min and 21 seconds reported in this paper. This huge difference concerns the different stop conditions used to end the additional greedy algorithm in test case selection and test case prioritization problems. In the test case selection problem the additional greedy ends when the maximum code coverage is reached, thus, as reported by Harrold *et al.* [16] the execution time of $O\left(\mid T\mid \cdot \max\mid T_i\mid\right)$, where $\mid T\mid$ represents the size of the original test suite, while $\max\mid T_i\mid$ denotes the cardinality of the largest group of test cases which is able to reach the maximum coverage. For TCP the additional greedy algorithm does not end when the maximum coverage is reached but it is re-applied until all test cases are selected in order to obtain a complete test case ordering. Thus, for TCP the running time of the (re-started) additional greedy algorithm is $O\left(|T|\times|T|\right)$ motivating the higher execution time reported in this paper. These findings are particularly interesting since in previous works on multi-objective test case selection [24,31] the additional greedy algorithm turned out to be faster than genetic algorithms with the only exception of large programs [24]. For multi-objective TCP problems we highlight that genetic algorithms, and HGA in particular, are always faster than the additional greedy algorithm independently of the size of the program and the test suites. We also note that despite the lower running time, HGA is more cost-effective than the additional greedy algorithm ($\mathbf{RQ_1}$).

6   Threats to Validity

This section discusses the threats to the validity of our empirical evaluation, classifying them into *construct*, *internal*, and *external* validity.

Construct Validity. In this study, they are mainly related to the choice of the metrics used to evaluate the characteristics of the different test case prioritization algorithms. In order to evaluate the optimality of the experimented algorithms (HGA, and additional greedy) we used the $APFD_c$ [10], a well-know metric used in previous work on multi-objective test case prioritization [13,14]. Another construct validity threat involves the correctness of the measures used as test criteria: statement coverage, faults coverage and execution cost. To mitigate such a threat, the code coverage information was collected using two open-source profiler/compiler tools (GNU `gcc` and `gcov`). The execution cost was measured by counting the number of source code blocks expected to be executed by the test cases, while the original fault coverage information was extracted from the SIR repository [19].

Internal Validity. To address the random nature of the GAs themselves [1], we ran HGA 20 times for each subject program (as done in previous work [7,22,30]), and considered the mean $APFD_c$ scores. The tuning of the GA's parameters is another factor that can affect the internal validity of this work. In this study we used the same genetic operators and the same parameters used in previous work on test case prioritization [20,22].

External Validity. We considered 6 programs from the SIR, that were also used in most previous work on regression testing [4,7,22,26,31]. However, in order to corroborate our findings, replications on a wider range of programs and optimization techniques are desirable. Also, there may be optimization algorithms or formulations of the test case prioritization problem not considered in this study that could produce better results. In this paper we compared HGA with the additional greedy algorithm in order to evaluate the benefits of the proposed algorithms over the most used. Moreover, in order to make the results more generalizable, we evaluated all the algorithms with respect to solving two different formulations of the test case prioritization problem with two and three objectives to be optimized.

7   Conclusion and Future Work

This paper proposes a hypervolume-based genetic algorithm (HGA) to solve multi-criteria test case prioritization. Specifically, we use the concept of *hypervolume* [2], which is widely investigated in many-objective optimization, to generalize the traditional Area Under Curve (AUC) metrics used in previous work on test case prioritization [20–22]. Indeed, the proposed *hypervolume* metric condenses multiple testing criteria through the proportion of the objective space, while AUC based metrics can manage only one cumulative code coverage criterion per time [22].

To show the applicability of HGA we instantiated the TCP problem using three different testing criteria. The empirical study conducted on six real-world open source programs demonstrated that the proposed algorithm is not only much faster than greedy algorithms, but is also able to generate test case orderings allowing to reveal more regression faults at the same level of execution cost for large software programs. This denotes an important finding since previous search-based approaches based on AUC metrics did not statistically outperform greedy algorithms in terms of effectiveness [22].

Given the promising results obtained in this paper, we plan to apply the *hypervolume* metric when considering up to three testing criteria in order to investigate its scalability with respect to greedy algorithms for higher dimensional TCP problems. We also plan to replicate the study, considering more and different software systems and different coverage criteria to corroborate the results reported in this paper. Then, we plan to incorporate diversity measures proposed in previous studies on multi-objective test case selection [7,24] to improve the performances of HGA for software systems with highly redundant test suites, where greedy algorithms are particularly competitive. Finally, we plan to apply the proposed meta-heuristic also for other test case optimitization problems.

References

1. Arcuri, A., Briand, L.C.: A practical guide for using statistical tests to assess randomized algorithms in software engineering. In: Proceedings of International Conference on Software Engineering (ICSE), pp. 1–10. ACM (2011)
2. Auger, A., Bader, J., Brockhoff, D., Zitzler, E.: Theory of the hypervolume indicator: optimal μ-distributions and the choice of the reference point. In: Proceedings of SIGEVO workshop on Foundations of Genetic Algorithms (FOGA), pp. 87–102. ACM (2009)
3. Bryce, R.C., Colbourn, C.J., Cohen, M.B.: A framework of greedy methods for constructing interaction test suites. In: Proceedings International Conference on Software Engineering (ICSE), pp. 146–155 (2005)
4. Chen, T.Y., Lau, M.F.: Dividing strategies for the optimization of a test suite. Inf. Process. Lett. **60**(3), 135–141 (1996)
5. Cohen, M., Dwyer, M., Shi, J.: Constructing interaction test suites for highly-configurable systems in the presence of constraints: A greedy approach. IEEE Trans. Softw. Eng. **34**, 633–650 (2008)
6. Conover, W.J.: Practical Nonparametric Statistics, 3rd edn. Wiley, New York (1998)
7. De Lucia, A., Di Penta, M., Oliveto, R., Panichella, A.: On the role of diversity measures for multi-objective test case selection. In: Proceedings of International Workshop on Automation of Software Test (AST), pp. 145–151 (2012)
8. Do, H., Rothermel, G., Kinneer, A.: Empirical studies of test case prioritization in a junit testing environment. In: 15th International Symposium on Software Reliability Engineering, pp. 113–124. IEEE Computer Society (2004)
9. Durillo, J.J., Nebro, A.J.: jMetal: a java framework for multi-objective optimization. Adv. Eng. Softw. **42**, 760–771 (2011)
10. Elbaum, S., Malishevsky, A., Rothermel, G.: Incorporating varying test costs and fault severities into test case prioritization. In: Proceedings of International Conference on Software Engineering (ICSE), pp. 329–338. IEEE (2001)
11. Elbaum, S., Malishevsky, A.G., Rothermel, G.: Prioritizing test cases for regression testing. In: Proceedings of International Symposium on Software Testing and Analysis (ISSTA), pp. 102–112. ACM (2000)
12. Elbaum, S., Malishevsky, A.G., Rothermel, G.: Prioritizing test cases for regression testing. Softw. Eng. Notes **25**, 102–112 (2000)
13. Elbaum, S., Malishevsky, A.G., Rothermel, G.: Test case prioritization: a family of empirical studies. IEEE Trans. Softw. Eng. **28**(2), 159–182 (2002)
14. Elbaum, S., Rothermel, G., Kanduri, S., Malishevsky, A.: Selecting a cost-effective test case prioritization technique. Softw. Qual. J. **12**(3), 185–210 (2004)
15. Hao, D., Zhang, L., Zhang, L., Rothermel, G., Mei, H.: A unified test case prioritization approach. ACM Trans. Softw. Eng. Methodol. **24**(2), 10:1–10:31 (2014)

16. Harrold, M.J., Gupta, R., Soffa, M.L.: A methodology for controlling the size of a test suite. ACM Trans. Softw. Eng. Methodol. **2**, 270–285 (1993)
17. Huang, Y.C., Huang, C.Y., Chang, J.R., Chen, T.Y.: Design and analysis of cost-cognizant test case prioritization using genetic algorithm with test history. In: Proceedings of Annual Computer Software and Applications Conference (COMPSAC), pp. 413–418. IEEE (2010)
18. Hughes, E.: Evolutionary many-objective optimisation: many once or one many? IEEE Congr. Evol. Comput. **1**, 222–227 (2005)
19. Hyunsook Do, S.G.E., Rothermel, G.: Supporting controlled experimentation with testing techniques: an infrastructure and its potential impact. Empirical Softw. Eng.: Int. J. **10**, 405–435 (2005)
20. Islam, M., Marchetto, A., Susi, A., Scanniello, G.: A multi-objective technique to prioritize test cases based on latent semantic indexing. In: Proceedings of European Conf. on Software Maintenance and Reengineering (CSMR), pp. 21–30. IEEE (2012)
21. Li, Z., Bian, Y., Zhao, R., Cheng, J.: A fine-grained parallel multi-objective test case prioritization on GPU. In: Ruhe, G., Zhang, Y. (eds.) SSBSE 2013. LNCS, vol. 8084, pp. 111–125. Springer, Heidelberg (2013)
22. Li, Z., Harman, M., Hierons, R.M.: Search algorithms for regression test case prioritization. IEEE Trans. Softw. Eng. **33**(4), 225–237 (2007)
23. Malishevsky, A.G., Ruthruff, J.R., Rothermel, G., Elbaum, S.: Cost-cognizant test case prioritization. Technical report, Department of Computer Science and Engineering (2006)
24. Panichella, A., Oliveto, R., Di Penta, M., De Lucia, A.: Improving multi-objective test case selection by injecting diversity in genetic algorithms. IEEE Trans. Softw. Eng. **41**(4), 358–383 (2015)
25. Rothermel, G., Untch, R., Chu, C., Harrold, M.: Prioritizing test cases for regression testing. IEEE Trans. Softw. Eng. **27**(10), 929–948 (2001)
26. Rothermel, G., Harrold, M.J., von Ronne, J., Hong, C.: Empirical studies of test-suite reduction. Softw. Test. Verif. Reliab. **12**, 219–249 (2002)
27. Srikanth, H., Williams, L., Osborne, J.: System test case prioritization of new and regression test cases. In: International Symposium on Empirical Software Engineering (2005)
28. Vargha, A., Delaney, H.D.: A critique and improvement of the cl common language effect size statistics of mcgraw and wong. J. Educ. Behav. Stat. **25**(2), 101–132 (2000)
29. Yoo, S., Harman, M.: Regression testing minimization, selection and prioritization: a survey. Softw. Test. Verif. Reliab. **22**(2), 67–120 (2012)
30. Yoo, S., Harman, M.: Pareto efficient multi-objective test case selection. In: Proceedings of International Symposium on Software Testing and Analysis (ISSTA), pp. 140–150. ACM (2007)
31. Yoo, S., Harman, M.: Using hybrid algorithm for Pareto efficient multi-objective test suite minimisation. J. Syst. Softw. **83**(4), 689–701 (2010)
32. Zhang, L., Hao, D., Zhang, L., Rothermel, G., Mei, H.: Bridging the gap between the total and additional test-case prioritization strategies. In: Proceedings of International Conference on Software Engineering (ICSE), pp. 192–201. IEEE (2013)

Optimizing Aspect-Oriented Product Line Architectures with Search-Based Algorithms

Thainá Mariani[1][(✉)], Silvia Regina Vergilio[1], and Thelma Elita Colanzi[2]

[1] Federal University of Parana, Curitiba, PR, Brazil
{tmariani,silvia}@inf.ufpr.br
[2] State University of Maringa, Maringá, PR, Brazil
thelma@din.uem.br

Abstract. The adoption of Aspect-Oriented Product Line Architectures (AOPLA) brings many benefits to the software product line design. It contributes to improve modularity, stability and to reduce feature tangling and scattering. Improvements can also be obtained with a search-based and multi-objective approach, such as MOA4PLA, which generates PLAs with the best trade-off between different measures, such as cohesion, coupling and feature modularization. However, MOA4PLA operators may violate the aspect-oriented modeling (AOM) rules, impacting negatively on the architecture understanding. In order to solve this problem, this paper introduces a more adequate representation for AOPLAs and a set of search operators, called SO4ASPAR (Search Operators for Aspect-Oriented Architectures). Results from an empirical evaluation show that the proposed operators yield better solutions regarding the fitness values, besides preserving the AOM rules.

Keywords: Aspects · SPL · Search-based design

1 Introduction

A Software Product Line (SPL) defines a set of software products that share features to satisfy a domain. In the SPL context, features are visible functionalities for the user. A feature can be designed like a variability, representing a variable functionality which may or not be present in a product. On the other hand, a feature can be a mandatory functionality, being present in every product. An SPL offers some artifacts to build products. The Product Line Architecture (PLA) is an important artifact that contains all the commonalities and variabilities of an SPL. The PLA is used to derive the architecture of each product [12].

The use of Aspect-Oriented Modeling (AOM) concepts in the PLA design is useful to modularize crosscutting features and has been adopted and investigated by many works [10,13–15,19,20,22]. These works show that the adoption of an Aspect-Oriented Product Line Architecture (AOPLA) contributes to improve modularity, stability and to reduce feature tangling and scattering.

In addition to this, the PLA design needs to consider different principles, such as cohesion, coupling and feature modularization. Hence, we can observe that the

M. Barros and Y. Labiche (Eds.): SSBSE 2015, LNCS 9275, pp. 173–187, 2015.
DOI: 10.1007/978-3-319-22183-0_12

PLA design is a complex task [12], related to several factors. Such task has been properly addressed in the Search-Based Software Engineering (SBSE) field. To this end, Colanzi et al. [4] introduced MOA4PLA (*Multi-objective Optimization Approach for PLA Design*), a search-based design approach for multi-objective optimization of PLAs. The approach aims at optimizing a PLA and generating a set of alternatives with the best trade-off among different objectives. MOA4PLA includes a meta-model to represent the PLA at the class diagram level, and a model to evaluate the PLA alternatives based on specific PLA attributes. Search based operators were also proposed to guide the optimization algorithms. They change the architecture by modifying its organization, i.e., by inserting, removing or moving its elements.

MOA4PLA has presented promising results [4]. However, we observe that it has some limitations when optimizing AOPLAs. The meta-model does not capture AOM particularities. The search operators may violate AOM rules, and these violations are propagated to the produced solutions. These violations reduce the AOM benefits and impact negatively in the architecture understanding.

To reduce such limitations and considering the AOM benefits, this paper proposes a way to represent AOPLAs and a set of search-based operators that aggregate AOM rules. Such proposed representation and operators are implemented and evaluated for AOPLA design, in the MOA4PLA context, but it can also be used with other search-based approaches for AO architectures in general, such as that ones described in [17]. This happens because the proposed operators include traditional operations such as move methods, move operators and so on [17], and feature-driven operations, specific for the PLA context [4].

An empirical evaluation of the proposed representation and search operators was conducted using the MOA4PLA approach and three AOPLAs. A qualitative analysis shows that the proposed operators preserve the AOM rules during the optimization, which contributes to improve the architecture quality. Moreover, a quantitative analysis shows improvement related to cohesion and feature modularization in the fitness values.

This paper is organized as follows. Section 2 presents MOA4PLA, the search-based approach used in this work. Sections 3 and 4 introduce, respectively, the representation adopted to AOPLA and the proposed search operators. Section 5 describes how the empirical study was conducted. Section 6 presents and analyses the obtained results. Finally, Sect. 7 contains some concluding remarks and possible future works.

2   Search-Based Design of PLAs

Search-based design approaches are found in the literature [17]. Most of them are based on Multi-Objective Algorithms (MOAs), that is, search-based algorithms that can properly deal with problems influenced by several factors. The works address the context of standard software design [1,18,21], and also PLA design context [4,9]. PLA design is part of software architecture design, so an approach proposed for PLA design is also valid for architectures in general. Considering this, we decided to implement our ideas in the PLA context, with the approach MOA4PLA [4], which is described in this section.

MOA4PLA uses search-based multi-objective algorithms guided by traditional search operators and an operator specific to improve feature modularization. As output, a set of PLA alternatives, with the best trade-off between the objectives, is generated. The approach also includes a meta-model to represent the PLA elements. The MOA4PLA activities are shown in Fig. 1.

The first activity is the *Construction of the PLA Representation*. The input is a PLA designed at the class diagram level. This diagram should contain the architectural elements and information about the SPL variabilities. From this input a PLA representation is generated, according to the meta-model of Fig. 2. A PLA contains architectural elements such as packages, interfaces, operations and their inter-relationships. Each architectural element is associated with feature(s) by using UML stereotypes. It can either be common to all SPL products or variable, appearing only in some product(s). Variable elements are associated with variabilities that have variation points and their variants.

In the activity *Definition of the Evaluation Model*, a model to evaluate the PLA alternatives is defined according to the needs and priorities of the architect.

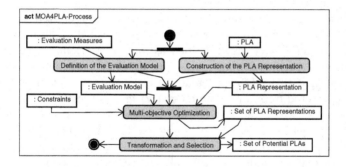

Fig. 1. MOA4PLA activities [4].

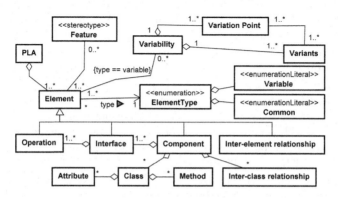

Fig. 2. MOA4PLA meta-model [4].

In this work we use two objectives also used by Colanzi et al. in [4]. The first objective (CM) is related to conventional metrics, which evaluate basic design principles, such as cohesion and coupling. Cohesion measures how strongly-related are the functionalities inside an element. Coupling evaluate the interdependency level of an element, which is measured by the relationships between architectural elements. The second objective (FM) is related to feature-driven metrics, specific to the SPL context. FM evaluates the architecture modularization level by measuring the feature scattering, feature interaction and feature-based cohesion [19]. Feature scattering measures the number of elements in which a feature is present. It considers that a feature scattered in many elements impacts negatively on modularity. Feature interaction measures the number of features interacting in common architectural elements, which worsen the modularization. Feature-based cohesion indicates that an element associated with many features is not stable because a modification in any of the associated features may impact the other ones. Briefly, these two objectives aim at analyzing if the obtained solutions (alternatives PLAs) are likely to represent proper designs from the point of view of high cohesion, low coupling, reuse and feature-based modularity. More details about how FM and CM are calculated can be found in [4].

In the *Multi-Objective Optimization* activity, the PLA representation obtained in the first activity is optimized according to the constraints informed by the architect. Here, the multi-objective algorithms are selected and then executed. The MOA4PLA search operators are herein called traditional operators and its main functionality are described as following: (i) *move method* moves a method from a class to another; (ii) *move attribute* moves an attribute from a class to another; (iii) *add class* creates a class and moves to it a method or an attribute selected from a random class; (iv) *move operation* moves an operation from an interface to another; (v) *add package* creates a package, creates an interface inside this package and moves an operation from a random interface to the created one; and (vi) the *feature-driven* operator selects a crosscutting feature to be modularized and, to do this, all elements associated with the selected crosscutting feature are moved to a modularization package.

After the operators application, each generated PLA is evaluated by the evaluation model defined in the previous activity. As output, a set of PLA representations with the best trade-off between the objectives (CM and FM) is generated. In the last activity *Transformation and Selection*, each PLA representation obtained by the previous activity is converted to a class diagram. At last, the architect can select one of these PLAs to be adopted for the SPL.

As mentioned before, MOA4PLA can be applied to AOPLAs, however it presents some limitations mainly related to the meta-model to represent the solutions and search operators. However, we did not find approaches related to search-based design of AOPLAs. Found works [10,13–15,19,20,22] show the importance of AOPLAs, highlighting the benefits provided: to improve modularity, stability, feature tangling and scattering.

Due to these benefits and the lack of works regarding search-based design of AOPLAs, we introduce in the next sections a new way to represent AOPLAs, and operators that consider AOM rules.

3 Representation of AOPLAs

To allow the optimization of AOPLAs by MOA4PLA, a representation of the AOM elements in class diagrams is needed. The required elements are aspects, advices, join points, pointcuts and crosscutting relationship. An aspect is a module responsible for encapsulating a crosscutting concern. Such aspect is similar to a class, because contains methods, attributes and can be part of inheritance. An aspect defines join points, advices and pointcuts. A join point is an execution point of a system, such as a call procedure which needs functionalities delegated to an aspect. An advice is an aspect functionality and can be executed before, after or during a join point execution. A pointcut determines which join points crosscut which aspects. Finally, a crosscutting relationship is needed to connect aspects and its join points [11].

MOA4PLA uses a class diagram as input, therefore we searched for approaches to represent the AOM elements in this kind of diagram. UML does not offer specific support to modeling AOM elements, but it is commonly used for this goal [3]. That way, the AOM elements can be modeled in a class diagram, in which an aspect element is represented as a class with the $<<aspect>>$ stereotype. Such representation is coherent, since an aspect structure is similar to a class structure. The crosscutting relationship can be represented as a dependency with the $<<crosscutting>>$ stereotype [3]. We choose the notation presented by Pawlak et al. [16] to be adopted in this work. Such notation is sui table to represent the main AOM elements and it can be easily adapted to the MOA4PLA representation. The notation proposed by Pawlak et al. [16] presents stereotypes to represent aspects as classes and advices as methods. Such notation also introduces a crosscutting relationship that represents the connection between an aspect and its join points. A join point, in turn, can be a method of any class. Next we present the representations used for the AOM elements.

- **Aspect:** aspects are represented as classes with the $<<aspect>>$ stereotype;
- **Advice:** advices are represented as methods inside the corresponding aspect. An advice must have one of the following stereotypes with the described functionality: (i) $<<before>>$ prescribes the advice execution before a join point; (ii) $<<after>>$ prescribes the advice execution after a join point; (iii) $<<around>>$ prescribes the advice execution along with a joint point; and (iv) $<<replace>>$ prescribes the advice execution replacing the join point execution;
- **Crosscutting relationship:** it is represented by an unidirectional association with the $<<pointcut>>$ stereotype. Such relationship is necessary to connect an aspect and elements which have join points. In the relationship ends are informed which advices crosscut which join points. The ends should contain keywords with methods names (advices or join points) separated by commas, or the word *all* to all methods.

Figure 3 illustrates the presented notation. The example has aspect crosscutting join points that are in two different classes. The class *Aspect* with the $<<aspect>>$ stereotype represents the aspect and all its methods represent

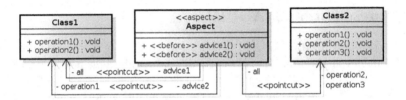

Fig. 3. Notation of Pawlak [16] for representing AOM elements.

advices. There are two crosscutting relationships between *Aspect* and *Class1*. One of them informs that the advice *advice1* crosscuts all the methods of *Class1*. The other informs that the advice *advice2* crosscuts *operation1*. That way, all the *Class1* methods are join points of the aspect. The crosscutting relationship between *Aspect* and *Class2* defines that all the advices crosscut the *operation2* and *operation3* methods, thus such methods are join points of the aspect.

4   Search Operators for AOPLAs

According to the chosen notation, violations in an AOPLA can occur if an aspect is disconnected from its advices and crosscutting relationships. This is a problem because advices define functionalities of an aspect, and crosscutting relationships associate the aspect with its join points. To prevent this problem, next, we introduce a set of search operators called *Search Operators for Aspect-Oriented Architectures* (SO4ASPAR) which avoid violations in AOPLAs.

SO4ASPAR is derived from the MOA4PLA operators by aggregating AOM rules. However, such rules can also be added to other similar search-based design operators. Nevertheless, the search operators which aggregate the AOM rules are named *Move_Method4ASPAR (Move Method for Aspect-oriented Architectures), Move_Attribute4ASPAR (Move Attribute for Aspect-oriented Architectures), Add_Class4ASPAR (Add Class for Aspect-oriented Architectures), Move_Operation4ASPAR (Move Operation for Aspect-oriented Architectures), Add_Package4ASPAR (Add Package for Aspect-oriented Architectures)* and *Feature_Driven4ASPAR (Feature_Driven for Aspect-oriented Architectures)*. Next we present the rules aggregated to these operators. They are specific to the elements aspect and join point.

4.1   Aspect Rules

Aspects are well-defined elements responsible for modularizing a concern. An aspect can contain advices, methods and attributes, which define the aspect functionalities. Two aspect rules were defined as follows:

1. **Advices, methods or attributes should not be moved from an aspect.** If one of these elements is moved to other elements, a modularized concern can become scattered in the architecture and consequently, the aspect lose its benefits regarding modularization and cohesion.

2. **Methods and attributes should not be moved to aspects**, because if they were, an aspect could be associated with additional concerns besides its main concern, losing its main modularization functionality.

In general, violations to both rules could occur using the conventional operators by moving elements from a class to another, since an aspect is structurally represented as a class and the conventional operators interpret an aspect as a class. Figure 4 presents an example of how an aspect structure can be violated if the operators do not aggregate the aspect rules. Figure 4(a) shows an aspect and a class before an application that moves a method. Figure 4(b) shows the same elements after such application, in which the *exitGame* method of *Game* was moved to the *CIPersistDataMgt* aspect. The application resulted in an AOM rule violation, because the aspect lost its main functionality of modularizing the *<<persistence>>* feature by getting associated also with the *<<play>>* feature.

Aspect rules are aggregated to operators which move methods or attributes. That way, such operators cannot move advices, methods or attributes from or to an aspect. Such rules are used to define the operators *Move_Method4ASPAR*, *Move_Attribute4ASPAR*, *Add_Class4ASPAR* and *Feature_Driven4ASPAR*.

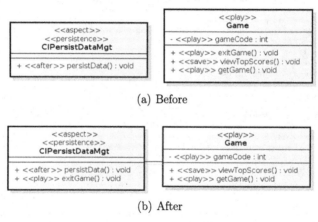

(a) Before

(b) After

Fig. 4. Example of an aspect violation.

4.2 Join Point Rule

The join point rule defines that when a joint point is moved to an element, a crosscutting relationship must be added/adapted between the aspect and the target element, and removed/adapted between the aspect and the source element. Such rule is used to move methods that represent join points, in order to avoid a join point disconnected of its crosscutting relationship with an aspect, since it complicates the identification of relations between these elements.

Join point rule is aggregated to search operators that move methods or operations. Based on this, such rule is used to define the search operators *Move_Method4ASPAR*, *Add_Class4ASPAR*, *Move_Operation4ASPAR*, *Add_Package4ASPAR* and *Feature_Driven4ASPAR*.

The join point rule procedure is detailed in Algorithm 1. It receives as input the join point, the aspect, the source element and the target element. Two steps are executed along to the search operators main functionality, more exactly after an operation for moving a join point from an element to another. The first step (lines 9–13) verifies the crosscutting relationship between the aspect and the source element. If the end cover only the join point name, the relationship is removed, otherwise the join point name is removed from the relationship end. The second step (lines 14–26) verifies if the target element has a crosscutting relationship that covers the advices related to the join point. In an affirmative case, the join point name is added in the relationship end. Otherwise, a crosscutting relationship, the advices, and join points names are added in these ends.

Algorithm 1. Join Point Rule

---

1 **Algorithm:** Join Point Rule

2 **Input:** *aspect, sourceElement, targetElement, joinPoint*

3 **begin**

4   *relationshipSourceElement* ← crosscutting relationship between *aspect* and *sourceElement* which defines *joinPoint*;

5   *advicesRSE* ← all advices of *relationshipSourceElement*;

6   *JoinPoints* ← all join points of *relationshipSourceElement*;

7   *RelationshipsTargetElement* ← all crosscutting relationships between *aspect* and *targetElement*;

8   *create* ← true;

9   **if** *JoinPoints* == 1 **then**

10   remove *relationshipSourceElement*;

11   **else**

12   remove *joinPoint* from *relationshipSourceElement*;

13   **end**

14   **foreach** *relationshipTargetElement* ∈ *RelationshipsTargetElement* **do**

15   *advicesRTE* ← advices from *relationshipTargetElement*;

16   **if** *advicesRTE* == *advicesRSE* **then**

17   add *joinPoint* in *relationshipTargetElement*;

18   *create* ← false;

19   *break*;

20   **end**

21   **end**

22   **if** *create* == *true* **then**

23   create a crosscutting relationship (*relationshipTargetElement*) between *aspect* and *targetElement*;

24   add *joinPoint* in *relationshipTargetElement*;

25   add *advicesRSE* in *relationshipTargetElement*;

26   **end**

27 **end**

Figure 5 presents an example of the join point rule. Figure 5(a) shows the organization before the application of *Move_Operation4ASPAR*. In such organization, the *CIPersistDataMgt* aspect and the *IPersistAlbumMgt* interface are connected by a crosscutting relationship, which in turn has in its ends the *removeAlbum* advice and the *removeAlbum* join point. Figure 5(b) shows the structure after the operator and join point rule application. The *removeAlbum* joint point was moved to *IPlayMedia* by *Move_Operation4ASPAR*. Consequently, the join point rule removed the relationship between *CIPersistDataMgt* and *IPersistAlbumMgt*, since it connected the aspect exclusively to the moved join point. Lastly, aiming to

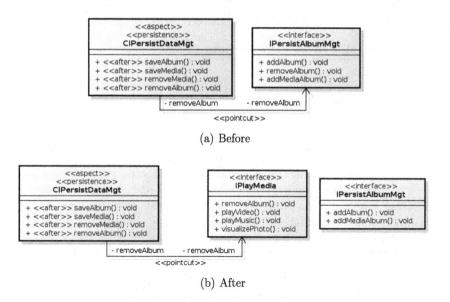

Fig. 5. Example of a joint point rule application.

connect the aspect and advice again with its join point, a crosscutting relationship was inserted between *CIPersistDataMgt* and *IPlayMedia*.

5   Empirical Study Description

To allow evaluation, we extended OPLA-Tool that provides automated support to use MOA4PLA [4]. This tool works with jMetal [8]. The extension receives as input an XMI file, representing the class diagram, according to the proposed representation. SO4ASPAR operators were implemented as mutation operators in the NSGA-II [5]. The fitness functions CM and FM (Sect. 2) and the procedure to set the initial population are the same used in the related work [4]. The used fitness functions do not consider the AOM elements, like aspects and crosscutting relationships in the calculation. However, such elements can impact also other elements like classes and interfaces, which are considered in such functions.

The evaluation goal is to verify if the proposed search operators can optimize an AOPLA as the traditional MOA4PLA search operators and, at the same time, preserve the AOM rules. Such empirical study was guided by the following research question: "How are the SO4ASPAR results when compared with traditional operators of MOA4PLA?" From this general question we derived the following other two questions:

–**RQ1:** How are the results considering the fitness values of the solutions?
–**RQ2:** How are the results considering AOM rules violations?

To answer these questions, some experiments were conducted. One experiment with the MOA4PLA traditional operators, named here SO (from Search

Table 1. PLAs characteristics.

PLA	Fitness (FM, CM)	Packages	Interfaces	Classes	Features	Aspects	Pointcuts
AGM	(727, 6.1)	11	18	30	12	2	7
MM	(1074, 4.1)	10	18	14	14	2	8
BET	(1411, 90.0)	56	30	109	16	6	7

Operators), and the second experiment with SO4ASPAR and using the introduced representation. In order to answer RQ1 we conducted a quantitative analysis. In such analysis we used hypervolume [23] as the main quality indicator and the Kruskal Wallis [6] non-parametric statistical test. Hypervolume was used because it is able to evaluate solution sets generated by multi-objective algorithms and also because it is one of the most used quality indicators in the literature [2]. To answer RQ2 we conducted a qualitative analysis. In such analysis we took into account that the architect will choose just one solution (AOPLA) from the set of non-dominated solutions. Hence, we choose the solution of each experiment with the lowest Euclidean Distance (ED) to be analyzed. ED measures the distance between a solution and the ideal solution for the problem. In this work, the ideal solution has the values for FM and CM equals to 0. Results from these quantitative and qualitative analyses are presented in the next section.

We used the following three academic AOPLAs: (i) Arcade Game Maker (AGM), (ii) Mobile Media (MM); and (iii) Electronic Tickets in Urban Transportation (BET). AGM [19] is an SPL which contains a set of arcade games operating in various environments. MM [19] is an SPL to manage photos, videos and music in mobiles. BET [7] is an SPL to manage urban transportation, including payments, trips, gates and others. We adapted such AOPLAs by using the notation presented in Sect. 3. Table 1 presents some characteristics of the used AOPLAs, such as the original fitness and numbers of classes, features, aspects and so on.

SO and SO4ASPAR experiments were conducted for each AOPLA, resulting in 6 experiments. For each experiment 30 runs were performed. The parameters needed are the population size, number of generations and mutation rate. Their values were set considering previous performed parameters tuning for each AOPLA. That way, AGM and MM have the population size of 50 individuals, 300 generations and 90 % of mutation rate. BET has also population of 50 individuals, but 100 generations and 100 % of mutation rate.

5.1   Threats to Validity

The main threat of this work is the size of the AOPLAs. They have few elements and are non-commercial. However, mostly of the time just feature models are available and the owners do not publish a complete SPL documentation. Nevertheless, the used AOPLAs offer support to comparisons between the operators.

The notation used in the AOPLA representation has a limitation. Such notation represents join points by names. This is a problem because join points with

Table 2. Number of solutions in the pareto fronts.

PLA	PF_{true}	PF_{known}	
		SO	SO4ASPAR
AGM	12	19	12
		(0)	(12)
MM	32	24	32
		(0)	(32)
BET	13	13	13
		(0)	(13)

Table 3. Hypervolume results.

PLA	Experiment	Average (Std.Dev.)	Kruskal (p-value)
AGM	SO	10.4734 (0.0157)	TRUE
	SO4ASPAR	**0.6126** (0.1191)	(4.28E-11)
MM	SO	0.7928 (0.0409)	TRUE
	SO4ASPAR	**0.9262** (0.0293)	(3.17E-11)
BET	SO	0.8668 (0.0375)	FALSE
	SO4ASPAR	**0.8905** (0.0367)	(0.06)

a same name can be swapped by the operators. However, the adopted notation is, among the notations found in the literature, the one that better represent the aspects elements used in this work. Finally, the used algorithms are non-deterministic. To reduce such threat we conducted 30 independent runs for each experiment. Besides that, we also used common quality indicators usually used in the literature in multi-objective approaches.

6 Results and Analysis

In this section the results obtained by the experiments are quantitatively (Sect. 6.1) and qualitatively (Sect. 6.2) analyzed.

6.1 Quantitative Results

Firstly and in order to answer RQ1, our analysis used two sets: PF_{known} and PF_{true}. The PF_{known} front of each experiment is the union of the fronts obtained by all 30 runs. The PF_{true} front in this case is the approximated PF_{true}, which is the union of all PF_{known} obtained for each AOPLA. The union of several fronts results in a set of the non-dominated and non-repeated solutions from these fronts. Table 2 shows the number of solutions present in PF_{true} and PF_{known}. The number of solutions of PF_{known} that belong to PF_{true} is presented in parenthesis.

Results of Table 2 show that PF_{true} is composed only by solutions achieved by SO4ASPAR for all AOPLAs. That way, all solutions found by SO are dominated by solutions found by SO4ASPAR. Regarding the original AOPLAs, we observe that most of the achieved solutions dominated the original ones.

Figure 6 shows the sets PF_{known} found for each AOPLA. That way, it is possible to analyze how the experiments optimize the objectives. Figure 6(a) shows such fronts for AGM, Fig. 6(b) for MM, and Fig. 6(c) for BET.

Results presented in Fig. 6 shows that SO4ASPAR experiments found, in general, solutions with the best trade-off between the objectives. We can observe that preserving AOM rules improves feature modularization and also cohesion.

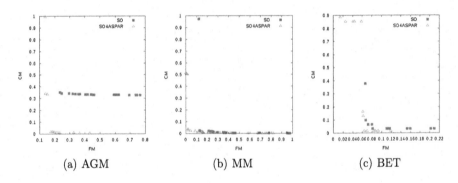

(a) AGM   (b) MM   (c) BET

Fig. 6. PF_{known} found by the experiments.

Conceptually, an aspect is a well-defined and cohesive element which can modularize a feature. That way, preserving its structure allows that such benefits remain in the generated solutions, which can be tracked to the obtained fitness values. Although the aspects elements are not evaluated by the MOA4PLA metrics, the movement of aspects elements (methods, advices, attributes) to classes may worsen the fitness value, since a feature modularized by an aspect can be scattered in the AOPLA, which also worsen the classes cohesion.

Hypervolume was also used to analyze the results. Table 3 shows the obtained results for each AOPLA in each experiment. Hypervolume average, calculated among the 30 runs, and the standard deviation are shown in Column 3. The best average found for each AOPLA is highlighted. Column 4 presents if there is statistic difference (Kruskal Wallis test with 5 % of significance) between the hypervolume values of the experiments.

Table 3 shows that, for the AGM and MM AOPLAs, the hypervolume averages calculated for the conducted experiments are statistically different. That way, for these AOPLAs, SO4ASPAR operators provide better results than SO. For BET AOPLA, both experiments do not present statistical difference and, therefore, they are considered equivalent. We observed that due to the large number of elements existing in such AOPLA (see Table 1) the impact of the aspects elements is minimal related to all other elements, so it was not possible to improve the results considerably.

Results presented in this section allows answering RQ1. In this sense, results regarding Pareto Fronts show that using the proposed operators improves the fitness values (related to feature modularization and cohesion). Finally, hypervolume results show that the SO4ASPAR results is quantitatively better or equivalent than using SO operators.

6.2 Qualitative Results

Qualitative results were obtained by analyzing the organization of aspects elements in the solutions found by the experiments. Therefore, we can verify if the organization of such elements is in accordance to the AOM rules. Firstly, an analysis was conducted with the AGM AOPLA. The SO solution with the lowest ED has the fitness (FM: 631, CM: 4.083) and the SO4ASPAR solution has the fitness (FM: 595, CM: 3.083). Figure 7 shows excerpts containing the organization of the aspects elements in the original AOPLA and in the obtained solutions.

Figure 7(a) presents the *ExceptionControlMgt* aspect whose advice *throwException* crosscuts the *initialize* join point of the *IInitializationMgt* interface. Figure 7(b) shows how these elements are in the SO solution. The *initialize* join point was moved to *Interface12146*, so the crosscutting relationship related to such join point was lost. Figure 7(c) shows the same elements in the SO4ASPAR solution. In such solution, the join point also was moved, but the crosscutting relationship was added between the aspect and the target interface (*Interface3546*). That way, the AOM rules were preserved.

A second analysis was conducted with the MM AOPLA. The SO solution with the lowest ED has the fitness (FM: 884, CM: 4.071). And, the fitness of the solution that has the lowest ED found by SO4ASPAR is (FM: 773, CM: 4.076). Figure 8 shows some aspects elements of the original AOPLA and the solutions found.

Figure 8(a) shows some elements of the original MM AOPLA, which has the *PersistDataMgt* aspect, for which its advice *saveAlbum* crosscuts the (*addAlbum*

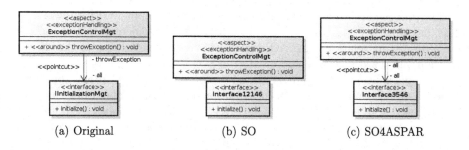

(a) Original   (b) SO   (c) SO4ASPAR

Fig. 7. Aspects elements of the AGM PLA.

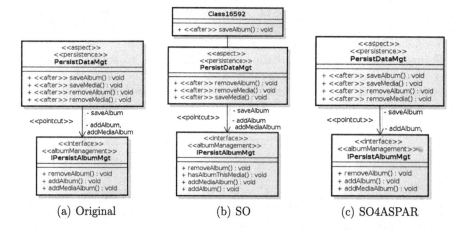

(a) Original   (b) SO   (c) SO4ASPAR

Fig. 8. Aspects elements of the MM AOPLA.

and *addMediaAlbum*) join points that are in the *IPersistAlbumMgt* interface. Figure 8(b) shows these elements in the SO solution. The advice *saveAlbum* was moved to *Class16592*. Hence, the aspect lost its functionality and, moreover, the crosscutting relationship between *PersistDataMgt* and *IPersistAlbumMgt* became incoherent. Figure 8(c) shows the same elements in the SO4ASPAR solution. In this case, the elements remain as in the original AOPLA.

Besides the analysis presented for the lowest ED solutions, we analyzed most part of the other solutions and in all of them, no violations occurred. Therefore, we can answer RQ2, by concluding that the SO operators violated AOM rules, while the SO4ASPAR operators showed that the organizations of elements which follow the AOM rules are more understandable.

7   Concluding Remarks

This paper contributes to search-based design of AOPLAs by introducing a representation for AOPLA and search operators named SO4ASPAR (*Search Operators to Aspect-Oriented Architectures*), which aggregate the AOM rules. This set of operators allows the aspect-oriented architecture optimization by search-based design approaches. The generated solutions does not violate AOM rules.

The proposed representation takes into account the input AOPLA given by a class diagram, and allows representations of the AOM elements, such as aspects and crosscutting relationships. AOM rules were defined according to the chosen notation, and used to define and create the SO4ASPAR operators.

The operators were implemented and evaluated with MOA4PLA approach. Experiments were performed with the traditional MOA4PLA operators (SO) and the proposed search operators (SO4ASPAR). A quantitative analysis showed an improvement in the fitness values (feature modularization and cohesion) of the solutions generated by SO4ASPAR. Regarding the hypervolume quality indicator, SO4ASPAR presented better or statistically equivalent results to SO. A qualitative analysis showed that the AOM rules were preserved by the SO4ASPAR experiments and violated by the SO experiments. For the SO4ASPAR experiments, the organization of the aspects elements in the generated AOPLAs is more similar to the original ones.

Future works include the creation of new operators to aggregate rules of other modeling approaches, like architectural styles. Furthermore, the addition of AOM metrics in the fitness function must also be investigated. Such metrics can evaluate more accurately the AOM benefits. Other experiments should be conducted with other AOPLAs.

References

1. Bowman, M., Briand, L., Labiche, Y.: Solving the class responsibility assignment problem in object-oriented analysis with multi-objective genetic algorithms. IEEE Trans. Softw. Eng. **36**, 817–837 (2010)
2. Bringmann, K., Friedrich, T., Klitzke, P.: Two-dimensional subset selection for hypervolume and epsilon-indicator. In: GECCO (2014)

3. Clements, P., Bachmann, F., Bass, L., Garlan, D., Ivers, J., Little, R., Merson, P., Nord, R., Stafford, J.: Documenting Software Architectures: Views and Beyond, 2nd edn. Addison Wesley, Boston (2011)
4. Colanzi, T.E., Vergilio, S.R., Gimenes, I.M.S., Oizumi, W.N.: A search-based approach for software product line design. In: SPLC (2014)
5. Deb, K., Pratap, A., Agarwal, S., Meyarivan, T.: A fast and elitist multiobjective genetic algorithm: NSGA-II. IEEE Trans. Evol. Comput. **6**, 182–197 (2002)
6. Derrac, J., Garcìa, S., Molina, D., Herrera, F.: A practical tutorial on the use of nonparametric statistical tests as a methodology for comparing evolutionary and swarm intelligence algorithms. Swarm Evol. Comput. **1**, 3–18 (2011)
7. Donegan, P.M., Masiero, P.C.: Design issues in a component-based software product line. In: SBCARS (2007)
8. Durillo, J.J., Nebro, A.J.: jmetal: a java framework for multi-objective optimization. Adv. Eng. Softw. **42**, 760–771 (2011)
9. Guizzo, G., Colanzi, T.E., Vergilio, S.R.: A pattern-driven mutation operator for search-based product line architecture design. In: Le Goues, C., Yoo, S. (eds.) SSBSE 2014. LNCS, vol. 8636, pp. 77–91. Springer, Heidelberg (2014)
10. Jingjun, Z., Xueyong, C., Guangyuan, L.: Mapping features to architectural components in aspect-oriented software product lines. In: CSSE (2008)
11. Kiczales, G., Lamping, J., Mendhekar, A., Maeda, C., Lopes, C., Loingtier, J.M., Irwin, J.: Aspect-oriented programming. In: ECOOP, pp. 220–242 (1997)
12. van der Linden, F., Schmid, K., Rommes, E.: Software Product Lines in Action: The Best Industrial Practice in Product Line Engineering. Springer, Secaucus, NJ, USA (2007)
13. Nyben, A., Tyszberowicz, S., Weiler, T.: Are aspects useful for managing variability in software product lines? a case study. In: SPLC (2005)
14. Oizumi, W., Contieri Jr., A., Correia, G., Colanzi, T., Ferrari, S., Gimenes, I., Oliveira Jr., E., Garcia, A., Masiero, P.: On the proactive design of product-line architectures with aspects: an exploratory study. In: COMPSAC (2012)
15. Oldevik, J.: Can aspects model product lines? In: AOSD (2008)
16. Pawlak, R., Duchien, L., Florin, G., Legond-Aubry, F., Seinturier, L., Martelli, L.: A UML notation for aspect-oriented software design. In: AOM (2002)
17. Räihä, O.: A survey on search-based software design. Comput. Sci. Rev. **4**(4), 203–249 (2010)
18. Räihä, O.: Genetic Algorithms in software architecture synthesis. Ph.D. thesis, University of Tampere, Tampere, Finland (2011)
19. Sant'Anna, C.N.: On the modularity of aspect-oriented design : a concern-driven measurement approach. Ph.D. thesis, Pontificial Catolic University of Rio de Janeiro, Rio de Janeiro, RJ (2008)
20. Saraiva, D., Pereira, L., Batista, T., Delicato, F.C., Pires, P.F., Kulesza, U., Araújo, R., Freitas, T., Miranda, S., Souto, A.L., Coelho, R.: Architecting a model-driven aspect-oriented product line for a digital tv middleware: a refactoring experience. In: Babar, M.A., Gorton, I. (eds.) ECSA 2010. LNCS, vol. 6285, pp. 166–181. Springer, Heidelberg (2010)
21. Simons, C., Parmee, I., Gwynllyw, R.: Interactive, evolutionary search in upstream object-oriented class design. IEEE Trans. Softw. Eng. **36**(6), 798–816 (2010)
22. Tizzei, L., Rubira, C., Lee, J.: An aspect-based feature model for architecting component product lines. In: EUROMICRO (2012)
23. Zitzler, E., Thiele, L.: Multiobjective evolutionary algorithms: a comparative case study and the strength Pareto approach. IEEE Trans. Evol. Comput. 3 (1999)

Adaptive Neighbourhood Search
for the Component Deployment Problem

Aldeida Aleti[1]($\boxtimes$) and Madalina Drugan[2]

[1] Faculty of Information Technology, Monash University, Melbourne, Australia
aldeida.aleti@monash.edu
[2] Artificial Intelligence Lab, Vrije Universiteit Brussel, Brussels, Belgium
mdrugan@vub.ac.be

Abstract. Since the establishment of the area of search-based software engineering, a wide range of optimisation techniques have been applied to automate various stages of software design and development. Architecture optimisation is one of the aspects that has been automated with methods like genetic algorithms, local search, and ant colony optimisation. A key challenge with all of these approaches is to adequately set the balance between exploration of the search space and exploitation of best candidate solutions. Different settings are required for different problem instances, and even different stages of the optimisation process.

To address this issue, we investigate combinations of different search operators, which focus the search on either exploration or exploitation for an efficient variable neighbourhood search method. Three variants of the variable neighbourhood search method are investigated: the first variant has a deterministic schedule, the second variant uses fixed probabilities to select a search operator, and the third method adapts the search strategy based on feedback from the optimisation process. The adaptive strategy selects an operator based on its performance in the previous iterations. Intuitively, depending on the features of the fitness landscape, at different stages of the optimisation process different search strategies would be more suitable. Hence, the feedback from the optimisation process provides useful guidance in the choice of the best search operator, as evidenced by the experimental evaluation designed with problems of different sizes and levels of difficulty to evaluate the efficiency of varying the search strategy.

Keywords: Adaptive neighbourhood search · Component deployment optimisation

1 Introduction

One of the main aims of search-based software engineering (SBSE) is the automation of software design and development [14]. Ideally, the system developer would only have to submit requirements models, which would be used to generate the entire software system. Although many stages of software design and development have been automated, such as architecture design optimisation [1,3], code

© Springer International Publishing Switzerland 2015
M. Barros and Y. Labiche (Eds.): SSBSE 2015, LNCS 9275, pp. 188–202, 2015.
DOI: 10.1007/978-3-319-22183-0_13

generation and repair [25], and software test case generation [4], a system that performs the enormous task of completely automating the process of software development from requirements does not exist, at least not yet. Nevertheless, each individual effort in the automation of specific stages brings us one step closer to the ultimate goal of SBSE.

The decision regarding the architecture of the system, being one of the most creative and important steps of software development [3] affects the quality of the final software system. Designing a software architecture that does not only satisfy the functional requirements, but that is at the same time optimal in terms of quality attributes, such as performance and reliability is not an easy task. The concept of software architecture is defined as 'the fundamental concepts or properties of a system in its environment embodied in elements, relationships, and in the principles of its design and evolution' [15]. In this paper we focus on embedded systems, where the architecture is composed of software components, hardware units, interactions of software components, and communications between hardware units. The allocation of software components into the hardware units and the assignment of interactions to the communication network, known as the component deployment problem is among design decision that have to be made at this stage. The search space of this problem is very large. For instance, in a system with 10 hardware units and 60 software components there are $20^{60} \approx 1.15 \times 10^{78}$ possible options, which are clearly beyond a human's capacity to handle at a reasonable amount of time.

This has lead to the application of a wide range of search-based methods in software architecture design [3], to deal with the complexity of software systems, the enormous design space and the effect of design decisions on quality attributes. Furthermore, search-based methods may produce architectures that a system designer would have not been able to think of, helping with the creative process. These efforts include methods like linear programming [9,23], genetic algorithms [1,17,20], and local search [13]. The majority of these approaches consider experimental studies to determine the success of the optimisation strategy based on a set of selected problem instances. The no-free-lunch theorems tell us that 'for any algorithm, any elevated performance over one class of problems is exactly paid for in performance over another class' [26].

More specifically, the performance of an optimisation algorithm highly depends on the fitness landscape of the targeted optimisation problem. Examples of landscape features are the number and distribution as well as the sizes of the optima, the location of the global optimum, and plateaus. A fitness landscape with a single optimum is easy to search with a local search method. On the other extreme, problems with many local optima and an isolated global optimum create a fitness landscape that is rugged and hard to explore. A plateau symbolises the presence of neighbouring solutions with equal fitness, where the progress of a search algorithm potentially stagnates.

The choice of neighbourhood structure determines whether the fitness landscape is easy to search. For example, if the fitness difference between any two neighbouring solutions is on average small then the landscape is more likely to be suited for a wide range of local search operators. In contrast, if significant fitness difference is encountered in the neighbourhood, different operators will produce different quality results, and the choice of the operator becomes important.

For new problems, like the Component Deployment, the structure of the fitness landscape that arises from different search operators is not known. A poor choice of the neighbourhood operator may lead to suboptimal algorithm performance. Ideally, the neighbourhood operator should be adapted during the search-based on the structure of the fitness landscape. In this work, we investigate three strategies for varying the neighbourhood operator: a deterministic schedule, where the change is controlled by a deterministic rule, a variable schedule, where operators are selected based on predefined probabilities, and an adaptive strategy, which uses feedback from the optimisation process.

2   Component Deployment Optimisation

The component deployment problem refers to the allocation of software components to the hardware nodes, and the assignment of inter-component communications to network links. Formally, we define the software components as $C = \{c_1, c_2, ..., c_n\}$, $n \in \mathbb{N}$. The execution of the software system is initiated in one software component (with a given probability), and during its execution uses many other components connected via communication links, which are assigned with a transition probability [16]. A software component has a memory size sz expressed in KB (kilobytes), workload wl, which is the computational requirement of a component expressed in MI (million instructions), and initiation probability q_0, which is the probability that the execution of a system starts from the component. Software components interact to perform various tasks. Each interaction from component c_i to c_j is annotated with the following properties: (i) data size ds_{ij} in kilobytes, referring to the amount of data transmitted from software component c_i to c_j during a single communication event, and (ii) next-step probability p_{ij} the probability that the execution of component c_i ends with a call to component c_j.

The hardware architecture is composed of a distributed set of hardware hosts, denoted as $\mathcal{H} = \{h_1, h_2, ..., h_m\}$, $m \in \mathbb{N}$. Each hardware host is annotated with the following properties: (i) memory capacity (cp) expressed in kilobytes, (ii) processing speed (ps), which is the instruction-processing capacity of the hardware unit, expressed in million instructions per second (MIPS), and (iii) failure rate (fr), which characterises the probability of a single hardware unit failure [7].

The hardware hosts are connected via links denoted as $\mathcal{N} = \{n_1, n_2, ...n_s\}$, with the following properties: (i) data rate (dr$_{ij}$), which is the data transmission rate of the bus, expressed in kilobytes per second (KBPS), and (ii) failure rate (fr$_{ij}$) is the exponential distribution characterising the data communication failure of each link.

The way the components are deployed affects many aspects of the final system, such as the processing speed of the software components, how much hardware is used or the reliability of the execution of different functionalities [5,21], which constitute the quality attributes of the system. Formally, the component deployment problem is defined as $D = \{d \mid d : C \rightarrow \mathcal{H}\}$, where D is the set of all functions assigning components to hardware resources.

2.1 Objective Function

The reliability evaluation obtains the mean and variance of the number of visits of components in a single execution and combines them with the failure parameters of the components. Failure rates of *execution elements* can be obtained from the hardware parameters, and the time taken for the execution is defined as a function of the software-component workload and processing speed of its hardware host. The reliability of a component c_i can be computed by Eq. 1, where $d(c_i)$ denotes the hardware host where component c_i is deployed.

$$R_i = e^{-\text{fr}_{d(c_i)} \cdot \frac{\text{wl}_i}{\text{ps}_{d(c_i)}}}. \tag{1}$$

where $d(c_i)$ is the deployment function that returns the hardware host where component c_i has been deployed. The reliability of a *communication element* is characterised by the failure rates of the hardware buses and the time taken for communication, defined as a function of the bus data rates dr and data sizes ds required for software communication. The reliability of the communication between component c_i and c_j is defined as

$$R_{ij} = e^{-\text{fr}_{d(c_i)d(c_j)} \cdot \frac{\text{ds}_{ij}}{\text{dr}_{d(c_i)d(c_j)}}}. \tag{2}$$

The probability that a software system produces the correct output depends on the number of times it is executed. The *expected number of visits* for each component $v : C \rightarrow \mathbb{R}_{\geq 0}$ is $v_i = q_i + \sum_{j \in \mathcal{I}} v_j \cdot p_{ji}$, where $\mathcal{I}$ denotes the index set of all components. The transfer probabilities p_{ji} can be written in a matrix form $P_{n \times n}$, where n is the number of components. Similarly, the execution initiation probabilities q_i can be expressed with matrix $Q_{n \times 1}$. The matrix of expected number of visits for all components $V_{n \times 1}$ can be calculated as $V = Q + P^T \cdot V$.

The reliability of a software system is also influenced by the failure rate of the network links used during the execution of the system. The more frequently the network is used, the higher is the probability of producing an incorrect output. It should be noted that the execution of a software system is never initiated in a network link, and the only predecessor of link l_{ij} is component c_i. Hence, the expected number of visits of network links $v : C \times C \rightarrow \mathbb{R}_{\geq 0}$ is calculated as $v_{ij} = v_i \cdot p_{ij}$. Finally, the reliability of a deployment architecture $d \in D$ is calculated as:

$$R = \prod_{i=1}^{n} R_i^{v_i} \prod_{i,j \text{ (if used)}} R_{ij}^{v_{ij}}. \tag{3}$$

2.2   Constraints

The problem is naturally constrained, since not all possible deployment architectures can be feasible. For the purpose of this work, we consider three constraints: allocation, memory and communication.

Allocation constraint takes care of the allocation of all software components into hardware resources. Formally, this constraint is modelled as

$$\sum_{j=1}^{m} x_{ij} = 1, \quad \forall i = 1, \ldots, n, \tag{4}$$

where x_{ij} is 1 if the software component i is deployed on the hardware unit j, and 0 otherwise.

Hardware memory capacity deals with the memory requirements of software components and makes sure that there is available memory in the hardware units. Processing units have limited memory, which enforces a constraint on the possible components that can be deployed into each hardware host. Formally, the memory constraint is defined as

$$\sum_{i=1}^{n} sz_i x_{ij} \leq cp_j, \quad \forall j \in \{1, \ldots, m\}. \tag{5}$$

   Communication constraint is responsible for the communication between software components. If the transition probability between two software components i and j is positive, $p_{ij} > 0$, these two components will communicate with a certain probability. Therefore, either they should be deployed on the same hardware unit, or on different units that are connected with a communication link (bus) with a positive data rate, $dr_{ij} > 0$. This is modelled as follows:

$$x_{ik} + x_{jl} \leq 1, \quad \text{if } p_{ij} > 0 \text{ and } dr_{kl} \leq 0. \tag{6}$$

2.3   Related Work

For many decades, researchers have been developing evermore sophisticated algorithms to solve the component deployment problem [3]. Notable examples are genetic algorithms [18,19], ant colony optimisation [5,24] and heuristics [6]. Aleti et al. [5] formulated the component deployment problem as a biobjective optimisation problem with data transmission reliability and communication overhead as objectives. Memory capacity constraints, location and colocation constraints were considered in the formulation, which was solved using P-ACO [12] as well as MOGA [11]. P-ACO was found to produce better solutions in the initial optimisation stages, whereas MOGA continued to produce improved solutions long after P-ACO had stagnated.
   A Bayesian learning method was developed by Aleti and Meedeniya [6] and applied to the formulation defined by Aleti et al. [5]. The probabilities of a

solution being part of the non-dominated set was calculated as the ratio of non-dominated solutions produced in the current generation and the overall number of solutions in the generation. Compared to NSGA-II [10] and P-ACO, the Bayesian method was found to produce approximation sets with higher hypervolume values.

Meedeniya et al. [18] applied NSGA-II to the robust optimisation of the CDP considering a varying response time. In reality, vehicles and their ECUs are exposed to temperature differences and similar external factors, which causes the software components to react differently at each invocation. The formulation by Meedeniya et al. [18] treats response time and reliability as probability distributions and presents solutions which are robust with regards to the uncertainty.

In the work by Thiruvady et al. [24], one of the most successful ACO solvers, Ant Colony System (ACS) is combined with constraint programming (CP) to optimise problem instances with different degrees of constrainedness. The constraints considered are limited memory of a hardware unit, collocation restrictions of software components on the same hardware units, and communication between software components. Furthermore, the authors explore the alternative of adding a local search to ACS and CP-ACS. When the search space is extremely constrained, the feasible areas form isolated islands between which the CP solver finds it hard to navigate, unless it is allowed to cross through an infeasible space using relaxation mechanisms. For this reason, ACS outperforms the CP-hybrid in the component deployment optimisation problem, especially when the colocation constraint is very tight.

Both constraints and the objective function affect the suitability of optimisation methods in solving the component deployment problem. The choice of the search operator becomes essential in the efficiency of the optimisation process. In many cases, different search operators may be optimal at different stages of the optimisation process, which motivated this work. Using feedback from the search to adjust the neighbourhood operator has the potential for avoiding getting stuck in a local optimum, or in an infeasible area of the search space.

3   Varying the Neighbourhood Operator for the Component Deployment Problem

Variable neighbourhood search is a general, successful and powerful local search-based method for difficult optimization problems. Local search (LS) based metaheuristics starts from an initial solution and iteratively generates new solutions using a neighbourhood strategy. Each step, a solution that improves over the existing best-so-far solution is chosen. The local search stops when there is no possible improvement, i.e. in a local optimum. Because LS can be stuck in local optima, some advanced local search algorithms consist in alternating (randomly or adaptively) the neighbourhood of the current solution.

The suitability of a local search method for solving an optimisation problem instance depends on the structure of the fitness landscape of that instance. A fitness landscape in the context of combinatorial optimisation problems refers to the (i) search space S, composed of all possible solutions that are connected through (ii) the search operator, which assigns each solution $s \in S$ to a set of neighbours $N(s) \subset S$, and the fitness function $F : S \rightarrow \Re$. As the neighbourhood of a solution depends on the search operator, a given problem can have any number of fitness landscapes. The neighbourhoods can be very large, such as the ones arising from the crossover operator of a genetic algorithm, while a 2-opt operator of a permutation problem has a neighbourhood that is relatively limited in size.

3.1 Neighbourhood Strategies

We vary the application of three different neighbourhood operators: OneFlip, kOpt and Perturb. The search starts with a randomly initialised solution, where components are randomly allocated to hardware hosts.

kOpt exchanges the host allocations of k components. In this work, the value of k is equal to 2. Formally, the 2Opt operator produces a new solution d'_i from existing d_i by switching the mapping of two components, e.g. for selected k, l: $d'_i = [d_i(c_1), d_i(c_2), ..., d_i(c_k)..., d_i(c_l), ..., d_i(c_n)]$ while the original solution is $d_i = [d_i(c_1), d_i(c_2), ..., d_i(c_l)..., d_i(c_k), ..., d_i(c_n)]$. With this operator, from one solution d_i we can generate $\binom{n}{2}$ possible new solutions.

OneFlip neighbourhood operator changes the allocation of a single component. Formally, the OneFlip operator produces a new solution d'_i from existing solution d_i by changing the mapping of one components, e.g. for selected k: $d'_i = [d_i(c_1), d'_i(c_2), ..., d_i(c_k), ..., d_i(c_n)]$ while the original parent solution is $d_i = [d_i(c_1), d_i(c_2), ..., d_i(c_k), ..., d_i(c_n)]$. From one solution d_i, we can generate $2n$ new solutions corresponding to the n positions and 2 values for each position.

Perturb changes the allocation of a random component into a random host. The application of this neighbourhood operator creates a new solution d'_i from existing solution d_i by changing the mapping of one components, e.g. for a random k: $d'_i = [d_i(c_1), d'_i(c_2), ..., d_i(c_k), ..., d_i(c_n)]$ while the original parent solution is $d_i = [d_i(c_1), d_i(c_2), ..., d_i(c_k), ..., d_i(c_n)]$. From one solution d_i, we can generate $k_1 n$ new solutions corresponding to the n positions and k_1 values for each position in d_i.

3.2 Adaptive Neighbourhood Search for the Component Deployment Problem

Each operator is applied until a local optimum is found. The solution is then evaluated (line 7 in Algorithm 1) and the change in fitness is recorded. The adaptive neighbourhood uses the change in fitness as feedback for adjusting the operator selection probabilities. At the beginning, all operators have equally probability of being selected. The selection probabilities are updated over the iterations based on operator performance. The main steps of these methods are described in Algorithm 1. The feedback is used to decide whether to continue to use the current operator or switch to a different one, as shown in Algorithm 2.

Algorithm 1. Neighbourhood operators.

```
    procedure ONEFLIP(S)
 2:     S* = S
        localOptimum = TRUE
 4:     for all c < C do
            h = RANDOMLYSELECTHOST(H)
 6:         S' = ASSIGNCOMPONENTTOHOST(S, c, h)
            EVALUATE(S')
 8:         if S' > S* then
                S* = S'
10:         end if
        end for
12:     improvement = FITNESSDIFFERENCE(S, S*)
        S = S*
14:     RETURN(improvement)
    end procedure
16: procedure KOPT(S, k)
        S* = S
18:     localOptimum = TRUE
        for c = 0; c < |C| − k; c + + do
20:         S' = ASSIGNCOMPONENTTOHOST(S, c, d(c + k))
            S' = ASSIGNCOMPONENTTOHOST(S, c + k, d(c))
22:         EVALUATE(S')
            if S' > S* then
24:             S* = S'
            end if
26:     end for
        improvement = FITNESSDIFFERENCE(S, S*)
28:     S = S*
        RETURN(improvement)
30: end procedure
    procedure PERTURB(S)
32:     c = RANDOMLYSELECTCOMPONENT(C)
        h = RANDOMLYSELECTHOST(H)
34:     S' = ASSIGNCOMPONENTTOHOST(S, c, h)
        EVALUATE(S')
36:     if S' > S* then
            S* = S'
38:     end if
        improvement = FITNESSDIFFERENCE(S, S*)
40:     S = S*
        RETURN(improvement)
42: end procedure
```

The mechanism used for the selection of the neighbourhood operator is a fitness proportionate method (line 4 in Algorithm 2). Each operator is assigned a selection probability proportionate to its quality (line 14 in Algorithm 2). For the purpose of this work, the fitness change in the solution modified by an operator

---

Algorithm 2. Adaptive neighbourhood search.

---
    procedure AN
2:     S = RANDOMLYALLOCATE(C, H)
      N = SELECTNEIGHBOURHOODOPERATOR($P(N)$)
4:    **if** N == OneFlip **then**
       $Q(N)$=ONEFLIP(S)
6:    **end if**
     if N == KOpt **then**
8:     $Q(N)$=KOPT(S, k)
     end if
10:   **if** N == Perturb **then**
      $Q(N)$=PERTURB(S)
12:   **end if**
     REPORTFEEDBACK($Q(N)$)
14:   RETURN(S)
    end procedure

---

is used to updates the operator's quality. Given the operator's quality $Q(N)$, the update rule for the operator's selection probability $P(N)$ is calculated as

$$P(N) = \alpha P(N) + (1 - \alpha)Q(N), \qquad (7)$$

where α is a parameter that controls the influence of previous versus immediate performance. Higher values for α increase the effect of previous performance, whereas lower values focus on immediate effects. In this study, α was set to 0.9. Formally, the operators quality is calculated as:

$$Q(N) = \frac{|f(S) - f(S^*)|}{f(S)} \qquad (8)$$

where $f(S)$ is the quality of the solution at the start of the search, and $f(S^*)$ is the quality of the optimised solution.

The deterministic neighbourhood strategy, performs a variable neighbourhood search by applying the three neighbourhood operators sequentially, in the order given in Algorithm 3. We have selected this order arbitrarily and can be changed by the user. Another alternative would have been to select at random one of these operators.

The variable neighbourhood search, on the other hand, assigns equal probabilities to OneFlip and kOpt. The main steps are listed in Algorithm 3. At each iteration, VN selects one of the two operators with equal probability. The Perturb operator is the most disruptive operator since it can make the largest changes in the search space. Therefore, Perturb is applied after the OneFlip or kOpt with a very small probability, which ensures that the search does not get trapped in a local optimum.

Algorithm 3. Deterministic and variable neighbourhood search operators.

```
    procedure DN
2:      S = RANDOMLYALLOCATE(C, H)
        ONEFLIP(S)
4:      PERTURB(S)
        KOPT(S, k)
6:      RETURN(S)
    end procedure
8:
    procedure VN
10:     S = RANDOMLYALLOCATE(C, H)
        r = RANDOM([0,1])
12:     if r > 0.5 then
            ONEFLIP(S)
14:     end if
        if r < 0.5 then
16:         KOPT(S, k)
        end if
18:     p = RANDOM([0,1])
        if p < 0.01 then
20:         PERTURB(S)
        end if
22:     RETURN(S)
    end procedure
```

4   Experiments

To evaluate the efficiency of the proposed methods for varying the neighbourhood search operator, we have designed a set of experiments with problems of different sizes and level of difficulty. The design of experiments and the analysis of results is described in the following sections.

4.1   Experimental Design

The problems used for the experiments consist of a number of randomly generated instances with varying complexity and constrainedness. The memory constraint takes its tightness from the ratio of components to hardware hosts - the fewer hosts, the less 'space' there is for components. The smallest instances consist of 10 hosts and 23 software components whereas the largest instances consist of 62 hardware hosts and 130 software components. All algorithms were allowed 50 000 function evaluations, and all trials were repeated 30 times to account for the stochastic behaviour of the algorithms. Results from the 30 runs were analysed and compared using the Kolmogorov-Smirnov (KS) non-parametric test [22]. Furthermore, the effect size was reported for each experiment.

The validity of the presented experiments may be questioned on the grounds that the results may only reflect the performance of the algorithms in certain problem instances, and there is a chance that the approaches may perform differently for other problems. In the design of experiment, we aimed at reducing this threat by generating problem instances of different sizes and characteristics. Instead of manually setting specific problem properties, we developed a problem generator integrated in ArcheOpterix [2]. The problem generator and the problem files can be downloaded from http://users.monash.edu.au/~aldeidaa/ ArcheOpterix.html. As a result, the experiments set themselves apart from an instance-specific setting to a broader applicability.

4.2   Results

The experiments were performed on a 64-core 2.26 GHz processor computer. There was little difference in the run-times of the different optimisation schemes for the same problem instances. The main difference in run-time was observed between the problem instances with different size. Solving the smaller instances was faster, since the evaluation of the quality attributes takes less time. The distributions of the fitness values (reliability function in Eq. 3) of the 30 runs are visualised as boxplots for Adaptive Neighbourhood (AN), Variable neighbourhood (VN), deterministic neighbourhood (DN) and local search (LS). The middle lines represent the median value for each case. The means and standard deviations for all problem instances and optimisation schemes are shown in Table 1. AN outperforms the other strategies in the majority of the problem instances, which indicates that using feedback from the search to adapt the neighbourhood operator benefit the optimisation process (Fig. 1).

Table 1. The mean and standard deviation of the 30 trials of adaptive neighbourhood search (AN), variable neighbourhood search (VN), deterministic neighbourhood search (DN) and local search (LS).

	AN		VN		DN		LS	
Problem	Mean	Std. dev	Mean	Std. dev	Mean	Std. dev	Mean	Std. dev
H10C23	0.999871	0.000000	0.999871	0.000000	0.998980	0.000057	0.999871	0.000000
H20C45	0.999993	0.000000	0.999979	0.000004	0.999965	0.000009	0.999993	0.000000
H25C54	**0.999981**	0.000000	0.999980	0.000000	0.999935	0.000010	0.999979	0.000000
H30C65	**0.999780**	0.000002	0.999746	0.000007	0.999615	0.000048	0.999743	0.000005
H35C74	**0.999986**	0.000000	0.999980	0.000001	0.999912	0.000023	0.999983	0.000000
H42C85	**0.999777**	0.000039	0.999770	0.000027	0.999759	0.000037	0.999737	0.000045
H55C107	**0.999796**	0.000004	0.999771	0.00007	0.999679	0.000006	0.999667	0.000043
H62C130	**0.999974**	0.000009	0.999932	0.000008	0.999918	0.000016	0.999919	0.000013

As the adaptive neighbourhood strategy consistently outperforms the three other optimisation schemes, we use the Kolmogorov-Smirnov (KS) nonparametric test [22] to check for a statistical difference. The 30 results of the repeated trials for each of the problem instances were submitted to the KS analysis. The adaptive neighbourhood search (AN) was compared to the other

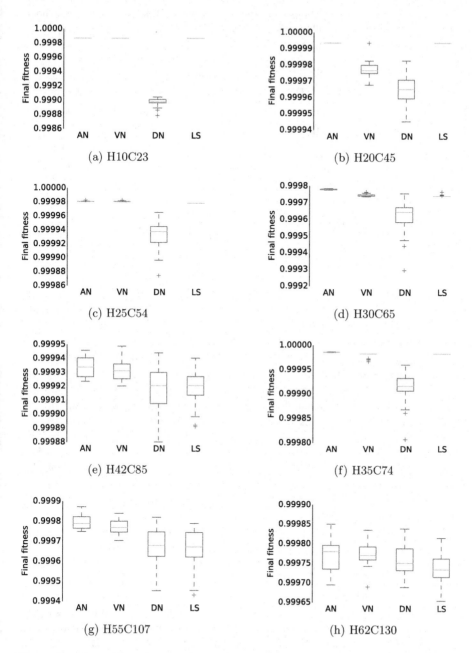

Fig. 1. Boxplots of fitness values (reliability function in Eq. 3) for Adaptive Neighbourhood (AN), Variable neighbourhood (VN), deterministic neighbourhood (DN) and local search (LS).

Table 2. The KS test values and effect size of the 30 trials of adaptive neighbourhood search vs. variable neighbourhood search (AN vs. VN), adaptive neighbourhood search vs. deterministic neighbourhood search (AN vs. DN) and adaptive neighbourhood search vs. local search (AN vs. LS).

	KS test			Effect size		
Problem	AN vs. VN	AN vs. DN	AN vs. LS	AN vs. VN	AN vs. DN	AN vs. LS
H10C23	1	≤ 0.01	1	0.00	0.99	0.00
H20C45	≤ 0.01	≤ 0.01	1	0.92	0.91	0.00
H25C54	0.02	≤ 0.01	≤ 0.01	0.99	0.95	0.99
H30C65	≤ 0.01	0.05	≤ 0.01	0.95	0.92	0.98
H35C74	≤ 0.01	≤ 0.01	≤ 0.01	0.97	0.98	0.99
H42C85	0.01	0.03	0.03	0.91	0.92	0.94
H55C107	≤ 0.01	0.02	≤ 0.01	0.90	0.99	0.90
H62C130	0.01	0.04	0.05	0.92	0.90	0.93

three optimisation schemes, with a null hypothesis of an insignificant difference between the performances (AN vs. VN, AN vs. DN, and AN vs. LS). The results of the tests are shown in Table 2.

All KS tests, used for establishing that there is no difference between independent datasets under the assumption that they are not normally distributed, result in a rejection of the null hypothesis at a 95 % confidence level in the majority of the cases. AN and LS have the same performance in two problems H20C45 and H10C23. The search space of these two instances is relatively small, and the problems can be solved to high quality with local search. For larger and more complex search spaces, the local search method fails at finding good results. The deterministic neighbourhood search method has the worst performance out of the four optimisation schemes. Clearly, applying the three operators sequentially does not benefit the search, although for the large problem instances, varying the neighbourhood produces better results than local search, even if it is done in a deterministic way.

Since statistical significance depends on the sample size, we also compute the effect size for each comparison (AN vs. VN, AN vs. DN, and AN vs. LS), as shown in Table 2. The effect of the sample size is measured using the Cohen's d estimation [8], which considers the pooled standard deviation. In reporting the effect size, we follow the guidelines proposed by Cohen [8]: a 'small' effect size is 0.2, a 'medium' effect size is 0.5, and a 'large' effect size is 0.8. In essence, the effect size indicates the number of standard deviations difference between the means of the samples. The effect size for the problem instances that show statistical significance in terms of the KS test was above 0.9. As a results, it can be concluded that the difference in the performance of the optimisation schemes is meaningful, and that the AN strategy is the most successful search method for the component deployment problem.

5   Conclusion

This paper propose an adaptive variable neighbourhood search for component deployment components that uses multiple neighbourhood operators to escape local optimum. These operators are adaptively selected such that the operator that improves the most the fitness value and most frequently the current solution is selected the most often. Two other versions of this variable neighbourhood search algorithm alternate uniformly at random or deterministically the three operators. We test the three proposed algorithms and a simple version of multiple restarts local search on several instances of component deployment problems with different level of difficulty. The experimental results show that the adaptive variable neighbourhood algorithm outperforms the other algorithms. We conclude that the local search algorithms are useful optimization algorithms for component deployment problems.

Acknowledgements. This research was supported under Australian Research Council's Discovery Projects funding scheme, project number DE 140100017.

References

1. Aleti, A.: Designing automotive embedded systems with adaptive genetic algorithms. Autom. Softw. Eng. **22**, 199–240 (2015)
2. Aleti, A., Björnander, S., Grunske, L., Meedeniya, I.: ArcheOpterix: an extendable tool for architecture optimization of AADL models. In: Model-based Methodologies for Pervasive and Embedded Software, pp. 61–71. ACM and IEEE Digital Libraries (2009)
3. Aleti, A., Buhnova, B., Grunske, L., Koziolek, A., Meedeniya, I.: Software architecture optimization methods: a systematic literature review. IEEE Trans. Softw. Eng. **39**(5), 658–683 (2013)
4. Aleti, A., Grunske, L.: Test data generation with a kalman filter-based adaptive genetic algorithm. J. Syst. Softw. **103**, 343–352 (2015)
5. Aleti, A., Grunske, L., Meedeniya, I., Moser, I.: Let the ants deploy your software - an ACO based deployment optimisation strategy. In: ASE, pp. 505–509. IEEE Computer Society (2009)
6. Aleti, A., Meedeniya, I.: Component deployment optimisation with bayesian learning. In: ACM Sigsoft Symposium on Component based Software Engineering, pp. 11–20. ACM (2011)
7. Assayad, I., Girault, A., Kalla, H.: A bi-criteria scheduling heuristic for distributed embedded systems under reliability and real-time constraints. In: Dependable Systems and Networks, pp. 347–356. IEEE Computer Society (2004)
8. Cohen, J.: Statistical Power Analysis for the Behavioral Sciences. Lawrence Erlbaum Associates, Hillsdale (1988)
9. Coit, D.W., Konak, A.: Multiple weighted objectives heuristic for the redundancy allocation problem. IEEE Trans. Reliab. **55**(3), 551–558 (2006)
10. Deb, K., Pratap, A., Agarwal, S., Meyarivan, T.: A fast elitist multi-objective genetic algorithm: NSGA-II. IEEE Trans. Evol. Comput. **6**, 182–197 (2000)

11. Fonseca, C.M., Fleming, P.J., et al.: Genetic algorithms for multiobjective optimization: formulation, discussion and generalization. In: ICGA, vol. 93, pp. 416–423 (1993)

12. Guntsch, M., Middendorf, M.: Solving multi-criteria optimization problems with population-based ACO. In: Fonseca, C.M., Fleming, P.J., Zitzler, E., Deb, K., Thiele, L. (eds.) EMO 2003. LNCS, vol. 2632, pp. 464–478. Springer, Heidelberg (2003)

13. Harman, M., Afshin Mansouri, S., Zhang, Y.: Search-based software engineering: trends, techniques and applications. ACM Comput. Surv. **45**(1), 11:1–11:61 (2012)

14. Harman, M., McMinn, P.: A theoretical and empirical study of search-based testing: local, global, and hybrid search. IEEE Trans. Softw. Eng. **36**(2), 226–247 (2010)

15. ISO/IEC. IEEE international standard 1471 2000 - systems and software engineering - recommended practice for architectural description of software-intensive systems (2000)

16. Kubat, P.: Assessing reliability of modular software. Oper. Res. Lett. **8**(1), 35–41 (1989)

17. Malek, S., Medvidovic, N., Mikic-Rakic, M.: An extensible framework for improving a distributed software system's deployment architecture. IEEE Trans. Softw. Eng. **38**(1), 73–100 (2012)

18. Meedeniya, I., Aleti, A., Avazpour, I., Amin, A.: Robust archeopterix: architecture optimization of embedded systems under uncertainty. In: Software Engineering for Embedded Systems, pp. 23–29. IEEE (2012)

19. Meedeniya, I., Aleti, A., Grunske, L.: Architecture-driven reliability optimization with uncertain model parameters. J. Syst. Softw. **85**(10), 2340–2355 (2012)

20. Meedeniya, I., Buhnova, B., Aleti, A., Grunske, L.: Architecture-driven reliability and energy optimization for complex embedded systems. In: Heineman, G.T., Kofron, J., Plasil, F. (eds.) QoSA 2010. LNCS, vol. 6093, pp. 52–67. Springer, Heidelberg (2010)

21. Meedeniya, I., Buhnova, B., Aleti, A., Grunske, L.: Reliability-driven deployment optimization for embedded systems. J. Syst. Softw. **84**, 835–846 (2011)

22. Pettitt, A.N., Stephens, M.A.: The kolmogorov-smirnov goodness-of-fit statistic with discrete and grouped data. Technometrics **19**(2), 205–210 (1977)

23. Shan, S., Gary Wang, G.: Reliable design space and complete single-loop reliability-based design optimization. Reliab. Eng. Syst. Saf. **93**(8), 1218–1230 (2008)

24. Thiruvady, D., Moser, I., Aleti, A., Nazari, A.: Constraint programming and ant colony system for the component deployment problem. Procedia Comput. Sci. **29**, 1937–1947 (2014)

25. Weimer, W., Forrest, S., Le Goues, C., Nguyen, T.V.: Automatic program repair with evolutionary computation. Commun. ACM **53**(5), 109–116 (2010)

26. Wolpert, D.H., Macready, W.G.: No free lunch theorems for optimization. IEEE Trans. Evol. Comput. **1**(1), 67–82 (1997)

Transformed Search Based Software Engineering: A New Paradigm of SBSE

He Jiang[✉], Zhilei Ren, Xiaochen Li, and Xiaochen Lai

School of Software, Dalian University of Technology, Dalian, China
{jianghe,zren,laixiaochen}@dlut.edu.cn,
lil989@mail.dlut.edu.cn

Abstract. Recent years have witnessed the sharp growth of research interests in Search Based Software Engineering (SBSE) from the society of Software Engineering (SE). In SBSE, a SE task is generally transferred into a combinatorial optimization problem and search algorithms are employed to achieve solutions within its search space. Since the terrain of the search space is rugged with numerous local optima, it remains a great challenge for search algorithms to achieve high-quality solutions in SBSE. In this paper, we propose a new paradigm of SBSE, namely Transformed Search Based Software Engineering (TSBSE). Given a new SE task, TSBSE first transforms its search space into either a reduced one or a series of gradually smoothed spaces, then employ search algorithms to effectively seek high-quality solutions. More specifically, we investigate two techniques for TSBSE, namely search space reduction and search space smoothing. We demonstrate the effectiveness of these new techniques over a typical SE task, namely the Next Release Problem (NRP). The work of this paper provides a new way for tackling SE tasks in SBSE.

Keywords: Search based software engineering · Search space transformation · Search space reduction · Search space smoothing · Next release problem

1 Introduction

Since Harman and Jones proposed the conception of Search Based Software Engineering (SBSE) in 2001 [1], SBSE has attracted a great amount of research interests from the society of Software Engineering (SE). As shown in the SBSE repository[1], up to Feb. 3, 2015, 1389 relevant research papers involving over 659 authors around the world have been published.

As stated in [1, 2], a SE task in SBSE is firstly transferred into an optimization problem for solving and then various search algorithms are employed to seek solutions within its search space, a high-dimensional rugged space consisting of points (solutions). Some typical search algorithms include Evolutionary Algorithms (EA, e.g., Genetic Algorithms, Genetic Programming, and Memetic Algorithms), Ant Colony Algorithms (ACO), Tabu Search (TS), Simulated Annealing (SA), Particle Swarm Optimization (PSO), Hill Climb (HC), etc. Up to now, SBSE has covered most SE tasks across all the

---

[1] SBSE repository: http://crestweb.cs.ucl.ac.uk/resources/sbse_repository/.

© Springer International Publishing Switzerland 2015
M. Barros and Y. Labiche (Eds.): SSBSE 2015, LNCS 9275, pp. 203–218, 2015.
DOI: 10.1007/978-3-319-22183-0_14

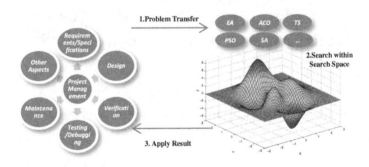

Fig. 1. Roadmap of SBSE

stages of the software lifecycle, including requirement/specification, design, verification, testing/debugging, maintenance, and software project management (see Fig. 1).

Since the search spaces in SBSE are usually rugged with numerous local optima, search algorithms are apt to get trapped into poor local optima. In this paper, we propose a new paradigm of SBSE named Transformed Search Based Software Engineering (TSBSE) to tackle this challenge. In TSBSE, the search spaces are transformed so as to either constrain search algorithms within promising regions or provide better initial solutions for search algorithms. More specifically, we present two techniques for search space transformation, namely search space reduction and search space smoothing. Taking the Next Release Problem (NRP) as a case study, we investigate how to resolve SE tasks within TSBSE.

The remainder of this paper is structured as follows. In Sect. 2, we present the new SBSE paradigm TSBSE. Then in Sect. 3 we present the related work of the NRP. In Sects. 4 and 5, we present the detailed technique of search space smoothing over NRP and the experimental results, respectively. In Sect. 6, we discuss the threats to validity. Finally, we conclude this paper and discuss the future work in Sect. 7.

2 Transformed Search Based Software Engineering

In this section, we introduce the new paradigm of SBSE, namely Transformed Search Based Software Engineering (TSBSE). A key challenge lying in SBSE is that search algorithms in SBSE may easily get trapped into poor local optima, due to the rugged terrain of search spaces with numerous local optima. Therefore, TSBSE aims to tackle the above challenge by transforming the search spaces. As shown in Fig. 2, given a SE task, TSBSE firstly transfers it into a combinatorial optimization problem. Then, TSBSE transforms the related search space to facilitate the process of searching solutions. More specifically, two techniques are available for search space transformation, namely search space reduction and search space smoothing. Third, search algorithms, e.g., EA, ACO, TS, SA, PSO, are employed to search within the transformed search space. In the following part, we illustrate more details of search space reduction and search space smoothing.

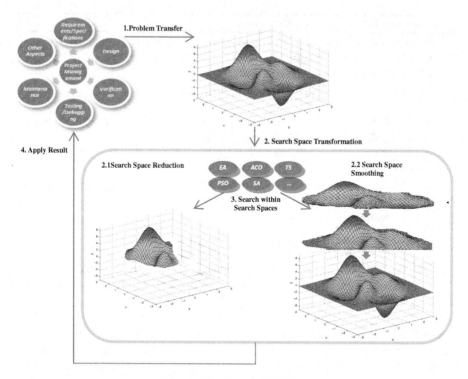

Fig. 2. Roadmap of TSBSE

Search Space Reduction. In SBSE, a search space may consist of numerous local optima and, search algorithms are apt to get trapped into poor local optima. The basic idea of search space reduction in TSBSE is to constrain search algorithms in a reduced search space consisting of high-quality solutions. In such a way, search algorithms could better find high-quality solutions within reasonable running time.

Some related studies [3, 4] in the literature can be viewed as the applications related to search space reduction. For example, in [3], Xuan et al. proposed a backbone based multilevel algorithm to solve NRP. They constrain a shared common part of optimal solutions and reduce the search space into smaller ones. Then, they employ Simulated Annealing to iteratively search for high-quality solutions.

In Fig. 3, we present the pseudo code of the search space reduction. First, in each reduction level, the search algorithm is applied on the current reduced search space to produce a set of high quality solutions $\Gamma_k{}'$. Then, the search space is reduced according to the solutions $\Gamma_k{}'$, e.g., by fixing the common parts of the solutions (lines 2–6 of Algorithm 1). Second, after the search space reduction phase, the search algorithm is applied on the final reduced search space, to obtain a local optimum $\Gamma_{\delta+1}{}'$ (line 7 of Algorithm 1). Third, the local optimum $\Gamma_{\delta+1}{}'$ is transferred gradually back to the feasible solution to the original search space (lines 8–10 of Algorithm 1). During the refinement procedure, the best solution achieved so far is recorded. After the refinement phase, the best solution is returned (line 11 of Algorithm 1).

Algorithm 1: Search Space Reduction

Input: search space Π, search algorithms A, maximum number α of reduction levels, a set of solutions Γ

Output: best solution

```
 1  begin
 2  │   for k = 1 to α do
 3  │   │   Obtain a set of solutions Γₖ by A in Πₖ
 4  │   │   Calculate high quality part Γₖ′ of Γₖ
 5  │   │   Reduce the search space to Πₖ₊₁ by Γₖ′
 6  │   end
 7  │   Obtain a local optimum Γ_{α+1}′ in the reduced search space Π_{α+1} by A
 8  │   for k = α to 1 do
 9  │   │   Refine the solution with Γₖ₊₁′ and Γₖ′ in level k
10  │   end
11  │   return the best solution achieved
12  end
```

Fig. 3. Pseudo Code of Search Space Reduction

Search Space Smoothing. In SBSE, the terrain of a search space is usually rugged with many poor local optima. Hence, the solutions of search algorithms may heavily depend on the initial solutions fed into search algorithms. For example, Hill Climbing may easily get trapped into a poor local optimum, if it is initialized with a random solution. The idea of search space smoothing is to transform a search space into a series of gradually smoothed ones. In the most smoothed search space, search algorithms are apt to achieve high-quality solutions. Then, the resulting solutions are fed into the second smoothed search space as its initial solutions. Since the terrains of the two search spaces are similar in shape, these initial solutions could lead search algorithms to better hit new high-quality solutions. In such a way, we eventually return to the original search space and achieve the final solutions.

Figure 4 presents the process of search space smoothing over a one-dimensional search space. The original search space is smoothed into two smoothed search spaces. First, a solution is initialized in the most smoothed search space (smoothed search

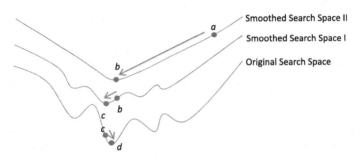

Fig. 4. Illustration of search space smoothing over one-dimensional search space

---

Algorithm 2: Search Space Smoothing

Input: search space Π, search algorithms A, maximum number β of smoothing levels, a set of solutions Γ

Output: best solution

1 **begin**
2 | Generate a smoothed search space Π_0
2 | Generate initial solutions Γ_0 in Π_0
3 | **for** $k = 1$ to β **do**
4 | | Tune the search space to Π_k, towards the original, rugged space.
5 | | Assign the current best solutions Γ_{k-1} as the initial solution
6 | | Apply A with Γ_{k-1} in Π_k to get the current best solutions Γ_k
7 | **end**
8 | **return** the best solution achieved
9 **end**

Fig. 5. Pseudo Code of search space smoothing

space II) and a local optimum b is achieved. Then, the solution b is used as the initial solution in smoothed search space I, and a local optimum c can be achieved. Finally, the solution c is used as the initial solution in the original search space and the final solution d is eventually returned.

In Fig. 5, we present the pseudo code of the search space smoothing. First, we generate a smoothed search space $\prod_0$, in which the initial solutions Γ_0 is generated (lines 1–2 of Algorithm 2). Then, the search is conducted over a series of search spaces, which are transferred gradually back towards the original, rugged search space (lines 3–7 of Algorithm 2). More specifically, at each iteration, the search space is firstly tuned, and the best solutions up to the previous iteration is regarded as the initial solutions. The algorithm is then applied on the current tuned search space with these initial solutions to obtain the current best solutions. Finally, after the search space is transferred to the original search space, the best solution in the original search space is returned (line 8 in Algorithm 2).

Some early studies [5] in the literature demonstrate that combinatorial optimization problems could be better solved by search space smoothing. However, as to our knowledge, no related work has been done in SBSE. Since for most tasks in SBSE, it is still a challenge on how to prevent search algorithms from getting trapped into poor local optima. We believe that search space smoothing is a promising technique to solve the above problem and may significantly improve the effectiveness of search algorithms in SBSE.

3 Related Work

3.1 The Next Release Problem

Bagnall et al. [6] first proposed the Next Release Problem (NRP) to balance the profits of customers and the developing costs of requirements in the next release of software systems. Besides customer profits, a variety of problem objectives have been proposed in literature, such as component prioritization [7], fairness [8], etc. According to the number of problem objectives, we can classify the NRP into two categories, namely single-objective NRP (or the NRP for short) and multi-objective NRP (or MONRP for short).

For the category of single-objective NRP, Bagnall et al. [6] apply numerous search-based algorithms, including greedy algorithms, local search, etc., on five randomly generated instances to solve the NRP. In this work, they model the problem as searching for the maximum profits from customers within a predefined cost bound of a software system. The problem can be formalized as follows [6]:

$$\text{Maximize} \sum\nolimits_{i \subseteq S} w_i \text{ subject to } \text{cost}\left(\cup_{i \in S}\hat{R}_i\right) \leq B, B \leq Z^+ \tag{1}$$

where S is a set of customers, $\hat{R}$ is a set of requirements, w_i is the importance of the ith customer, and $\text{cost}\left(\cup_{i \in S}\hat{R}_i\right)$ means the cost of satisfying all the requirements $\hat{R}$ of the ith customer. The cost should be within some bounds B.

Following the problem definition, Greer and Ruhe [9] propose a genetic algorithm-based approach to iteratively generate the final decision of the NRP. Jiang et al. [10] propose an ant colony optimization algorithm with a local search operator (first found hill climbing) to approximately solve the NRP. A backbone-based multi-level algorithm is proposed in [3]. In this paper, Xuan et al. iteratively reduce the search space by adding the common part of the customers and customers with zero cost to the requirements selection into the combined backbone (approximate backbone and soft backbone). Then they refine the final decision according to the solution in the reduced search space and the combined backbone. Baker et al. [7] extend the NRP with the component selection and ranking, and explore both greedy and simulated annealing algorithms to this problem. Moreover, Ngo-The and Ruhe [11] propose a two-phase optimization approach, which combine integer programming and genetic programming, to allocate the resources of software releases. Paixão et al. proposed a recoverable robust approach for [12] and extands the NRP with a novel formulation which considers the production of robust solutions [13, 14]. Fuchshuber et al. [15] modify the hill climbing algorithm with some patterns observed from the terrain visualization. Araújo et al. [16] draw machine learning models into the NRP. Harman et al. [17] analyze the NRP from the perspective of requirement sensitivity analysis. In this paper, we propose the framework of search space transformation for SBSE, and take the single-objective NRP as a case study. In contrast to solving the problems directly, we smooth the search space to improve the search ability of existing algorithms.

For the category of multi-objective NRP, Zhang et al. [18] first take multi-factors in requirements engineering into consideration and apply the genetic algorithm-based multiobjective optimization to the MONRP. Many related work extend MONRP by balancing factors between the benefits and fairness [19], sensitivity [20] robustness [21], or uncertainty [22]. Besides, Saliu and Ruhe [23] aim at optimizing release plans from both the business perspectives and the implementation perspectives. Zhang et al. [24] seek to balance the requirements needs of today with those of the future. Veerapen et al. [25] evaluate integer linear programming approach on both the single-objective and multi-objective NRP. A recent work by Zhang et al. [26] conduct comprehensive empirical study of different search algorithms across different real world datasets in NRP. Another review is conducted by Pitangueira [27].

3.2 Search Space Reduction for the NRP

Search space reduction is an effective approach to search high quality solutions for SBSE in the framework of search space transformation. A typical application of search space reduction has been studied in [3].

In [3], Xuan et al. propose a Backbone-based Multilevel Algorithm (BMA) to solve the NRP. The BMA employs multilevel reductions to iteratively reduce the problem scale and refine the final optimal solution. For each level, BMA combines approximate backbone with soft backbone to build a part of final optimal solution and reduce the search space by removing the common part of the optimal customers. The approximate backbone is employed to fix the common part of local optima of several local search operators. While the soft backbone is employed to augment the approximate backbone by adding the customers who provide profits with zero cost to the requirements selection. Based on the backbones, BMA resolves the large scale problem to a small one and search solution to it efficiently. Finally, BMA constructs a solution to the original instance by combining the approximate backbone, the soft backbone, and the current solution to the reduced instance together. The experiments show that search space reduction with backbones can significantly reduce the problem scale, meanwhile improves the quality of solutions for NRP without time cost.

4   Search Space Smoothing for the NRP

In this section, we present the main idea of search space smoothing for the NRP, and propose the algorithm framework. More specifically, we first introduce the motivation of search space smoothing. Then, we demonstrate how to realize the search space smoothing framework.

4.1 The Motivation

The motivation of search space smoothing is intuitive and simple, which is usually described analogously as "seeing the forest before trees" [28]. The idea of search space smoothing is to capture the general characteristics of the search space first, and gradually gain more details of the search terrain. This process is realized by transferring the search terrain from a smooth on towards the original rugged one. To achieve the performance improvement with search space smoothing, researchers have proposed various approaches. Among these approaches, most adopt the instance perturbation techniques, to realize the gradual transfer from smooth search terrains to the original rugged ones. Through a series of instance perturbations, search space smoothing intends to avoid the search from being stuck by locally optimal traps. With the help of well-defined smoothing strategies, search space smoothing is able to conduct such search space transferring at the cost of only a few extra parameters. In the existing literatures, there exist several smoothing approaches, such as power law smoothing, sigmoidal smoothing, etc. In this study, we take the power law smoothing as an example, to investigate the possibility of realizing the search space smoothing.

As mentioned in Sect. 2, the objective of the NRP is to maximize the revenue of the selected customer subset. Following the existing search space smoothing studies [5, 28], we propose the following smoothing formula:

$$w_i(\alpha) = \begin{cases} \bar{w} + (w_i' - \bar{w})^{\alpha}, & w_i' \geq \bar{w} \\ \bar{w} - (\bar{w} - w_i')^{\alpha}, & w_i' < \bar{w} \end{cases}, \tag{2}$$

where w' is the normalized revenue of the ith customer, $\bar{w}$ indicates the normalized average revenue of all the customers, and α is a parameter that controls the degree of smoothing. By introducing the parameter, smoothed instances could be generated. In Fig. 6, we provide the illustration of the influence caused by the smoothing parameter. In the figure, the x- and y- axes represent the normalized revenue and the smoothed revenue calculated with Eq. 2, respectively. The curves in the figure correspond to different configurations of the parameter. It is obvious that when $\alpha \gg 1$, all the revenues tend to be equal, meanwhile when α is 1, the instance would degenerate to the original instance. By adaptively controlling α, the search terrain could be fine-tuned accordingly.

In Fig. 7, we present the pseudo code of the search space smoothing framework for the NRP. The framework works in an iterative paradigm, according to certain schedule of the parameter α. For example, suppose the simplest schedule: let α decreases linearly from 5 to 1. At each iteration, we first construct a smoothed instance according to Eq. 2 (line 7 of Algorithm 3). Then, with the best solution up to the previous iteration as the initial solution, we apply the embedded algorithm to improve the incumbent solution (lines 8–9 of Algorithm 3). As α decreases towards 1, the search space gets transferred towards the original space. Finally, when the main loop terminates, the best solution achieved is returned (line 11 of Algorithm 3).

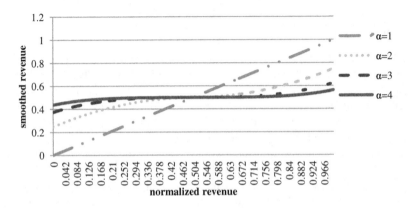

Fig. 6. Revenue Smoothing Transformation Scheme

Algorithm 3: Search Space Smoothing for NRP

Input: Embedded Algorithm A
Output: optimized solution s
1 **begin**
2   **for** *each customer i* **do**
3 | Normalize all the revenues so that $0 \leq \omega_i' \leq 1$
4   **end**
5   Generate initial solutions
6   **for** α *in predefined schedule* **do**
7   Set the revenue vector with respect to Eq. 2
8   Assign the initial solution with the current best solution
9   Apply A with the smoothed instance for optimization
10   **end**
11   **return** best solution achieved
12 **end**

Fig. 7. Pseudo Code of the search space smoothing framework for NRP

We could observe that, search space smoothing does not make assumptions about the algorithm which is embedded in the framework. Hence, it is easy to implement search space smoothing based variants that adopt other algorithms. For the following section, we would examine the flexibility of search space smoothing with a simple evolutionary search algorithm.

4.2 Search Space Smoothing Based Memetic Algorithm

After introducing the background information of the search space smoothing framework, we proceed to adapt the smoothing techniques for solving the NRP. In this subsection, we embed a simple Memetic Algorithm (MA) into the search space smoothing framework (denoted as SSS-MA). The reason we choose MA as the embedded algorithm is that, MA could be viewed as the combination of genetic algorithm and local search techniques. By balancing the intensification ability of local search and the diversification of the genetic operators, MAs have achieved promising performances in various problem domains [29, 30].

The pseudo code of SSS-MA is presented in Fig. 8. Similar to the existing genetic algorithms, MA is a population based iterative process. The population consists of a set of solutions to the NRP instance, each of which is encoded as a Boolean vector. MA realizes the problem solving procedure with two phases, i.e., the initialization phase and the main loop phase. First, all the individuals are randomly initialized and evaluated (line 2 of Algorithm 4). Then, for the second phase, the population is iteratively evolved to optimize the individuals. At each iteration, we first modify the parameter α if necessary. In this study, we consider a simple schedule, i.e., decrease α linearly from 5 to 1. After the smoothed instance is constructed (lines 4–5 of Algorithm 4), genetic operators such as crossover and mutation are applied over each individual. In this

---

Algorithm 4: Search Space Smoothing based Memetic Algorithm for NRP

Input: maximum iterator n*Iter*, population size n*Pop*, elitism rate *eRate*, mutation rate m*Rate*

Output: best solution achieved

1 **begin**
2   initialization
3   **for** $i \leftarrow 1$ *to* n*Iter* **do**
4         $\alpha \leftarrow \left\lfloor 6 - \dfrac{5 \times i}{nIter} \right\rfloor$
5   Modify instance variables with Eq. 2
6   **for** n*Pop* $\times$ (1 − *eRate*) **do**
7   Randomly select two individuals as parents
8   Apply uniform crossover
9   Apply bit-flipping mutation over the offspring
10   Apply hill climbing over the offspring
11   **end**
12   Apply elitism selection
13   **end**
14   **return** best solution achieved
15 **end**

Fig. 8. Pseudo Code of SSS-MA

study, uniform crossover and bit-flipping mutation are employed to produce the offspring individuals (lines 7–9 of Algorithm 4). Furthermore, in addition to the genetic operators, MA features the use of local search operators (line 10 of Algorithm 4). In this study, we apply a bit-flipping based hill climbing procedure as the local search operator. After all the operators have been applied, all the individuals and their offspring undergo a selection operator, to construct the population for the next iteration (line 12 of Algorithm 4). In this study, the truncation based selection mechanism is adopted. With the selected individuals, the evolution process continues the following iterations, until certain stopping criteria are met.

5 Experiments

In this section, we present the extensive experiments, to demonstrate the effectiveness of search space smoothing applied to the NRP. More specifically, we first present the preliminary information of the experiments. Then, numerical experiments are conducted over the benchmark instances. We compare the SSS-MA with the baseline MA, to examine the performance of the proposed algorithm. Finally, we investigate why search space smoothing works by illustrate the anytime performance of SSS-MA.

Before presenting the experimental results, we first briefly give the background information of the experiments. In this study, the algorithms are implemented in C++, compiled with g++ 4.9. The experiments are conducted on a PC with an Intel Core i5

3.2 GHz CPU and 4 GB memory, running GNU/Linux with kernel 3.16. For the benchmark instances, there are two classes from [3] and [6], respectively.

To evaluate the performance of SSS-MA, we consider two comparative algorithms. First, we adopt the basic MA as the baseline algorithm. The only difference between MA and SSS-MA lies in the smoothing mechanism. By comparing the two algorithms, we are able to examine the usefulness of search space smoothing. Second, besides MA, we employ the solution achieved by the backbone guided algorithm BMA [3] as the reference to evaluate the effectiveness of SSS-MA objectively, since BMA is among the best heuristics for the NRP. Next, since there are parameters in both MA and SSS-MA, we have to conduct the parameter tuning task. In this study, we choose to tune the elitism ratio and the mutation rate, and fix the rest parameters for the two algorithms. The reason for this experiment scheme is that, during the implementation, we find that these two parameters have the major influence on the performance. In particular, we employ the automatic tuning tool irace [31]. The parameter settings for the algorithms are summarized in Table 1.

Table 1. Parameter setup for MA and SSS-MA

Parameter	MA	SSS-MA
Maximum iteration	5000	5000
Population size	10	10
Elitism rate	0.51	0.27
Mutation rate	0.02	0.01

5.1   Numerical Results

After the preliminary experiment, we proceed to carry out the numerical experiments. For each benchmark instances, we independently execute the two algorithms for 10 times, and report the results in Table 2. The table is organized as follows. The first column indicates the instances. The second column presents the best known solution quality achieved by BMA. Then, in columns 3–5 and 6–8, the results for MA and SSS-MA are given, respectively. For each algorithm, we list the maximum and the mean of the solution quality, as well as the average time in seconds. From the table, several interesting observations could be drawn. First, from the effectiveness aspect, SSS-MA is able to achieve solutions with better quality than SSS-MA. Over the 39 instances, SSS-MA outperforms MA over 36 instances, in terms of the best solution quality. When we compare the average solution quality of the two algorithms, similar observations could be found. For both the two comparison scenarios, the conclusion that SSS-MA outperforms MA is supported by the nonparametric Wilcoxon's two-sided signed rank test (with p-values < 0.0001). In particular, SSS-MA obtains solutions that are better than the currently best known solutions over 6 instances. Second, from the efficiency aspect, SSS-MA is slower than MA over all the instances. The reason for this phenomenon might be that, for SSS-MA, especially during its beginning iterations, the search is conducted over the smoothed terrain, it is possible

Table 2. Results

Instance	BMA	MA			SSS-MA		
	Best	Best	Average	Time	Best	Average	Time
nrp1-0.3	1201	**1204**	1191.1	1.22	1200	1189.2	2.59
nrp1-0.5	1824	**1836**	1812.8	1.38	1834	1784.2	2.62
nrp1-0.7	2507	2507	2507	1.15	2507	2507	2.42
nrp2-0.3	4726	4007	3927.7	5.57	**4365**	4179.8	13.53
nrp2-0.5	7566	7034	6840.7	7.16	**7353**	7202.2	15.79
nrp2-0.7	10987	10585	10419	7.85	**10683**	10589.5	16.56
nrp3-0.3	7123	6846	6756	7.25	**7001**	6894.2	14.70
nrp3-0.5	10897	10566	10522.2	7.95	**10758**	10644.6	15.75
nrp3-0.7	14180	13867	13819.5	7.78	**13990**	13953	15.58
nrp4-0.3	9818	8950	8841.6	17.96	**9164**	9003.8	29.72
nrp4-0.5	15025	14609	14457.6	20.22	**14794**	14613.6	32.95
nrp4-0.7	20853	19996	19906.6	22.60	**20205**	20117.4	35.76
nrp5-0.3	17200	14873	14564.3	19.33	**15417**	15165.7	40.68
nrp5-0.5	24240	22409	22204.5	14.95	**22785**	22616.3	34.89
nrp5-0.7	28909	27494	27283.6	10.41	**27854**	27761.8	28.75
nrp-e1-0.3	7572	7396	7344.5	12.95	**7539**	7460.8	20.63
nrp-e1-0.5	10664	10607	10555	15.16	**10740**	10676.3	22.90
nrp-e2-0.3	7169	7053	6984.2	15.04	**7097**	7046.2	22.16
nrp-e2-0.5	10098	10021	9964.8	17.93	**10081**	10021.7	25.27
nrp-e3-0.3	6461	6345	6305	10.00	**6385**	6329.4	16.59
nrp-e3-0.5	9175	9090	9034.5	11.55	**9095**	9054.2	18.35
nrp-e4-0.3	5692	5553	5525.1	10.66	**5633**	5576.7	16.24
nrp-e4-0.5	8043	7982	7919	12.46	**7989**	7965.4	18.14
nrp-m1-0.3	10008	9573	9490.6	17.31	**9735**	9627	28.26
nrp-m1-0.5	14588	14416	14305.7	20.38	**14607**	14470.4	32.44
nrp-m2-0.3	8272	8044	7927.6	16.70	**8128**	8030.6	25.49
nrp-m2-0.5	11975	11970	11879.1	20.28	**12045**	11979.7	29.43
nrp-m3-0.3	9559	9302	9226.6	15.22	**9470**	9332	26.40
nrp-m3-0.5	14138	14123	14045.9	17.85	**14289**	14167.7	30.00
nrp-m4-0.3	7408	7197	7123.8	13.85	**7288**	7211.5	21.87
nrp-m4-0.5	10893	10836	10774.7	16.53	**10940**	10875.1	24.92
nrp-g1-0.3	5938	5917	5862	9.24	**5930**	5897.4	15.04
nrp-g1-0.5	8714	8657	8610.4	11.00	**8701**	8669.5	17.08
nrp-g2-0.3	4526	4474	4452.2	8.34	**4495**	4477.1	12.42
nrp-g2-0.5	6502	6447	6436.4	9.91	**6489**	6455.5	14.09
nrp-g3-0.3	5802	**5749**	5722.7	8.50	5739	5711.9	14.37
nrp-g3-0.5	8402	8327	8293.7	9.77	**8359**	8308.9	15.90
nrp-g4-0.3	4190	4149	4134.9	6.88	**4173**	4143.2	10.79
nrp-g4-0.5	6030	6002	5977.4	7.86	**6010**	5977.8	11.93

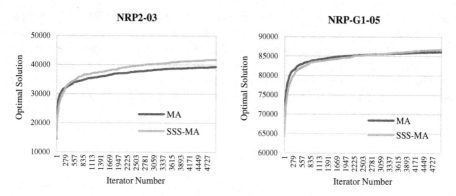

Fig. 9. Performance Comparison between MA and SSS-MA

that the hill climbing operator may be more time consuming. However, we can see that the times for the two algorithms are in the same order of magnitude.

5.2 Anytime Performance Comparison

In the previous subsection, we have observed that SSS-MA outperforms MA in terms of solution quality. However, SSS-MA is more time consuming accordingly. In this subsection, we intend to investigate the dynamic characteristics of the two algorithms, by visually comparing their anytime performance. We choose nrp-2-0.3 and nrp-g1-0.5 as the typical instances, and plot the anytime performance curves of MA and SSS-MA. In Fig. 9, the x-axis indicates the number of iterations elapsed, and the y-axis indicates the average solution quality achieved by the two algorithms.

From the figure, we find that for the beginning iterations, MA outperforms SSS-MA. For example, over nrp2-0.3, after 200 iterations, the solution quality of MA is 31559, while that of SSS-MA is 30089. However, as the search terrain gets transferred back to the original terrain, the solution obtained by SSS-MA is improved accordingly. After 400 iterations, SSS-MA is able to achieve better solutions compared to MA. These observations demonstrate that SSS-MA is able to avoid locally optimal traps to some extent. Similar observations could be found over NRP-g1-0.5. Similar phenomenon could be observed on the other instance we examine. Based on the anytime performance comparison, we partially confirm that the reason for the slow convergence of SSS-MA is caused by the smoothing operation.

6 Threats to Validity

In this paper, we demonstrate the effectiveness of search space smoothing, one of the techniques in TSBSE, on a typical SE task the NRP. However, there are some threats to validity: First, we validate the effectiveness of search space smoothing in TSBSE on 39 instances in the NRP and demonstrate the effectiveness of search space reduction with several related work. The proposed technique should be validated with more real world data set and SE tasks. Second, we smooth the search space in the NRP with a typical search space smoothing technique, the power law smoothing, which has been successfully applied in several research work [28, 29]. With this technique, we improve the optimal solution of the NRP with some time costs. However, the search space smoothing technique may slightly affect the results of our case study. In the future, we should validate and compare more search space smoothing techniques for SE tasks, and propose more time efficient formulas.

7 Conclusion and Future Work

In this paper, we address the conception of Transformed Search Based Software Engineering (TSBSE). Taking the Next Release Problem from the requirements engineering as a case study, we investigate the feasibility of applying search space smoothing for SBSE. The contributions of this study are tri-fold. First, we propose the conception of the TSBSE, which unifies the techniques such as search space reduction and search space smoothing. To the best of our knowledge, this is the first time such conception is issued in the software engineering community. Second, we develop a Search Space Smoothing based Memetic Algorithm (SSS-MA). We demonstrate that, with minor modification, algorithms could be embedded into the search space smoothing framework. Furthermore, numerical results reveal that, the proposed algorithm is able to update several best known solutions over the benchmark of the NRP instances. For the future work, we are interested in the following directions. First, SSS-MA tends to be slower than directly executing the embedded algorithm. Hence, how to accelerate the problem solving process deserves more efforts. Second, in the existing literature, there exist several smoothing schemes. Comparisons between these schemes seem interesting. Third, we would explore the possibility of extending the search space smoothing framework to more problems in software engineering.

Acknowledgement. This work is supported in part by the National Natural Science Foundation of China under Grants 61175062, 61370144, and 61403057, and in part by China Postdoctoral Science Foundation under Grant 2014M551083.

References

1. Harman, M., Jones, B.: Search-based software engineering. Inf. Softw. Technol. **43**(14), 833–839 (2001)
2. Harman, M., Mansouri, A., Zhang, Y.: Search based software engineering: trends, techniques and applications. ACM Comput. Surv. **45**(1), 11–75 (2012). Article 11
3. Xuan, J., Jiang, H., Ren, Z., Luo, Z.: Solving the large scale next release problem with a backbone-based multilevel algorithm. IEEE TSE **38**(5), 1195–1212 (2012)
4. Ren, Z., Jiang, H., Xuan, J., Luo, Z.: An accelerated limit crossing based multilevel algorithm for the p-Median problem. IEEE TSMCB **42**(2), 1187–1202 (2012)
5. Jun, G., Huang, X.: Efficient local search with search space smoothing: A case study of the traveling salesman problem (TSP). IEEE Trans. Syst. Man Cybern. **24**(5), 728–735 (1994)

6. Bagnall, A.J., Rayward-Smith, V.J., Whittley, I.M.: The next release problem. Inf. Softw. Technol. **43**(14), 883–890 (2001)
7. Baker, P., Harman, M., Steinhofel, K., Skaliotis, A.: Search based approaches to component selection and prioritization for the next release problem. In Software Maintenance, pp. 176–185 (2006)
8. Finkelstein, A., Harman, M., Mansouri, S.A., Ren, J., Zhang, Y.: A search based approach to fairness analysis in requirement assignments to aid negotiation, mediation and decision making. Requirements Eng. **14**(4), 231–245 (2009)
9. Greer, D., Ruhe, G.: Software release planning: an evolutionary and iterative approach. Inf. Softw. Technol. **46**(4), 243–253 (2004)
10. Jiang, H., Zhang, J., Xuan, J., Ren, Z., Hu, Y.: A hybrid ACO algorithm for the next release problem. In: SEDM, pp. 166–171 (2010)
11. Ngo-The, A., Ruhe, G.: Optimized resource allocation for software release planning. IEEE Trans. Software Eng. **35**(1), 109–123 (2009)
12. Paixão, M.H.E., de Souza, J.T.: A recoverable robust approach for the next release problem. In: Ruhe, G., Zhang, Y. (eds.) SSBSE 2013. LNCS, vol. 8084, pp. 172–187. Springer, Heidelberg (2013)
13. Paixão, M., Souza, J.: A scenario-based robust model for the next release problem. In: GECCO, pp. 1469–1476 (2013)
14. Paixão, M., Souza, J.: A robust optimization approach to the next release problem in the presence of uncertainties. J. Syst. Softw. **103**, 281–295 (2014)
15. Fuchshuber, R., de Oliveira Barros, M.: Improving heuristics for the next release problem through landscape visualization. In: Le Goues, C., Yoo, S. (eds.) SSBSE 2014. LNCS, vol. 8636, pp. 222–227. Springer, Heidelberg (2014)
16. Araújo, A.A., Paixão, M.: Machine learning for user modeling in an interactive genetic algorithm for the next release problem. In: Le Goues, C., Yoo, S. (eds.) SSBSE 2014. LNCS, vol. 8636, pp. 228–233. Springer, Heidelberg (2014)
17. Harman, M., Krinke, J., Medina-Bulo, I., Palomo-Lozano, F., Ren, J., Yoo, S.: Exact scalable sensitivity analysis for the next release problem. TOSEM **23**(2), 19 (2014)
18. Zhang, Y., Harman, M., Mansouri, S.A.: The multi-objective next release problem. In: GECCO, pp. 1129–1137. ACM (2007)
19. Finkelstein, A., Harman, M., Mansouri, S.A., Ren, J., Zhang, Y.: A search based approach to fairness analysis in requirement assignments to aid negotiation, mediation and decision making. Requirements Eng. **14**(4), 231–245 (2009)
20. Harman, M., Krinke, J., Ren, J., Yoo, S.: Search based data sensitivity analysis applied to requirement engineering. In: GECCO, pp. 1681–1688. ACM (2009)
21. Gueorguiev, S., Harman, M., Antoniol, G.: Software project planning for robustness and completion time in the presence of uncertainty using multi objective search based software engineering. In: GECCO, pp. 1673–1680. ACM (2009)
22. Li, L., Harman, M., Letier, E., Zhang, Y.: Robust next release problem: handling uncertainty during optimization. In: GECCO, pp. 1247–1254 (2014)
23. Saliu, M.O., Ruhe, G.: Bi-objective release planning for evolving software systems. In: FSE, pp. 105–114 (2007)
24. Zhang, Y., Alba, E., Durillo, J.J., Eldh, S., Harman, M.: Today/future importance analysis. In: GECCO, pp. 1357–1364. ACM (2007)
25. Veerapen, N., Ochoa, G., Harman, M., Burke, E.K.: An integer linear programming approach to the single and bi-objective next release problem. Inf. Softw. Technol. **65**, 1–13 (2015)
26. Zhang, Y., Harman, M., Ochoa, G., Ruhe, G., Brinkkemper, S.: An empirical Study of meta-and hyper-heuristic search for multi-objective release planning. RN **14**, 07 (2014)

27. Pitangueira, A.M., Maciel, R.S.P., Barros, M.: Software requirements selection and prioritization using SBSE approaches: A systematic review and mapping of the literature. J. Syst. Softw. **103**, 267–280 (2014)
28. Coy, S.P., Golden, B.L., Runger, G.C., Wasil, E.A.: See the forest before the trees: fine-tuned learning and its application to the traveling salesman problem. IEEE SMCA. **28**, 454–464 (2014)
29. Fraser, G., Arcuri, A., McMinn, P.: A Memetic Algorithm for whole test suite generation. J. Syst. Softw. **103**(2), 311–327 (2014)
30. Moscato, P., Cotta, C., Mendes, A.: Memetic algorithms. In: Onwubolu, G.C., Babu, B.V. (eds.) New Optimization Techniques in Engineering, pp. 53–85. Springer, Berlin, Heidelberg (2004)
31. Lopez-Ibanez, M., Dubois-Lacoste, J., Stutzle, T., et al.: The irace package, iterated race for automatic algorithm configuration. IRIDIA, Universite Libre de Bruxelles, Belgium, Technical Report TR/IRIDIA/2011-004 (2011)

SBSE Challenge Papers

Regression Test Case Prioritisation for Guava

Yi Bian[2]($\boxtimes$), Serkan Kirbas[3,4], Mark Harman[1], Yue Jia[1], and Zheng Li[2]

[1] CREST, Department of Computer Science, University College London,
Malet Place, London WC1E 6BT, UK
[2] Department of Computer Science, Beijing University of Chemical Technology,
Beijing 100029, People's Republic of China
marvinbian@yeah.net
[3] Department of Computer Science, Brunel University London, Kingston Lane,
Uxbridge, London UB8 3PH, UK
[4] Computer Engineering Department, Bogazici University, 34342
Bebek, Istanbul, Turkey

Abstract. We present a three objective formulation of regression test prioritisation. Our formulation involves the well-known, and widely-used objectives of Average Percentage of Statement Coverage (APSC) and Effective Execution Time (EET). However, we additionally include the Average Percentage of Change Coverage (APCC), which has not previously been used in search-based regression test optimisation. We apply our approach to prioritise the base and the collection package of the Guava project, which contains over 26,815 test cases. Our results demonstrate the value of search-based test case prioritisation: the sequences we find require only 0.2 % of the 26,815 test cases and only 0.45 % of their effective execution time. However, we find solutions that achieve more than 99.9 % of both regression testing objectives; covering both changed code and existing code. We also investigate the tension between these two objectives for Guava.

Keywords: Regression testing · Test case prioritisation · NSGA-II

1 Introduction

Test Case Prioritisation (TCP) reorders a sequence of test cases, based on testing objectives [1–3,6–8]. Most previous work on test case prioritisation has been single objective, though it has been argued that much more work is needed on multiple active approaches [11]. Yoo et al. [9] extended single objective test case selection to the multiple objective paradigm, but there is far less work on multi objective prioritisation [12–15].

This paper introduces a multi objective formulation of the test prioritisation problem, in which we include an additional objective which, perhaps surprisingly, has not previously been studied in any multi objective regression test optimisation work. That is, in addition to statement coverage, and execution time, which

© Springer International Publishing Switzerland 2015
M. Barros and Y. Labiche (Eds.): SSBSE 2015, LNCS 9275, pp. 221–227, 2015.
DOI: 10.1007/978-3-319-22183-0_15

have been widely studied, we also use coverage of changed code as an objective, since this is clearly critical in regression test optimisation. Our formulation therefore balances the tension between coverage of (specifically) changed code against all code, while seeking to minimise the overall execution time.

We apply our approach to Guava [4], an open source Java project containing several google versions of core Java utility libraries. These libraries provide day-to-day functionalities including collections, data caching, concurrency support, string manipulation[1]. In this work, we selected test suites for one of the major package of Guava, com.google.common.collect, which contains 26,815 test cases. We chose to test this package because it provides the core data collection that are used in every Java program, such as, list, set, maps, tables etc. [5].

2   Our Approach to Test Case Prioritisation

This section presents our algorithm representation and fitness functions to test case prioritisation problem. Given a test suite T with n elements, and a set of n objectives, $f_1, ..., f_n$. We seek to find a new permutation of T, $T' = < t'_1, ..., t'_n >$ where $\exists i \in \{1, ..., n\} \wedge f_i(T') > f_i(T'')$ [11].

We use NSGA-II [10], with a permutation encoding in which the N test cases are given a sequence number from 0 to $N - 1$. We used rank selection, order crossover, and order-changing mutation operators in the NSGA-II. Figure 1 shows an example of the order crossover operator. It first randomly selects two points and then swaps elements between these points and order the remainder from the beginning of the position. The crossover rate is 0.1 and mutation rate is 0.001.

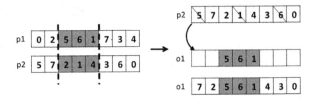

Fig. 1. An example of the order crossover

We have considered three objectives in test case prioritisation. The first one is Average Percentage of Change Coverage (APCC). APCC allows us to prioritise tests focused on the code that has been added or modified recently. To extract the code change information, we first extract the current version of Guava from the git repository and then use the "Blame" function to determine which lines have been changed. Given a line number as input, the "Blame" function returns the previous revision numbers in which if the line was added or a modified.

---

[1] https://code.google.com/p/guava-libraries/.

We mark the line as "changed" if the date of the revision returned is after the previous release of the Guava library. APCC is defined as follow:

$$APCC = (1 - \frac{TC_1 + TC_2 + \cdots + TC_M}{NM} + \frac{1}{2N}) * 100\,\% \tag{1}$$

In this formula, N is the number of test cases, M is total number of changed statements, and TC_i denotes the identifier of the test case that first covers the changed statement i in the execution sequence. A higher APCC value means the given test sequence cover more source code changed faster.

In addition to prioritising for the objective of covering changed code, we also include two more standard (and previously studied) objectives: Average Percentage of Statements Covered (APSC) and Effective Execution Time (EET) [14]. APSC has been widely used in TCP work [8], which measures the rate of average number of lines of code covered by given execution of test sequence. Effective Execution Time (EET) calculates execution time required for the test sequence to achieve 100\,% of the test objectives (so, 100\,% of either APCC, APSC or both depending on the problem formulation). Let ET_i be the execution time of test case i, and N_{length} is the number of test cases that achieve the test objectives, EET is defined as follow:

$$EET = \sum_{i=0}^{N_{length}} ET_i \tag{2}$$

3   Experiments and Results

In order to understand the impact of the newly introduced APCC metric, we have carried out three different multiple objective experiments, as set out in Table 1.

Table 1. Three groups of experiments are conducted

Group	Optimisation Objectives
G1	APSC and EET
G2	APCC and EET
G3	APSC, APCC and EET

All experiments were run on a CentOS 5.11 with 8 Intel E5426 CPU cores and 16G memory. In each experiment, there are 26,815 test cases in the optimisation sequences for 62 classes in the collection package. We manually extracted the code change information as explained in the approach section. Based on this Git analysis, we found that 140 lines have changed in the latest git commit. As Guava is quite mature and stable now and there are some latest git commits about one or two years ago, so there wasn't many major changes to the collection package.

For our search, we use the popular and widely-used NSGA-II algorithm. We experimented with three different population sizes: 100, 200, and 500, Each with a generation upper limit (termination condition) of 1000 generations. We also terminate the search if the sum value of average change in different optimisation objectives is smaller than 0.0001 in 10 consecutive generations. We compared the original sequence and average results from a set of random sequences. We generated 100,000 random sequences, from which we construct a pareto front using elite sorting based APSC, APCC and EET, repeating this process 100 times, so that 10,000,000 random test sequences are constructed in total.

The results for each of the three experiments are presented in Table 2. In Table 2, the APSC APCC and EET columns show the average best fitness value respectively over 100 runs. The Length and Time(s) show the number of selected tests to achieve maximum coverage (all statement coverage for G1 and G3 and statement coverage for G2) and execution time on average. The generation and front set columns show the average number of generations and the size of pareto front. The original row reports the results of running the default test suite where the random row shows the results using random generated sequence as a baseline. In the experiments involving random generation, the time spent (recorded in the sixth column) is that time on the fitness function calculation and elite sorting of randomly generated individuals.

The results of our experiments suggest that prioritisation can be very effective for Guava, finding test sequences that achieve coverage of both test adequacy criteria with only a tiny fraction of the budget required by the entire test suite. That is, both 100 % APCC and APSC can be achieved with 0.2 % of test cases and 0.45 % of total execution time for the entire suite. For the Guava developer this highlights the value of prioritising test cases in order to maximise early coverage of both changed and unchanged statements.

Table 2. Average value of objectives in different group of experiments

Strategy		APSC	APCC	EET(s)	Length	Time(s)	Generation	Front set
original		24.8085 %	9.1243 %	210.47	26808.00	-	-	-
random		86.1261 %	89.7498 %	188.26	24031.36	442.02	-	19.30
100	G1	99.9584 %	-	1.13	80.65	71.82	800.09	2.39
	G2	-	99.9834 %	0.39	22.94	4.06	82.40	1.24
	G3	99.9563 %	99.9900 %	1.40	111.32	71.48	721.30	4.84
200	G1	99.9674 %	-	1.03	59.02	99.65	477.70	2.78
	G2	-	99.9925 %	0.28	7.13	5.47	34.57	1.66
	G3	99.9657 %	99.9921 %	1.08	65.76	107.39	432.58	5.61
500	G1	99.9709 %	-	0.96	49.93	180.33	214.70	2.73
	G2	-	99.9927 %	0.28	7.00	12.91	31.50	1.77
	G3	99.9692 %	99.9923 %	0.94	48.15	210.27	223.69	7.43

Table 3. The $p-value$ of Mann-Whitney-Wilcoxon test and Vargha and Delaney $\widehat{A}_{12}$ between two different set of TCP experiment groups

Group	100 vs. 200		100 vs. 500		200 vs. 500	
	MWW	VDA	MWW	VDA	MWW	VDA
G1	3.24E-08	0.7263	2.71E-20	0.8778	6.10E-10	0.7533
G2	2.32E-30	0.9687	9.67E-33	0.9877	1.66E-07	0.7142
G3	1.67E-13	0.8018	1.39E-23	0.9097	7.09E-07	0.7030

Table 4. The total number of test cases in one group and intersection number between two different groups

		100			200			500			Total
		G1	G2	G3	G1	G2	G3	G1	G2	G3	
100	G1	-	430	2060	624	71	2221	489	64	571	2591
	G2		-	1008	295	59	1101	237	52	265	1260
	G3			-	1223	140	8889	823	134	945	10758
200	G1				-	65	1337	420	59	483	1486
	G2					-	142	63	30	66	167
	G3						-	859	142	995	11933
500	G1							-	49	448	935
	G2								-	49	165
	G3									-	1066

The 100, 200, 500 rows show the overall results of three experiments running with population size of 100, 200 and 500 respectively. We used the $Mann-Whitney-Wilcoxon$ test with $Bonferroni\ correction$ to check the $hypervolume$ distribution of pareto front sets in different population size and then we compare the significants between these results by using Vargha and Delaney $\widehat{A}_{12}$ effect. The results are in Table 3. In Table 3, MWW and VDA show the p-value and the $\widehat{A}_{12}$ value. The results show that the hypervolume of the pareto front generated from three different population settings has significant differences with a high effect size.

We also calculated the number of similar test cases used by the different sequences as shown in Table 4. In order to avoid double counting, we combined the test cases with the same statement coverage which reduced the number of test cases considered from 26,815 to 14,516 different test cases. In Table 4, the number on each cell denotes the number of test cases in the intersection of the two different test sequences (row and column values) considered and the last column is the total number of those test cases in the sequences. Again the results are total number over all 100 runs.

The results indicate that, as we might expect, covering all objectives (G3) is similar to covering statements with minimal execution time (G1). This is because there are relatively few changed statements, so covering all statements and all changed statements is very much similar to covering all statements; the former subsumes the latter. However, targeting the coverage of *only* the changed statements at minimal cost, yields very different test suites that either attempting statement coverage alone or both statement coverage and changed statement coverage.

In the future we will consider to include the fault information based on Guava project to verify which combine of objectives is more effective for testing the errors in Guava project. Also we need to include more objective to satisfy the requirements of industrial needed, for example, adding the mutation testing to measure the errors detection ability between test sequences or considering to give a higher the coverage value for the test sequence that can quickly coverage the most important classes in project. At last we are also considering to use GPGPU technology to accelerate the TCP process which will obviously improve the efficiency of regression testing.

4   Conclusions and Actionable Findings

In our experiments, we extended multi-objective test case prioritisation process to consider coverage of changed statements and applied it to test prioritisation for Guava's collection package. Our experiments revealed that prioritisation can dramatically reduce the size of test sequences required to achieve early coverage of changed statements (and all statements) for Guava developer. Also targeting only coverage of the changed statements yields very different test sequences to targeting coverage of all statements.

References

1. Yoo, S., Harman, M.: Regression testing minimization, selection and prioritisation: a survey. Softw. Test. Verification Reliab. **22**(2), 67–120 (2012)
2. Rothermel, G., Untch, R.H., Chu, C., Harrold, M.J.: Prioritizing test cases for regression testing. IEEE Trans. Softw. Eng. **27**(10), 929–948 (2001)
3. Huang, P., Ma, X., Shen, D., Zhou, Y.: Performance regression testing target prioritisation via performance risk analysis. In: Proceedings of the 36th International Conference on Software Engineering, pp. 60–71. ACM, May 2014
4. Guava Project Web Site. https://github.com/google/guava
5. http://blog.takipi.com/google-guava-5-things-you-never-knew-it-can-do/
6. Jiang, B., Chan, W.K.: On the integration of test adequacy, test case prioritisation, and statistical fault localization. In: 2010 10th International Conference on Quality Software (QSIC), pp. 377–384. IEEE (2010)
7. Elbaum, S., Malishevsky, A.G., Rothermel, G.: Test case prioritisation: a family of empirical studies. IEEE Trans. Softw. Eng. **28**(2), 159–182 (2002)
8. Li, Z., Harman, M., Hierons, R.M.: Search algorithms for regression test case prioritisation. IEEE Trans. Softw. Eng. **33**(4), 225–237 (2007)

9. Yoo, S., Harman, M.: Pareto efficient multi-objective test case selection. In: Proceedings of the 2007 International Symposium on Software Testing and Analysis, pp. 140–150. ACM (2007)
10. Deb, K., Pratap, A., Agarwal, S., et al.: A fast and elitist multiobjective genetic algorithm: NSGA-II. IEEE Trans. Evol. Comput. **6**(2), 182–197 (2002)
11. Harman, M.: Making the case for MORTO: multi objective regression test optimization. In: ICST Workshops, pp. 111–114 (2011)
12. Sun, W., Gao, Z., Yang, W., et al.: Multi-objective test case prioritization for GUI applications. In: Proceedings of the 28th Annual ACM Symposium on Applied Computing. pp. 1074–1079. ACM (2013)
13. Snchez, A.B., Segura, S., Ruiz-Corts, A.A.: Comparison of test case prioritization criteria for software product lines. In: 2014 IEEE Seventh International Conference on Software Testing, Verification and Validation (ICST), pp. 41–50. IEEE (2014)
14. Li, Z., Bian, Y., Zhao, R., Cheng, J.: A fine-grained parallel multi-objective test case prioritization on GPU. In: Ruhe, G., Zhang, Y. (eds.) SSBSE 2013. LNCS, vol. 8084, pp. 111–125. Springer, Heidelberg (2013)
15. Epitropakis, M.G., Yoo, S., Harman, M., Burke, E.K.: Empirical evaluation of pareto efficient multi-objective regression test case prioritisation. In: Proceedings of the 2015 International Symposium on Software Testing and Analysis, pp. 234–245. ACM (2015)

Continuous Test Generation on Guava

José Campos[1](✉), Gordon Fraser[1], Andrea Arcuri[2,3], and Rui Abreu[4,5]

[1] Department of Computer Science, The University of Sheffield, Sheffield, UK
{jose.campos,gordon.fraser}@sheffield.ac.uk
[2] Scienta, Oslo, Norway
[3] University of Luxembourg, Luxembourg City, Luxembourg
aa@scienta.no
[4] PARC, Palo Alto, USA
[5] University of Porto, Porto, Portugal
rui@computer.org

Abstract. Search-based testing can be applied to automatically generate unit tests that achieve high levels of code coverage on object-oriented classes. However, test generation takes time, in particular if projects consist of many classes, like in the case of the Guava library. To allow search-based test generation to scale up and to integrate it better into software development, *continuous test generation* applies test generation incrementally during continuous integration. In this paper, we report on the application of continuous test generation with EvoSuite at the SSBSE'15 challenge on the Guava library. Our results show that continuous test generation reduces the time spent on automated test generation by 96 %, while increasing code coverage by 13.9 % on average.

Keywords: Search-based testing · Automated unit test generation · Continuous integration · Continuous test generation

1 Introduction

To support software testers and developers, tests can be generated automatically using various techniques. Search-based testing is well suited for the task of generating unit tests for object-oriented classes, where a test typically consists of a sequence of method calls. Although search-based unit test generation tools have been successfully applied to large projects [4], performance is not one of the strengths of search-based test generation: Every fitness evaluation requires costly test execution. For example, we found that our EvoSuite [2] search-based unit test suite generator requires somewhere around 2 minutes of search time to achieve a decent level of coverage on most classes, and more time for the search to converge. While 2 minutes may not sound particularly time consuming, it is far from the instantaneous result developers might expect while writing code. Even worse, a typical software project has more than one class — for example, Guava version 18 has more than 300 classes, and consequently generating tests for 2 minutes per class would take more than 10 h.

© Springer International Publishing Switzerland 2015
M. Barros and Y. Labiche (Eds.): SSBSE 2015, LNCS 9275, pp. 228–234, 2015.
DOI: 10.1007/978-3-319-22183-0_16

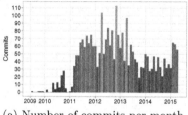

(a) Number of commits per month.

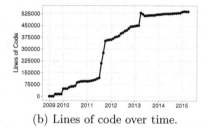

(b) Lines of code over time.

Fig. 1. Activity of the Guava library based on the Git log.

In practice, however, generating tests for an entire software project of this size may not be required frequently. Instead, software projects evolve and grow over size. For example, Fig. 1a shows that the Guava library is actively developed, with many commits per month. However, not every class is changed every day, and the software takes time to grow (Fig. 1b). An opportunity to exploit this incremental nature of software is offered by the regular build and test phases applied every day as part of continuous integration. *Continuous test generation* [1] is the synergy of automated test generation with continuous integration: Tests are generated during every nightly build, but resources are focused on the most important classes, and test suites are built incrementally over time. CTG supports the application of *test suite augmentation* [7,8], but importantly addresses the time-budget allocation problem of individual classes, is not tied to an individual coverage criterion, and is applicable for incremental test generation, even if the system under test did not change. In this paper, as part of the SSBSE'15 challenge, we describe the application of continuous test generation on the Guava library.

2   Continuous Test Generation (CTG)

Experimentation on automated test generation typically (e.g., [4]) consists of applying a tool to an entire software project, and to allocate the same amount of time to every artifact (e.g., class under test). In practice, even if one would restrict this test generation to code that has been changed since the last time of test generation, the computational effort (e.g., CPU time and memory used) to generate tests may exceed what developers are prepared to use their own computers for while they are working on them. However, integration and testing is often performed on remote continuous integration systems — these continuous integration systems are well suited to host continuous test generation.

Continuous integration is often invoked on every commit to a source code repository, or for nightly builds which test all the changes performed since the last nightly build. Applying test generation during continuous integration creates a scheduling problem: Which classes should be tested, and how much time should be spent on each class? For example, in order to distinguish trivial classes from more complex classes, EVOSUITE uses the number of branches in the class to allocate a time budget proportional to the size of a class. The choice of which class to test can be based on change information: First, as new or modified code is more likely to be faulty [6], EVOSUITE prioritises changed classes, and allocates more time to them. Second, EVOSUITE monitors the coverage progress of each class: As long as invoking EVOSUITE leads to increased coverage, it is invoked even if the class has not been changed. However, once EVOSUITE can no longer increase coverage, we can assume that all feasible goals have been covered and stop the invocation of the tool on those classes.

As a further optimisation, we exploit the fact that a test generation tool may be repeatedly applied to the same classes, with or without changes. Instead of initialising the initial population of the genetic algorithm in EVOSUITE completely randomly, we can include the previous version of the test suite as one individual of the initial population of the genetic algorithm.

To assess the effectiveness of CTG, we consider the following scenario: CTG is invoked after every commit to the source code repository as part of continuous integration. To simulate this scenario, we selected all compiled Git commits to the Guava project between version 17 and 18. In total 126 (out of 148) different versions of Guava have been selected. This represents 45,025 classes in total, and an average of 357 classes per version. We configured CTG with an amount of time proportional to the number of classes in each project, i.e., one minute per class under test. We compare two configurations of CTG: The baseline configuration (*Simple*) tests each class for one minute for every invocation. The advanced configuration (*History*) allocates budget based on change and coverage history, and reuses past results. We repeated each experiment five times (more repetitions were not possible due to the computational costs of the experiment).

In the first commit, the number of classes tested by both configuration is the same, and thus so is the time spent on test generation (Fig. 2b) and the achieved coverage (Fig. 2a). Between commits 1 and 11, only nine classes have been changed which allowed the History strategy to reduce the time spent on test generation from 253 minutes (at first commit) to 8 minutes (at commit

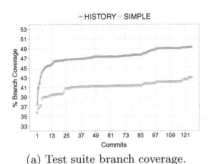
(a) Test suite branch coverage.

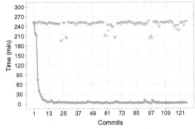
(b) Time spent on test generation.

Fig. 2. Branch coverage, and time spent on test generation for the Guava open source case study over the course of 126 commits. For each commit we report the average branch coverage over all classes and over the five runs for "History", and "Simple" strategies.

number 11). During the same time the coverage increased from 0.37 to 0.46, while during the same period the Simple strategy just increased coverage from 0.35 to 0.39 on average, spending on average 250 minutes per commit. After 126 commits, History achieved 49 % branch coverage on average, having spent a total of 1,333 minutes on test generation. On the other hand, Simple just achieved 43 % coverage with 30,937 minutes spent on test generation. This means that History achieved a relative improvement of +13.9 % in branch coverage within −95.7 % of Simple's time.

3   Guava's Challenges

Although the previous section showed that a CTG strategy based on *History* is able to achieve more coverage than a *Simple* strategy, even after 126 commits EvoSuite only covered 49 % of the total number of branches. In this section we discuss the challenges of testing the Guava project. Figure 3 visualises the coverage achieved by EvoSuite after 10 minutes of test generation (averaged over 30 runs) in a tree-map, where the size of a box is proportional to the number of branch coverage goals in that class, and the colour represents the coverage achieved. EvoSuite identified 359 testable (i.e., top-level public classes) out of 468 source files. In total there are 1,692 classes including member classes, anonymous classes, but the latter are tested as part of their containing classes. Overall, there seems to be a large number of classes with high coverage, and some classes where EvoSuite failed to achieve any substantial coverage.

Figure 3 contains two noticeable problematic classes, `MapMakerInternalMap` and `LocalCache`, which both have around no coverage, but represent a large share of the area in the figure. `MapMakerInternalMap` consists of only six methods which all simply return a Boolean value, but also has a complex constructor that receives a `MapMaker` instance, and a total of 52 internal classes (including interfaces, abstract classes, and enum classes). As EvoSuite considers all methods of inner classes as target methods equal to the methods of the main class under test, most of the time is spent on trying to instantiate these inner classes. However, these classes all have several generic type parameters, and EvoSuite struggles to efficiently resolve these[1]. A further problem for `MapMakerInternalMap` lies in the constructor, as the top right hand corner of Fig. 3 shows that EvoSuite struggles to cover `MapMaker` for similar reasons, and so it rarely manages to instantiate a valid instance to pass into the `MapMakerInternalMap` constructor; even if it does, this needs to satisfy many constraints before the entire constructor executes without exception. The `LocalCache` class similarly has a complex constructor that requires complex dependencies with generic types, and many inner classes with further generic type parameters. Clearly, adding a more sophisticated generic type system or treating inner classes separately would lead to higher coverage.

---

[1] Note that Java would allow ignoring these type parameters, but we argue that this would severely degrade the usefulness of the generated tests to developers, and might miss important coverage scenarios [5].

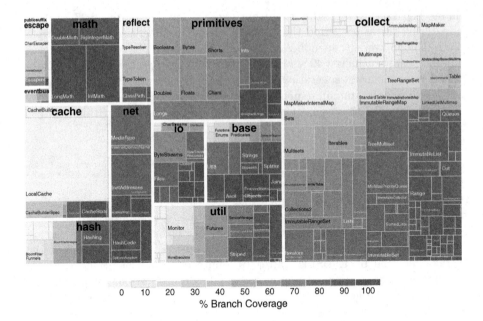

Fig. 3. Branch coverage for the Guava version 18. The area of each box is proportional to the number of branches in each class, and the colour represents the coverage achieved in 10 minutes, averaged over 30 repetitions.

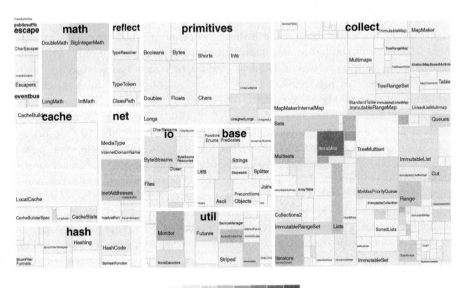

Fig. 4. Number of undeclared thrown exceptions for the Guava version 18. (Results are based on 30 repetitions).

Beside achieving a certain degree of code coverage, EvoSuite can also find faults in the system under test [3]. Typical examples are methods crashing by throwing unexpected exceptions. Even in the case of Guava, many potential faults were found, as shown in Fig. 4. For example, there are 14 distinct exceptions in class `Iterables` alone. However, a closer look at some of these exceptions show that those were expected, although not declared in the signature (e.g., with the `throws` keyword) of those methods. Java does not enforce to declare expected unchecked exceptions (e.g., input validation) in the signatures, although those are very important for a library to understand its behaviour in case of wrong inputs. To complicate the matter even further, a developer might mention the expected exceptions (e.g., a `NullPointerException` if an input parameter is null) only in the JavaDocs, using the tag `@Throws`. However, JavaDocs do not become part of the compiled bytecode. Therefore, if a developer fails to write proper method declarations, an automated testing tool cannot distinguish between real, critical faults and expected failing input validations.

4   Conclusions

In this paper, we have presented the results of applying EvoSuite on the *Guava* library. Using a continuous test generation approach reduces the amount of time spent on test generation dramatically, while leading to overall higher coverage. On the majority of classes, EvoSuite achieves a substantial degree of coverage, but a closer look revealed problems with generic types and inner classes, which pose new research and engineering challenges to be faced in the future. To learn more about EvoSuite, visit our Web site at: http://www.evosuite.org/.

Acknowledgments. This work is supported by the EPSRC project "EXOGEN" (EP/K030353/1) and by the National Research Fund, Luxembourg (FNR/P10/03).

References

1. Campos, J., Arcuri, A., Fraser, G., Abreu, R.: Continuous test generation: enhancing continuous integration with automated test generation. In: IEEE/ACM International Conference on Automated Software Engineering (ASE), ASE 2014. pp. 55–66. ACM, New York (2014)
2. Fraser, G., Arcuri, A.: EvoSuite: automatic test suite generation for object-oriented software. In: ACM SIGSOFT European Software Engineering Conference and the ACM SIGSOFT Symposium on the Foundations of Software Engineering (ESEC/FSE), ESEC/FSE 2011, pp. 416–419. ACM, New York (2011)
3. Fraser, G., Arcuri, A.: 1600 faults in 100 projects: automatically finding faults while achieving high coverage with EvoSuite. Empirical Softw. Eng. (EMSE) **20**(3), 611–639 (2013)
4. Fraser, G., Arcuri, A.: A large-scale evaluation of automated unit test generation using EvoSuite. ACM Trans. Softw. Eng. Methodol. (TOSEM) **24**(2), 8:1–8:42 (2014)

5. Fraser, G., Arcuri, A.: Automated test generation for java generics. In: Winkler, D., Biffl, S., Bergsmann, J. (eds.) SWQD 2014. LNBIP, vol. 166, pp. 185–198. Springer, Heidelberg (2014)
6. Graves, T.L., Karr, A.F., Marron, J.S., Siy, H.: Predicting fault incidence using software change history. IEEE Trans. Softw. Eng. (TSE) 26(7), 653–661 (2000)
7. Santelices, R., Chittimalli, P.K., Apiwattanapong, T., Orso, A., Harrold, M.J.: Test-suite augmentation for evolving software. In: IEEE/ACM International Conference on Automated Software Engineering (ASE), ASE 2008, pp. 218–227. IEEE Computer Society, Washington, DC (2008)
8. Xu, Z., Kim, Y., Kim, M., Rothermel, G., Cohen, M.B.: Directed test suite augmentation: techniques and tradeoffs. In: ACM SIGSOFT Symposium on the Foundations of Software Engineering (FSE), FSE 2010, pp. 257–266. ACM, New York (2010)

Generating Readable Unit Tests for Guava

Ermira Daka[1], José Campos[1(⊠)], Jonathan Dorn[2], Gordon Fraser[1],
and Westley Weimer[2]

[1] Department of Computer Science, The University of Sheffield, Sheffield, UK
`jose.campos@sheffield.ac.uk`
[2] University of Virginia, Charlottesville, Virginia, USA

Abstract. Unit tests for object-oriented classes can be generated automatically using search-based testing techniques. As the search algorithms are typically guided by structural coverage criteria, the resulting unit tests are often long and confusing, with possible negative implications for developer adoption of such test generation tools, and the difficulty of the test oracle problem and test maintenance. To counter this problem, we integrate a further optimization target based on a model of test readability learned from human annotation data. We demonstrate on a selection of classes from the Guava library how this approach produces more readable unit tests without loss of coverage.

Keywords: Readability · Unit testing · Automated test generation

1 Introduction

Search-based testing can support developers by generating unit tests for object-oriented classes automatically. Developers need to read these generated tests to provide test oracles, or when investigating test failures. These are difficult manual tasks, which are influenced by the representation of the tests. For example, consider the unit tests generated by EVOSUITE [4] shown in Fig. 1. Both test cases cover the method `listeningDecorator` in class `MoreExecutors` taken from the Guava library, but they are quite different in presentation. Which of the two would developers prefer to see — i.e., which one of the two is more *readable*?

An automated unit test generation tool would typically ignore this question, as most tools are driven by structural criteria (e.g., branch coverage). To overcome this issue, we introduced [2] a *unit test readability model* that quantifies the readability of a unit test. The model is learned from human annotation data, and is integrated into the search-based EVOSUITE unit test generation tool, in order to guide it to generate more readable tests. For example, even though the first test in Fig. 1 is longer, it is deemed less readable as it has very long lines and more identifiers. In this paper, we demonstrate readability optimized unit test generation using the Guava library.

M. Barros and Y. Labiche (Eds.): SSBSE 2015, LNCS 9275, pp. 235–241, 2015.
DOI: 10.1007/978-3-319-22183-0_17

```
Executor executor0 = MoreExecutors.directExecutor();
int int0 = 0;
ScheduledThreadPoolExecutor scheduledThreadPoolExecutor0 = new
    ScheduledThreadPoolExecutor(int0);
int int1 = 0;
ScheduledExecutorService scheduledExecutorService0 =
    MoreExecutors.getExitingScheduledExecutorService(scheduledThreadPoolExecutor0);
ListeningExecutorService listeningExecutorService0 =
    MoreExecutors.listeningDecorator((ExecutorService) scheduledThreadPoolExecutor0);
```

```
// Undeclared exception!
try {
  ListeningExecutorService listeningExecutorService0 =
      MoreExecutors.listeningDecorator((ExecutorService) null);
  fail("Expecting exception: NullPointerException");

} catch(NullPointerException e) {
  //
  // no message in exception (getMessage() returned null)
  //
}
```

Fig. 1. Two versions of a test that exercise the same functionality in the Guava class `MoreExecutors`, but have a different appearance and readability.

2   Measuring Unit Test Readability

Because readability relates to human subjective experience, machine learning has previously been applied to learn models of readability from user annotations of code snippets. A classifier of code readability was learned by Buse and Weimer [1], and later refined by Posnett et al. [5], by mapping each code snippet to a set of syntactic features and then using machine learning on the feature vectors and user annotation.

In principle these code readability models also apply to unit tests, which are essentially small programs. However, the features of unit tests can differ substantially from regular code. For example, complex control flow is less common for unit tests (in particular automatically-generated ones). Furthermore, the classifiers used in previous work are not sufficient to guide test generation — for this we needed a regression (numeric value predictive) model.

To generate such a model, we collected [2] 15,669 human judgments of readability (in a range of 1–5) on 450 unit test cases using Amazon Mechanical Turk[1]. Participants were required to pass a Java qualification test to ensure familiarity with the language. The unit tests underlying this study were collected from manually-written and automatically-generated tests for several open source Java projects (Apache commons, poi, trove, jfreechart, joda, jdom, itext and guava). We defined a set of 116 initial syntactic features of unit tests, and through feature selection ultimately learned a formal model based on 24 features, including line width, aspects of the identifiers, and byte entropy. The model's ratings are predictive of human annotator judgments of test case readability.

---

[1] http://aws.amazon.com/mturk/.

For a given unit test we can extract a vector of values for these features, which allows the application of machine learning techniques. The model is trained on the feature vectors together with the user ratings, and when used for prediction the model produces a readability rating for a given feature vector.

3   Generating Readability Optimized Tests

EVOSUITE [4] uses a genetic algorithm to evolve individual unit tests or sets of unit tests, typically with the aim to maximize code coverage of a chosen test criterion. Over the time, we have collected ample anecdotal evidence of aspects developers disliked about the automatically-generated tests, and EVOSUITE now by default applies a range of different optimizations to the tests generated by the genetic algorithm. For example, redundant statements in the sequences of statements are removed, numerical and string values are minimized, unnecessary variables are removed, etc. However, the readability of a test may be an effect of the particular choice of parameters and calls, such that only generating a completely different test, rather than optimizing an existing one, would maximize readability.

To integrate the unit test readability model into EVOSUITE, we explored the following approaches: (1) As code coverage remains a primary objective for the test generation, the readability model can be integrated as a secondary objective. If two individuals of the population have the same fitness value, during rank selection the one with the better readability value is preferred. (2) Because readability and code coverage may be conflicting goals (e.g., adding a statement may improve coverage, but decrease readability), classical multi-objective algorithms (e.g., NSGA-II [3]) can be used with coverage and readability as independent objectives.

However, EVOSUITE's post-processing steps may complicate initial readability judgments: An individual that seems unreadable may become more readable through the post-processing (and vice-versa). Therefore, we consider the following solutions: (1) Measure the readability of tests not on the search individuals, but on the result of the post-processing steps. That is, the fitness value is measured in the style of Baldwinian optimization [6] on the improved phenotype, without changing the genotype. This can be applied to the scenario of a secondary objective as well as to multi-objective optimization. (2) Optimize readability as another post-processing step, using an algorithm that generates alternative candidates and ranks them by readability [2].

4   Generating Readable Tests for Guava

To study these approaches for readability optimization in detail, we selected five classes from Guava randomly, and generated tests as described in the previous section. Figure 2 summarizes the overall results (over 5 runs) in terms of the modeled readability scores for these five different classes with and without

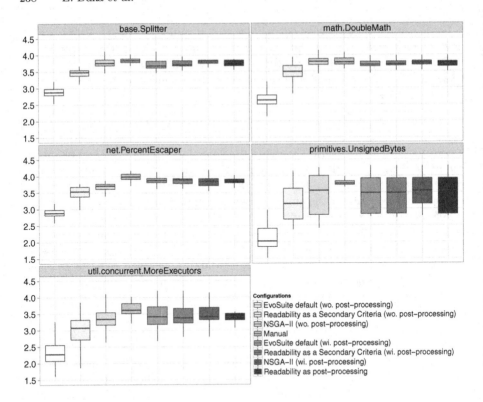

Fig. 2. Readability scores of manually-written and automatically-generated test cases in 7 different configurations.

optimization with both post-processing and no post-processing techniques. Furthermore, the readability values of the manually-written tests for these classes are included for reference.

The first three boxes of each plot show substantial improvement over the default configuration by including the readability model as a secondary objective or as a second fitness function. In all five classes, the multi-objective optimization achieves the most readable tests. However, note that without post-processing, these tests do not yet have assertions (which according to the model have a negative effect on readability). Despite this, in all five classes the average readability of the manually written tests (fourth box) is slightly higher.

Boxes 5–7 show a similar pattern when applying EvoSuite's post-processing steps. However, we can see the large effects EvoSuite's many post-processing steps have, as the generated tests approach the readability of manual tests. For Splitter and DoubleMath the improvement over the default is significant at $\alpha = 0.05$ (calculated by using Wilcoxon test), on UnsignedBytes and MoreExecutors there is an improvement although not significant. On PercentEscaper there is no significant difference. The final box shows the results of a post-processing step driven by the readablity model, which is generally slightly below NSGA-II, but on the other hand is computationally much cheaper. We note that using the readability model in a post-processing step is generally on par with the multi-objective optimization.

These results demonstrate that our search-based approach can produce test cases that are competitive with manual tests in terms of modeled readability.

4.1   User Agreement

To validate whether users agree with these optimizations, we selected 50 pairs of test cases for the selected 5 classes, where the tests in each pair cover the same coverage objective, and each pair consists of one test generated using EVOSUITE's default configuration, whereas the other one is optimized. Half of the pairs were selected from the configurations that do use post-processing, and half from the configurations that do not. We used Amazon Mechanical Turk to run a forced-choice survey, showing a random subset of pairs to each participant. As when building the model, participants were required to pass a Java qualification test.

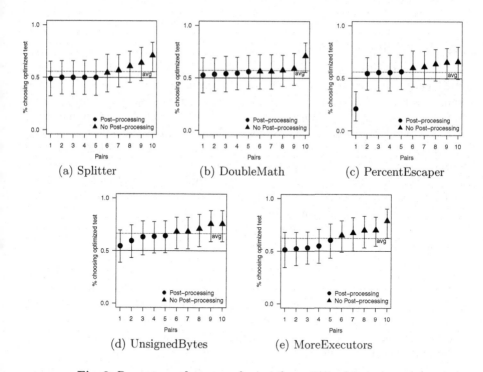

(a) Splitter   (b) DoubleMath   (c) PercentEscaper

(d) UnsignedBytes   (e) MoreExecutors

Fig. 3. Percentage of users preferring the optimized test cases

Figure 3 summarizes the 2,250 responses we received from 79 different participants. The error bars indicate the 95 % confidence interval around the rate at which the participants preferred the optimized test. Overall, the participants preferred the optimized test 59 % of the time ($p < 0.01$ calculated with Fleiss' kappa test). In four of the classes (`Splitter`, `DoubleMath`, `UnsignedBytes`, and `MoreExecutors`) we can see this preference at the level of individual tests. For example, we have 95 % confidence that participants preferred the `UnsignedBytes` tests generated without post-processing at a rate higher than random chance. For pairs generated without post-processing the preference is generally clearer than for those with post-processing, where for these classes the difference in readability is generally small.

Notably, there is one pair of tests for class `PercentEscaper` where the users preferred the default version to the one optimized using the readability model. The model predicts that the shorter, optimized test is preferable to the longer test produced by EvoSuite's default configuration, which contains an exception. However, this exception has a clear and easily to interpret message shown in a comment in the test, which the users seem to count as readable — which is not something a syntactic readability model could do.

Although human preference for our tests is modest, it is present, and our readability improvements are orthogonal to the structural coverage of the generated test suite.

4.2   Test Suite Generation

To see how results generalize, we generated test suites for all 359 top-level, public classes in Guava. Because the use of post-processing steps during fitness evaluation has high computational costs, we applied the readability optimization as a post-processing step, and compare the result to the default configuration with the regular post-processing steps. Calculated after 20 repetitions, there are 235 out of the 359 classes where the optimization leads to higher average readability values, and 162 cases are significant at $\alpha = 0.05$; there are 38 classes where readability is worse, with 8 of them being significant. On average, the readability score (averaged over all tests in a test suite) is increased by 0.14 ($\hat{A}_{12} = 0.76$), without affecting code coverage.

5   Conclusions

While there has been significant research interest in test input generation in general and test case generation in particular, the readability of the resulting tests is rarely considered. Anecdotal evidence suggests that readability is a factor in the adoption of automatically-generated tests. We evaluate multiple approaches to incorporate a learned model of test readability, based on human annotations, into a test suite generation algorithm. We find that post processing approaches are competitive with more expensive search strategies. We can produce test suites that are equally powerful with respect to structural coverage metrics but are more readable. In a modest but statistically significant manner, humans prefer our readability-optimized test cases.

Acknowledgment. Supported by EPSRC project EP/K030353/1 (EXOGEN).

References

1. Buse, R.P., Weimer, W.R.: A metric for software readability. In: Proceedings of the 2008 International Symposium on Software Testing and Analysis, ISSTA 2008, pp. 121–130. ACM, New York, NY, USA (2008)
2. Daka, E., Campos, J., Fraser, G., Dorn, J., Weimer, W.: Modeling readability to improve unit tests. In: European Software Engineering Conference and ACM SIG-SOFT Symposium on the Foundations of Software Engineering, ESEC/FSE 2015 (2015)
3. Deb, K., Pratap, A., Agarwal, S., Meyarivan, T.: A fast and elitist multiobjective genetic algorithm: NSGA-II. Trans. Evol. Comp 6(2), 182–197 (2002)
4. Fraser, G., Arcuri, A.: EvoSuite: automatic test suite generation for object-oriented software. In: European Conference on Foundations of Software Engineering (ESEC/FSE), pp. 416–419 (2011)
5. Posnett, D., Hindle, A., Devanbu, P.: A simpler model of software readability. In: Working Conference on Mining Software Repositories (MSR), pp. 73–82 (2011)
6. Whitley, D., Gordon, V.S., Mathias, K.: Lamarckian evolution, the Baldwin effect and function optimization. In: Davidor, Y., Männer, R., Schwefel, H.-P. (eds.) PPSN 1994. LNCS, vol. 866. Springer, Heidelberg (1994)

Testing Django Configurations Using Combinatorial Interaction Testing

Justyna Petke[(⊠)]

CREST Centre, University College London, London, UK
j.petke@ucl.ac.uk

Abstract. Combinatorial Interaction Testing (CIT) is important
because it tests the interactions between the many parameters that make
up the configuration space of software systems. We apply this testing
paradigm to a Python-based framework for rapid development of web-
based applications called Django. In particular, we automatically create
a CIT model for Django website configurations and run a state-of-the-art
tool for CIT test suite generation to obtain sets of test configurations.
Our automatic CIT-based approach is able to efficiently detect invalid
configurations.

1 Introduction

Software testing is a challenging and highly important task. It is widely believed
that half the costs of software projects are spent on testing. Search-based software engineering (SBSE) techniques have also been successfully applied to the
problem [6]. Moreover, over half of the literature on the whole field of SBSE is
concerned with testing [7]. In order to apply an automated test method to the
problem at hand, one might require information about the inner workings of the
system to be tested. Such white-box testing techniques [3,8,11,16,17] generate
test suites that systematically exercise the program, for instance, to cover all
program branches. These, however, require knowledge of inner workings of the
system under test, setup could take significant amount of time, while resultant
test suite might not be better than the one generated manually [4].

The vast majority of software systems can be configured by setting some
top-level parameters. For checking system behaviour under the different settings,
knowledge of the inner workings of such systems is not necessarily required. This
is a situation where black-box testing methods, such as Combinatorial Interaction Testing (CIT), come in handy. The aim of an automated technique for
software configurations is to generate a test suite that exercises various system
settings. Testing all possible combinations of parameters is infeasible in practice.
There exist, for instance, a model for the Linux kernel that contains over 6000
features that can be set[1]. Even if all these took Boolean values, 2^{6000} configurations would have had to be generated in order to test them all. In order to

---

[1] Linux kernel feature model is available at: https://code.google.com/p/linux-
variability-analysis-tools/source/browse/2.6.28.6-icse11.dimacs?repo=formulas.

© Springer International Publishing Switzerland 2015
M. Barros and Y. Labiche (Eds.): SSBSE 2015, LNCS 9275, pp. 242–247, 2015.
DOI: 10.1007/978-3-319-22183-0_18

avoid this combinatorial explosion problem, techniques such as CIT have been introduced.

Combinatorial Interaction Testing (CIT) aims to test a subset of configurations, yet preserve high fault detection rate when compared with a set of all possible parameter combinations. It is a light-weight black-box testing technique that allows for efficient and effective automated test configuration generation [12]. Several studies have shown that CIT test suites are able to discover all the known interaction faults of the system under test [1,10,15,18]. Hence, we have chosen this method to test Django, a very popular Python-based framework for rapid development of web-based applications.

Django[2] was designed to help developers create database-driven websites as quickly as possible. Among popular sites using it are: Instagram, Mozilla and The Washington Times. Django is written in Python and comes with its own set of unit tests. A global settings file is also provided and contains parameters that can be configured in any Django-based web application. The set of values for some of the Django settings is potentially infinite, since they admit strings. We have thus concentrated on Boolean parameters only. We used CIT to test the various combinations of Django's Boolean settings available and discovered several invalid configurations.

2   Background

Combinatorial interaction testing (CIT) has been used successfully as a system level test method [1,2,9,10,14,15,18]. CIT combines all t-combinations of parameter inputs or configuration options in a systematic way so that we know we have tested a measured subset of the input or configuration space. A CIT test suite is usually represented as a covering array (CA): $CA(N; t, v_1^{k_1} v_2^{k_2} ... v_m^{k_m})$, where N is the size of the array, t is its strength, sum of $k_1, ..., k_m$ is the number of parameters and each v_i stands for the number of values for each of the k_i parameters.

Suppose we want to generate a pairwise interaction test suite for an instance with 3 parameters, where the first parameter can take 4 values, the second one can only take 3 values and the third parameter can take 5 values. Then the problem can be formulated as: $CA(N; 2, 4^1 3^1 5^1)$. Furthermore, in order to test all combinations one would need $4 * 3 * 5 = 60$ test cases. If, however, we cover all interactions between any two parameters, then we only need 20 test cases. Such a test suite is called a 2-way or pairwise test suite.

There are several approaches for covering array generation. The two most popular ones use either simulated-annealing (SA) or a greedy algorithm. The SA-based approach is believed to produce smaller test suites, while the greedy one is regarded to be faster [5]. A state-of-the-art CIT tool that implements an SA-based algorithm is Covering Arrays by Simulated Annealing (CASA)[3]. It is relatively mature in the CIT area, so we chose it for our experiments.

---

[2] Django is available at: https://www.djangoproject.com/.
[3] CASA is available at: http://cse.unl.edu/~citportal/.

3 Setup

In order to generate a CIT test suite for Django, we need to first find the parameters that we can configure. The source distribution of Django comes with a top-level settings file called GLOBAL_SETTINGS.PY, an extract of which is shown in Fig. 1. There are 137 parameters defined. In order to ease tester effort we only consider Boolean ones. Otherwise, we would have to inspect each non-Boolean parameter to identify which values are allowed (theoretically each parameter of type *string* can take infinitely many values). This can be done as a future step.

```
# Whether a user's session cookie expires when the Web browser is closed.
SESSION_EXPIRE_AT_BROWSER_CLOSE = False
# The module to store session data
SESSION_ENGINE = 'django.contrib.sessions.backends.db'
```

Fig. 1. An extract from Django's GLOBAL_SETTINGS.PY file.

We construct a CIT model for GLOBAL_SETTINGS.PY automatically by counting the number of Boolean parameters. There are 23 such parameters. Hence the CIT model is: $CA(t; 2^{23})$. We produce test configurations for $t = 2$ and $t = 3$ using the CASA tool, that is, we produce a pairwise test suites and a test suite that covers all value combinations between any three parameters. Higher-strength CIT is feasible [13], however, pairwise testing is the most popular both in the literature as well as in the industry. 3-way testing is not as frequently used and there are only few studies focusing on higher-strength CIT[4].

Next, we automatically construct multiple copies of the SETTING.PY file based on the CIT test configurations that will be substituted in turn with the default settings file that is created whenever a Django project is started. We first ran the unit test suite to check if all tests pass. We do not know whether these exercise all possible Django configurations. Next, we evaluate each CIT test case by first running the Django development server. Afterwards we re-run the tests and invoked two websites: 'Welcome to Django' page and the 'polls' website, which is the default website used in Django tutorials[5]. We chose these two webpages since they are the most basic ones and hence any fault-triggering test case for these will likely produce a fault for more complex webpages. We use MacBook Air with 1.7 GHz Intel Core i7 processor and 8 GB of RAM.

We emphasise that each step is automated (except for voting which could be automated as well): from parameter extraction through model generation and test case generation to actual testing of the system. Therefore, the whole process could potentially be applied to any other configurable software system, without knowledge of the inner workings of such a system.

---

[4] This is partially due to the fact that the higher interaction strength t is required, the larger the number of test cases that need to be generated. Pairwise testing is believed to be good enough, especially since several empirical studies have shown that 6-way testing can discover all the known faults [10].

[5] Django tutorials are available at: https://www.djangoproject.com/.

4   Results

The source distribution of Django comes with its own test suite. It is composed of unit tests that perform 9242 checks on the MacBook Air laptop used. Thus, we first ran the existing test suite to check if all of them pass. It is possible that some of these test various Django configurations, but we have not investigated this. The original test suite did not reveal any faults.

The CASA tool, which uses simulated-annealing, produced 8 test configurations that cover all pairwise interactions between the 23 parameters extracted from GLOBAL_SETTINGS.PY settings file in less than a second. 2^{23} tests would have been needed to test all possible combinations of parameter settings. 3-way test suite was created within 42 sec. The CIT test suites generated are the smallest possible for the chosen criteria[6]. We have created the default project, as presented in part 1 of Django's 'Writing your first Django app' tutorial, and substituted the SETTINGS.PY file with the automatically generated variants in turn. In 4 out of 8 configurations, from the pairwise test suite, an error occurred. An explanation, however, was provided by Django as shown in Fig. 2.

```
Django version 1.9.dev20150502163522, using settings 'mysite.settings'
Starting development server at http://127.0.0.1:8000/
Quit the server with CONTROL-C.
CommandError: You must set settings.ALLOWED_HOSTS if DEBUG is False.
```

Fig. 2. An error caught by Django.

Before moving forward, we have added a constraint to the CIT model that the parameter 'ALLOWED_HOSTS' must be set to '['127.0.0.1', 'localhost']' if the 'DEBUG' parameter is False. We re-generated and re-run the tests and they all passed. Next, we invoked the 'Welcome Page' after starting the server for each of the different test setting configurations generated using CASA. We repeated the experiment with the 'polls' website described in the Django tutorial. If the voting page opened properly, we also posted a vote. Since our results were similar for both 'Welcome Page' and 'polls' websites, we report only those for the 'polls' website. We mention differences where applicable.

Our experiments revealed that most of the combinations of configuration values were invalid. For the pairwise test suite 6 out of the 8 test configurations did not allow for the 'polls' webpage to be invoked. In particular, in 4 cases HTTP error 301 was thrown and the website did not load within pre-specified amount of time (10 s). In 2 cases security HTTP error 400 was thrown with the following message: 'You're accessing the development server over HTTPS, but it only supports HTTP'.

The 3-way test suite for the 'polls' website consisted of 23 test cases. 4 runs produced correct results; 11 produced HTTP error 301 and timed-out; and security HTTP error 400 was observed 6 times. Additionally, two configurations

---

[6] The smallest known test suite sizes for various CIT models are available at: http://www.public.asu.edu/~ccolbou/src/tabby/catable.html.

triggered an error that only occurred when invoking the 'polls' webpage, but not the 'Welcome to Django' one. It was triggered by pressing the voting button, causing redirection to 'Forbidden page' and throwing HTTP error 403.

We tried to find the minimal configurations causing each type of error. We first extracted configurations that were set to the same values in all the settings files causing the same type of error. We then compared these against the default settings to find changes. In the case of the HTTP 301 error, there was only one line that all the relevant settings files had in common, namely 'PREPEND_WWW = True', which was set to 'False' in the default settings file. We checked that indeed it was the cause of the HTTP 301 error. Moreover, we found a post online from a user of Django, who had encountered the same problem. It took him 5 days to figure out the root cause of this error manually. Using the same approach, we found that the security HTTP error 400 was caused by 'SECURE_SSL_REDIRECT = True' and 'Forbidden page' HTTP 403 errors were caused by 'CSRF_COOKIE_SECURE = True'. This is not to say that the three configurations are always invalid. In Django documentation for 'PREPEND_WWW' parameter, for instance, it states 'This is only used if CommonMiddleware is installed'.

This small experiment has shown that even though Django server seems to be well-tested, one needs to be careful when modifying the default settings. CIT can provide a quick way of finding invalid configurations for a particular Django project.

5   Conclusions

Many real-world software systems are highly configurable. Combinatorial interaction testing (CIT) techniques have been developed specifically for such systems. CIT test suites cover all interactions between any set of t parameters. Different parameter values can be set, for instance, via modifying a top-level settings file. An example of such a system is a very popular framework for rapid web development called Django. By applying CIT techniques to test basic websites written in Django automatically we discovered that under many test configurations invoking a basic website produces errors. Moreover, each step of our approach is (or could be) automated and does not involve any knowledge of the inner workings of the Django system. Therefore, it can be applied to any other configurable software system.

References

1. Cohen, D.M., Dalal, S.R., Fredman, M.L., Patton, G.C.: The AETG system: an approach to testing based on combinatorial design. IEEE Trans. Software Eng. **23**(7), 437–444 (1997)
2. Cohen, M.B., Colbourn, C.J., Gibbons, P.B., Mugridge, W.B.: Constructing test suites for interaction testing. In: Proceedings of the International Conference on Software Engineering, pp. 38–48, May 2003

3. Fraser, G., Arcuri, A.: Whole test suite generation. IEEE Trans. Software Eng. **39**(2), 276–291 (2013). http://doi.ieeecomputersociety.org/10.1109/TSE.2012.14
4. Fraser, G., Staats, M., McMinn, P., Arcuri, A., Padberg, F.: Does automated white-box test generation really help software testers? In: International Symposium on Software Testing and Analysis, ISSTA 2013, Lugano, Switzerland, July 15–20, 2013, pp. 291–301 (2013). http://doi.acm.org/10.1145/2483760.2483774
5. Garvin, B.J., Cohen, M.B., Dwyer, M.B.: Evaluating improvements to a meta-heuristic search for constrained interaction testing. Empirical Software Eng. **16**(1), 61–102 (2011)
6. Harman, M., Jia, Y., Zhang, Y.: Achievements, open problems and challenges for search based software testing (keynote). In: 2015 IEEE Eighth International Conference on Software Testing, Verification and Validation (2015)
7. Harman, M., Mansouri, S.A., Zhang, Y.: Search-based software engineering: Trends, techniques and applications. ACM Comput. Surv. **45**(1), 11 (2012). http://doi.acm.org/10.1145/2379776.2379787
8. Harman, M., McMinn, P.: A theoretical and empirical study of search-based testing: Local, global, and hybrid search. IEEE Trans. Software Eng. **36**(2), 226–247 (2010)
9. Kuhn, D.R., Okun, V.: Pseudo-exhaustive testing for software. In: SEW. pp. 153–158. IEEE Computer Society (2006)
10. Kuhn, D.R., Wallace, D.R., Gallo, A.M.: Software fault interactions and implications for software testing. IEEE Trans. Software Eng. **30**(6), 418–421 (2004)
11. McMinn, P.: Search-based software test data generation: a survey. Softw. Test. Verif. Reliab. **14**(2), 105–156 (2004). http://dx.doi.org/10.1002/stvr.294
12. Petke, J., Cohen, M., Harman, M., Yoo, S.: Practical combinatorial interaction testing: empirical findings on efficiency and early fault detection. IEEE Trans. Software Eng. **99**, 1–1 (2015)
13. Petke, J., Cohen, M.B., Harman, M., Yoo, S.: Efficiency and early fault detection with lower and higher strength combinatorial interaction testing. In: European Software Engineering Conference and the ACM SIGSOFT Symposium on the Foundations of Software Engineering. ESEC/FSE 2013, pp. 26–36. ACM, Saint Petersburg, Russian Federation, August 2013
14. Qu, X., Cohen, M.B., Rothermel, G.: Configuration-aware regression testing: an empirical study of sampling and prioritization. In: Proceedings of the International Symposium on Software Testing and Analysis, pp. 75–86 (2008)
15. Qu, X., Cohen, M.B., Woolf, K.M.: Combinatorial interaction regression testing: A study of test case generation and prioritization. In: ICSM, pp. 255–264. IEEE (2007)
16. Tillmann, N., de Halleux, J.: White-box testing of behavioral web service contracts with Pex. In: Proceedings of the 2008 Workshop on Testing, Analysis, and Verification of Web Services and Applications, held in conjunction with the ACM SIGSOFT International Symposium on Software Testing and Analysis (ISSTA 2008), TAV-WEB 2008, Seattle, Washington, USA, 21 July 2008, pp. 47–48 (2008). http://doi.acm.org/10.1145/1390832.1390840
17. Tonella, P.: Evolutionary testing of classes. In: Proceedings of the ACM/SIGSOFT International Symposium on Software Testing and Analysis, ISSTA 2004, Boston, Massachusetts, USA, 11–14 July 2004, pp. 119–128 (2004). http://doi.acm.org/10.1145/1007512.1007528
18. Yilmaz, C., Cohen, M.B., Porter, A.: Covering arrays for efficient fault characterization in complex configuration spaces. IEEE Trans. Software Eng. **31**(1), 20–34 (2006)

Synthesis of Equivalent Method Calls in Guava

Andrea Mattavelli[1]([✉]), Alberto Goffi[1], and Alessandra Gorla[2]

[1] Università Della Svizzera Italiana (USI), Lugano, Switzerland
{andrea.mattavelli,alberto.goffi}@usi.ch
[2] IMDEA Software Institute, Madrid, Spain
alessandra.gorla@imdea.org

Abstract. We developed a search-based technique to automatically synthesize sequences of method calls that are functionally equivalent to a given target method. This paper presents challenges and results of applying our technique to Google Guava. Guava heavily uses Java generics, and the large number of classes, methods and parameter values required us to tune our technique to deal with a search space that is much larger than what we originally envisioned. We modified our technique to cope with such challenges. The evaluation of the improved version of our technique shows that we can synthesize 188 equivalent method calls for relevant components of Guava, outperforming by 86 % the original version.

1 Introduction

Reusable software libraries frequently offer distinct functionally equivalent API methods in order to meet different client components' needs. This form of *intrinsic* redundancy in software [3] has been successfully exploited in the past for various purposes, such as to automatically produce test oracles [1] and to increase the reliability of software systems [2]. Even when completely automated in their internals, these techniques require developers to manually identify functionally equivalent sequences of method calls within the system. This activity can be tedious and error prone, and may thus be a showstopper for a widespread adoption of these techniques.

To support developers in this manual task, we developed a search-based technique that can automatically synthesize and validate sequences of method calls that are *test-equivalent* to a given target method [7]. This paper reports the results of using our prototype implementation SBES to automatically synthesize functionally equivalent method calls for the Google Guava library, and more precisely for its extensive set of collections. Guava collections heavily use Java generics, a language feature that was not supported in our original work. Moreover, the high number of classes, methods and parameter values made the search space large, and as a consequence more challenging for our search-based technique. We cope with such challenge by means of memetic algorithms.

We evaluated SBES on 220 methods belonging to 16 classes of the Google Guava collections library. Compared to the old version of our prototype, the support of Java generics and the use of memetic algorithms allow to find 86 % more *true* functionally equivalent method sequences.

© Springer International Publishing Switzerland 2015
M. Barros and Y. Labiche (Eds.): SSBSE 2015, LNCS 9275, pp. 248–254, 2015.
DOI: 10.1007/978-3-319-22183-0_19

2   Synthesis of Equivalent Sequences of Method Calls

Our search-based technique aims to automatically synthesize a sequence of method invocations whose functional behavior is equivalent to a target method. For example, given the method put(key,value), which inserts a new key-value pair in a Guava Multimap instance, our technique may be able to synthesize Multimap m=new Multimap(); m.putAll(key, new List().add(value)) as a possible equivalence. Producing solutions that would be equivalent for all possibly infinite inputs and states, is a well-known undecidable problem. The problem becomes tractable, though, by reducing the number of potential executions to a finite set. Therefore, our technique deems as equivalent two sequences of method calls that produce identical results and lead to identical states on a given set of test inputs, which we refer to as *execution scenarios*. This definition of equivalence is based on the *testing equivalence* notion defined by De Nicola and Hennessy [4].

We implemented our technique in a tool for Java called SBES (Search-Based Equivalent Synthesis) that manipulates source code. SBES employs an iterative two-phase algorithm to generate sequences of method calls that are equivalent to a given input method m. In the first phase—the *Synthesis* phase—it generates a candidate sequence eq whose behavior is equivalent to m on the existing set of execution scenarios. In order to do that, SBES generates a stub class that extends the class declaring m, and encloses all execution scenarios and an artificial method method_under_test, which acts as the main driver for the synthesis:

```
1  public void method_under_test() {
2    if (distance(exp_s[0], act_s[0])==0 && distance(exp_s[1], act_s[1])==0 &&
3        distance(exp_r[0], act_r[0])==0 && distance(exp_r[1], act_r[1])==0)
4      ; // target
5  }
```

SBES aims to generate a sequence of method calls eq that covers the TRUE branch of this artificial method. The condition evaluates whether the *return value* and the *state reached* by executing eq in each execution scenarios are test-equivalent to executing m. Arrays act_r and exp_r store the return values of eq and m respectively. Similarly, act_s and exp_s store the corresponding reached states. The synthesis phase may lead to spurious results, since it considers only a finite set of execution scenarios. Therefore, in the second phase of the algorithm— the *Validation* phase—SBES aims to remove spurious results by looking for counterexamples (that is, previously unknown scenarios for which eq and m are not test-equivalent). In this phase, SBES automatically generates a slightly different stub class with the following artificial method:

```
1  public void method_under_test(Integer key, String value) {
2    ArrayListMultimap clone = deepClone(this);
3    boolean expect = this.put(key, value);
4    boolean actual = clone.putAll(key, new ArrayList().put(value));
5    if (distance(this,clone)>0 || distance(expect,actual)>0)
6      ; // target
7  }
```

SBES aims once again to generate a sequence of method calls that can cover the TRUE branch. In this case, though, the condition asserts the *non* equivalence between m and eq. The code shows the stub based on the example of the Guava

Multimap class, the target method put(key,value), and the candidate equivalence putAll(key, new List().add(value)). If this phase produces a counterexample, the algorithm iterates, adding the counterexample to the initial set of scenarios. Otherwise, SBES returns *eq* as the final result.

In both phases, SBES exploits a custom version of EvoSuite as a search-based engine [5]. We modified EvoSuite such that it has the TRUE branch of method_under_test as the sole goal to cover. Since the condition of the artificial method branch is a conjunction of atomic clauses, the fitness function evaluates the branch distance of each clause separately, aiming to generate an individual whose all clauses evaluate to TRUE. The branch distance of each atomic clause is computed using numeric, object or string distance functions depending on the involved type. EvoSuite does not have a proper notion of *object* distance, and as a consequence it is unable to effectively guide the evolution when a branch condition evaluates an object. Using method equals to compare objects would yet fail at providing any guidance, since this method returns a boolean value, and thus flattens the fitness landscape [8]. To overcome this issue, we implemented a notion of distance that *quantifies* the difference between two objects. To calculate such distance, we compute the distance of all the object's fields. For non-primitive fields, we recursively call the object distance function on them. As a result, the distance between two objects amounts to the sum of the distance of all the inspected fields. Two objects are deemed as identical if their distance is zero. We refer the interested reader to our previous paper for further details on SBES [7].

3   Extending SBES to Deal with Google Guava

In our previous work we demonstrated the effectiveness of SBES on few, selected Java classes such as Stack and a set of classes from the GraphStream library. Using SBES on Google Guava was challenging for at least two reasons. First, Guava contains more than 335 classes and 5,400 methods. The combinatorial explosion of classes, parameters, and method calls only considering the library itself is enormous. Second, most of the classes in the library are implemented using generic types. Generic types allow developers to abstract algorithms and data structures, but their presence increases the complexity of the synthesis process. Ignoring generic types exacerbates the combinatorial explosion mentioned before, since type erasure substitutes generics with the base class java.lang.Object. Yet, by considering generic types we must concatenate method calls that both satisfy and adhere to the generic types specified at class instantiation time, increasing the complexity of the generation process.

To cope with Guava, we extended SBES along two lines. First, we added generic-to-concrete type replacement to our prototype. In those cases where the execution scenarios declare and use concrete classes rather than generic types, we exploit such information. For example, suppose to synthesize equivalences for method Multimap<K,V>.put(key,value), with the following initial execution scenario: Multimap<Integer,String> m=new Multimap();m.put(15, "String"). Since in the execution scenario the generic types K and V are replaced with Integer and String respectively, we can safely replace all the occurrences of the generic types with the concrete classes in the stub class. By resolving generic types, EvoSuite obtains more information to guide the search towards better individuals, without wasting time to find syntactically valid concrete classes. The second extension tries to mitigate the combinatorial explosion of method calls and parameters. In our previous evaluation we observed that in order to find valid solutions, it is necessary to invoke methods either in a specific order or with specific parameter values. To efficiently synthesize such sequences of method calls, we exploit *memetic algorithms*. Memetic algorithms combine both global and local searches to generate better individuals, thus accelerating the evolution towards a global optimum. EvoSuite already supports memetic algorithms [6], in Sect. 4 we briefly discuss how we found the optimal configuration of memetic search.

4 Experimental Evaluation

The purpose of evaluating SBES on the Google Guava library was twofold. First, we wanted to show that many methods of the Guava API have equivalent sequences of method calls. Second, we wanted to demonstrate that SBES can effectively synthesize such equivalent sequences. In particular, we wanted to assess whether the improvements that we brought to SBES with respect to our previous work could identify substantially more correct solutions.

Experimental Setup. We limited our evaluation to the classes declared in package collect, and in particular we selected a random set of concrete classes for which we identified a list of equivalences in previous studies [1–3]. As a result, we selected 16 subject classes with a total of 220 methods under analysis. These classes represented a challenge for SBES since they declare a high number of methods, which strains the search process. Moreover, these classes make an extensive use of generic types. For each target method we first evaluated the effectiveness—measured in terms of *true* synthesized solutions—of the original version of SBES. We then evaluated the effectiveness of SBES with generic-to-concrete type replacement, which we refer to as $SBES^G$. Finally, we evaluated the effectiveness of combining the generic-to-concrete support and memetic search. We refer to this version as $SBES^{G,M}$. We ran the experiments by feeding the prototype with the class under analysis, the target method, and an initial execution scenario, which consists of one test case that was either extracted from the existing test suite, or generated automatically with EvoSuite. For each target method, we iterated the entire synthesis process 20 times—regardless of the success of the first phase—with a search budget of 180 seconds for both the first and second phase. The search budgets were validated in our previous evaluation [7].

Table 1. Guava classes considered with their number of methods under evaluation and equivalences synthesized by the three prototype versions $SBES$, $SBES^G$, and $SBES^{G,M}$

Class	Methods	$SBES$		$SBES^G$		$SBES^{G,M}$	
		TP	FP	TP	FP	TP	FP
ArrayListMultimap	15	7	1	13	1	12	3
ConcurrentHashMultiset	16	5	0	9	1	6	2
HashBasedTable	16	3	6	3	8	2	8
HashMultimap	15	7	0	9	2	13	1
HashMultiset	16	6	0	15	3	19	5
ImmutableListMultimap	11	1	1	2	1	2	0
ImmutableMultiset	8	3	0	1	0	3	0
LinkedHashMultimap	15	6	1	9	1	12	3
LinkedHashMultiset	16	5	1	19	2	19	6
LinkedListMultimap	15	6	2	10	1	11	0
Lists	8	18	0	17	3	15	1
Maps	9	6	0	5	0	8	0
Sets	10	12	2	15	0	21	0
TreeBasedTable	15	0	8	4	8	3	10
TreeMultimap	14	4	1	9	3	8	2
TreeMultiset	20	12	5	32	13	34	10
Total	**220**	**101**	**28**	**172**	**47**	**188**	**50**

Results. Table 1 summarizes the results of our experiments.[1] For the selected target methods of Google Guava, SBES, SBES^G, and SBES^{G,M} could successfully synthesize 101, 172 and 188 equivalent sequences of method calls respectively. SBES^G finds 70 % more equivalences than the base version. Such result confirms that generic-to-concrete type replacement can indeed reduce the search space without reducing potential behaviors of the class, ultimately improving the synthesis process. Similarly, memetic algorithms successfully improve the synthesis process: SBES^{G,M} can generate 9 % more solutions than SBES^G. However, the effectiveness of memetic algorithms largely depends on the frequency at which EvoSuite performs the local search [6]. If the local search occurs too often, it steals search budget from the global search. On the other hand, if the local search occurs infrequently, it does not bring much benefits. To find the optimal configuration, we ran SBES^{G,M} such that the local search was done once every 10, 50, 75, 85, and 100 generations. As expected, a frequent local search degrades the effectiveness of the approach. With 10 generations we obtained the worst result (we synthesized 30 equivalences less than SBES^G, i.e., -17%), and obtained consistently better results for the other configurations up to the opti-

---

[1] A replication package is available at http://star.inf.usi.ch/sbes-challenge.

mal rate of once every 75 generations. After this threshold, local search seems not to be frequent enough, since the effectiveness decreased again $(-7\%$ w.r.t. the optimal configuration).

For all runs we manually validated the solutions. While on the one hand SBES^G and SBES^{G,M} identify more truly equivalent solutions (reported as TP in Table 1) than SBES, they also produce more false positives (FP in Table 1). In some cases, as for HashBasedTable, TreeBasedTable, and TreeMultiset, this is due to the inability of EvoSuite to generate a syntactically valid test case as a counterexample. The validation phase, thus, fails in invalidating even the most trivial spurious candidate. In the reminder of the cases, instead, false positives are due to a major limitation of the technique: the behavior of the target branch in the artificial method during the validation phase is comparable to a flag variable. In fact, the object distance during the validation phase is zero for all generated solutions, except for those corner cases in which the behavior of the candidate is not equivalent. As a consequence, the evolution in the second phase lacks any guidance. This is a limitation of our approach, and we are actively working to overcome such issue.

5 Conclusion

This paper introduces significant improvements over our previous work on the automatic synthesis of functionally equivalent sequences of method calls [7]. The experiments on 220 methods belonging to 16 classes of the Google Guava library show that generic-to-concrete type replacement and memetic algorithms allowed the new prototype to outperform the previous version by 86% in terms of true equivalences synthesized.

Acknowledgment. This work was supported in part by the Swiss National Science Foundation with projects SHADE (grant n. 200021-138006) and ReSpec (grant n. 200021-146607). The authors would like to thank Mauro Pezzè and Paolo Tonella for their contributions to the previous version of the technique.

References

1. Carzaniga, A., Goffi, A., Gorla, A., Mattavelli, A., Pezzè, M.: Cross-checking oracles from intrinsic software redundancy. In: International Conference on Software Engineering (ICSE), pp. 931–942. ACM (2014)
2. Carzaniga, A., Gorla, A., Mattavelli, A., Perino, N., Pezzè, M.: Automatic recovery from runtime failures. In: International Conference on Software Engineering (ICSE), pp. 782–791. IEEE (2013)
3. Carzaniga, A., Mattavelli, A., Pezzè, M.: Measuring software redundancy. In: International Conference on Software Engineering (ICSE), pp. 156–166. IEEE (2015)
4. De Nicola, R., Hennessy, M.: Testing equivalences for processes. Theoret. Comput. Sci. **34**(1–2), 83–133 (1984)

5. Fraser, G., Arcuri, A.: EvoSuite: automatic test suite generation for object-oriented software. In: Symposium on the Foundations of Software Engineering (FSE), pp. 416–419. ACM (2011)
6. Fraser, G., Arcuri, A., McMinn, P.: A memetic algorithm for whole test suite generation. J. Syst. Softw. **103**, 311–327 (2015)
7. Goffi, A., Gorla, A., Mattavelli, A., Pezzè, M., Tonella, P.: Search-based synthesis of equivalent method sequences. In: Symposium on the Foundations of Software Engineering (FSE), pp. 366–376. ACM (2014)
8. Harman, M., Hu, L., Hierons, R.M., Wegener, J., Sthamer, H., Baresel, A., Roper, M.: Testability transformation. IEEE Trans. Softw. Eng. (TSE) **30**(1), 3–16 (2004)

Object-Oriented Genetic Improvement for Improved Energy Consumption in Google Guava

Nathan Burles[1]([✉]), Edward Bowles[1], Alexander E.I. Brownlee[2],
Zoltan A. Kocsis[2], Jerry Swan[1], and Nadarajen Veerapen[2]

[1] University of York, York YO10 5DD, UK
nathan.burles@york.ac.uk
[2] University of Stirling, Stirling FK9 4LA, UK

Abstract. In this work we use metaheuristic search to improve Google's Guava library, finding a semantically equivalent version of com.google.common.collect.ImmutableMultimap with reduced energy consumption. Semantics-preserving transformations are found in the source code, using the principle of subtype polymorphism. We introduce a new tool, OPACITOR, to deterministically measure the energy consumption, and find that a statistically significant reduction to Guava's energy consumption is possible. We corroborate these results using JALEN, and evaluate the performance of the metaheuristic search compared to an exhaustive search—finding that the same result is achieved while requiring almost 200 times fewer fitness evaluations. Finally, we compare the metaheuristic search to an independent exhaustive search at each variation point, finding that the metaheuristic has superior performance.

Keywords: Genetic Improvement · Object-oriented programming · Subclass substitution · Liskov Substitution Principle · Energy profiling

1 Introduction

Across all scales of computing, from mobile devices to server farms, there is widespread interest in minimizing energy requirements. For a given program, it is likely that there are many functionally-equivalent programs exhibiting a variety of different non-functional properties. Previous work by Sahin et al. [13] has measured the effect of 6 popular refactorings on 9 real Java programs, concluding that the effect of these refactorings on energy usage are highly end-application dependent and that commonly-applied predictive metrics are of little practical use. This is therefore a strong motivator for the application of techniques from Search Based Software Engineering (SBSE). In this article, we use metaheuristic search to find semantically equivalent programs with reduced energy consumption. Semantics preserving transformations are achieved via the behavioral equivalence that is central to object-orientation.

© Springer International Publishing Switzerland 2015
M. Barros and Y. Labiche (Eds.): SSBSE 2015, LNCS 9275, pp. 255–261, 2015.
DOI: 10.1007/978-3-319-22183-0_20

Related Work. Although there are a number of works in Genetic Programming (GP) and Grammatical Evolution (GE) that claim to be 'Object Oriented' [1,2,8,12,15], we are not aware of any concerned with the central pillar of Object Orientation, viz. the Liskov Substitution Principle (LSP) [7] as exemplified by subtype polymorphism. In this respect, the closest work we are aware of is that of the SEEDS framework of Manotas et al. [9], in which alternative subtypes of container classes are substituted into bytecode in order to minimize power consumption. The search mechanism that is employed in SEEDS is that of a separate exhaustive search at each object allocation location: our approach differs by using a genetic approach to assign subclasses to constructor invocations. It is certainly therefore the first work deserving of the title of 'Object-Oriented Genetic Improvement'. Related work in a non-SBSE context is the interesting use of strong-typing corresponding to different operating modes (e.g. 'battery level high') [4], allowing the programmer to delineate differing responses to operating conditions (e.g. opting to render a low resolution image when energy is low).

2 Implementation

In outline, the improvement process is as follows:

1. Parse the source file designated for improvement, yielding an Abstract Syntax Tree (AST). Identify *variation points*, i.e. source nodes in the AST corresponding to the creation of Guava container objects.
2. Obtain the complete set of possible target substitutions T (i.e. all the container classes within the Guava, Apache Collections[1], and the Java 8 util package). For each source node S_i in the AST, find the subset of possible target substitutions $t(S_i) \subseteq T$ which are actually valid.
3. Given a sequence of the k source nodes $[S_1, \ldots, S_k]$ from the AST, the search space is then given by all combinations from $[t(S_1), \ldots, t(S_k)]$. The solution representation is thus an assignment $i \mapsto s \in t(S_i), 1 \leq i \leq k$, represented as an element $r \in \mathbb{Z}^k$, with constraints $0 \leq r_i < |t(S_i)|$.
4. Given such an assignment, the AST node for each variation point can be replaced with its target substitution and the correspondingly mutated source file can be written out to disk.
5. The program containing the mutated source is then compiled and evaluated by a measure related to its energy consumption. By this means, combinatorial search is performed in the space of these representations using the Genetic Algorithm metaheuristic [6], in order to find the sequence of substitutions which minimize energy consumption.

Variation Points. The open-source Java framework Google Guava implements a variety of concrete subclasses of java.util.Collection. There are well-known tradeoffs in performance characteristics between different collection subclasses:

---

[1] Guava v18.0, Apache Collections v4.0.

for example, finding a specific element in a linked list is $\mathcal{O}(n)$ but in a hash-set it is $\mathcal{O}(1)$. We selected com.google.common.collect.ImmutableMultimap as a testcase for improvement, since it features a number of instantiations of Collection subclasses. Source file parsing (and subsequent re-generation, described below) was done with a popular open-source library com.github.javaparser.JavaParser[2]. Within this file, three types of syntax fragments were identified for use as variation points: calls to constructors (e.g. new LinkedHashMap<>()); calls to Guava factory classes (e.g. Maps.newHashMap()); and calls to Guava static creator methods (e.g. ImmutableList.of()). These were filtered to include only fragments creating a collection object, i.e., one implementing java.util.Collection, java.util.Map or com.google.common.collect.Multimap. In total, 5 variation points were found, with between 5 and 45 possible substitutions each.

Mutating the Source Code. For each variation point, one of three approaches to determining the interface of the created object was used: the method's return type for return statements; the declared type for variable declarations. For other expressions, the least-general interface implemented by the class was used: one of Map, Set, List, Multimap, Multiset or Collection. The potential substitutions for a variation point are classes implementing the appropriate interface in Guava, Apache Collections, java.util, and java.util.concurrent. Excluded were abstract and inner classes, and those expecting a particular type (e.g. Treecollections require elements implementing Comparable). A modified version of JavaParser's SourcePrinter performed the required code substitution at each variation point in ImmutableMultimap's source. A careless programmer might depend on functionality not guaranteed by the LSP, e.g. relying on a collection being sorted, despite this not being part of the superclass type specification that is actually visible at the point at which such reliance is made. This is a logical error on behalf of the programmer, and strictly speaking necessitates that they rewrite the code. Although we do not cater for such programming errors in our experiments, the best that can be done in such cases is to include any existing unit tests as a constraint on the search.

Measuring Energy Consumption. During the evolutionary process the fitness function was the energy consumption measured using a new tool, OPACITOR, designed to make measurements deterministic. OPACITOR traces the execution of Java code, using a modified version of OpenJDK, generating a histogram containing the number of times each Java opcode was executed—allowing very similar programs to be distinguishable. A model of the energy costs of each Java opcode, created by Hao et al. [5], is then used to calculate the total number of Joules used. As the Just-In-Time compilation (JIT) feature of the Java Virtual Machine (JVM) is non-deterministic, it is disabled during evolution. Similarly, Garbage Collection (GC) is non-deterministic and so the JVM is allocated enough memory to avoid GC. During the final testing, after evolution has completed, these features are re-enabled to ensure that the results remain valid on

---

[2] During development we discovered and fixed a bug in the hashCode implementation of the Node class in the com.github.javaparser.JavaParser library.

an unmodified JVM. It should be noted that a significant benefit of OPACITOR, compared to other approaches which require timing or physical energy measurement, is that it is unaffected by anything else executing on the experimental system. This means that it can be parallelised, or executed simultaneously with other programs, without difficulty. In previous work [14] we successfully used JALEN [11] to calculate the energy required, and compare two algorithms; during the final testing we have used this technique as a corroboration that OPACITOR is effective and generates reliable measurements.

3 Experiments

The first experiment performed was the use of a metaheuristic to search for a solution with reduced energy consumption. We elected to use a Genetic Algorithm (GA) [6] to search the space of solutions, since this is known to be a useful approach for a variety of assignment problems [3]. The solution representation used is a vector of integers $r \in \mathbb{Z}^k$. The representation itself is constrained with the required constraints $0 \leq r_i < |t(S_i)|$.

The GA was configured with a population of 500, running for 100 generations. New populations were generated using an elitism rate of 5 %, single-point crossover with a rate of 75 %, and one-point mutation with a rate of 50 % with candidates selected using tournament selection with arity 2. These parameters were selected, after preliminary investigations, in order to provide sufficient genetic diversity to the evolution without requiring an excessive number of fitness evaluations as each evaluation takes in the order of 10 s on a 3.25 GHz CPU. During experimentation we ran the GA five times, with a different seed to the random number generator, in order to test the robustness of the evolution.

A second experiment ran an exhaustive search on the entire search space of 674,325 possible solutions, using 32 3.25 GHz cores to allow it to finish within 2.5 days, in order to determine how close the GA came to finding an ideal solution.

The final experiment ran an exhaustive search independently on each variation point, following the example of Manotas et al. [9] but on source code instead of bytecode, before combining each of the substitutions at the end.

4 Results

Statistical testing was carried out using the Wilcoxon/Mann Whitney U Statistical Tests and Vargha-Delaney Effect size tests (as implemented in the ASTRAIEA framework [10]). The results were obtained with 100 samples in each dataset. The result of each of the runs of the GA was the same set of substitutions, and so this set was used thereafter.

When considering a full exhaustive search of the entire problem space of 674,325 possible combinations of substitutions, performed to gauge the effectiveness of the GA, the best set of substitutions were the same as those found

Table 1. Energy (J) required to exercise the various methods provided by the ImmutableMultimap class 10,000 times (mean of 100 runs, and standard deviation σ), as well as the p-values (p) and effect size measures (e) comparing our result to the original or the result of an independent exhaustive search at each variation point.

Measurement technique	GA	Original			Independent exhaustive		
	J	J	p	e	J	p	e
OPACITOR	216.49	298.58	–	–	266.43	–	–
OPACITOR with JIT and GC	11.15	14.75	<.001	0.93	13.45	<.001	0.85
	σ2.06	σ1.13			σ1.15		
JALEN	11.81	15.25	<.001	0.94	13.46	<.001	0.82
	σ2.18	σ1.00			σ0.66		

by the GA. The use of a GA therefore provided a speed-up of almost 200 while still successfully finding the best possible result.

The combined results of the original library, our improved version, and the version using only independent exhaustive search are shown together in Table 1. During the evolution, with JIT disabled and GC avoided, the best solution found used 216.49 J. This compares with 298.58 J required by the original, and 266.43 J required by the solution found using an exhaustive search independently on each variation point. As the measurements in this case are deterministic, and thus generate only one observation for each version, no statistical tests are necessary.

The GA required approximately 3,500 fitness evaluations to find its best solution (the number of evaluations varied slightly between different evolutionary runs), while the exhaustive search at each variation point required only 105 evaluations. Although using the GA was therefore significantly slower than the approach used in similar work [9], the final result is also significantly better.

More interestingly, similarly impressive results were also obtained when non-determinism was reintroduced post-evolution—with JIT enabled and the JVM's memory allocation unmodified (allowing for GC when necessary). In this case the GA's solution required 11.15 J, compared with 14.75 J for the original and 13.45 J for the independent exhaustive search. As the energy measurement is no longer deterministic, the p-values and effect size measures vary accordingly. Vargha and Delaney suggest that a value of 0.71 indicates a large difference between data sets, and so the results demonstrate that the GA's solution provides a significant improvement over both the original and the independent exhaustive search.

To help corroborate that the model-based energy measurement provides realistic results, we used JALEN (with JIT and GC) to compare the three versions of ImmutableMultimap. The results support the assertion that OPACITOR provides realistic and reliable energy measurements, as well as the hypothesis that performing the evolution using the deterministic measure would map correctly to results generated in a non-deterministic, realistic environment.

5   Conclusion

We have introduced 'Object-Oriented Genetic Improvement', a technique by which non-functional properties such as time or energy consumption may be optimised by substituting suitable alternative subclasses to constructor invocations. By virtue of subclass adherence to the 'Liskov Substitution Principle' [7], we can make semantics-preserving changes to source code in order to take advantage of the vastly different performance characteristics displayed by different collection implementations. We applied this technique to the com.google.common.collect.ImmutableMultimap class, part of Google's Guava library, using a new tool, OPACITOR, to evaluate the energy consumption of candidate solutions.

Our results showed that significant improvements could be made, with the best solution providing a saving of approximately 24 %. The results generated by OPACITOR were corroborated using JALEN, which uses time and CPU utilisation as a proxy for energy consumption. Thus, the results show that the substitutions improve both the energy consumption and the execution time of the class. We further compared the results of our technique to those obtained using an approach used in related work [9]—a separate exhaustive search at each variation point—and found that although the number of fitness evaluations increased using a GA, the performance of the final result was significantly improved. This shows that the variation points within code are not always independent. This is intuitively the case for ImmutableMultimap—two of the identified variation points instantiate the BuilderMultimap private class which exists within ImmutableMultimap, while other variation points exist within the BuilderMultimap sub-class. An independent exhaustive search at each variation point may therefore decide to substitute BuilderMultimap for a more efficient alternative, even though more efficient subclass substitutions can be made within the private class.

Acknowledgement. Work funded by UK EPSRC grant EP/J017515/1. Data available at https://github.com/nburles/burles2015object.

References

1. Abbott, R.J.: Object-oriented genetic programming, an initial implementation. In: Proceedings of the 6th International Conference on Computational Intelligence and Natural Computing, North Carolina, USA (2003)
2. Bruce, W.S.: Automatic generation of object-oriented programs using genetic programming. In: Proceedings of the 1st Annual Conference on Genetic Programming, pp. 267–272. MIT Press, Cambridge (1996)
3. Chu, P.C., Beasley, J.E.: A genetic algorithm for the generalised assignment problem. Comput. Oper. Res. **24**(1), 17–23 (1997)
4. Cohen, M., Zhu, H.S., Senem, E.E., Liu, Y.D.: Energy types. In: Proceedings of the ACM International Conference on Object Oriented Programming Systems Languages and Applications, OOPSLA 2012, pp. 831–850. ACM, NY (2012)

5. Hao, S., Li, D., Halfond, W.G., Govindan, R.: Estimating mobile application energy consumption using program analysis. In: 35th International Conference on Software Engineering, pp. 92–101. IEEE (2013)
6. Holland, J.H.: Adaptation in Natural and Artificial Systems: An Introductory Analysis with Applications to Biology, Control and Artificial Intelligence. MIT Press, Cambridge (1992)
7. Liskov, B.: 'Data abstraction and hierarchy' (keynote address). SIGPLAN Not. **23**(5), 17–34 (1987)
8. Lucas, S.: Exploiting reflection in object oriented genetic programming. In: Keijzer, M., O'Reilly, U.-M., Lucas, S., Costa, E., Soule, T. (eds.) EuroGP 2004. LNCS, vol. 3003, pp. 369–378. Springer, Heidelberg (2004)
9. Manotas, I., Pollock, L., Clause, J.: Seeds: a software engineer's energy-optimization decision support framework. In: Proceedings of the 36th International Conference on Software Engineering, pp. 503–514. ACM, NY (2014)
10. Neumann, G., Swan, J., Harman, M., Clark, J.A.: The executable experimental template pattern for the systematic comparison of metaheuristics. In: Proceedings of the 2014 Conference Companion on Genetic and Evolutionary Computation Companion, pp. 1427–1430. ACM (2014)
11. Noureddine, A., Bourdon, A., Rouvoy, R., Seinturier, L.: Runtime monitoring of software energy hotspots. In: Proceedings of the 27th IEEE/ACM International Conference on Automated Software Engineering, pp. 160–169. IEEE (2012)
12. Oppacher, Y., Oppacher, F., Deugo, D.: Evolving java objects using a grammar-based approach. In: Proceedings of the 11th Annual Conference on Genetic and Evolutionary Computation, pp. 1891–1892. ACM, NY (2009)
13. Sahin, C., Pollock, L., Clause, J.: How do code refactorings affect energy usage? In: Proceedings of the 8th ACM/IEEE International Symposium on Empirical Software Engineering and Measurement, pp. 36:1–36:10. ACM, NY (2014)
14. Swan, J., Burles, N.: TEMPLAR - a framework for template-method hyper-heuristics. In: Machado, P., Heywood, M.I., McDermott, J., Castelli, M., García-Sánchez, P., Burelli, P., Risi, S., Sim, K. (eds.) EuroGP 2015. LNCS, vol. 9025, pp. 205–216. Springer, Switzerland (2015)
15. White, T., Fan, J., Oppacher, F.: Basic object oriented genetic programming. In: Mehrotra, K.G., Mohan, C.K., Oh, J.C., Varshney, P.K., Ali, M. (eds.) IEA/AIE 2011, Part I. LNCS, vol. 6703, pp. 59–68. Springer, Heidelberg (2011)

Automated Transplantation of Call Graph and Layout Features into Kate

Alexandru Marginean$^{(\boxtimes)}$, Earl T. Barr, Mark Harman,
and Yue Jia

Department of Computer Science, CREST Centre, UCL, London, UK
alexandru.marginean.13@ucl.ac.uk

Abstract. We report the automated transplantation of two features currently missing from Kate: call graph generation and automatic layout for C programs, which have been requested by users on the Kate development forum. Our approach uses a lightweight annotation system with Search Based techniques augmented by static analysis for automated transplantation. The results are promising: on average, our tool requires 101 min of standard desktop machine time to transplant the call graph feature, and 31 min to transplant the layout feature. We repeated each experiment 20 times and validated the resulting transplants using unit, regression and acceptance test suites. In 34 of 40 experiments conducted our search-based autotransplantation tool, μSCALPEL, was able to successfully transplant the new functionality, passing all tests.

1 Introduction

We recently introduced a search based technique for automated software transplantation [2,7]. Guided by dependence analysis and testing, our approach uses a variant of genetic programming to identify and extract useful functionality from a donor program, and transplant it into a (possibly unrelated) host program. We implemented our approach as a tool called μSCALPEL, which is publicly available [1].

In this challenge paper, we illustrate the way in which realistic, scalable, and useful real-world transplantation can be achieved using μSCALPEL. We apply our tool to the SSBSE 2015 Challenge program Kate[1], a popular text editor based on KDE. Its rich feature set and available plugins make it a popular, lightweight IDE for C developers. We perform two automated transplantations using μSCALPEL. In the first one, we transplant call graph drawing ability from the GNU utility program cflow, to augment Kate with the ability to construct and display call graphs.

This is a useful feature for a lightweight IDE, like Kate, and would clearly be nontrivial to implement from scratch. Using our search based autotransplantation, μSCALPEL, the developer merely needs to identify the entry point of the source code in the donor program (cflow in this case) and the tool will do

---

[1] http://kate-editor.org.

© Springer International Publishing Switzerland 2015
M. Barros and Y. Labiche (Eds.): SSBSE 2015, LNCS 9275, pp. 262–268, 2015.
DOI: 10.1007/978-3-319-22183-0_21

the rest; extracting the relevant code, matching names spaces between host and donor and executing regressions, unit and acceptance tests. Like much previous work on genetic programming [12], our approach relies critically on the availability of high quality test suites. We do not directly address this issue in the present paper, but believe that existing achievements in Search Based [5] and other [4] test data generation techniques will help us to ensure that this reliance is reasonable and practical.

Our second transplantation incorporates a pretty printer for C, which Kate only partially supports and which its users have requested. At the time of writing, we deployed a new version of Kate that incorporates these features. We hope to be able to report on the uptake of this 'genetically improved' Kate at the conference.

Our work is closely related to recent achievements in genetic improvement, which have been able to dramatically speed up real world systems [9,14,15], port between languages [8], balance memory consumption and execution time [16], reduced energy consumption [3,13] and fix bugs [10]. Most closely related to our approach is work on auto-specialisation using transplantation [11] and grow and graft genetic improvement [6]. Whereas auto-specialisation transplants from different versions of the same system (or closely related systems) and grow and graft transplants newly grown simple features, μSCALPEL transplants large-scale features (and subsystems) from one or more donors into an unrelated host.

2   The μSCALPEL Transplantation Framework

We presented a framework for transplanting a feature between two unrelated systems and a tool to implement our approach [1] in our recent ISSTA paper [2], so we provide merely a summary here to make the paper self-contained. Given a host H program that is lacking a feature of interest, a donor program D, that implemented the feature, and a lightweight annotation system, our tool, μSCALPEL, attempts to autotransplant the feature from D into H. The feature of interest in the donor is called the Organ. From the entry of the donor, there are one or more path that reaches the Organ Entry point, called veins.

Our approach uses Genetic Programming (GP), augmented by static analysis, for extracting, configuring, and transplanting the organ into the host environment. GP explores combinations of statements on the vein, and in the host–donor variable mappings, that will enable the organ to execute in the host environment, guided by testing. The first stage of our approach uses context insensitive slicing on the call graph of the donor program to construct a map, with the key being the variables available in the vein, and the values being the variables in scope at the implantation point in the host [2]. GP is used to transplant the feature in the host system, having the host–donor map, and the code base represented by these context insensitive slices. The search space has two dimensions: the variable mapping and the statements available to form the transplant itself. The tool that implements out approach, μSCALPEL, is publicly available [2].

3 Applying Autotransplantation to Kate

We chose two popular, real world systems, as the donor programs: GNU cflow[2], and GNU Indent[3]. The former generates call graphs for C programs, a feature that is missing from Kate; the latter pretty prints C source files, with far fewer restrictions than Kate's existing built-in indentation functionality. Kate's existing indentation feature fails to wrap a line that is too long, for example. It simply adds space or tabs in a programming language independent manner, whereas GNU's Indent exploits language awareness to provide far better formatting functionality.

μSCALPEL requires user to provide an implantation point in H, and the entry point of the feature in D. We chose one of the Kate plugins as the implantation point. We start from the time date plugin template[4], and annotate the entry point in Kate, in the function 'void TimeDatePluginView:: slotInsertTimeDate()' of the plugin. This function is called every time the user selects the menu element corresponding to the current plugin. We chose this point as the implantation point for allowing the user to chose whenever wants to generate the call graphs. The annotation added in the host is: 'void TimeDatePluginView::slotInsertTimeDate() { /* IP */' .

For the cflow donor, the desired functionality is to transplant the tree form of the call graphs. Thus, we label the function 'tree_output()' as the organ entry in the donor system. The organ generates the call graph of a C program and displays it in the tree format (option '-T' from cflow). The annotation is: 'void tree_output(){ /*OE*/'. For the Indent donor, the desired functionality is to enable Kate to completely format a C source file. We want to format the current opened document in the Kate's main page. Thus, we label the function 'indent_single_file()' as the organ entry point. This function reformats the source file, according to the settings of GNU Indent. The annotation is: 'exit_values_ty indent_single_file(BOOLEAN using_stdin){/*OE*/'. The developer need only provide μSCALPEL with these simple annotations and suitable test cases and the reminder of the transplantation process is entirely automated.

We used several different test suites to validate our transplant. First, we execute the original regression test suite, available with Kate. Since this test suite does not execute the organ, we augmented it with test cases specifically aimed at executing the organ. Second, we generated an acceptance test suite, aimed at checking the transplanted functionality when executed in the host. As with all approaches to GP, the test cases are used to guide the search for suitable code.

Provision of these test cases remains the responsibility of the software engineer. Such tests, or a large subset thereof, would be likely required by a human transplantation process in any case, so this is not a significant additional burden. Furthermore, even were such costs attributed to the autotransplantation process,

---

[2] http://gnu.org/software/cflow.

[3] http://gnu.org/software/indent.

[4] https://techbase.kde.org/Development/Tutorials/Kate/KTextEditor_Plugins.

it would be likely easier, in many cases, to define suitable test cases to *check* a transplant than it would be to *generate* one from scratch while ensuring it is sufficiently tested. In order to estimate the human cost, we recorded the elapsed developer time required to construct the isolation, acceptance, and regression++ test cases that are specifically required to validate the transplantation, thereby providing an upper bound on human effort. Our estimation for annotations and the test suites is one hour for both of the transplants.

For all our test suites we provide coverage information. Table 2 shows the results of our tests for both donor programs. We also manually generated the ice-box test suite, used by the GP in the process of transplanting the feature.

4   Experiments and Results

We seek to answer three research questions. **RQ1)** Can we transplant the two desired features into Kate, without breaking the original functionality of Kate? **RQ2)** Do the transplanted features (organs) provide the desired functionality inside Kate? **RQ3)** What is the computational effort required by automatic transplantation? We repeat each of the transplantation experiments 20 times, executing μSCALPEL on a Ubuntu 14.10 machine, 64-bit architecture, 16 GB ram, and 8 cores processor.

Table 2 presents the number of runs in which for every test suite, all test cases pass. We report the number of successful runs for the regression, augmented regression, and acceptance test suites individually and also report the coverage achieved by test cases (of the entire Kate system, and of just the transplanted organ). This coverage data is that reported by the publicly available coverage metric tool gcov. Table 2a shows the results of the test suites for cflow donor transplant, while Table 2b shows the results of the test suites for Indent donor transplant. For cflow, 16 out of 20 runs where unanimously successful, while for Indent 18 out of 20 runs were unanimously successful.

We deem a transplantation attempt to be successful if (and only if) all the test cases from the corresponding test suite passed. The row labelled 'Unanimously' reports the number of transplantation attempts in which *all* test cases passed in all test suites. The line 'Isolation' reports the results of the isolation test suite, which is used by the GP algorithm for evolving the organ (as opposed to being used for valuation purposes).

Observe that even were we to find that automated transplantation was only successful one a few of the 20 attempts, then this would be sufficient to demonstrate the feasibility of autotransplantation in general. The testing process can be used to validate any transplantation attempt, allowing the software engineer to discard any and all failed attempts. As a result show, autotransplantation achieves a much higher success rate than this, minimal, feasibility requirement. Overall, we have evidence that autotransplantation is feasible for the popular real world system Kate. We now turn to the specific research questions, we posed to answer them.

RQ1 Table 2 revels that for both of the transplants, all the regression test cases passed. However, the organs were not executed by the existing regression test suites, so we manually augmented them to generate the regression++ test suites. Organ coverage for the regression++ test suites is: 59 % for cflow, and 58 % for Indent. For cflow 17 out of 20 transplantation attempts passed all test in these augmented test suites, while for Indent, 18 out of 20 pass all. Clearly one can never do enough regression testing, but these results provide release some confidence. In future work we plan to use automated search based software testing [5] to further improve autotransplantation regression testing.

Table 1. Runtime data, averaged over 20 runs.

Donor	Time(min.)	
	Avg	Std Dev
GNU cflow	101	31
GNU Indent	31	6

RQ2 For cflow 18 out of 20 transplants passed all acceptance tests, while for Indent 19 out of 20 pass, giving confidence that μSCALPEL has successfully transplanted code, such that the desired functionality is available to host program.

RQ3 Table 1 reports the timing information for the transplants. On average, transplanting the call graph feature from cflow took 101 min, while the layout feature from Indent took 31 min. In less than 44 hours total time, we were able to complete all 40 repetitions of the two experiments. The human effort required to incorporate these two new features would surely have been considerably greater.

Table 2. Transplantation results. Figures marked with * exclude regression test cases that failed before the transplantation (only one for Kate).

(a) GNU cflow Donor

Category	Pass Rate	Coverage (%)	
		All	Organ
Unanimously	16	-	-
Isolation	18	-	-
Regression	20*	62	0
Regression++	17	74	59
Acceptance	18	52	59

(b) GNU Indent Donor

Category	Pass Rate	Coverage (%)	
		All	Organ
Unanimously	18	-	-
Isolation	19	-	-
Regression	20*	66	0
Regression++	18	78	68
Acceptance	19	48	68

A Flavour for the Transplants Produced by μSCALPEL Fig. 1 provides a flavour of the Indent transplant. Figure 1a shows portion of the vein, identified in the static slicing processing. The vein starts at the function main(), and ends at organ entry; the function indent_single_file(). The vein contains the function process_args(), which initialises globals, based on the command line parameters originally used in the donor Indent. Figure 1b shows the resulting code after the inlining process. The brackets capture the code corresponding to each original function. Figure 1c shows the code transplanted into Kate by one of the successful transplants. An α–renaming scheme is used to avoid namespace conflicts within the host, and between the inlined functions.

Some organ statements must be removed, due to failed test cases or incorrect binding to host variables. Some variables may even be unbindable, leading to

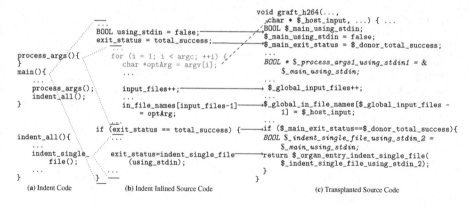

Fig. 1. Transplant operation in cflow donor transplant. Code snippet from the beginning of the graft. ⊣ means function inlining; optArg is mapped to $_host_input; → means statement replacement under α — renaming; grayed statements are deleted.

an uncompilable (or crashable) transplant. For example, the variables argc and argv simply cannot be bound to host variables, because Kate has no concept of 'command line argument'. Fortunately, GP discovers such issues. It removes the first for statement in Fig. 1b . The variable optArg is used for parsing the command line parameters of Indent. This variable was mapped at the variable $_host_input$, thereby correctly using input from Kate call graph computation.

5   Conclusions

We demonstrated that search based automated transplantation (a form of genetic improvement) can be used to automatically transplant non-trivial features (that are requested by users, but hitherto unimplemented by developers) into the large real-world system Kate.

References

1. Barr, E.T., Harman, M., Jia, Y., Marginean, A., Petke, J.: μSCALPEL (2014). http://crest.cs.ucl.ac.uk/autotransplantation/MuScalpel.html
2. Barr, E.T., Harman, M., Jia, Y., Marginean, A., Petke, J.: Automated software transplantation. In: ISSTA (2015, to appear)
3. Bruce, B., Petke, J., Harman, M.: Reducing energy consumption using genetic improvement. In: GECCO 2015 (2015)
4. Cadar, C., Sen, K.: Symbolic execution for software testing: three decades later. CACM **56**(2), 82–90 (2013)
5. Harman, M., Jia, Y., Zhang, Y.: Achievements, open problems and challenges for search based software testing (keynote). In: ICST (2015)
6. Harman, M., Jia, Y., Langdon, W.B.: Babel Pidgin: SBSE can grow and graft entirely new functionality into a real world system. In: Le Goues, C., Yoo, S. (eds.) SSBSE 2014. LNCS, vol. 8636, pp. 247–252. Springer, Heidelberg (2014)

7. Harman, M., Langdon, W.B., Weimer, W.: Genetic programming for reverse engineering (keynote paper). In: WCRE (2013)
8. Langdon, W.B., Harman, M.: Evolving a CUDA kernel from an nVidia template. In: IEEE CEC (2010)
9. Langdon, W.B., Harman, M.: Optimising existing software with genetic programming. TEVC **19**(1), 118–135 (2015)
10. Le Goues, C., Forrest, S., Weimer, W.: Current challenges in automatic software repair. SQJ **21**(3), 421–443 (2013)
11. Petke, J., Harman, M., Langdon, W.B., Weimer, W.: Using genetic improvement & code transplants to specialise a C++ program to a problem class. In: EuroGP (2014)
12. Poli, R., Langdon, W.B., McPhee, N.F.: A field guide to genetic programming (2008). published via http://lulu.com and freely available at http://www.gp-field-guide.org.uk
13. Schulte, E., Dorn, J., Harding, S., Forrest, S., Weimer, W.: Post-compiler software optimization for reducing energy. In: ASPLOS, pp. 639–652 (2014)
14. Sidiroglou-Douskos, S., Misailovic, S., Hoffmann, H., Rinard, M.C.: Managing performance vs. accuracy trade-offs with loop perforation. In: FSE, pp. 124–134 (2011)
15. Sitthi-amorn, P., Modly, N., Weimer, W., Lawrence, J.: Genetic programming for shader simplification. ACM TOG **30**(6), 152:1–152:11 (2011)
16. Wu, F., Harman, M., Jia, Y., Krinke, J., Weimer, W.: Deep parameter optimisation. In: GECCO 2015 (2015)

Grow and Serve: Growing Django Citation Services Using SBSE

Yue Jia[✉], Mark Harman, William B. Langdon,
and Alexandru Marginean

CREST, Department of Computer Science, University College London,
WC1E 6BT, Malet Place, London, UK
yue.jia@ucl.ac.uk

Abstract. We introduce a 'grow and serve' approach to Genetic Improvement (GI) that grows new functionality as a web service running on the Django platform. Using our approach, we successfully grew and released a citation web service. This web service can be invoked by existing applications to introduce a new citation counting feature. We demonstrate that GI can grow genuinely useful code in this way, so we deployed the SBSE-grown web service into widely-used publications repositories, such as the GP bibliography. In the first 24 hours of deployment alone, the service was used to provide GP bibliography citation data 369 times from 29 countries.

1 Introduction

Reusing bespoke features developed for a specific system on other systems requires a substantial amount programmers' effort. This effort can be reduced by implementing the features as web services, thereby using standard protocols to share data and to provide functionality to client applications. We argue that such service-based architecture, where available, provides a useful possible deployment mechanism for genetic improvement. We use a variant of the 'grow and graft' genetic improvement approach [5] to grow a new feature implemented in Python, which can then subsequently be served as a Django service module. Such web services can be easily invoked by existing applications to introduce new features. We call this approach 'grow and serve'; it is 'grow and graft' genetic improvement *without the graft*.

Our approach is a form of genetic improvement [6,9,11,15], which has been used for code migration [7], improving energy efficiency [3,10,13], memory/speed trade-offs [16], automated repair [1,9], and performance improvement [8,11,12,14,15]. More specifically we use the 'grow and graft' approach [5], in which new functionality is grown in isolation and subsequently grafted into an existing system. However, in previous work, the grafting phase has specialised the previously grown code for the system into which it is to be grafted. Similar specialisation is also required in genetic improvement by program transplantation [2,12]. However, in our approach, the grafting phase is not only highly

© Springer International Publishing Switzerland 2015
M. Barros and Y. Labiche (Eds.): SSBSE 2015, LNCS 9275, pp. 269–275, 2015.
DOI: 10.1007/978-3-319-22183-0_22

general, it also becomes trivial; the extra functionality we grow simply becomes a web service module running on the Django framework.

This paper follows the result reporting style used in our previous work on 'grow and graft' genetic improvement, reporting on the guidance required for the grow stage as we did previously [5]. However, the primary claim of the present paper is that we have been able to grow *useful* functionality that was not previously available. For this reason we chose to grow an application that we believe may be useful to some readers. Our agenda is to migrate genetic improvement research from demonstration examples, grown in the laboratory and of primarily scientific interest, to real-world usable code. Our starting point for this outward genetic improvement spread is our own academic community, since we believe we might hope to understand some of their requirements.

Specifically, we use our tools to provide a citation reporting service. The reader can use this to augment existing webpages with citation information, served by Django, genetically improved by the incorporation of the citation service module we grew. We make this available, so that the reader can investigate the code produced by genetic improvement, but also so that he or she can, for example, automatically augment any publication listing websites with citation information.

Citation numbers can provide helpful information in publication repositories. However, this information is missing from many publication repositories (such as the GP bibliography, the mutation and the SBSE repositories). It is not straightforward for the provider of the bibliography to provide citation information, for example from Google Scholar, without considerable effort or supporting technology. We believe that this makes this an interesting and worthwhile candidate for our genetic improvement approach. To demonstrate the usefulness of this new functionality, we have used it to augment the GP bibliography website (and others) with this functionality, an instance of 'GP for GP'; using GP to envolve an improvement to the website concerned with GP. We recorded the first 24 hours of deployment usage, finding that the service was used to provide GP bibliography citation data 369 times from 29 countries.

2   Approach Used to Grow and Serve a Citation Service

Django is an open source web application framework with a stateless service with which we provide a simple URL link to query the number of citations for a publication. The URL takes the title of the publication and returns the number of citations it has attracted. We use the Google Scholar website to source citation information, but our approach could equally be applied to other citation data providers, such as Microsoft Academic Search or Research Gate.

Django turns features implemented in Python into web applications or web services. Therefore, we grow the citation service as Python code using the 'grow' phase of our 'grow and graft' approach [5]. The 'graft' phase becomes trivial; we simply copy the automatically-grown Python code into an existing Django template running on an Apache server. Our GP system implements a strongly-typed GP that takes a grammar file and a test harness as input and outputs a program that passes all the tests specified in the test harness.

The grammar file specifies a set of data types and potential APIs suggested by the developer as likely to be useful to GP. Retrieving citation information is clearly not straightforward, and we do not expect the GP to discover this for itself. Rather, we provide GP with several different types of APIs that it may find useful. These can be divided into four categories: handling HTTP requests, parsing HTML trees, string manipulation, and list manipulation. All of these functionaries are Python built-in functions or are supported by widely-used packages (such as the `lxml` and `requests` models).

Our approach is therefore to give the GP phase 'hints', in the form of pre-existing code that may be useful. As we have argued previously [5], we believe that these hints would be trivial for the human programmer to provide, but almost impossible for GP to discover by itself. As such, the provision of such hints represents an ideal trade-off between human and machine-based effort.

The GP system was designed to evolve imperative programs, formed by a sequential list of assignments and functional calls [5]. We adapted the system to evolve Python code by converting the object-oriented APIs into an imperative form. For example, function $foo.bar(arg)$ is turned into function $foo\_bar(foo, arg)$.

We manually created these functions, to expedite experimentation. However, the process we followed was entirely algorithmic and therefore could have been fully automated. These functions are provided in the test harness file. The test harness also includes the functional tests and fitness computation components for evaluating the evolved code segments. At each generation, GP evolves a population of code segments and inserts them into the test harness. The test harness is executed and evaluated for fitness.

Fitness Functions: We experimented with 8 different fitness functions, composed of a set of 22 equally-weighted fitness components. The default (starting) fitness value is set zero, which denotes a completely useless candidate solution. The fitness value is subsequently incremented, based on the candidate solution's ability to satisfy each of the different fitness components.

The first set of components are the 'essential' fitness requirements; that the new code must pass the test cases that capture correct functionality. We designed five black-box functional tests to cover the different possible forms of input and feedback from the source of citation data, as shown in Table 1. We increase the fitness value by 1 if the execution of a test completes without raising an exception. The fitness value is further increased by 1 if the evolved function also returns the expected output. This gives us 10 essential fitness components; 2 for each of the 5 tests, shown in Table 1.

Our grow and graft genetic improvement research agenda starts with a fundamental assumption: For many programming tasks, it will prove to be easier for the programmer to specify a few criteria for successful solutions, than it will be for the programmer to *generate* the solutions from scratch. This notion

Table 1. The 5 Functional Black Box Test Cased Used for Essential Fitness

1	Characristic	Input	Expected Output
1	Full Title	'Higher Order Mutation Testing'	return 'Cited by 102'
2	Key Words	'Babel Pidgin'	return 'Cited by 5'
3	1 Citation	'Genetic Improvement for Adaptive Software Engineering'	return 'Cited by 1'
4	0 Citation	'Achievements, open problems and challenges for search based software testing'	return 'No Citation'
5	Bad Title	'sdfsdsdf sdoi jsdlkfjsdljlksdlkadslkfsadjlsdfkljsdflksd'	return 'No Citation'

that 'checking is easier than generating' goes the very heart of the motivation for SBSE itself [4]. We think of these criteria for successful solutions as 'hints' provided by the programmer to the GP.

We designed three sets of assistant fitness functions to provide these hints (See Fig. 1). These functions are classified according to our assessment of human effort required to provide them. The set of 'Inclusion' fitness functions specify the names of functions that might be included in a successful solution. We do not give the GP any information about the parameters to pass nor the expected results with these fitness components. The programmer simply has to identify a set of candidate functions which may (or may not) prove to be useful in a candidate solution. We believe that this requires very little human effort, since most programmers will be readily able to call to mind a set of such possible candidate functions for any given programming task. In the case of the problem in hand, the functions we make available with the 'Inclusion' fitness are simply the data structure manipulation functions likely to be useful in any solution.

1	Inclusion	Call to request get
2	Inclusion	Call to generate html tree
3	Inclusion	Call to search html tree
4	Inclusion	Call to filter list
5	Inclusion	Call to concat
6	Ordering	concat before send
7	Ordering	generate html after input
8	Ordering	search html after generated
9	Ordering	filter list after search
10	Necessary	concat gives correct link
11	Necessary	Correct call to Google Scholar
12	Necessary	result contains citation data

Fig. 1. The 12 Fitness Component Hints

The 'Order' fitness components denote a slightly more sophisticated requirement of human effort. They capture constraints on the ordering in which included calls are performed. Clearly, this requires more thought on the part of the programmer. However, we believe that even novice programmers are aware of simple ordering constraints such as 'concatenating partial results together before passing onto the output'. It may even be possible for non-programmers to provide this kind of hint.

Finally, the most sophisticated fitness components are the 'necessity conditions', which denote pre-and post-conditions on the states of computation. These can be thought of as intermediate white box assertion checks that complement the essential black box test cases. Providing such assertions requires more effort from the programmer, but it may help to guide the GP to solutions faster. Perhaps, more importantly, these assertions may provide a useful interface between human understanding and search-based automation. The assertions can be used to constrain solutions such that they satisfy the programmer's conception of expected behaviour at key checkpoints in the computation.

Without such assertions, a perfectly valid solution may be evolved that passes all black box tests, yet remains incomprehensible to the human programmer. Ultimately, such evolved 'source' code may become 'the new object code', removing this concern for all programmers who are content to trust the backend object code that emerges from the 'compilation' process [6]. However, in the intermediate period during which we seek uptake of ideas like genetic improvement, such checkpoints may provide a useful human-machine interface.

Experiment: We used the default crossover, mutation, and elitism operators from the original babel pidgin system [5] with values 0.5, 1.0 and 0.05 respectively and population size 200. The GP terminates when best fitness remains unchanged for 30 generations. We run our experiments on an iMac running OSX 10.10. To speed up the evaluation, we cached the Google Scholar webpage test case results for faster fitness evaluation. This cached call is replaced by an external Google Scholar enquiry link in the final version evolved. All experiments were repeated 30 times to allow for inferential statistical comparison of results.

Results: The results are shown in Fig. 2. Fitness components are labelled as follows: E: Essential, I: Inclusion, O: Ordering and N: Necessity. In Fig. 2 we list the eight choices of fitness components in increasing order of sophistication, loosely denoting the programmer effort required to provide the hints to the GP. We analyse the results using a nonparametric two-tailed binomial test to compare success achieved using the essential fitness, E, with each and all of those we achieved using more sophisticated fitness. We use the Hochberg correction in order to account for the fact that we are performing seven different inferential statistical tests.

Fitness Used	Successful runs in 30 trials	Time in seconds	f=Fitness evaluations
E	0 (p=N/A)	204	6,306
EI	0 (p=N/A)	281	7,400
EO	0 (p=N/A)	379	10,226
EN	0 (p=N/A)	348	9,686
EIO	1 (p=0.500)	425	10,806
ENI	0 (p=N/A)	438	11,133
ENO	9 (**p=0.020**)	443	11,633
ENIO	16 (**p=0.002**)	499	12,700

Fig. 2. Results for Growing Django service

With an α level of 0.05, the widely-used threshold for statistical significance, this corrected statistical test indicates that the result for ENIO and for ENO is significantly different to that for E (with a Vargha-Delaney $\hat{A}_{12}$ effect sizes 0.76 and 0.65 respectively). Overall, the results indicate the importance of ordering constraints, and the power of providing the necessity constraints to capture simple pre- and post-conditions.

Encouragingly, the results also suggest that, perhaps, these more sophisticated pre-and post-conditions are not always required in order to find successful solutions. Since the approach can be repeated multiple times, and the programmer can and use fitness to reject inadequate solutions, we need only be successful on one occasion within reasonable time, after repeated executions. Since a successful solution is found using EIO fitness after only 425 sec, we have tentative evidence that useful functionality can be grown in isolation and deployed as a service using relatively modest programmer hints.

3 Deployment, Conclusions and Future Work

We deployed the service on the Microsoft Azure cloud, incorporating it into the GP[1] and Mutation testing repositories[2]. We also made the citation counting service available as text-returning[3] and image-returning[4] services for others to use. We believe that 'grow and serve' may prove to be widely applicable: The approach will be applicable to any software framework, such as Django, into which behaviour-describing modules can be deployed.

References

1. Arcuri, A., Yao, X.: A novel co-evolutionary approach to automatic software bug fixing. In: CEC, pp. 162–168 (2008)
2. Barr, E.T., Harman, M., Jia, Y., Marginean, A., Petke, J.: Automated software transplantation. In: ISSTA (2015), to appear
3. Bruce, B.R., Petke, J., Harman, M.: Reducing energy consumption using genetic improvement. In: GECCO (2015, to appear)
4. Harman, M., Jones, B.F.: Search based software engineering. IST **43**(14), 833–839 (2001)
5. Harman, M., Jia, Y., Langdon, W.B.: Babel Pidgin: SBSE can grow and graft entirely new functionality into a real world system. In: Le Goues, C., Yoo, S. (eds.) SSBSE 2014. LNCS, vol. 8636, pp. 247–252. Springer, Heidelberg (2014)
6. Harman, M., Langdon, W.B., Jia, Y., White, D.R., Arcuri, A., Clark, J.A.: The GISMOE challenge: constructing the pareto program surface using genetic programming to find better programs (keynote paper). In: ASE, pp. 1–14 (2012)
7. Langdon, W., Harman, M.: Evolving a CUDA kernel from an nVidia template. In: CEC, pp. 1–8, July 2010
8. Langdon, W.B., Harman, M.: Optimising existing software with genetic programming. TEC **19**(1), 118–135 (2015)
9. Le Goues, C., Nguyen, T., Forrest, S., Weimer, W.: Genprog: a generic method for automatic software repair. TSE **38**(1), 54–72 (2012)
10. Li, D., Tran, A.H., Halfond, W.G.J.: Making web applications more energy efficient for OLED smartphones. In: ICSE, pp. 527–538 (2014)

---

[1] http://www.cs.bham.ac.uk/~wbl/biblio/.
[2] http://crestweb.cs.ucl.ac.uk/resources/mutation_testing_repository/index.php.
[3] http://yuejia.cloudapp.net/gpcitation/publication-title/.
[4] http://yuejia.cloudapp.net/gpcitation/img/publication-title/.

11. Orlov, M., Sipper, M.: Flight of the FINCH through the Java wilderness. TEC **15**(2), 166–182 (2011)
12. Petke, J., Harman, M., Langdon, W.B., Weimer, W.: Using genetic improvement and code transplants to specialise a C++ program to a problem class. In: Nicolau, M., Krawiec, K., Heywood, M.I., Castelli, M., García-Sánchez, P., Merelo, J.J., Rivas Santos, V.M., Sim, K. (eds.) EuroGP 2014. LNCS, vol. 8599, pp. 137–149. Springer, Heidelberg (2014)
13. Schulte, E., Dorn, J., Harding, S., Forrest, S., Weimer, W.: Post-compiler software optimization for reducing energy. In: ASPLOS, pp. 639–652 (2014)
14. Sitthi-amorn, P., Modly, N., Weimer, W., Lawrence, J.: Genetic programming for shader simplification. ACM TOG **30**(6), 152:1–152:11 (2011)
15. White, D.R., Arcuri, A., Clark, J.A.: Evolutionary improvement of programs. TEC **15**(4), 515–538 (2011)
16. Wu, F., Weimer, W., Harman, M., Jia, Y., Krinke, J.: Deep parameter optimisation. In: GECCO (2015, to appear)

Specialising Guava's Cache to Reduce Energy Consumption

Nathan Burles[1](✉), Edward Bowles[1], Bobby R. Bruce[2], and Komsan Srivisut[1]

[1] University of York, York YO10 5DD, UK
{nathan.burles,eab530,ks1077}@york.ac.uk
[2] CREST Centre, University College London, London WC1E 6BT, UK
r.bruce@cs.ucl.ac.uk

Abstract. In this article we use a Genetic Algorithm to perform parameter tuning on Google Guava's Cache library, specialising it to OpenTripPlanner. A new tool, OPACITOR, is used to deterministically measure the energy consumed, and we find that the energy consumption of OpenTripPlanner may be significantly reduced by tuning the default parameters of Guava's Cache library. Finally we use JALEN, which uses time and CPU utilisation as a proxy to calculate energy consumption, to corroborate these results.

Keywords: Parameter tuning · Library specialisation · Energy profiling · Reduced power consumption

1 Introduction

The practice of releasing software with configurable parameters is common. This is due to the widely accepted belief that few pieces of software are truly optimal for all situations and therefore an interface is required to allow a more optimal solution to be deployed. Configurable parameters allow developers to release software for general use instead of developing multiple versions, each tailored to a specific environment.

The issue with this model is that few know how to properly tune parameters. To do so requires in-depth knowledge of the software to be configured and the domain in which it is to be deployed. It is for this reason Automatic Parameter Tuning is advantageous. Automated Parameter Tuning is the automatic process of tweaking software parameters until optimal (or near optimal) configurations are found depending on non-functional (and occasionally functional) properties desired by the user.

Research into parameter tuning has focused primarily on execution time [9,17–19], memory consumption [17], and occasionally functional attributes such as output precision [7]. The rise in mobile computing technology [6] with limited battery life, and growth in large server farms responsible for consuming large amounts of energy [10] has sparked a new wave of research into energy efficient software [2,7,12,15]. For this reason we wish to use SBSE to tune and specialise parameters to reduce energy consumption.

This paper will outline a method of optimising parameters to reduce energy consumption using Genetic Algorithms (GAs) to tune Google Guava's[1]

---

[1] Available at https://github.com/google/guava.

M. Barros and Y. Labiche (Eds.): SSBSE 2015, LNCS 9275, pp. 276–281, 2015.
DOI: 10.1007/978-3-319-22183-0_23

CacheBuilder class as used by OpenTripPlanner[2]. Guava's Cache is similar to a map, in that it stores a set of associated keys and values. They differ mainly in their approach to persistence—a map retains all stored associations until they are explicitly removed, whereas a Cache generally evicts entries automatically in order to conserve memory.

The ECJ Toolkit. We have chosen to use ECJ [11] to implement the GA as it is one of the most popular Java-based toolkits for evolutionary computation [4,20]. Using ECJ requires little setup, only the configuration of parameters; the selection of the desired Evolutionary Algorithm, the Evolutionary Algorithm parameters (population size, mutation rate, etc.), and the desired fitness evaluation function. For our requirements ECJ serves as a black-box Evolutionary Algorithm which we trust to be fully tested and reliable.

2   Related Work

Previous work in tuning parameters to reduce energy consumption has been successful, albeit in a round-about manner. In 2011 Hoffmann et al. introduced PowerDial [7], a system for dynamically modifying trade-offs between accuracy in computation and use of system resources during load peaks. Though not directly reducing energy consumption per se, the framework aims to reduce the amount of computing infrastructure required to manage load peaks in server farms that translates to significant reductions in energy consumption (as well as capital costs).

Optimising other non-functional attributes using automatic parameter tuning has also been successful. Wu et al. [21] used Genetic Algorithms to tune both "shallow" and "deep" parameters for both execution time and memory consumption in the widely used *dlmalloc* memory allocator. They were able to show clear trade-offs between these two attributes with possible configuration options resulting in up to 21 % reduction in memory consumption and a 12 % reduction in execution time.

Although it is a relatively new area of interest, using SBSE techniques such as GAs to reduce energy consumption has previously been used by both Schulte et al. in 2014 [15] and Bruce et al. in 2015 [2] to reduce energy consumption as a post- and pre-compilation process respectively.

3   Implementation

The improvement process is as follows:

1. Find variation points within the CacheBuilder class, i.e. the declaration of default values for parameters, and identify the valid values for each of these parameters, for example integers: int initialCapacity = ?, or enumerated types: Strength keyStrength = Strength.{strong, weak, soft}.
2. Generate a template version of the CacheBuilder class to allow the variation points to be easily replaced by the respective element in a solution vector.
3. Given k parameters, the solution representation is a vector containing k integers $[S_1, \ldots, S_k]$, where S_k is in the range identified earlier.

---

[2] Available at http://www.opentripplanner.org.

4. Given an assignment, the default parameter values can be replaced and the modified source file can be written out to disk. The library containing the mutated parameters is compiled and evaluated as part of OpenTripPlanner by a measure related to its energy consumption.

Variation Points. The first two items in the process are performed manually, as the most reliable way to determine valid values for the parameters is by reading the API documentation. In total, due to dependencies and mutual exclusions, there are 9 parameters which may be modified—6 integer values and 3 binary or ternary values.

Mutating the Source Code. For each variation point, the range of potential substitution values were selected to be appropriate. For example the *initial-Capacity* and *maximumSize* parameters were assigned the range [0, 100000], whereas *keyStrength* was assigned the range [0, 1] (mapping to {strong, weak}) and *valueStrength* the range [0, 2] (mapping to {strong, weak, soft}). As a template version of the `CacheBuilder` class has been created, the substitution values can be directly inserted and written to disk—using an enumeration where appropriate for the selection of reference strengths.

Measuring Energy Consumption. We have used a new tool, OPACITOR, to measure the energy consumption during the evolutionary process. OPACITOR is designed to make measurements deterministic, meaning that multiple runs are no longer required and very similar algorithms can be accurately compared. Using a modified version of OpenJDK, OPACITOR counts the number of times each Java opcode was executed. Combined with a model of the energy costs of each Java opcode, created by Hao et al. [5], the tool is then able to calculate the number of Joules used.

In order for a Java program running in a standard environment to be deterministic, various features of the Java Virtual Machine (JVM) must be disabled—namely Just-In-Time compilation (JIT) and Garbage Collection (GC). It is not appropriate to explicitly disable GC, and so instead the initial memory allocated to the JVM is increased to the point that GC does not occur. These features are re-enabled after the evolution has completed, to allow a comparison to occur under realistic conditions.

An important benefit of a model- and trace-based tool such as OPACITOR, when compared to more common approaches such as timing or physical energy measurement, is that is can be run concurrently with other programs without any detrimental effects. This means that fitness evaluations can be executed in parallel on a multi-core system.

Previous work [16] used JALEN [14] to successfully calculate the energy required by Quicksort. JALEN uses time and CPU utilisation as a proxy to calculate energy consumption, and so we have used this tool to corroborate the results generated by OPACITOR during the final comparison.

4   Experiments

We used a metaheuristic search to specialise Guava's Cache library to suit Open-TripPlanner with the property of reduced energy consumption. We decided to use a GA [8] to search the space of solutions, since this has been shown to be an effective approach for a number of assignment problems [3]. The solution representation used is a vector of integers $r \in \mathbb{Z}^k$. The representation is constrained such that each integer falls within its respective bounds, for example a boolean parameter $r_{bool} \in [0,1]$ or a size parameter may be $r_{size} \in [1,100000]$ (limited to ensure the memory requirement does not exceed that available to the experimental machine).

The GA was configured with a population of 100, running for 100 generations. New populations were generated using an elitism rate of 5 %, single-point crossover with a rate of 75 %, and one-point mutation with a rate of 25 % with candidates selected using tournament selection with arity 2. These parameters were selected, after preliminary investigations, in order to provide a sufficient opportunity for the evolution to proceed without requiring an excessive number of fitness evaluations as each evaluation takes over 2 min on a 3.25 GHz CPU. During experimentation we ran the GA five times, with a different seed to the random number generator, in order to test the robustness of the evolution.

5   Results

Statistics were generated using the ASTRAIEA statistical testing framework [13] which performs tests in accordance with the guidelines of Arcuri and Briand [1], namely the Wilcoxon/Mann Whitney U Statistical Tests and Vargha-Delaney Effect size tests. The results were obtained with 100 samples in each dataset. The result of each of the runs of the GA was a similar set of parameter settings, differing only in the exact integers used for the size parameters, and so the first results generated were used for the final comparison between the original library and our specialised version.

The results of the final comparison between Cache versions are shown in Table 1. During the evolution, with JIT disabled and GC avoided, the best set of parameters found used 13596.94 J. This compares favourably with 13857.65 J required by the original version, although it may not initially appear to be a particularly sizeable reduction. This is due to the overhead incurred by Open-TripPlanner when initially loading mapping and transit data—this is unaffected

Table 1. Energy (J) required to exercise Guava's Cache library, as used by OpenTrip-Planner (mean of 100 runs, and standard deviation σ), as well as the p-values (p) and effect size measures (e) comparing our result to the original.

| Measurement technique | GA | Original | | | OpenTripPlanner |
	J	J	p	e	Overhead (J)
OPACITOR	13596.94	13857.65	–	–	10027.24
OPACITOR with JIT and GC	807.69 σ1.57	888.82 σ1.75	<.001	1.00	652.98 σ1.27
JALEN	783.79 σ2.18	815.50 σ1.84	<.001	1.00	662.45 σ1.48

by the Guava Cache, and so these measurements are also included in Table 1 to allow a more useful comparison. Subtracting this overhead shows the improvement more representatively—the evolved version used 3569.70 J and the original version used 3830.41 J. As the measurements in this case are not subject to noise, only one measurement for each of the versions is generated and thus no statistical tests are required.

More interestingly, significant results were also found when noise was reintroduced—enabling JIT and using the JVM's default memory allocation settings (allowing for GC when necessary). In this case the GA's solution required 807.69 J, compared with 888.82 J for the original (or 154.71 J and 235.84 J respectively after subtracting the overhead). As the energy measurement now contains noise, due to the non-determinism of JIT and GC, the p-values and effect size measures are calculated. Vargha and Delaney suggest that a large difference between data sets is indicated by a value of 0.71, and so the results show that a significantly improved version of Guava's Cache has been found by the GA.

To help corroborate these figures, and support the assertion that OPACITOR provides realistic results, we used JALEN (with JIT and GC) to provide additional measurements. The results generated by JALEN can be seen to support the results provided by OPACITOR.

6   Conclusion

We have demonstrated a method of optimising parameters to reduce energy consumption using Genetic Algorithms, applied to Google Guava's `CacheBuilder` class as used by OpenTripPlanner and using a new tool, OPACITOR, to evaluate the energy consumption.

Our results showed that specialising libraries to software packages can provide significant improvements, with the best solution in this case providing a saving of approximately 9 %. The results generated by OPACITOR were corroborated using JALEN, which uses time and CPU utilisation as a proxy for energy consumption. As such, it is reasonable to claim that specialising the library has improved both the energy consumption and the execution time of the software using it. Modifying the Cache's default parameters also has an effect on the memory consumption, and so future work should investigate the trade-off between energy/time and memory.

Acknowledgement. Work funded by UK EPSRC grant EP/J017515/1. Data available at https://github.com/nburles/burles2015specialising.

References

1. Arcuri, A., Briand, L.: A hitchhiker's guide to statistical tests for assessing randomized algorithms in software engineering. Softw. Test. Verif. Reliab. **24**(3), 219–250 (2012)
2. Bruce, B.R., Petke, J., Harman, M.: Reducing energy consumption using genetic improvement. In: GECCO (2015, to aappear)
3. Chu, P.C., Beasley, J.E.: A genetic algorithm for the generalised assignment problem. Comput. Oper. Res. **24**(1), 17–23 (1997)

4. Gagné, C., Parizeau, M.: Genericity in evolutionary computation software tools: principles and case-study. Int. J. Artif. Intell. Tools **15**(02), 173–194 (2006)
5. Hao, S., Li, D., Halfond, W.G., Govindan, R.: Estimating mobile application energy consumption using program analysis. In: 35th International Conference on Software Engineering, pp. 92–101. IEEE (2013)
6. Heggestuen, J.: Business insider: one in every 5 people in the world own a smartphone, one in every 17 own a tablet (2013). http://www.businessinsider.com/smartphone-and-tablet-penetration-2013-10. Accessed 3 May, 2015
7. Hoffmann, H., Sidiroglou, S., Carbin, M., Misailovic, S., Agarwal, A., Rinard, M.: Dynamic knobs for responsive power-aware computing. ACM SIGPLAN Not. **46**, 199–212 (2011). ACM
8. Holland, J.H.: Adaptation in Natural and Artificial Systems: An Introductory Analysis with Applications to Biology, Control and Artificial Intelligence. MIT Press, Cambridge (1992)
9. Katagiri, T., Kise, K., Honda, H., Yuba, T.: FIBER: a generalized framework for auto-tuning software. In: Veidenbaum, A., Joe, K., Amano, H., Aiso, H. (eds.) ISHPC 2003. LNCS, vol. 2858, pp. 146–159. Springer, Heidelberg (2003)
10. Koomey, J.: Growth in data center electricity use from 2005 to 2010, August 2011
11. Luke, S., Panait, L., Balan, G., et al.: A java-based evolutionary computation research system, March 2004. http://cs.gmu.edu/~eclab/projects/ecj
12. Manotas, I., Pollock, L., Clause, J.: SEEDS: a software engineer's energy-optimization decision support framework. In: Proceedings of the 36th International Conference on Software Engineering, pp. 503–514. ACM Press, New York (2014)
13. Neumann, G., Swan, J., Harman, M., Clark, J.A.: The executable experimental template pattern for the systematic comparison of metaheuristics. In: Proceedings of the 2014 Conference Companion on Genetic and Evolutionary Computation Companion, pp. 1427–1430. ACM (2014)
14. Noureddine, A., Bourdon, A., Rouvoy, R., Seinturier, L.: Runtime monitoring of software energy hotspots. In: Proceedings of the 27th IEEE/ACM International Conference on Automated Software Engineering, pp. 160–169. IEEE (2012)
15. Schulte, E., Dorn, J., Harding, S., Forrest, S., Weimer, W.: Post-compiler software optimization for reducing energy. In: Proceedings of the 19th International Conference on Architectural Support for Programming Languages and Operating Systems, pp. 639–652. ACM (2014)
16. Swan, J., Burles, N.: Templar-a framework for template-method hyper-heuristics. In: Machado, P., Heywood, M.I., McDermott, J., Castelli, M., García-Sánchez, P., Burelli, P., Risi, S., Sim, K. (eds.) EuroGP 2015. LNCS, vol. 9025, pp. 205–216. Springer, Heidelberg (2015)
17. Tăpuş, C., Chung, I.H., Hollingsworth, J.K., et al.: Active harmony: towards automated performance tuning. In: Proceedings of the 2002 ACM/IEEE Conference on Supercomputing, pp. 1–11. IEEE Computer Society Press (2002)
18. Vuduc, R.W., Demmel, J.W., Bilmes, J.: Statistical models for automatic performance tuning. In: Alexandrov, V.N., Dongarra, J., Juliano, B.A., Renner, R.S., Tan, C.J.K. (eds.) ICCS 2001. LNCS, vol. 2073, pp. 117–126. Springer, Heidelberg (2001)
19. Whaley, R.C., Dongarra, J.J.: Automatically tuned linear algebra software. In: Proceedings of the 1998 ACM/IEEE Conference on Supercomputing, pp. 1–27. IEEE Computer Society (1998)
20. White, D.R.: Software review: the ECJ toolkit. Genet. Program Evolvable Mach. **13**(1), 65–67 (2012)
21. Wu, F., Weimser, W.: Deep parameter optimisation. In: GECCO (2015, to appear)

Multi-objective Module Clustering for Kate

Matheus Paixao$^{(\boxtimes)}$, Mark Harman, and Yuanyuan Zhang

CREST Centre, University College London, London, UK
matheus.paixao.14@ucl.ac.uk

Abstract. This paper applies multi-objective search based software remodularization to the program Kate, showing how this can improve cohesion and coupling, and investigating differences between weighted and unweighted approaches and between equal-size and maximising clusters approaches. We also investigate the effects of considering omnipresent modules. Overall, we provide evidence that search based modularization can benefit Kate developers.

Keywords: Software module clustering · Multi-objective optimization · Search based software engineering

1 Introduction

This paper reports on experiments with multi-objective search based software re-modularization through module clustering applied to the system Kate [1], a C/C++ editor for KDE platforms. Both unweighted and weighted data were considered, as well as omnipresent modules. We follow the approach initially introduced by Mitchell and Mancoridis [2], in which a Module Dependency Graph (MDG) is remodularized to improve cohesion and coupling, as more recently amended and extended by Praditwong et al. [3] to the multi-objective optimization paradigm. In the unweighted MDG, an edge between two modules denotes a dependency between these modules. For a weighted MDG, an edge denotes the strength of the dependency, which is represented by the edge weight [4]. By using the MDG, the optimization algorithm can then search for a partition of this graph that optimizes the considered quality metrics.

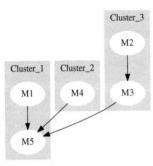

Fig. 1. Modularization example

Search based modularization seeks partitions that cluster modules to favour high cohesion and low coupling. Consider the simple example (shown in Fig. 1), in which edges denote inter-module dependencies. A simple solution would be $X = <1, 3, 3, 2, 1>$. This vector of modules assignments denotes a modularization solution of the five modules into three clusters. Modules m_1 and m_5 are in cluster c_1, m_2 and m_3 in c_3, and finally m_4 in c_2. The MDG that represents these five modules is depicted with this modularization solution in Fig. 1.

© Springer International Publishing Switzerland 2015
M. Barros and Y. Labiche (Eds.): SSBSE 2015, LNCS 9275, pp. 282–288, 2015.
DOI: 10.1007/978-3-319-22183-0_24

The set of fitness functions considered by the two approaches are presented next:

- **Maximizing Clusters (MCA)**   – **Equal-size Clusters (ECA)**
  - cohesion (max)   cohesion (max)
  - coupling (min)   coupling (min)
  - number of clusters (max)   number of clusters (max)
  - MQ (max)   MQ (max)
  - number of isolated clusters (min) cluster size difference (min)

The metrics of cohesion and coupling are related to the dependencies between modules. Cohesion is the sum of the weights of all edges that start and finish in the same cluster. On the other hand, coupling is the sum of the weights of all edges that start in a cluster and finish in another cluster. MQ means Modularization Quality [2], which is the metric used in the previous single objective works. An isolated cluster is the one that has only one module inside it. To illustrate each fitness function of both MCA and ECA, consider the modularization example given in Fig. 1. The set of metrics would be assigned as *cohesion: 2, coupling: 2, number of clusters: 3, MQ: 0.66, isolated clusters: 1, cluster size difference: 1.*

2   Modularizing Kate Using SBSE

Kate's source code is organized in two folders, *src* and *session*, where each folder accommodates some classes. First, the call graph of each function and the inheritance graph between classes were extracted using Doxygen [5]. Kate's unweighted and weighted MDGs were created from these graphs, where each class is considered a module, and a function call or inheritance represents a dependency between modules. The weight of an edge in the weighted MDG is the number of functions calls between the classes. For the unweighted MDG, all edges have the same weight of 1. The clusters are the folders the classes are in. The original Kate's unweighted MDG can be seen in Fig. 2. Function calls are represented by continuous black arrows and inheritance relationships by dashed red arrows. As can be seen, Kate has only two clusters, corresponding to *src* and *session*.

We used the Two-Archive Genetic Algorithm [6], configured based on previous work [3] with crossover probability 0.8 and mutation probability $0.004 \log_2(M)$, where M is the number of modules. The population size used was $10M$, and the algorithm was executed for 10000 generations.

We used both MCA and ECA optimization approaches, each of which was executed 30 times. Each execution generates a pareto front. In order to compare the two approaches, the solution with highest cohesion was selected as a representative of each execution. This set of representative solutions was then used to compute the average and standard deviations of each quality metric. We also performed non-parametric statistical testing and effect size assessment using a paired Wilcoxon and Vargha-Delaney tests, respectively, as recommended in guidance on assessing algorithms differences for SBSE [7,8]. These tests were carried out using the systematic metaheuristic comparison tool Astraiea [9].

Space is limited to six pages. Although this paper is self-contained, the interested reader can find more examples of modularization results, analysis and

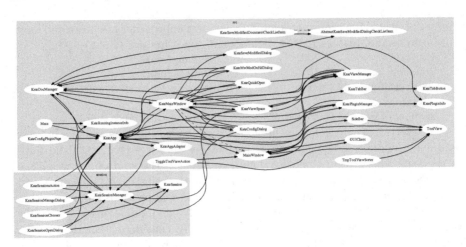

Fig. 2. Kate's original unweighted modularization, where continuous black arrows represent function calls and dashed red arrows represent inheritance (Color figure online).

discussion in the complementary Technical Report [10]. We also make available Kate's modularization data at www0.cs.ucl.ac.uk/staff/m.paixao/kateMod/, to support replication and further studies. Finally, the multi-objective software module clustering tool we developed for this work will be made available in the near future. We pose and answer three research questions, which occupy the remainder of this paper.

RQ$_1$: How much can Kate's modularization be improved for the unweighted and weighted MDGs?

Table 1 presents the results for both MCA and ECA approaches for the unweighted and weighted MDGs in comparison to Kate's original modularization. In case of statistical difference between MCA and ECA, the value is highlighted and the effect size is presented. As one can see, both multi-objective approaches were able to find solutions with better quality metrics than the original modularization for the two different datasets. Regarding cohesion, coupling and MQ, MCA could improve such metrics in 16.3 %, 83 % and 7.88 % for unweighted data, and 3.93 %, 46.8 % and 70.41 % for weighted data, respectively. Considering ECA, these values are similar, 16.4 %, 83.7 % and 1.65 % for unweighted, and 3.49 %, 41.57 % and 60.35 % for weighted.

For the other quality metrics, MCA and ECA also presented similar results for both datasets, which suggests that these two different approaches did not find very different results for this case study. In fact, almost no statistical difference was detected between MCA and ECA, as can be visually seen in the plots of the solutions found in Fig. 3.

Table 1. Quality metrics results for the unweighted and weighted MDGs in comparison to Kate's original modularization

	Fitness	Kate's Original	MCA	ECA	Effect Size
Unweighted	Cohesion	51	59.30 ± 1.10	59.37 ± 1.08	-
	Coupling	10	1.70 ± 1.10	1.63 ± 1.08	-
	Number of Clusters	2	2.57 ± 0.92	2.37 ± 0.87	-
	MQ	1.308	1.42 ± 0.28	1.33 ± 0.36	-
	Isolated Clusters	0	0.53 ± 0.76	-	-
	Cluster Difference	11	-	14.03 ± 7.79	-
Weighted	Cohesion	250	259.83 ± 4.62	258.73 ± 5.23	-
	Coupling	21	11.17 ± 4.62	12.27 ± 5.23	-
	Number of Clusters	2	5.90 ± 1.04	**6.97 ± 1.54**	0.22
	MQ	1.69	2.88 ± 0.46	2.71 ± 0.55	-
	Isolated Clusters	0	2.27 ± 1.26	-	-
	Cluster Difference	19	-	21.23 ± 2.03	-

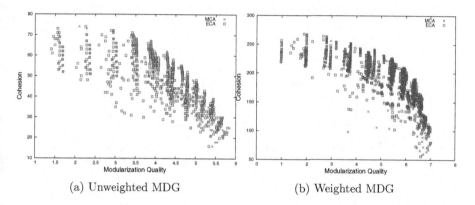

(a) Unweighted MDG   (b) Weighted MDG

Fig. 3. MCA and ECA solutions location for the unweighted and weighted data

RQ$_2$: What difference do omnipresent modules make?

For almost all systems, there is usually a subset of modules that have more dependencies than the average. These modules have been called omnipresent [11] because they belong to the whole system, rather than to a single cluster.

Based on previous works [11], omnipresent modules were handled using thresholds. By choosing an omnipresent threshold $o_t = 3$, for example, modules that have 3 times more dependencies than the average are considered omnipresent. Two different thresholds were used in this work, $o_t = 3$ and $o_t = 2$. After identified, the omnipresent modules are isolated from the MDG, and not considered during the optimization process. Because the results for both unweighted and weighted datasets when considering omnipresent modules are similar, only the unweighted results will be discussed. Table 2 presents such results.

Table 2. Quality metrics results for the unweighted dataset and different thresholds for omnipresent modules

	Fitness	Kate's Original	MCA	ECA	Effect Size
$o_t = 3$	Cohesion	34	35.60 ± 1.36	35.47 ± 1.54	-
	Coupling	5	3.40 ± 1.36	3.53 ± 1.54	-
	Number of Clusters	2	5.07 ± 1.44	4.77 ± 1.69	-
	MQ	1.32	3.32 ± 1.02	3.11 ± 1.18	-
	Isolated Clusters	0	0.27 ± 0.44	-	-
	Cluster Difference	16	-	12.63 ± 4.03	-
$o_t = 2$	Cohesion	29	27.20 ± 0.95	27.67 ± 0.91	-
	Coupling	0	1.80 ± 0.95	1.33 ± 0.91	-
	Number of Clusters	2	**5.70 ± 1.04**	4.17 ± 1.75	0.73
	MQ	1.40	**3.96 ± 0.69**	2.93 ± 1.17	0.76
	Isolated Clusters	0	0.00 ± 0.00	-	-
	Cluster Difference	17	-	6.03 ± 2.99	-

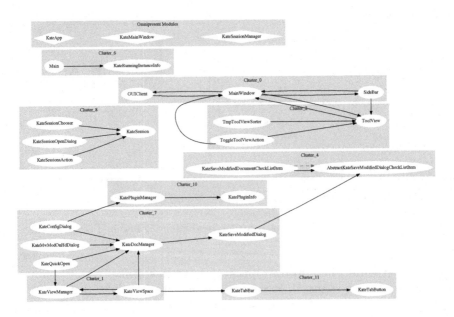

Fig. 4. Example of solution generated for the unweighted dataset and $o_t = 2$

For both $o_t = 3$ and $o_t = 2$, the improvements for cohesion and coupling were small. However, since the MQ metric had improvements of 151.5 % and 182.8 %, and the number of clusters was much bigger, a better overall modularization was achieved. Both approaches had almost the same performance for both thresholds, for almost no statistical difference was detected.

As an answer to RQ_2, there is nearly no difference in the behavior of the multi-objective approach when omnipresent modules are considered. It tends to improve all metrics, with both MCA and ECA presenting similar results. However, the magnitude of the improvement is smaller. This might happen because the isolation of omnipresent modules reduces the search space, making the original solution closer to the optimal.

RQ$_3$: Can the multi-objective module clustering provide useful advice?

Figure 4 presents an example of solution found for the unweighted dataset and omnipresent threshold $o_t = 2$. Despite not being shown in this paper, the solutions for the other scenarios achieved similar modularization. We can see that this solution does capture intuitive clustering of functionality (even though it is computed structurally with no knowledge of purpose of intent). For instance, 'Tool', 'Plugins' and 'Tab' all appear to be related, and they were clustered together by the SBSE approach. Also the 'session' cluster, which appeared to make some sense in the original clustering, has been retained by the algorithm.

3   Conclusion and Future Works

This paper demonstrated that, by applying a multi-objective module clustering approach, it was possible to improve Kate's original modularization for several quality metrics. The optimization technique had basically the same performance for both unweighted and weighted datasets, as well as considering omnipresent modules. The generated solutions were also able to provide useful advice about Kate's modularization. As future research directions, it is expected to apply the multi-objective module clustering approach to other systems.

References

1. Kate (2015). http://kate-editor.org/. Accessed in April, 2015
2. Mancoridis, S., Mitchell, B.S., Rorres, C., Chen, Y.F., Gansner, E.R.: Using automatic clustering to produce high-level system organizations of source code. In: IWPC, vol. 98, pp. 45–52. Citeseer (1998)
3. Praditwong, K., Harman, M., Yao, X.: Software module clustering as a multi-objective search problem. IEEE Trans. Softw. Eng. **37**(2), 264–282 (2011)
4. Mahdavi, K., Harman, M., Hierons, R.M.: A multiple hill climbing approach to software module clustering. In: Proceedings of the International Conference on Software Maintenance, ICSM 2003, pp. 315–324. IEEE (2003)
5. Doxygen (2015). http://www.stack.nl/~dimitri/doxygen/index.html. Accessed in April, 2015
6. Praditwong, K., Yao, X.: A new multi-objective evolutionary optimisation algorithm: the two-archive algorithm. In: 2006 International Conference on Computational Intelligence and Security, vol. 1, pp. 286–291. IEEE (2006)
7. Arcuri, A., Briand, L.: A hitchhiker's guide to statistical tests for assessing randomized algorithms in software engineering. Softw. Test. Verif. Reliab. **24**(3), 219–250 (2014)

8. Harman, M., McMinn, P., de Souza, J.T., Yoo, S.: Search based software engineering: techniques, taxonomy, tutorial. In: Meyer, B., Nordio, M. (eds.) Empirical Software Engineering and Verification. LNCS, vol. 7007, pp. 1–59. Springer, Heidelberg (2012)

9. Neumann, G., Swan, J., Harman, M., Clark, J.A.: The executable experimental template pattern for the systematic comparison of metaheuristics. In: Proceedings of the 2014 Conference Companion on Genetic and Evolutionary Computation Companion, pp. 1427–1430. ACM (2014)

10. Paixao, M., Harman, M., Zhang, Y.: Improving the module clustering of a c/c++ editor using a multi-objective genetic algorithm. RN **15**(02), 01 (2015)

11. Mancoridis, S., Mitchell, B.S., Chen, Y., Gansner, E.R.: Bunch: a clustering tool for the recovery and maintenance of software system structures. In: Proceedings of the IEEE International Conference on Software Maintenance, (ICSM 1999), pp. 50–59. IEEE (1999)

SBSelector: Search Based Component Selection for Budget Hardware

Lingbo Li[✉], Mark Harman, Fan Wu, and Yuanyuan Zhang

CREST, Department of Computer Science, University College London,
Malet Place, London WC1E 6BT, UK
lingbo.li.13@ucl.ac.uk

Abstract. Determining which functional components should be integrated to a large system is a challenging task, when hardware constraints, such as available memory, are taken into account. We formulate such problem as a multi-objective component selection problem, which searches for feature subsets that balance the provision of maximal functionality at minimal memory resource cost. We developed a search-based component selection tool, and applied it to the KDE-based application, *Kate*, to find a set of *Kate* instantiations that balance functionalities and memory consumption. Our results report that, compared to the best attainment of random search, our approach can reduce at most 23.70 % memory consumption with respect to the same number components. While comparing to greedy search, the memory reduction can be up to 19.04 %. *SBSelector* finds a instantiation of *Kate* that provides 16 more components, while only increasing memory by 1.7 %.

1 Introduction

Using Component Based Software Engineering (CBSE) [6], a new software edition (or instance) can be developed by composing pre-existing components, each of which contributes new functionalities to the system. In an ideal world, we would simply include all components, thereby yielding maximal functionality. However, in practice, resource constraints need to be taken into account. In this paper, we focus on the resource constraint of memory consumption.

There are many component selection methods that use an iterative selection/rejection model to filter components based on pre-defined rules/criteria (i.e., stakeholders' requirements) or expert experience [4]. From Requirements Engineering perspective of view, the component selection problem is also known as the Next Release Problem (NRP) [1,10], which can be addressed using search-based techniques. Previous work on SBSE formulations of component selection [2] proposed a single-objective NRP model to select components, later Zhang et al. [12] introduced Multi-Objective NRP (MONRP), and Li et al. [9] extended MONRP with a simulation-based approach to address uncertainty. Kwong et al. [8] also demonstrated how NRP can be re-deployed for multi objective component selection. In their work, selecting highly rated components and the coupling and cohesion relationships among components were considered as improving optimisation objectives.

© Springer International Publishing Switzerland 2015
M. Barros and Y. Labiche (Eds.): SSBSE 2015, LNCS 9275, pp. 289–294, 2015.
DOI: 10.1007/978-3-319-22183-0_25

In this paper, we develop and implement a tool *SBSelector*, which uses a multi-objective SBSE approach to component selection, and apply it to the large, real world system *Kate*, a text editor written in C++. *Kate* is a configurable multi-platform text editor [7]. It can be extended by 'plug-in' type components to enrich its functionality. Some plug-ins are written in native C++, while others are written in Python. There is a special C++ plug-in called Pâté that switches on/off functionality to support Python-based plug-ins. There are currently 37 plugins available, yielding a component selection search space of 2^{37} candidate instances; already too many to support exhaustive exploration, thereby motivating search-based approach.

2 Component Selection as an Instance of MONRP

This section briefly outlines the problem formulation and implementation.

Objectives: There are two objectives which are taken into account. Both of them aim to maximise the users' satisfaction. The first objective is to maximise the number of enabled supplement components of *Kate*: $Maximize\ Component(\vec{x}) = \sum_{i=1}^{n}(x_i)$. In general, the more components are integrated, the more features are available for users to increase their satisfaction. The second objective is defined as minimising the worst-case memory consumption of *Kate*: $Minimize\ Memory(\vec{x}) = \max_{1 \le j \le m} memory(\vec{x})$. Where n is the number of components, and m is the number of simulations. The decision vector $\vec{x} = \{x_1, \cdots, x_n\} \in \{0,1\}^n$ determines the inclusion of components in the system: x_i is 1 if component i is selected and 0 otherwise. The function $memory(\vec{x})$ denotes one evaluation of memory consumption for decision vector $\vec{x}$.

Algorithmic and Implementation Details: The optimisation process is implemented in a Java-based Linux toolkit, *SBSelector*, which directly modifies the configuration file to select components. Since *SBSelector* is a component selection tool, there are no changes made to the source code of the software, making *SBSelector* easily applicable to other Linux software.

The core of *SBSelector* adopts Non-dominated Sorting Genetic Algorithm-II (NSGA-II) [3]. Initially, *SBSelector* generates and evaluates solution population P_0 with size N randomly. Each individual is a component configuration representing the selection of components. Tournament selection, single point crossover, and bit-flip mutation are then applied to reproduce a new population P_0'. Each generated offspring solution in P_0' is evaluated, and merged into P_0, which is then sorted by non-dominated sorting, thereby, producing a new population P_1 with size N for next generation. The population evolves until a termination condition is met. In our experiments, the evolution terminates when the pre-defined generation number is reached. The main evaluation process of *SBSelector* is presented in Algorithm 1.

In each simulation, *Kate* is executed for 1.5 s, and its memory consumption is measured every 100 ms through analysing the results of standard Unix utility, *ps*. *SBSelector* evaluates the dependence constraints, using a 'repair method' [11] to ensure that all dependence constraints are met.

Algorithm 1. SBSelector evaluation process

Require: the solution (configuration) S for evaluation
    $com\_num = CountSelectedComponents(S)$
    $memories = \emptyset$
    for $i = 1, .., m$ **do**
        $memory = EvaluateMemory(S)$
        $memories = memories \cup \{memory\}$
    end for
    $max\_memory = GetMax(memories)$
    $SetFitnessOne(S, com\_num)$
    $SetFitnessTwo(S, max\_memory)$
    return S

---

3 Experiments and Results

In this paper, to evaluate the feasibility and effectiveness of *SBSelector*, we answer the following Research Questions:

RQ1 Does the extra memory consumed by enabling all plugins of *Kate* simply equal to the summation of the extra memory consumed by enabling each plugin one at a time?

    We ask this question as a baseline for this work. If two plugins share some libraries, it is likely that the extra memory consumed by enabling both plugins will be less than the sum of the extra memories consumed by enabling each of them. Therefore, if we observe that the extra memory needed by *Kate* with all plugins enabled is much less than the summation of that with each plugin enabled, there might be hidden shared dependencies between these plugins. This motivates the use of search of optimisation to find the combination of enabled plugins.

RQ2 How effectively can *SBSelector* find optimised combination of enabled plugins compared to random search and a greedy strategy selection?

    Without SBSE, human developers (or users) may include components randomly or greedily based on the memory consumed. We use random search as well as greedy search and compare the optimised combination of components given by NSGA-II against the result of random search and greedy search, to understand how much improvement we can achieve with search based techniques. The initial population size of NSGA-II is set to 50, and the total number of evaluations is 2500. The random search is performed as a sanity check [5], thus the total number of evaluations is the same with that of NSGA-II. Since the Greedy search is deterministic, it is executed once only.

RQ3 Given some mandatory plugins, can *SBSelector* still find combinations of optional plugins that only trade a little amount of memory consumption?

    In reality, some of the components are mandatory to the software or to the user, thus can not be excluded. In this question, we want to know whether the fixed inclusion has any impact to the effectiveness of *SBSelector*. We evaluate *SBSelector* for one particular scenario *S1*, where all Python plugins, 'Search and Replace', and 'SQL Plugin' are essential for Python developers. The result of *S1* is compared to scenario *S2* where all components are open to select.

In order to provide the experiment results in the form of statistical power, we execute our experiments for 10 times. In this case, 10 executions proved to provide a sufficient statistical power to avoid Type two errors, since the results were so strongly better than random search, the baseline against which we compared. All experiments were performed using a machine with dual Intel Core i5 3.20 GHz CPU and 4 GB RAM. The operating environment is Ubuntu 13.04 with Qt 4.8.4, KDE Development Platform 4.11.5, and KIO Client 2.0.

Answer to *RQ1*: The sum of all plugins' individual memory consumption is 45776.4 Kbytes, meanwhile, the extra memory consumed by *Kate* with all the plugins enabled is 22127.6 Kbytes. Specially, Pâté is the most expensive plugin (consumed 14255.6 Kbytes), while the Python program language based plugins are the cheapest. They use very little memory when they are enabled. The probable reason of this interesting finding is that, Pâté is the infrastructure of Python program language based plugins. It has to provide comprehensive invokable interface for those Python based plugins. Moreover, Python is a lightweight dynamic programming language, which means the loading memory consumed by these Python based plugins may be negligible. Consequently, enabling Pâté means nearly all required Python based underlying libraries are loaded. In summary, the result reveals that there are some plugins sharing the underlying libraries consuming less memory together. This promotes the applicability of our tool for the user without exact source code level knowledge of *Kate*.

Answer to *RQ2*: The results are plotted in two figures for two types of attainment: the best attainment (Fig. 1a) and the median attainment (Fig. 1b) surfaces for three approaches: NSGA-II, random search, and greedy search. It can be observed that, in both best and median attainments, there is an obvious gap between the attainment surfaces generated by NSGA-II and random search. The gap is considerably larger when the number of enabled plugins is between 24 and 34. Up to 23.79 % memory can be saved by proper component selection. To perform a statistics comparison between random search and NSGA-II, we use hypervolume indicator to represent the quality of the results. Wilcoxon signed-rank test is performed and its outcome denotes that there is a significant difference between the Pareto-front generated by NSGA-II and random search (p-value = 0.004, Vargha-Delaney effect size = 1). This indicates that our tool *SBSelector* outperforms the simulated human behaviour in terms of finding the solutions with more components while consume less amount of memory.

When human developers or users select components using greedy strategy, assuming they have the knowledge of the memory usages of all individual plugins, the outcome is better than random selection and close to the outcome of NSGA-II. Figure 1 exhibits that, with some basic information, greedy strategy can find, though not optimal, considerably better solutions than random search. Despite good solutions found by greedy search, NSGA-II constantly outperforms greedy search. Specially, with respect to including exact 27 components, the memory reduction from the greedy solution to the best solution found by NSGA-II is 19.04 %. In other words, without knowledge of the exact dependencies among underlying libraries, greedy strategy may mislead the software developer to suboptimal solutions. Such loss will be amplified with the growth of the scale of the

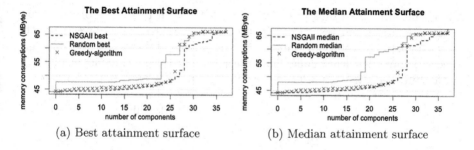

(a) Best attainment surface   (b) Median attainment surface

Fig. 1. Answer to *RQ2*. Comparison of 10-run attainment surfaces for NSGA-II, random search, greedy search.

problem. The Wilcoxon signed-rank test result indicates that the Pareto-front generated by NSGA-II and greedy search are moderately significantly different (p-value = 0.064, Vargha-Delaney effect size = 0.3). In Summary, comparing to simulated human behaviour, search based techniques can effectively find more memory-efficient component combinations. The amount of economized memory can be up to 23.79 %.

Answer to *RQ3*: In order to evaluate the effectiveness and applicability of our tool, we apply our tool in the scenario where *Kate* is used by a Python programmer. The result of *S1* and the comparison with the best attainment surface of *S2* is presented in Fig. 2.

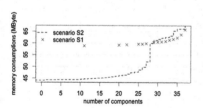

Fig. 2. Anwser to *RQ3* The comparison between the Pareto front of *S1* and the best attainment surface of *S2*.

When enabling 11 mandatory plugins in *S1*, *Kate* consumes 58, 840 KBytes, which is the minimum memory consumption for *S1* as shown in Fig. 2. As the number of included plugins gradually increases, the memory consumption of the best solutions found by NSGA-II grows insignificantly. For instance, after including exact 16 optional plugins, the memory consumption of *Kate* only increases 1.7 %. Surprisingly, when including more than 19 optional plugins, NSGA-II found better solutions in *S1* than that found in *S2*. This is because making 11 plugins mandatory significantly reduces the search space, thus NSGA-II can focus more on the rest solutions and performs better at certain areas. In summary, the answer to *RQ3* is, *SBSelector* is applicable and effective in practise when some plugins are mandatory.

4   Conclusions

In this paper, we demonstrated that component selection problem can be treated as an instance of MONRP, and addressed it using search based techniques.

The results presented illustrate the trade-off between two types of user experiences. Moreover, our results can be used to support to further investigate the hidden implicit relationships among *Kate*'s plugins. The results also highlight some solutions that, when embedding the same number of components, our approach can reduce the memory consumption by up to 23.79 %. In one specific use case, *SBSelector* can find a solution that provides 16 more components while only increase 1.7 % memory consumption. Future work will investigate applying our tool to large scale software systems (i.e., Chrome and Firefox), and consider the topic as well as the popularity of components as an added constraint & objectives.

References

1. Bagnall, A.J., Rayward-Smith, V.J., Whittley, I.M.: The next release problem. Inf. Softw. Technol. **43**(14), 883–890 (2001)
2. Baker, P., Harman, M. Steinhofel, K., Skaliotis, A.: Search based approaches to component selection and prioritization for the next release problem. In: Proceedings of the 22nd IEEE International Conference on Software Maintenance (ICSM 2006), pp. 176–185. IEEE Computer Society, Washington, DC (2006)
3. Deb, K., Pratap, A., Agarwal, S., Meyarivan, T.: A fast and elitist multiobjective genetic algorithm: NSGA-II. Trans. Evol. Comput. **6**(2), 182–197 (2002)
4. Fahmi, S.A., Choi, H.-J.: A study on software component selection methods. In: Proceedings of the 11th International Conference on Advanced Communication Technology, ICACT 2009, vol. 1, pp. 288–292. IEEE Press, Piscataway (2009)
5. Harman, M., McMinn, P., de Souza, J.T., Yoo, S.: Search based software engineering: techniques, taxonomy, tutorial. In: Meyer, B., Nordio, M. (eds.) Empirical Software Engineering and Verification. LNCS, vol. 7007, pp. 1–59. Springer, Heidelberg (2012)
6. Heineman, G.T., Councill, W.T. (eds.): Component-based Software Engineering: Putting the Pieces Together. Addison-Wesley Longman Publishing Co. Inc., Boston (2001)
7. Kate. http://kate-editor.org/. Accessed in April 2015
8. Kwong, C.K., Mu, L.F., Tang, J.F., Luo, X.G.: Optimization of software components selection for component-based software system development. Comput. Ind. Eng. **58**(4), 618–624 (2010)
9. Li, L., Harman, M., Letier, E., Zhang, Y.: Robust next release problem: handling uncertainty during optimization. In: Proceedings of the 2014 Conference on Genetic and Evolutionary Computation, GECCO 2014, pp. 1247–1254. ACM, New York (2014)
10. Zhang, Y., Finkelstein, A., Harman, M.: Search based requirements optimisation: existing work and challenges. In: Rolland, C. (ed.) REFSQ 2008. LNCS, vol. 5025, pp. 88–94. Springer, Heidelberg (2008)
11. Zhang, Y., Harman, M., Lim, S.L.: Empirical evaluation of search based requirements interaction management. Inf. Softw. Technol. **55**(1), 126–152 (2013). Special section: Best papers from the 2nd International Symposium on Search Based Software Engineering 2010
12. Zhang, Y., Harman, M., Afshin Mansouri, S.: The multi-objective next release problem. In: Proceedings of the 9th Annual Conference on Genetic and Evolutionary Computation (GECCO 2007), pp. 1129–1137. ACM, New York (2007)

Search-Based Bug Report Prioritization for Kate Editor Bugs Repository

Duany Dreyton[(✉)], Allysson Allex Araújo, Altino Dantas, Átila Freitas,
and Jerffeson Souza

Optimization in Software Engineering Group, State University of Ceará,
Doutor Silas Munguba Avenue, 1700, Fortaleza 60714-903, Brazil
{duany.dreyton,allysson.araujo,altino.dantas,jerffeson.souza}@uece.br,
atila.freitas@aluno.uece.br
http://goes.uece.br

Abstract. The prioritization of bugs in online repositories can be considered a complex and important task. Thus, providing an automatic strategy to deal with this challenge can be useful and significantly collaborate with the repository use. In this paper, a search-based approach to prioritize bugs in the Kate Editor Bugs Repository is proposed, taking into account some valuable information given by the repository users about the bugs. Experiments demonstrate the proposed approach can be calibrated to fit particular scenarios and can produce intelligent bug orders.

Keywords: Bugs prioritization · Genetic algorithm · SBSE · Kate editor

1 Introduction

Bug repositories have a vital role in software quality, specially in open source projects. As advantages, one can mention the large participation of users publishing code problems, suggesting enhancements and commenting on bug reports [1]. However, as large scale systems become even more common, the number of bugs in repositories grows significantly. Thus, the management of all these information may be considered as a complex task to deal with, including the decision about which bugs have more urgency to be fixed. Usually, a developer has to decide on its own, among all bugs, which should be fixed early, based on some personal criteria. Therefore, it is important for a bug repository to offer an intelligent bug prioritization process, which can stimulate developers to select the most important bugs to fix.

Search Based Software Engineering (SBSE) proposes the use of artificial intelligence techniques to solve complex problems in Software Engineering [2,3]. Prioritization is an activity frequently exploited by SBSE, given the many opportunities to be applied in the software development process [4,5]. However, there are no previous works which have directly investigated bugs prioritization in open

© Springer International Publishing Switzerland 2015
M. Barros and Y. Labiche (Eds.): SSBSE 2015, LNCS 9275, pp. 295–300, 2015.
DOI: 10.1007/978-3-319-22183-0_26

bug repositories using SBSE concepts. Anyway, other studies have been conducted to automatically prioritize bugs to be fixed. In [6] the use of a machine learning technique was proposed, namely Support Vector Machines, to build a bug priority recommender. Similarly, in [7], a classification based approach for automatic bug priority prediction using Support Vector Machine and Naïve Bayes classification algorithms was developed.

Kate Editor is a popular multi-platform and multi-document text editor, part of KDE environment, with plug-in support and written in C/C++. The website for Kate Editor project[1] contains links to the source code repository and an online bug repository. In the Kate Editor Bugs Repository, several information could be useful to allow an automated prioritization of bugs, such as the bug severity, priority level, precedence between bugs, current state, change history and the comments offered by the repository users.

Thereby, considering information about the bugs provided by the repository users, in this paper a formulation to bug prioritization in the Kate Editor Bugs Repository applying a Genetic Algorithm it is proposed and evaluated.

2   Problem Formulation

Consider $B = \{b_1, b_2, b_3, \cdots, b_N\}$ the set of all available bugs, where N is the number of bugs present in the repository. Consider $P = \{p_1, p_2, p_3, \cdots, p_M\}$ a specific order of bugs from set B, where M is a parameter previously defined by the repository administrator which represents the number of bugs presented as solution. Thus, the proposed optimization formulation is presented next:

$$
\begin{aligned}
&\text{Maximize} \quad (\alpha \times relevance(P) + \beta \times importance(P) - \gamma \times severity(P)) \\
&\text{subject to} \quad pos(P, b_i) < pos(P, b_j), if\ b_i \prec b_j\ and\ b_j \in P
\end{aligned} \tag{1}
$$

where $pos(P, b_i)$ returns the position of bug b_i in P if $b_i \in P$, and ∞ otherwise.

The $relevance(P)$ function considers the votes of the repository users to measure how relevant is to solve all bugs present in P. This is obtained by the following function:

$$
relevance(P) = \sum_{i=1}^{N} votes_i \times isIn(P, b_i) \tag{2}
$$

where $votes_i$ stores the normalized number of votes given by the repository users to bug b_i. The $isIn(P, b_i)$ function indicates whether b_i is in P, thus, it returns 1 if $b_i \in P$, and 0 otherwise.

The $importance(P)$ function aims at encouraging the early resolution of bugs considered to have higher priority by the repository users, given by:

$$
importance(P) = \sum_{i=1}^{N} priority_i \times (M - pos(P, b_i) + 1) \times isIn(P, b_i) \tag{3}
$$

---

[1] http://kate-editor.org/.

where $priority_i$ indicates the priority value given by repository users to bug b_i. $importance(P)$ increases as the bugs with higher priority are anticipated in P.

The $severity(P)$ function represents the impact of the early resolution of the bugs with highest severity. Thus, the solution is proportionally penalized according to this relation, where the bugs considered as more severe to the project have to be prioritized as soon as possible in the solution, as follows:

$$severity(P) = \sum_{i=1}^{N} severity_i \times pos(P, b_i) \times isIn(P, b_i) \qquad (4)$$

where $severity_i$ is the severity value assigned by the users to bug b_i. A lower value of $severity$ is reached when bugs with more severity are allocated in the initial positions.

It is important to highlight the freedom to configure the weights α, β and γ according to the faced scenario. For instance, if the context requires a solution that prioritizes the *relevance* over *importance* and *severity*, it could be appropriate to set $\alpha = 2$, $\beta = 1$ and $\gamma = 1$, for example.

In summary, the proposed approach aims at prioritizing bugs, considering votes, priority and severity values assigned to the bugs by repository users, respecting the precedence constraint. Thus, it is expected that the approach finds valid bug fix orders with high *relevance* and *importance*, but with low *severity* to the project.

3   Prioritizing Bugs for Kate Editor Bugs Repository

In order to apply the optimization process to prioritize bugs in the Kate Editor Bugs Repository, the following data extraction process was performed: three different bug states were considered, the *Unconfirmed* bugs, recently added into the repository, but still not officially confirmed, the *Confirmed* bugs, those considered as valid and available to be fixed and the *Reopened* bugs, those which at some point were closed, but had to be reopened. Unconfirmed bugs are considered in this approach because they can potentially become confirmed.

During data analysis, the relevant information, present in the repository, to be used in the proposed model were identified as follows:

1. Number of votes, which represents the relevance of a bug to the community;
2. Priority, which aims at defining the level of importance of a certain bug. This value is quantified as {Very Low (VLO): 0.2, Low (LO): 0.4, Normal (NOR): 0.6, High (HI): 0.8, Very High (VHI): 1.0};
3. Severity, responsible for measuring how serious is a bug, or if it is a request for a new feature. This value is quantified as {Wishlist: 0.1, Minor: 0.25, Average: 0.4, Crash: 0.55, Major: 0.70, Severe: 0.85, Critical: 1.0}.
4. Precedence, when a bug fix depends on the previous bug or a set of bugs.

In relation to extraction process, the number of votes were obtained using data scraping techniques. The priority and severity values were obtained through the JSON API[2] provided by the repository. Thereby, three datasets were generated collecting up all bugs with states previously defined for different time intervals, as follows:

- **dataset-1**: 303 bugs, present in the repository on April 27th, 2013;
- **dataset-2**: 407 bugs, present in the repository on April 27th, 2014;
- **dataset-3**: 543 bugs, present in the repository on April 9th, 2015.

Regarding the Genetic Algorithm settings, it was used a canonical version available in JMetal Framework [8] with the following configurations: $1,000$ individuals per population, $1,000,000$ evaluations of fitness, single point crossover with 90 % crossover rate, bitflip mutation with $\frac{1}{M}$ mutation rate and binary tournament selection. These parameters were empirically obtained by preliminary tests. Represented as an array of integers, each individual is a vector P where the index represents the position of a bug b_i. Solutions that does not satisfy the precedence constraints are discarded.

In order to demonstrate the influence of each weight configuration (see Eq. 1) in the search process, three different configurations were considered: $\{\alpha = 2, \beta = 1, \gamma = 1\}$, $\{\alpha = 1, \beta = 2, \gamma = 1\}$ and $\{\alpha = 1, \beta = 1, \gamma = 2\}$.

For each weight configuration, M and dataset, the GA was executed 30 times to deal with the stochastic nature of the algorithm [9]. In terms of results, the average and standard deviation of values of *relevance*, *importance* and *severity* were collected. To support replication, all datasets, results and source code were made available online for public access[3].

Therefore, the experiments were conducted in order to answer the following research questions:

RQ_1: *Is the proposed approach sensible to different weight configurations?*

RQ_2: *What is the result of applying the proposed approach in the Kate Editor Bugs Repository considering a balanced weight configuration?*

3.1   Results and Analysis

Table 1 shows the average and standard deviation of *relevance*, *importance* and *severity* values for each dataset and different weight configurations using a P with 30 bugs.

When weights $\{\alpha = 2, \beta = 1, \gamma = 1\}$ are used, a higher *relevance* value is reached for the three datasets. Considering dataset-1 alone, the increase was 1.54 % and 2.75 % in relation to the other weight configurations. In the second configuration, $\{\alpha = 1, \beta = 2, \gamma = 1\}$, the *importance* gets more influence and, consequently, results presented higher *importance* values for all datasets. Analyzing specifically the dataset-2, it reached 0.688 of *importance* value. This represents a gain of 6.34 % in relation to $\{\alpha = 2, \beta = 1, \gamma = 1\}$ and 1.92 % to $\{\alpha = 1, \beta = 1, \gamma = 2\}$. Finally, using $\{\alpha = 1, \beta = 1, \gamma = 2\}$, the *severity* is

---

[2] https://docs.python.org/3.4/library/json.html.
[3] http://goes.uece.br/duanydreyton/ssbsechallenge2015/en/.

Table 1. Average and standard deviation of *relevance, importance* and *severity* values for each dataset and different weight configurations, with $M = 30$.

Weight Configurations		$\alpha = 2, \beta = 1, \gamma = 1$	$\alpha = 1, \beta = 2, \gamma = 1$	$\alpha = 1, \beta = 1, \gamma = 2$
dataset-1	Relevance	**0.859±0.064**	0.846±0.075	0.836±0.063
	Importance	0.649±0.021	**0.691±0.011**	0.680±0.014
	Severity	0.124±0.014	0.121±0.013	**0.110±0.007**
dataset-2	Relevance	**0.870±0.045**	0.833±0.059	0.827±0.0777
	Importance	0.647±0.017	**0.688±0.017**	0.675±0.0147
	Severity	0.128±0.012	0.124±0.013	**0.113±0.010**
dataset-3	Relevance	**0.851±0.050**	0.840±0.054	0.841±0.042
	Importance	0.646±0.016	**0.707±0.013**	0.673±0.015
	Severity	0.146±0.016	0.141±0.018	**0.118±0.015**

considered twice more important than the other objectives. For dataset-3, it was possible to reach a *severity* of 0.118, which represents a reduction of 19.18 % to $\{\alpha = 2, \beta = 1, \gamma = 1\}$ and 16.31 % to $\{\alpha = 1, \beta = 2, \gamma = 1\}$.

Given these results, it is possible to answer RQ_1, by attesting the solutions are properly influenced by the weights, enabling the opportunity to configure which options better suit specific scenarios.

Table 2 shows the first five prioritized bugs of the best solution found using a balanced weight configuration, that is, $\{\alpha = 1, \beta = 1, \gamma = 1\}$, in order to answer RQ_2.

Table 2. Information of the first five prioritized bugs of the best found solution using $\{\alpha = 1, \beta = 1, \gamma = 1\}$ in dataset-3 with $M = 30$.

Order	ID's	Description	Votes (relevance)	Priority (importance)	Severity (severity)
1	267618	[PATCH] Kate sidebar does not appear with old sessions	41	1.0	0.55
2	343329	Remote files open up empty	131	0.6	0.7
3	226905	Add support for mime-type sections to. kateconfig files	20	1.0	0.1
4	241502	Kate find bar and split view	40	1.0	0.1
5	313455	JJ Autobracket plugin does not replicate all the functionality of the built in function	219	0.6	0.4

As can been seen, the first prioritized bug have 41 votes, 1.0 and 0.55 for priority and severity values, respectively. In relation to the first, the second bug has more votes and a small advantage in severity, but with a lower priority value. Analyzing the third bug, the values of votes and severity are considerably smaller than the previous ones, but it has the maximum of priority value.

It is important to mention that even a bug with high number of votes do not necessarily should be in the initial positions in P, given that Eq. 2 is not influenced by the position of a bug. The complete list of prioritized bugs in P is available in the supporting webpage.

4   Conclusions

As bugs repositories became more spread and large, the necessity of prioritizing bugs becomes more imminent, presenting itself as a complex task.

The objective of this paper was to propose a formulation and apply a Genetic Algorithm to prioritize bugs in the Kate Editor Bugs Repository. Each objective of the proposed model is related to a valuable information given by the repository users about the bugs. Experimental results demonstrated the proposed approach is sensitive to different weight configurations, allowing the user to adjust the option which better suits the faced scenario.

As future works, one can consider the evaluation of prioritization produced by this proposed approach by experts to validate the produced ranking; the adaptation of the proposed approach to other bugs repositories; the application of other meta-heuristics and the building of a multi-objective version of the approach.

References

1. Anvik, J., Hiew, L., Murphy, G.C.: Who should fix this bug?. In: Proceedings of the 28th international conference on Software engineering, pp. 361–370. ACM (2006)
2. Harman, M.: The current state and future of search based software engineering. In: 2007 Future of Software Engineering, pp. 342–357. IEEE Computer Society (2007)
3. Harman, M., McMinn, P., de Souza, J.T., Yoo, S.: Search based software engineering: techniques, taxonomy, tutorial. In: Meyer, B., Nordio, M. (eds.) Empirical Software Engineering and Verification. LNCS, vol. 7007, pp. 1–59. Springer, Heidelberg (2012)
4. Tonella, P., Susi, A., Palma, F.: Interactive requirements prioritization using a genetic algorithm. Inf. Softw. Technol. 55(1), 173–187 (2013)
5. Vidal, S.A., Marcos, C., Díaz-Pace, J.A.: An approach to prioritize code smells for refactoring. Automated Software Engineering, pp. 1–32 (2014)
6. Kanwal, J., Maqbool, O.: Managing open bug repositories through bug report prioritization using svms. In: Proceedings of the International Conference on Open-Source Systems and Technologies, Lahore, Pakistan (2010)
7. Kanwal, J., Maqbool, O.: Bug prioritization to facilitate bug report triage. J. Comput. Sci. Technol. 27(2), 397–412 (2012)
8. Durillo, J.J., Nebro, A.J.: jmetal: A java framework for multi-objective optimization. Adv. Eng. Softw. 42(10), 760–771 (2011)
9. Arcuri, A., Briand, L.: A hitchhiker's guide to statistical tests for assessing randomized algorithms in software engineering. Softw. Test. Verif. Reliabi. 24(3), 219–250 (2014)

Inferring Test Models from Kate's Bug Reports Using Multi-objective Search

Yuanyuan Zhang$^{(\boxtimes)}$, Mark Harman, Yue Jia, and Federica Sarro

CREST, Department of Computer Science, University College London,
Malet Place, London WC1E 6BT, UK
yuanyuan.zhang@ucl.ac.uk

Abstract. Models inferred from system execution logs can be used to test general system behaviour. In this paper, we infer test models from user bug reports that are written in the natural language. The inferred models can be used to derive new tests which further exercise the buggy features reported by users. Our search-based model inference approach considers three objectives: (1) to reduce the number of invalid user events generated (over approximation), (2) to reduce the number of unrecognised user events (under approximation), (3) to reduce the size of the model (readability). We apply our approach to 721 of *Kate*'s bug reports which contain the information required to reproduce the bugs. We compare our results to start-of-the-art *KLFA* tool. Our results show that our inferred models require 19 tests to reveal a bug on average, which is 98 times fewer than the models inferred by *KLFA*.

Keywords: SBSE · NLP · Topic modelling · Model inference · NSGA-II

1 Introduction and Background

Many systems allow users to submit bug reports when they encounter unexpected behaviour. Developers need to validate and fix these issues, based on these bug reports. Unfortunately, not all of the bug-fixes work as expected. A recent study suggests that up to 24 % of post-release bug-fixes of large software systems are incorrect and some of the generated patches even introduce additional faults into the software [1,2]. These bad bug fixes not only affect the reliability of the software source code but also have negative impact on their users [1].

Generating additional tests that exercise the reported buggy features could improve software developers' confidence in their bug fixes. In this paper, we adapt an event-based model inference approach for such test enhancement using search-based algorithms. Event-based model inference has been widely used in software testing [3,4]. This technique takes system logs as inputs and generates a finite state machine which recognises execution sequences observed from the log file. Such a log file is often automatically generated and contains a sequence of function calls.

© Springer International Publishing Switzerland 2015
M. Barros and Y. Labiche (Eds.): SSBSE 2015, LNCS 9275, pp. 301–307, 2015.
DOI: 10.1007/978-3-319-22183-0_27

In this work, our approach aims to infer models from user bug reports instead of using system logs. Bug reports submitted by users are written in natural language, many of which include a set of instructions that can be used to reproduce the bugs. An inferred model from these bug reports is a generalisation of the set of user events which has triggered software bugs. The model can be used to generate new test data targeting the user-reported buggy features of the system.

Traditional single objective inferencing approaches tend to suffer from two intertwined problems. The inferred model either misses some behaviour specified in bug reports (under generalising) and includes some infeasible behaviour (over generalising). To overcome this limitation, we adapted the multi-objective approach proposed by Tonella et al. [5] to balance these two conflicting objectives.

We apply our approach to the SSBSE 2015 Challenge program *Kate* [6], a popular multi-platform text editor. We provide empirical evidence that the model generated from our approach not only provides good trade-offs between under and over approximation but also provides a good level of fault detection ability.

2   Models Inference Framework

Our approach to bug-report model inference consists of four phases. The first phase extracts raw bug issue reports from the *Kate* bug tracking system. Then the second phase parses the raw data extracted to retrieve bug information, such as textual descriptions of the execution steps for bug reproduction, the related components, the status and severity of the bug. In the third phase, bug descriptions are used to identify execution trace information. In particular, we use topic modelling to mine and extract reproducible user events. In the final phase, we use two multi-objective search algorithms to infer models from the user events.

Phase 1 - Bug Report Extraction: *Kate* is a multi-platform text editor written in C/C++. The *KDE Bugtracking System* [7] is used by the *Kate* project to maintain and keep track of reported software bugs. A web crawler was implemented to collect raw HTML webpage data from the *KDE Kate* bug repository. There have been 5,583 bug issues reported (including those already resolved, verified and closed) since January 2000. Our crawler visits the webpage of each bug issue and saves it as raw bug report data.

Phase 2 - Raw Data Parsing: we extract bug descriptions for each bug issue by parsing the raw data according to a set of search rules. We manually developed the search rules based on HTML files to capture information about bug issue ID, status, component, importance, description. In particular, in the textual description, steps to reproduce are the most important part of the bug report. They provide valuable information for the developer in order to test and fix the issue. We retrieve such information from the *Kate* bug HTML files by locating content between the 'Steps to Reproduce' and 'Actual Results' keywords.

Phase 3 - Data Mining Trace Events: there are three steps in Phase 3: (1) preparing the training corpus; (2) clustering similar trace steps; (3) mapping trace events. First, since 'Steps to Reproduce' patterns are written in natural language, we need to refine the patterns to remove noise. The Natural Language ToolKit (NLTK) [8] was used to preprocess the raw patterns. NLTK is an open source library for Natural Language Processing (NLP) implemented in Python. We first tokenise the patterns from strings to vectors, then remove English language stop words, numbers and punctuation marks. Next, we stem tokens to their root form and filter out low-frequency words that only appear once. We save all the refined patterns together as corpus in the Vector Space Model (VSM), which will be used in the next step.

In the second step, we cluster similar preprocessed trace steps using a tool called *gensim* [9], an open source NPL topic modelling tool, supporting semantic topic detection. In order to cluster steps, we transform a pre-prepared training corpus into a term frequency-inverse document frequency (tf-idf) matrix and then project it into a Latent Semantic Indexing (LSI) space. For each trace step, we compute *similarity* against the transformed corpus. The *similarity* measure used is the *cosine* similarity between two vectors. The most similar steps are clustered. We repeatedly combine clusters if their similarity measure is greater than a predefined *similarity* threshold (*cosine* > *0.7* in the experiment on which we report here). At this stage, the user events are generated by locating shared common tokens in one cluster. We found some generated user events have the same semantics, for example, 'open_kate', 'start_kate' and 'launch_kate' all represent the same user behaviour. These events should be treated as one, otherwise the algorithm will generate many similar states. In the last step, we solve this problem by manually examining half of the user events and creating a mapping to transform duplicated user events.

Phase 4 - Model Inference: We use two multi-objective algorithms, a Genetic Algorithm and the NSGA-II algorithm to infer models from the user events generated. In this work, there are three objectives taken into account to optimise the inferred models. These objectives are those proposed by Tonella et al. [5]. The first objective is to minimise the amount of model behaviour which does not follow any existing trace events generated. This type of unobserved model behaviour is over approximation, which is unlikely to occur in reality. The second objective is to minimise the amount of behaviour which is not accepted by the model, namely under approximation. It is measured by the number of unrecognised trace events. The third objective is to minimise the number of states in a model, to ensure we favour simplicity where possible.

3 Experiments and Results

To evaluate the feasibility and effectiveness of our approach, we answer the following research questions: **RQ0:** What are the prevalence and the characteristics of the trace events generated? **RQ1:** What are the performance of multi-objective optimisation compared to the benchmark model inference technique, *KLFA* [10] in terms of the hypervolume, running time and the number of solutions? **RQ2:** What is the fault revealing ability of the models inferred?

In total, our approach takes 721 bug reports that contain 'Steps to Reproduce' patterns as inputs and generates 452 user event trace files containing 265 unique trace events. To answer RQ0, we manually analysed these events which can be divided into six categories, as shown in Table 1. As can be seen from the table, the user events generated from our approach cover a wide range of functionalities of *Kate*, from basic operations to advanced features.

Table 1. Example of user events generated

Category	Basic operation	Text editing	Programming
Examples	Start_Kate	copy_paste_text	select_haskell_mode
	open_multiple_files	change_input_method	show_javascript_console
	score_screen	fold_section	check_regular_expression
	drag_cursor	find_replace	fold_function
	resize_window	captialize_text	check_indentation
	close_file	set_bookmark_color	enter_vi_command
Category	Configuration	Plugins	Shortcut
Examples	change_keyboard_setting	enable_plugin_quickswitcher	ctrl_1
	change_background_color	enable_plug_xml	ctrl_g
	change_print_margin	enable_plugin_spellcheck	ctrl_o
	change_print_page_range	enable_plugin_tabbar	ctrl_r
	enable_command_line	enable_plugin_terminal	alt_right
	enable_static_word_wrap	enable_plugin_treeview	alt_tab

To answer RQ1, we adopt one of standard, widely-used measures of multi-objective solution quality - hypervolume. Hypervolume is the volume covered by the solutions in the objective space. It is the union of hypercubes of solutions on the Pareto front [11]. By using a volume rather than a count, this measure is less susceptible to bias when the numbers of points on the two compared fronts are very different. We also measure the running time of the algorithms and the number of solutions generated. For algorithms that produce good quality solutions, quick and diverse answers are an important algorithmic property for decision makers.

Table 2. Objectives and performance metrics results for GA, NSGA-II and KLFA

Performance / Algorithm	Objectives - Mean (Min, Max)			Quality Metrics - Mean	
	Over Approximation	Under Approximation	Size of Model	Running Time	No. of Solutions
GA	2 (0, 66)	219 (208, 225)	13 (2, 53)	3239.66s	25
NSGA-II	0.1 (0.0, 7)	215 (183, 226)	19 (1, 94)	2341.14s	17
KLFA	55707	4	289	556.30s	1

Table 2 shows the mean, lowest and highest values of three objectives and average running time and the number of solutions generated by GA and NSGA-II for 30 executions. As *KLFA* generates deterministic solutions, we only report the results with one run for *KLFA*. Figure 1 shows the distribution of models generated by three techniques, along three objectives, in the form of box plots. As can be seen from the results, both GA and NSGA-II are able to infer models which have a lower over-approximation account but relatively higher under-approximation account. By contract, the models inferred by *KLFA* have a very high over-approximation account. In terms of size of a model, both GA and NSGA-II are able to keep the size of a model small.

The statistical analysis of hypervolume results is reported in Table 3. We use Cliff's method [12] for assessing statistical significance and the Vargha-Delaney $\hat{A}_{12}$ metric for effect size measure where the result is significant (at the 0.05 α level). The results of all algorithms are significantly different. The effect size of the two search algorithms are very small and both of them outperform *KLFA*.

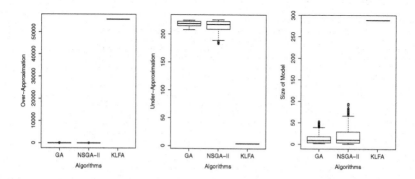

Fig. 1. Box plots of the over-approximation, under-approximation and size counts from the models inferred by multi-objective GA, NSGA-II and KLFA - 30 runs

Table 3. Hypervolume results of the statistical analysis for GA, NSGA-II and KLFA

Algorithm	Algorithm	Hypervolume	
		Cliff's method	Vargha-Delaney effect size
(x)	(y)	*p-value*	$\hat{A}_{12}$
GA	NSGA-II	1e-04	0.06
GA	KLFA	1e-04	1.00
NSGA-II	KLFA	1e-04	1.00

To answer RQ2, we investigate the fault-revealing ability of the models inferred. In software testing, the effectiveness of a test suite is assessed according to its ability to detect real bugs. We evaluate the fault-revealing ability of the models by checking the number of bug traces accepted by the models. If a bug trace is accepted by a model, it means the model can be used to generate test event traces to capture this bug. We have equally divided all valid bug reports into training and validation sets based on their submission time. We used the training set to infer models. We then check if the models inferred can capture the bug reported in the validation set. The training set contains 226 bug reports submitted between 07/2009 to 10/2012 , while the evaluation set contains 226 more recently submitted between 11/2012 and 02/2015. Table 4 shows the average number of bugs by each set of Pareto Front solution, the total number of bug detected and the average number of tests to be generated per bug revealed. Although *KLFA* generates find more bug in the validation set, it generates 500 times more tests traces. On the other hand, the models inferred using search only take less than 20 tests to reveal a bug on average where as *KLFA* takes 1,863. This makes former models preferable in place as the cost involved in checking the results of test sequence requires human effort.

Table 4. Results for fault-revealing ability of the models inferred

	Avg. # Traces (L = 4)	Avg. # Bugs Pareto Front	Total # Bugs	Avg. Test per bug revealed
GA	147	8	16	18
NSGA-II	116	6	22	19
KLFA	55,906	30	30	1863

4   Conclusion

We have studied the use of multi-objective search algorithm to infer models from software bug reports. The models inferred are well-balanced between the amount of over- and under-approximation of users behaviour. We also found that our approach generates smaller number of user event traces per bug revealed than *KLFA*, thereby these models are more preferable in practice. We believe that model inferencing techniques for documents written in natural language may prove to be widely applicable to many software documents, such as bug reports in our case.

Acknowledgements. We wish to express our gratitude to Paolo Tonella for his helpful suggestion and the search-based FSM tools provided.

References

1. Yin, Z., Yuan, D., Zhou, Y., Pasupathy, S., Bairavasundaram, L.: How do fixes become bugs? In: Proceedings of the 19th ACM SIGSOFT Symposium and the 13th European Conference on Foundations of Software Engineering (ESEC/FSE 2011), Szeged, Hungary, pp. 26–36. ACM, 5–9 September 2011
2. Buggy McAfee update whacks Wndows XP PCs: http://news.cnet.com/8301-1009_3-20003074-83.html

3. Krka, I., Brun, Y., Popescu, D., Garcia, J., Medvidovic, N.: Using dynamic execution traces and program invariants to enhance behavioral model inference. In: Proceedings of the ACM/IEEE 32nd International Conference on Software Engineering (ICSE 2010), Cape Town, South Africa, pp. 179–182. IEEE, 2–8 May 2010
4. Lorenzoli, D., Mariani, L., Pezzè, M.: Automatic generation of software behavioral models. In: Proceedings of the 30th International Conference on Software Engineering (ICSE 2008), Leipzig, Germany, pp. 501–510. ACM, 10–18 May 2008
5. Tonella, P., Marchetto, A., Nguyen, D.C., Jia, Y., Lakhotia, K., Harman, M.: Finding the optimal balance between over and under approximation of models inferred from execution logs. In: Proceedings of IEEE 5th International Conference on Software Testing, Verification and Validation (ICST), Montreal, QC, Canada, pp. 21–30. IEEE, 17–21 April 2012
6. The Kate Editor: http://kate-editor.org/
7. KDE Bugtraking System: https://bugs.kde.org/
8. The Natural Language ToolKit (NLTK): http://www.nltk.org/
9. Řehůřek, R., Sojka, P.: Software framework for topic modelling with large corpora. In: Proceedings of the LREC 2010 Workshop on New Challenges for NLP Frameworks, Valletta, Malta, pp. 45–50. ELRA, May 2010. http://is.muni.cz/publication/884893/en
10. Mariani, L., Pastore, F.: Automated identification of failure causes in system logs. In: Proceedings of the 19th International Symposium on Software Reliability Engineering (ISSRE 2008), Seattle, WA, USA, pp. 117–126. IEEE, 10–14 November 2008
11. Zitzler, E., Thiele, L.: Multiobjective evolutionary algorithms: a comparative case study and the strength pareto approach. IEEE Trans. Evol. Comput. $3(4)$, 257–271 (1999)
12. Cliff, N.: Ordinal Methods for Behavioral Data Analysis. Lawrence Erlbaum Associates Inc., New Jersey (1996)

Short Papers

Introducing Learning Mechanism for Class Responsibility Assignment Problem

Yongrui Xu[1], Peng Liang[1(✉)], and Muhammad Ali Babar[2]

[1] State Key Lab of Software Engineering, Wuhan University, Wuhan, China
{xuyongrui,liangp}@whu.edu.cn
[2] School of Computer Science, The University of Adelaide, Adelaide, Australia
ali.babar@adelaide.edu.au

Abstract. Assigning responsibilities to classes is a vital task in object-oriented design, which has a great impact on the overall design of an application. However, this task is not easy for designers due to its complexity. Though many automated approaches have been developed to help designers to assign responsibilities to classes, none of them considers extracting the design knowledge (DK) about the relations between responsibilities in order to adapt designs better against design problems. To address the issue, we propose a novel Learning-based Genetic Algorithm (LGA) for the Class Responsibility Assignment (CRA) problem. In the proposed algorithm, a learning mechanism is introduced to extract DK about which responsibilities have a high probability to be assigned to the same class, and the extracted DK is employed to improve the design qualities of generated solutions. An experiment was conducted, which shows the effectiveness of the proposed approach.

Keywords: CRA problem · Data mining · Genetic algorithm · The Baldwin effect

1 Introduction

In object-oriented design, assigning responsibilities to classes is a vital task, which has a great impact on the overall design of an application [1]. The main goal of Class Responsibility Assignment (CRA) is to find an optimal assignment of responsibilities (where responsibilities are presented in terms of methods and attributes) to classes and how objects should interact by using the methods [2]. Since the number of responsibilities can reach to hundreds and thousands in a normal industrial size system, and CRA depends heavily on human judgment and decision-making, it is challenging for designers to assign responsibilities to classes (especially for novice designers) [1].

Existing approaches on automated CRA can prevent novice designers from making improper software design [1–3]. In these automated approaches, quality metrics (e.g., structural metrics) are defined to evaluate the design qualities of generated solutions. However, several issues need to be considered for employing these automated CRA

This work is partially sponsored by the NSFC under Grant No. 61170025 and No. 61472286.

M. Barros and Y. Labiche (Eds.): SSBSE 2015, LNCS 9275, pp. 311–317, 2015.
DOI: 10.1007/978-3-319-22183-0_28

approaches: (1) in [4], the authors argued that no magic metrics for the evaluation of design quality had been found; (2) structural metrics seem to be 'cheating' the software engineer: they are 'improving the design' from the structural metrics standpoint, but these changes do not correspond to the expectations of designers [5]. Considering these, a new trend for evaluating CRA results is to compare the similarity between generated solutions and expert designs [2]. The reason of this comparison is that the designs produced by experienced designers (experts) follow design principles as much as possible, and expert designs possess the desired design properties.

As a reflection of this trend, we need to take a fresh look at the automated approach for CRA. The underlying reason of making generated solutions close to expert designs is that the designs produced by different experts are similar within the same context, and the best design practices (i.e., a type of implicit design knowledge (DK)) for the design problem may exist in these similar parts. If the implicit DK can be captured automatically and further used to generate software design solutions, it may adapt solutions better against design problems. To this end, a novel Learning-based Genetic Algorithm (LGA) is proposed in this paper, which introduces a learning mechanism for automated CRA. The contributions of this work are: (1) introduce learning mechanism for automated CRA, which adapts the generated solutions better against the design problems by considering the extracted DK; (2) propose a novel Genetic Algorithm (GA) based on the Baldwin effect, which considers relations between individuals to make better exploration and exploitation in the solution space. The proposed algorithm may also be applied to solve other software engineering (SE) problems with Search Based Software Engineering (SBSE) techniques.

2   Approach

In this section, we introduce the proposed Learning-based Genetic Algorithm (LGA) and the theories behind it. We also describe the procedure of applying LGA for CRA.

2.1   Learning-Based Genetic Algorithm (LGA)

Darwinism states that all species of organisms arise and develop through the natural selection of small, inherited variations that increase the individual's ability to compete, survive, and reproduce. However, Darwinism has been questioned that whether it is suitable for the phenomenon of microevolution [6]. Microevolution means changes can occur within existing species or gene pools without natural selection. To support microevolution, the Baldwin effect was proposed as a post-Darwinian mechanism of evolution [7]. The core mechanism of the Baldwin effect is the learning mechanism for individuals in response to changes in their environment.

Traditional GAs inspired by Darwinism are widely used in the field of SBSE, but they do not support microevolution well. Consequently, traditional GAs lead to isolations between candidate solutions, and cannot fully exploit the relations between candidate solutions to improve design qualities of final solutions. For instance, in a CRA problem, the relations between responsibilities in candidate solutions should be extracted as DK and be fully exploited to improve design qualities of individuals (i.e., candidate solutions) in the population. In addition, preferable individuals, which have better design qualities than others in a population, should evangelize their responsibility assignment as DK to other individuals, which leads to an adaptive change taking place simultaneously for most of the individuals of the population. To support microevolution of individuals with SBSE techniques, a Learning-based Genetic Algorithm (LGA) based on the Baldwin effect is proposed and shown in Fig. 1, which introduces a novel learning operator to support the learning mechanism for individuals.

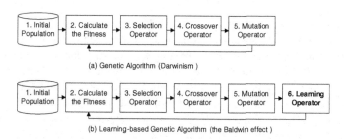

Fig. 1. Traditional Genetic Algorithm and Learning-based Genetic Algorithm

2.2 Solving CRA with LGA

In this section, we mainly show how to use the universal learning operator in LGA to extract implicit DK to improve design qualities for the CRA problem. **Step 1** to **Step 5** in Fig. 1 are omitted, which are detailed in [1, 2].

When **Step 5** in Fig. 1 is completed, a new generation is produced in both GAs. In LGA, according to the fitness of each individual, the individuals of this generation are further classified into three groups: preferable individuals group (PG), ordinary individuals group (OG), and inferior individuals group (IG). If the fitness of an individual is in the top 20 % of the generation, the individual may have good design qualities, and it belongs to PG. If the fitness is in the bottom 30 %, the individual may have poor design qualities, and it belongs to IG. The remaining individuals with moderate design qualities belong to OG. For CRA, individuals of IG should learn the DK extracted from individuals of PG to evolve these IG individuals, which is defined as "learning mechanism" in this paper. Figure 2 shows the four sub-steps about how to extract the DK according to the relations between responsibilities from individuals in PG, and how to apply the extracted DK for individuals in IG in order to make adaptive changes for these IG individuals.

Fig. 2. The procedure of learning in the learning operator

2.2.1   Construct Dataset from PG

A dataset which can be further used to extract DK is needed in our approach, and **Step 6.1** constructs this dataset from individuals in PG. The dataset is composed of records, and each record contains responsibilities which are assigned to the same class in a PG individual. For example, suppose there are five responsibilities (i.e., R_1 to R_5) that need to be assigned to classes. An individual *ind* in PG may assign R_1 and R_2 to *Class1*, and assign other responsibilities to *Class 2*. In this situation, two records exist for *ind*: {R_1, R_2} and {R_3, R_4, R_5}. Different with the genotype of *ind*, the two records are independent records in the constructed dataset. Hence, the dataset can be generated by combining records of all the individuals in PG.

2.2.2   Generate Frequent Itemsets and the Rule Set

In **Step 6.2**, we use the Apriori algorithm, an association algorithm from data mining, to discover the frequent itemsets of responsibilities from the dataset generated in **Step 6.1**. In data mining, a frequent itemset contains the elements, which have a high probability to appear together in records. When **Step 6.2** is completed, the DK about which responsibilities are always assigned to the same class in PG individuals can be discovered. For example, suppose {R_1, R_2} and {R_3, R_4, R_5} are two frequent itemsets acquired by the Apriori algorithm in **Step 6.2**, we then know R_1 and R_2 are often assigned to the same class in different PG individuals (similar case for R_3, R_4, and R_5).

However, it is not enough that the proposed approach can only be aware of which responsibilities have a high probability to be assigned to the same class in PG individuals. We need to discover and understand which responsibilities make other responsibilities be assigned to the same class in the frequent itemsets before introducing learning for individuals in IG. For instance, if {R_1, R_2} is a frequent itemset acquired in **Step 6.2**, we need to know whether R_1 leads to the assignment of R_2 to the same class with R_1 (i.e., $R_1 => R_2$), or vice versa (i.e., $R_2 => R_1$). Each situation above (e.g., $R_1 => R_2$) is called a rule, and a rule set is generated in **Step 6.3**. The generated rule set in **Step 6.3** contains the DK about how to optimize responsibilities assignment for design problems. In **Step 6.3**, all possible rules for each frequent itemset are generated, and we use *support, confidence*, and *lift* measures which are widely used in data mining to filter out uninteresting and repeated rules [8]. Suppose a rule has the form $X => Y$, the *support* of the rule is the proportion of records that contain both X and Y in the constructed dataset, and the *confidence* of this rule is the proportion of records that contain Y among the records that contain X. In addition, the *lift* measure calculates the relevance between X and Y in a rule. When **Step 6.3** is completed, the DK for design problems is automatically extracted with our approach, and individuals in IG can learn these DK from the rule set in **Step 6.4**.

2.2.3   Learn Adaptively for Individuals in IG

According to the *support* and *confidence* measure of each rule calculated in **Step 6.3**, the concept of learning rate is introduced for each rule. More specifically, a rule with higher values of *support* and *confidence* measures will have a higher learning rate, resulting that this rule has a higher probability to be learned by individuals in IG. In **Step 6.4**, each individual in IG tries to learn each rule in the generated rule set with the learning rate of that rule, and adaptively changes the individual itself with the rules that the IG individual decides to learn. For instance, if an individual in IG decides to learn the rule "$R_1 => R_2$", the individual will change itself, and assign R_2 to the class which contains R_1. However, each rule has its precondition, which should be satisfied before the rule is applied by individuals in IG. We define the precondition of a rule according to the left part of the rule. For example, in the rule "$R_1, R_2 \Rightarrow R_3$", the left part of the rule is $\{R_1, R_2\}$, and the precondition of the rule is that R_1 and R_2 should belong to the same class in an individual. If R_1 and R_2 are assigned in different classes in an individual in IG, this rule cannot be applied by this individual. In **Step 6.4**, individuals in IG apply the extracted DK from individuals in PG to make adaptive changes in order to better adapt against design problems.

With the novel learning operator in LGA, our proposed approach for CRA can fully exploit the use information between responsibilities, and extract the DK from individuals which have better design qualities in the population. In addition, our approach supports the microevolution mechanisms for the population, and allows individuals to adaptively change themselves to better adapt against the design problems.

3 Experiment

To evaluate the effectiveness of the proposed approach, we compare our approach with a GA based approach. The experiments were performed on a Dual Core@2.30 GHz with 10 GB of RAM. We use three software design problems (i.e., CBS, GDP, and SC) that are used in [3], which spans a range of size and complexity, to compare the similarity degree of the design solutions generated by the two approaches with the expert design. Expert designs can be found in [9]. *F-Score* is a cluster/classification evaluation measure that combines "*precision*" and "*recall*" from information retrieval, and existing CRA work [2] used it to calculate the similarity degree between two solutions, which is an appropriate measure for our purpose. The definition of the *F-Score* measure for the CRA problem can be found in [2], and higher *F-Score* value means the generated solution is closer to the expert design. Given the probabilistic nature of the algorithms, multiple runs are mandatory. For each problem instance, we run the evaluation 30 times for each algorithm to calculate the mean *F-Score* values of all the individuals in the population, and the mean value of the 30 *F-Score* values is used to represent the final *F-Score* value for an instance with corresponding algorithms. To enable a fair comparison, we used the same settings in each evaluation. The population size is 100, and for traditional genetic operators used in both algorithms, binary tournament is used as the default selection operator, swap mutation as the default mutation operator with reciprocal of chromosome lengths mutation probability, and single point crossover as the default crossover operator with crossover rate 0.9. The *F-Score* values of the three design problems with the two approaches are shown in Table 1. The results indicate that the proposed approach can generate solutions which are closer to expert design for all the three problems.

Table 1. *F-Score* values of design problems with different approaches

	CBS	GDP	SC
LGA for CRA	0.8347	0.7891	0.7019
GA for CRA	0.8289	0.7434	0.6583

4 Related Work

Traditional GAs inspired by Darwinism do not support learning during the evolutionary process. To tackle this problem, the authors in [10] introduced macroevolutionary algorithm (MA) for optimization problems. Similar to our proposed LGA, MA can also exploit the presence of links between "species" that represent candidate solutions to the optimization problem. However, the two approaches have essential difference on the evolutionary model: LGA is based on the Baldwin effect, while MA is inspired by macroevolution. In addition, many existing work also introduced machine learning (ML) techniques in evolutionary algorithms to generate better solutions for their problems [11–14], while our approach used an association algorithm in the search process. To our knowledge, it is the first time that a ML technique is employed for the CRA problem, which shows that introducing ML techniques in GAs can facilitate generating solutions closer to expert design.

5 Conclusions

In this paper, we propose a novel Learning-based Genetic Algorithm (LGA) for the CRA problem, which is based on the Baldwin effect. In LGA, an association algorithm is used to extract the implicit DK about which responsibilities have a high probability to be assigned to the same class, and the extracted DK is further employed to improve the design qualities of the individuals with poor design qualities in the population. An experiment was conducted to evaluate the effectiveness of our approach, and the results show that the approach can generate solutions closer to expert design. In the next step, a tool that supports LGA for CRA problem will be developed and LGA will be evaluated against the GA approach for CRA problem.

References

1. Bowman, M., Briand, L.C., Labiche, Y.: Solving the class responsibility assignment problem in object-oriented analysis with multi-objective genetic algorithms. IEEE Trans. Softw. Eng. **36**(6), 817–837 (2010)
2. Masoud, H., Jalili, S.: A clustering-based model for class responsibility assignment problem in object-oriented analysis. J. Syst. Softw. **93**(7), 110–131 (2014)
3. Smith, J.E., Simons, C.L.: The influence of search components and problem characteristics in early life cycle class modelling. J. Syst. Softw. **103**(5), 440–451 (2015)

4. Lanza, M., Marinescu, R.: Object-Oriented Metrics in Practice: Using Software Metrics to Characterize, Evaluate, and Improve the Design of Object-Oriented Systems, 1st edn. Springer, Heidelberg (2006)
5. de Oliveira, M., de Almeida, F., Horta, G.: Learning from optimization: a case study with apache ant. Inf. Softw. Technol. **57**(1), 684–704 (2015)
6. Kelly, K.: Out of Control: The New Biology of Machines, Social Systems and the Economic World, 1st edn. Basic Books, New York (1995)
7. Baldwin, J.M.: A new factor in evolution. Am. Nat. **30**(354), 441–451 (1896)
8. Merceron, A., Yacef, K.: Interestingness measures for association rules in educational data. In: Educational Data Mining, pp. 57–66 (2008)
9. Manual Designs. http://www.cems.uwe.ac.uk/ ~ clsimons/CaseStudies/ManualDesigns.pdf. Accessed on 01 July 2014
10. Marín, J., Solé, R.V.: Macroevolutionary algorithms: a new optimization method on fitness landscapes. IEEE Trans. Evol. Comput. **3**(4), 272–286 (1999)
11. Corazza, A., Di Martino, S., Ferrucci, F., Gravino, C., Sarro, F., Mendes, E.: Using tabu search to configure support vector regression for effort estimation. Empir. Softw. Eng. **18**(3), 506–546 (2013)
12. Amal, B., Kessentini, M., Bechikh, S., Dea, J., Said, L.B.: On the use of machine learning and search-based software engineering for Ill-defined fitness function: a case study on software refactoring. In: Le Goues, C., Yoo, S. (eds.) SSBSE 2014. LNCS, vol. 8636, pp. 31–45. Springer, Heidelberg (2014)
13. Minku, L., Yao, X.: An analysis of multi-objective evolutionary algorithms for training ensemble models based on different performance measures in software effort estimation. In: PROMISE 2013, Article No. 8 (2013)
14. Sarro, F., Di Martino, S., Ferrucci, F., Gravino, C.: A further analysis on the use of genetic algorithm to configure support vector machines for inter-release fault prediction. In: ACM SAC 2012, pp. 1215–1220 (2012)

Transformed Vargha-Delaney Effect Size

Geoffrey Neumann[1]([✉]), Mark Harman[2], and Simon Poulding[3]

[1] University of Stirling, Stirling, UK
gkn@cs.stir.ac.uk
[2] CREST Centre, University College London, London, UK
[3] Blekinge Institute of Technology, Karlskrona, Sweden

Abstract. Researchers without a technical background in statistics may be tempted to apply analytical techniques in a ritualistic manner. SBSE research is not immune to this problem. We argue that emerging rituals surrounding the use of the Vargha-Delaney effect size statistic may pose serious threats to the scientific validity of the findings. We believe investigations of effect size are important, but more care is required in the application of this statistic. In this paper, we illustrate the problems that can arise, and give guidelines for avoiding them, by applying a 'transformed' Vargha-Delaney effect size measurement. We argue that researchers should always consider which transformation is best suited to their problem domain before calculating the Vargha-Delaney statistic.

Keywords: Vargha and Delaney · Effect size · Threats to validity

1 Introduction

Software engineering researchers, and SBSE researchers in particular, have been increasingly adept at applying statistical analysis to their empirical data. In addition to measuring and reporting the statistical significance of the data, many researchers also rightly report an effect size. Statistical significance indicates how likely an observed difference between, for example, two randomized search algorithms is genuine rather than a result of chance. By contrast, the effect size provides an indication of the practical importance of any observed difference between the algorithms, while taking into account their inherent variability.

Vargha and Delaney's effect size measure [17] is regarded as a robust test when assessing randomized algorithms such as those used in SBSE [3]. The test returns a statistic, $\hat{A}$ (often denoted $\hat{A}_{12}$ in SBSE research), that takes values between 0 and 1; a value of 0.5 indicates that the two algorithms are stochastically equivalent, while values closer to 0 or 1 indicate an increasingly large stochastic difference between the algorithms.

One of the most attractive properties of the Vargha-Delaney test is the simple interpretation of the $\hat{A}$ statistic: for results from two algorithms, A and B, $\hat{A}_{AB}$ is simply the expected probability that algorithm A produces a superior value to algorithm B. If $\hat{A}_{AB} = 0.7$ then Algorithm A is expected to 'beat' Algorithm B 70 % of the time, which may lead us to conclude the Algorithm A

© Springer International Publishing Switzerland 2015
M. Barros and Y. Labiche (Eds.): SSBSE 2015, LNCS 9275, pp. 318–324, 2015.
DOI: 10.1007/978-3-319-22183-0_29

is 'better' than Algorithm B (and with a fairly large effect size). We can think of $\hat{A}_{AB}$ as a contest between algorithms A and B, repeated over a number of trial applications, with a draw counting equally for both algorithms. Other effect size statistics do not have this intuitive interpretation.

However, if we are to ensure this contest has a *correct* interpretation, we must be careful to compare the 'right' data values from the algorithms. In this paper we argue that the data observed for two techniques or algorithms may need to undergo transformation before we calculate the $\hat{A}$ statistic. While data transformations of the types we describe here are a common practice in statistics, we contend they are not applied in SBSE research as often as they should be. In the following section we demonstrate that the Vargha-Delaney test can be misinterpreted when it is applied to untransformed data, leading to serious threats to validity that can reverse the scientific findings of the study that contains them.

2   Misapplication of Vargha-Delaney Effect Size

Consider the illustrative data that might be obtained from two different algorithms, set out in Fig. 1(a), in which the problem demands that lower values are better than higher values. Suppose the values recorded in each trial are execution times in seconds. In this case, $\hat{A}_{AB} = 0.315$. As lower scores are better here, this would indicate that A is the clear winner out of A and B.

	Trial 1	Trial 2	Trial 3	Trial 4	Trial 5	Trial 6	Trial 7	Trial 8	Trial 9	Trial 10
Algorithm A	6.02	0.01	0.00	0.02	0.04	0.05	0.01	0.03	15.00	9.04
Algorithm B	0.05	0.05	2.00	0.09	0.08	0.06	0.05	0.09	0.09	0.08

(a) Untransformed Data

	Trial 1	Trial 2	Trial 3	Trial 4	Trial 5	Trial 6	Trial 7	Trial 8	Trial 9	Trial 10
Algorithm A	6.02	0.00	0.00	0.00	0.00	0.00	0.00	0.00	15.00	9.00
Algorithm B	0.00	0.00	2.00	0.00	0.00	0.00	0.00	0.00	0.00	0.00

(b) Transformed Data

Fig. 1. Illustrative Example of Three SBSE Algorithm Results

The analysis is deceptively simple, and in fact it is *oversimplified*. Unfortunately, many SBSE researchers (the present authors included) might have been tempted to simply apply $\hat{A}$ to raw (untransformed) data. This oversimplification can lead to serious threats to the construct validity of the scientific findings. To illustrate this threat to validity, suppose we are interested in execution time because our use-case involves a user who will become irritated should they have to wait too long for an answer. It is widely believed that response times lower than 100 ms are, for all practical purposes, imperceptible to users [4].

If this is our use-case, then we should, at least, first transform the data to reflect the fact that values lower than 100 ms are considered equally good (essentially 'instantaneous'). The transformed data for this response-time scenario is depicted in Fig. 1(b). In this more *use-case-compliant* analysis, $\hat{A}_{AB} = 0.615$, completely *reversing* the findings of the study; Algorithm A is now seen to be the loser, not the winner. As can be seen, applying Vargha-Delaney effect size to untransformed data can result in a potential threat to validity, able to undermine the scientific findings of the entire study. Transforming the data prior to the application of the Vargha-Delaney test addresses this threat.

We refer to this approach as *Pre-Transforming Data (PTD)*. It is one of two techniques discussed in this paper for avoiding these important threats to validity. As an alternative to transforming data before $\hat{A}$ is calculated, the comparisons that are performed during the $\hat{A}$ test could be modified. We refer to this as the *Modified Comparison Function* (MCF) technique. PTD is simpler to apply and normally sufficient, although the MCF technique is strictly more expressive, and so may be necessary in some scenarios. For example, when the quality of a result is a function of multiple values, pareto dominance could be incorporated into an MCF while PTD could not achieve this.

The key to the correct application of the Vargha-Delaney effect size measure lies in considering what it *means* for one algorithm to be superior to another. This is a question that goes to the very heart of any empirical investigation of algorithms. Non-parametric statistical tests such as Vargha-Delaney are championed because of a lack of assumptions. However, we have to be careful not to relinquish one set of questionable assumptions, only to tacitly incorporate another set of highly flawed assumptions. In particular, we ought not to be seduced by the apparent precision of our measurements, but should be ready to transform our data to represent the *appropriate precision* of the solution space. In the remainder of this paper we give guidelines to illustrate how researchers might choose different transformations for different scenarios.

3   Transforming Data and the $\hat{A}$ Comparison Function

Calculating $\hat{A}$ requires the comparison of each data point in one sample set with each data point in the other. The calculation is implemented in many statistical packages and is widely used. One advantage of using PTD is that the experimenter need not change the computation of $\hat{A}$ at all. Rather, they simply apply their existing $\hat{A}$ computation to the pre-transformed data, in order to avoid the threat to validity.

When PTD is used, $\hat{A}$ is calculated only after the data has been transformed using a many-to-one function, f_{ptd}. The function f_{ptd} captures the precision inherent in the judgement of whether one algorithm is superior to another for our proposed use-case. f_{ptd} can be used to 'bucket together' any observed values that should be considered equivalent for the purposes of algorithm comparison (such as all those timings lower than 100ms in response time).

By contrast, MCF modifies the way in which the comparisons themselves are performed. Given two numeric results x_1 and x_2, $\hat{A}$ simply determines which is true out of $x_1 > x_2$, $x_1 < x_2$ and $x_1 = x_2$. With the MCF technique, this comparison is replaced by a function, f_{mcf}, which takes, as input, two results x_1 and x_2. These may be simple numeric values or may be more complex data structures. f_{mcf} returns one of three possible outcomes (x_1 *is better than* x_2, x_1 *is worse than* x_2 and x_1 *equals* x_2).

In the remainder of this paper we consider possible ways in which f_{ptd} and f_{mcf} might be defined for different use-case scenarios, thereby illustrating our proposed approach to the transformed Vargha-Delaney effect size measure.

Using Moore's law: An observation originally made in 1965 by Gordon Moore stated that the number of transistors on a dense integrated circuit approximately doubles every two years [11]. There are various interpretations of the speed up implications achievable simply by advances in underlying hardware. However, if Algorithm A is faster than Algorithm B by 10 % we can safely assume that this 'advantage' is equivalent to less than 6 months of Moore's law. The precise determination of bucketing remains for the researcher to define and justify, but we might consider exponentially larger bucket sizes to take account of the erosion of performance advantages due to Moore's law.

Implementation differences: For problems concerning computational efficiency bucketing techniques could be set so that only improvements that are greater than those matched by mere implementation improvements are counted. Areas of implementation that we might consider include parallelization or hardware and software changes. In the case of parallelization it is possible to estimate how much time could be saved if a serial process were run in parallel. Amdahl's law [2] states that if a process is currently being run entirely sequentially and s is the proportion of time spent executing parts of the process that cannot be parallelized, then parallelizing it would cause it to run $1/(s + \frac{(1-s)}{N})$ times faster where N is the number of available processors. If the cost of additional parallel computation can be assessed, then this could be used to determine a threshold for bucketing.

Categorical Thresholds: In some situations there is a natural boundary that could be used as a threshold for equivalence bucketing. Often this will be a boundary between an unacceptable result and an acceptable result (as in the case of branch coverage distance [5]).

Singh and Kahlon [15] and Shatnawi [14] give thresholds for object oriented programming metrics such as information hiding, encapsulation, class complexity, inheritance, class size, cohesion and coupling. These metrics can be used to predict certain characteristics of 'poorly designed' programs (those above threshold have a 'code smell'). The fitness function that guides search-based refactoring to remove such smells might use the raw OOP metric value to guide it [7,12]. However, when it comes to assessing effect size, we should only consider a 'win' occurring when the metric value indicates the smell is removed (i.e. the metric value moves within threshold).

Thresholds can be defended and justified in many ways. There are often precedents of considering certain threshold values. For example Schneider [13] favours precision above 0.6 and recall above 0.7 (based on work by Ireson [9]), while McMinn states that the proportion of runs in which a branch is covered in 50 runs during testing needs to be more than 60 % [10]. PTD could be used here, accompanied by a justification of the transformation applied to the data based on these threshold values. Doing so will strengthen the conclusion validity by ruling out 'trivial wins'.

Time Scales: Ali et al. [1] review test case generation and state that a difference of a few minutes in how long a test case takes to run is unlikely to be of practical importance. One might characterise improvements in terms, of whether the difference is noticeable (100ms delay threshold), whether it can be used interactively (a few second delay), whether it can be achieved overnight (perhaps more suitable to regression test optimisation [18]) and so on. These could be used as thresholds for PTD.

Decomposition: If fitness is calculated from more than one metric then this provides many more options for Transformed VD. Many ideas from multi objective optimization, such as pareto dominance, could be explored even though the problem itself was not optimized as a multi objective problem. This could simply mean using a MCF, which only returns a difference between two solutions when one solution *pareto dominates* the other (it achieves at least equal performance in every objective and better performance in at least one objective [16]).

However, a much more sophisticated and problem specific MCF could be used. Objectives could be prioritized, each objective could have its own thresholds and conditional statements could be used so that the importance of one objective depends on the results of other objectives. In addition to objectives, fitness functions obtained by testing on a set of problem instances are also potentially decomposable. Comparisons could, for example, take into account growth functions across a set of problem instances of increasing complexity so that scalability can be compared. Hsu notes the importance of both objective prioritization and growth functions in software testing [8].

This discussion has highlighted many ways in which two solutions can be compared which cannot be replicated simply by pre-transforming the data, clearly demonstrating that this is one area in which the MCF technique provides much more power than both standard $\hat{A}$ and also PTD. However, PTD is simple: once transformed, the data can be compared using any existing VD test.

4 Conclusion

We have demonstrated how ritualistic application of the Vargha-Delaney $\hat{A}$ effect size may reverse technical findings, leading to a fundamentally flawed scientific analysis. The problem applies, not only to work on Search Based Software Engineering (SBSE) [6], but any work involving the comparison of randomised algorithms, although we chose to illustrate the problem using examples drawn from SBSE. This serious threat to validity cannot be overcome by simply avoiding the use of $\hat{A}$, because effect size reporting is essential. To address this problem, we proposed two approaches that enable the Vargha-Delaney measure to be applied to transformed data. Finally, we observe that although our paper focuses on the Vargha-Delaney effect size, there is no reason why these ideas could not be applied to other statistical tests used by SBSE researchers.

References

1. Ali, S., Briand, L.C., Hemmati, H., Panesar-Walawege, R.K.: A systematic review of the application and empirical investigation of search-based test case generation. IEEE Trans. Softw. Eng. **36**(6), 742–762 (2010)
2. Amdahl, G.M.: Validity of the single processor approach to achieving large scale computing capabilities. In: Proceedings of the Spring Joint Computer Conference, pp. 483–485. ACM, 18–20 April 1967
3. Arcuri, A., Briand, L.: A hitchhiker's guide to statistical tests for assessing randomized algorithms in software engineering. Softw. Test. Verif. Reliab. **24**, 219–250 (2012)
4. Department of Defense: US DOD MIL-STD 1472-F: Human engineering standard (1999)
5. Harman, M., Jia, Y., Zhang, Y.: Achievements, open problems and challenges for search based software testing (keynote). In: 8th IEEE International Conference on Software Testing, Verification and Validation (ICST 2014), Graz, Austria, April 2015
6. Harman, M., Jones, B.F.: Search based software engineering. Inf. Softw. Technol. **43**(14), 833–839 (2001)
7. Harman, M., Tratt, L.: Pareto optimal search-based refactoring at the design level. In: 9th Annual Conference on Genetic and Evolutionary Computation (GECCO 2007), pp. 1106–1113. ACM Press, London, July 2007
8. Hsu, H.Y., Orso, A.: Mints: a general framework and tool for supporting test-suite minimization. In: IEEE 31st International Conference on Software Engineering, ICSE 2009, pp. 419–429. IEEE (2009)
9. Ireson, N., Ciravegna, F., Califf, M.E., Freitag, D., Kushmerick, N., Lavelli, A.: Evaluating machine learning for information extraction. In: Proceedings of the 22nd international conference on Machine learning, pp. 345–352. ACM (2005)
10. McMinn, P.: How does program structure impact the effectiveness of the crossover operator in evolutionary testing? In: 2010 Second International Symposium on Search Based Software Engineering (SSBSE), pp. 9–18. IEEE (2010)
11. Moore, G.E., et al.: Cramming more components onto integrated circuits. Proc. IEEE **86**(1), 82–85 (1998)
12. O'Keeffe, M., ÓCinnédie, M.: Search-based refactoring: an empirical study. J. Softw. Maint. **20**(5), 345–364 (2008)
13. Schneider, K., Knauss, E., Houmb, S., Islam, S., Jürjens, J.: Enhancing security requirements engineering by organizational learning. Requirements Eng. **17**(1), 35–56 (2012)
14. Shatnawi, R.: A quantitative investigation of the acceptable risk levels of object-oriented metrics in open-source systems. IEEE Trans. Software Eng. **36**(2), 216–225 (2010)
15. Singh, S., Kahlon, K.: Object oriented software metrics threshold values at quantitative acceptable risk level. CSI Transact. ICT **2**(3), 191–205 (2014)

16. Srinivas, N., Deb, K.: Multi-objective function optimization using non-dominated sorting genetic algorithms. Evol. Comput. **2**(3), 221–148 (1995)
17. Vargha, A., Delaney, H.D.: A critique and improvement of the CL common language effect size statistics of McGraw and Wong. J. Educ. Behav. Stat. **25**(2), 101–132 (2000)
18. Yoo, S., Harman, M.: Regression testing minimisation, selection and prioritisation: a survey. J. Softw. Test. Verif. Reliab. **22**(2), 67–120 (2012)

Optimizing Software Product Line Architectures with OPLA-Tool

Édipo Luis Féderle[1], Thiago do Nascimento Ferreira[1(✉)],
Thelma Elita Colanzi[2], and Silvia Regina Vergilio[1]

[1] DInf - Federal University of Paraná, Curitiba CP: 19081, 81531-980, Brazil
edipofederle@gmail.com, {tnferreira,silvia}@inf.ufpr.br
[2] DIN - State University of Maringá, Maringá 87020-900, Brazil
thelma@din.uem.br

Abstract. MOA4PLA is an approach proposed for Product Line Architecture (PLA) design optimization, based on multi-objective algorithms and different metrics that consider specific PLA characteristics. To allow the practical use of MOA4PLA, this paper describes OPLA-Tool, a supporting tool that implements the complete MOA4PLA process. OPLA-Tool has a graphical interface used to choose algorithms, parameters, search operators used in the optimization, and to visualize the alternative PLAs (solutions), with their fitness values associated and corresponding class diagrams. The paper also describes an experiment conducted to evaluate the usefulness of OPLA-Tool. Results show that OPLA-Tool achieves its purpose and that improved solutions are obtained.

Keywords: SPL · Multi-objective algorithms · Architecture

1 Introduction

The Software Product Line (SPL) has been adopted in the industry, with focus on reuse of software artifacts, for building product families [10,12]. The Product Line Architecture (PLA) is an important artifact that contains all the commonalities and variabilities of a SPL. It is the basis to derive the products architectures. Then, the PLA needs to be generic and flexible, and we can conclude that the PLA design is not an easy task. It is impacted by many factors, and several problems may occur as a result of a poorly designed architecture, for example, instability, failure to meet business requirements, maintenance, scalability, implementation difficulties, and so on [6].

To help in this task, Colanzi et al. [3] introduced MOA4PLA, a *Multi-objective Optimization Approach for PLA Design*. Such approach encompasses a process, including: the construction of the PLA representation by using a metamodel; the definition of an evaluation model that includes a set of metrics that are specific for the PLA context; search operators to improve modularization and to be used by search-based and multi-objective algorithms. At the end, a set of PLA alternatives is produced, representing the best trade-off between the objectives.

© Springer International Publishing Switzerland 2015
M. Barros and Y. Labiche (Eds.): SSBSE 2015, LNCS 9275, pp. 325–331, 2015.
DOI: 10.1007/978-3-319-22183-0_30

MOA4PLA has presented good results, reported in the literature [2,3]. However, to allow the use of MOA4PLA, in practice, a supporting tool is fundamental.

In the literature, we can find some tools that could provide automated support for MOA4PLA. Darwin Tool [7] uses Genetic Algorithm to produce software architectures by adding/removing design patterns and Dearthóir Tool [1] optimizes software architectures using the heuristic Simulated Annealing. It restructures classes hierarchies and moves their methods to minimize and eliminate methods unused and code duplication. However, we can observe that such tools need adaptation to support MOA4PLA application. Also, they do not consider specific PLA characteristics.

In this sense, a tool, called OPLA-Tool (*Optimization for PLA Tool*), was proposed to support the use of MOA4PLA. OPLA-Tool implements the complete MOA4PLA process and allows the automated PLA optimization, contributing to reduce efforts in the PLA design. In addition to this, it makes easy experimental evaluation of MOA4PLA. In this way, this paper describes OPLA-Tool and presents an empirical study conducted in order to evaluate its usefulness by analysing the obtained solutions.

This paper is organized as follows. Section 2 reviews MOA4PLA and presents OPLA-Tool. Section 3 describes how the empirical study was conducted, presents and analyses the results. Finally, Sect. 4 concludes the paper.

2   OPLA-Tool

OPLA-Tool implements the MOA4PLA process, presented in Fig. 1(a). The modules that compose OPLA-Tool are presented in Fig. 1(b).

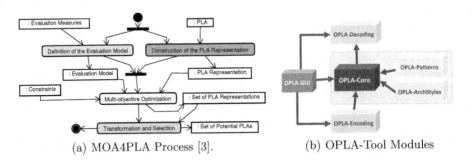

(a) MOA4PLA Process [3].   (b) OPLA-Tool Modules

Fig. 1. MOA4PLA Approach and OPLA-Tool

The module OPLA-GUI offers a graphical interface that allows the architect to select the input PLA, the search based algorithm parameters and operators. This module is also responsible for showing the results in terms of PLA alternative designs and theirs fitness. All input and output artifacts are XMI files, which is a standard used to allow information exchange by different UML tools.

The module OPLA-Encoding automated the step *Construction of the PLA Representation* (Fig. 1(a)). It receives as input a class diagram, XMI files, generated by Papyrus[1] (Eclipse plugin), which is used to create and edit UML models. The PLA design is encoded from class diagram (with classes, interfaces, attributes, methods, components and SPL variabilities including variation points and variants) to the representation used by the algorithm. More details about this representation are found in [3].

By using OPLA-GUI, the architect selects the metrics to be used in the evaluation model (*Definition of the Evaluation Model* step). Four objective functions are available in OPLA-Tool: (a) *CM* function provides basic indicator about cohesion, coupling and size; (b) *FM* function measures the feature modularization; (c) *Ext* function measures the extensibility degree of SPL in terms of the PLA abstraction [8]; and (d) *Eleg* function measures the design elegance [11].

The module OPLA-Core implements the *Multi-Objective Optimization* step. The algorithm searches for the best solutions (alternative PLAs), guided by the evaluation model previously defined and using MOA4PLA search operators, specific for PLA context [2,3]. In this first version of OPLA-Tool, two algorithms are available: NSGA-II and PAES. They were implemented by using jMetal [5], an object-oriented framework developed in Java and used in multi-objective optimization with metaheuristics. Modules OPLA-Patterns and OPLA-ArchStyles implement search operators related, respectively to, design pattern, such as Bridge and Strategy, and architectural styles, such as layered and client-server ones.

Figure 2 shows the main OPLA-Tool screens. In the General Configuration Tab the default settings, such as UML profile or temporary directory, are defined. In the Execution Configuration Tab the algorithms are selected and configured. The Results Tab presents the solutions found by the algorithm and corresponding objective values. The Non-Dominated Solutions Tab shows the found values relative to the non-dominated solutions generated. Finally, the architect visualizes the solutions in a readable form (class diagram) generated by OPLA-Decoding module (*Transformation and Selection* step), and selects the best one according to his/her needs. The tool does not implement any mechanism to help in this choice.

3 Empirical Study

An empirical study was performed aiming at evaluating whether OPLA-Tool is useful to support the automated MOA4PLA application in PLA design optimization. Differently from the experiments previously reported in [2,3], the experiment herein described was conducted with both algorithms implemented in OPLA-Tool: NSGA-II and PAES, and three objectives: *CM, FM, Ext*, related to basic design principles, feature modularization and PLA extensibility. The goal

---

[1] http://www.eclipse.org/modeling/mdt/papyrus/.

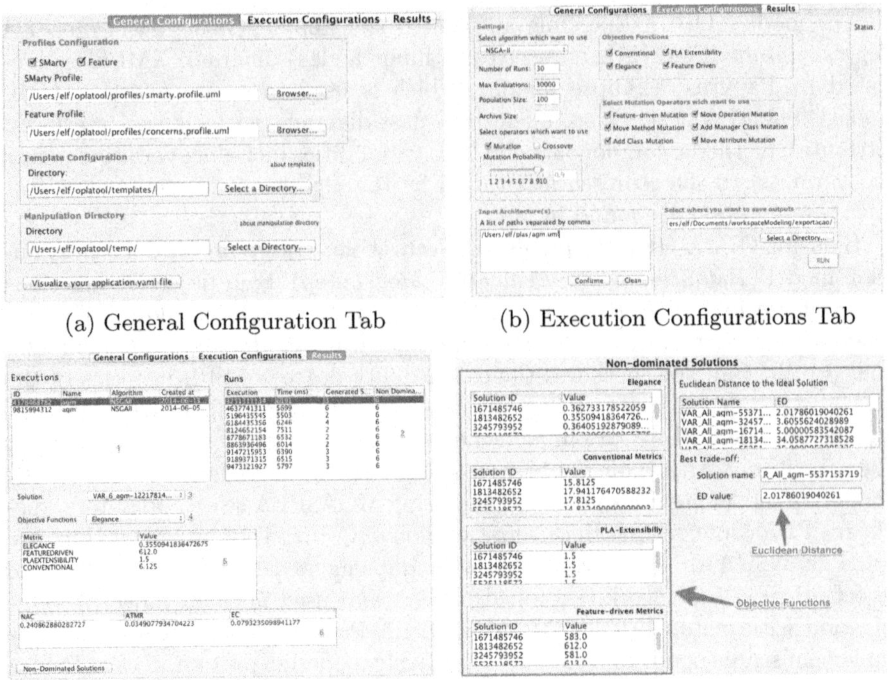

(a) General Configuration Tab

(b) Execution Configurations Tab

(c) Results Tab

(d) Non-Dominated Solutions

Fig. 2. Main screens in OPLA-Tool

is to compare both algorithms according to some common quality indicators, as well as, to evaluate the solutions obtained[2].

Three PLAs were used: Arcade Game Maker (AGM) [9] (original fitness $(CM, FM, Ext) = (6.1, 789, 1.5)$); Mobile Media (MM) [13] $(0.3, 221, 7)$; and Electronics Tickets for Urban Transport (BET) [4] $(0.02, 742, 3)$. We adopted the same parameters for the algorithms used by Colanzi et al. [3]: maximum number of evaluations: 30,000; population size: 100, 90 % for mutation rate. The algorithms were executed 30 times. The PF_k were obtained from the solutions of all these executions, by eliminating duplicate and dominated ones.

Below we analyse the results, which are presented in Table 1. This table presents the total number of solutions in PF_k found by each algorithm, as well as, the hypervolume values, with average and standard deviation. The same table also shows the results for the statistical test of Friedman (95 % significance) used to confirm whether there is difference in the use of one or another algorithm. In this case, only for AGM there was not statistical difference between both algorithms. PAES is the best for MM and BET in terms of hypervolume.

---

[2] The OPLA-Patterns and OPLA-ArchStyles modules were not used and will be evaluated in other studies.

Table 1. Number of solutions and *hypervolume*

PLA	PF_k		hypervolume		statistical test	
	NSGA-II	PAES	NSGA-II	PAES	p-value	difference?
AGM	11	20	0.00477 ± 0.00167	0.00308 ± 0.00209	0.06788	no
MM	6	7	0.00347 ± 0.00132	0.00642 ± 0.00221	0.00348	yes
BET	18	23	0.00652 ± 08.0E-4	0.00813 ± 3.6E-4	4.3204E-8	yes

Figure 3(a) and (b), produced by OPLA-Tool, show the fitness of the solutions (CM and FM) in the search space. For AGM (Fig. 3(a)), NSGA-II found a lower number of solutions but they are better distributed in the search space. It can also be noticed that some solutions of both algorithms are similar. For MM, the algorithms found a similar number of solutions, depicted in Fig. 3(b). However, PAES solutions are better, dominating all NSGA-II solutions. For BET, NSGA-II solutions are better and dominate PAES solutions. Picture with BET solutions is not shown due to lack of space.

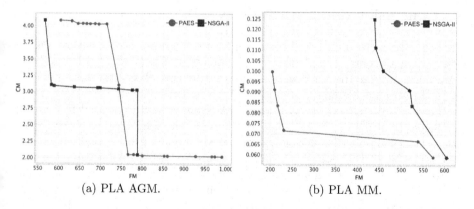

(a) PLA AGM.   (b) PLA MM.

Fig. 3. Solutions in the search space

An analysis of the fitness values of the obtained solutions show, in most cases, an improvement with respect to the values associated with the original PLA. For AGM, we observe that the NSGA-II solutions presented better fitness values for CM and FM, with respect to the original PLA. Only in one solution, the value of FM is equal to the original value. In all solutions the values for Ext are the same. For MM, all solutions had improvements over the CM function, however all solutions had worse results in FM function. For BET, all solutions had improvements in relation to CM function with worst results in FM function. For all PLAs, the values of Ext function remained the same.

Regarding PAES results, for AGM, all solutions are better in relation to its original CM values. In 20 solutions, 12 had improvements in FM. For MM, all solutions are better in relation to CM, and three solutions had improvements in FM. However, only one solution had bad values of FM and Ext. For BET, all solutions had improvements in relation to CM, with bad FM values. Again, for all PLAs, the values of Ext function did not change.

We also analyzed the solutions with best trade-off between the objectives (best ED values), and observed an improvement in the quality. For instance, by taking for AGM, the NSGA-II solution with best ED, we observe that in the original PLA, the GameBoard class has attributes and methods that are associated with three features: <<play>>, <<movement>> and <<collision>>. In the mentioned solution, the only attribute of GameBoard class, associated with <<collision>>, was moved to a new class (Class10881). The same happens with methods of original class associated with the feature <<collision>>. In this case, in the solution the features are better modularized.

This experiment allows us to state that OPLA-Tool is useful to automate the application of the complete MOA4PLA process. All MOA4PLA activities are supported by OPLA-Tool. Different algorithms and objective functions can be used, generating improved solutions with respect to the original PLA designs.

4   Conclusion and Future Work

This paper described OPLA-Tool, a tool for PLA optimization based on multi-objective algorithms. It implements the complete process of MOA4PLA and has a graphical interface to visualize the results, alternative class diagrams for a PLA to be optimized according to a model defined by the architect.

Three PLAs and the algorithms NSGA-II and PAES were used in a study conducted to evaluate the usefulness of the tool. The solutions presented better fitness values mainly considering traditional metrics and feature modularization. PAES presented the best hypervolume values for two PLAs, with statistical difference, and a greater number of solutions in most cases. However, NSGA-II solutions presented better fitness values when compared with the original ones.

Future work includes improvements in the OPLA-Tool mainly related to the visualization of the solutions, implementation of new algorithms and objectives. All these new facilities should be evaluated in future experiments. A future evaluation is to take into account the opinion of the architects of each PLA.

References

1. Cinneide, M.: Towards automated design improvement through combinatorial optimisation. In: Proceedings of Workshop on Directions in Software Engineering Environments (2004)
2. Colanzi, T.E., Vergilio, S.R.: A feature-driven crossover operator for product line architecture design optimization. In: Proceedings of COMPSAC 2014 (2014)
3. Colanzi, T.E., Vergilio, S.R., Gimenes, I.M.S., Oizumi, W.N.: A search-based approach for software product line design. In: Proceedings of SPLC 2014 (2014)

4. Donegan, P.M., Masiero, P.C.: Design issues in a component-based software product line. In: Brazilian Symposium on Software Components, Architectures and Reuse (SBCARS), pp. 3–16 (2007)

5. Durillo, J.J., Nebro, A.J., Alba, E.: The jMetal framework for multi-objective optimization: design and architecture. In: Proceedings of 2010 IEEE Congress on Evolutionary Computation (CEC), Barcelona, Spain, pp. 4138–4325, Julho 2010

6. Fowler, M.: Patterns of Enterprise Application Architecture. Addison-Wesley Longman, Amsterdam (2002)

7. Hadaytullah, S.V., Räihä, O., Koskimies, K.: Tool support for software architecture design with genetic algorithms. In: Proceedings of the 5th ICSEA (2010)

8. Oliveira Jr., E.D.: Systematic evaluation of software product line architectures. J. Univ. Comput. Sci. **19**, 25–52 (2013)

9. SEI: AGM (2015). http://www.sei.cmu.edu/productlines/ppl/

10. SEI: Product line hall of fame (2015). http://splc.net/fame.html

11. Simons, C., Parmee, I.: Elegant object-oriented software design via interactive, evolutionary computation. IEEE Transact. Syst. Man Cybern. **42**(6), 1797–1805 (2012)

12. Taylor, R.N., Medvidovic, N., Dashofy, E.M.: Software Architecture: Foundations Theory and Practice. Wiley, New York (2010)

13. Young, T.: Using AspectJ to Build a Software Product Line for Mobile Devices. Master's thesis, University of British Columbia (2005)

Exploring the Landscape of Non-Functional Program Properties Using Spatial Analysis

Matthew Patrick[1]([✉]) and Yue Jia[2]

[1] Department of Plant Sciences, University of Cambridge, Cambridge, UK
mtp33@cam.ac.uk
[2] Department of Computer Science, University College London, London, UK
yue.jia@ucl.ac.uk

Abstract. Deciding on a trade-off between the non-functional properties of a system is challenging, as it is never possible to have complete information about what can be achieved. We may at first assume it is vitally important to minimise the processing requirements of a system, but if it is possible to halve the response time with only a small increase in computational power, would this cause us to change our minds? This lack of clarity makes program optimisation difficult, as it is unclear which non-functional properties to focus on improving. We propose to address this problem by applying spatial analysis techniques used in ecology to characterise and explore the landscape of non-functional properties. We can use these techniques to extract and present key information about the trade-offs that exist between non-functional properties, so that developers have a clearer understanding of the decisions they are making.

Keywords: Spatial analysis · Fitness landscapes · Program optimisation

1 Introduction

Non-functional properties describe the way in which a system operates, rather than the actions the system performs [1]. Although two systems might be functionally equivalent, they may differ significantly in terms of their response time, power consumption and/or memory usage. These non-functional properties often conflict with one another. For example, reducing the response time may lead to increased power and memory requirements. The landscape of non-functional properties can be expressed as a Pareto surface of candidate programs [2], whereby no program is included that is surpassed on every non-functional property by some other program; each candidate program has the same functional properties, but expresses a different possible trade-off between non-functional properties. The task of the developer is to select a program from the Pareto surface that has the most desirable trade-off of non-functional properties.

It can be difficult for developers to understand the effect their decisions have on a system's non-functional properties whilst the system is still being built. For example, how is the developer to know which non-functional properties will be important

© Springer International Publishing Switzerland 2015
M. Barros and Y. Labiche (Eds.): SSBSE 2015, LNCS 9275, pp. 332–338, 2015.
DOI: 10.1007/978-3-319-22183-0_31

for each code unit before the units have been put together? This is why work on the non-functional properties of a system tends to occur towards the end of its development [1]. Yet, at this late stage, there is a limit to the improvements that can be made; it would be better for the developer to work on the non-functional properties in tandem with the functional ones. Development tools could apply techniques such as genetic programming to explore the Pareto optimal landscape [2]. In theory, the developer would only need to specify the functional properties of each module, then the tool will be able to suggest a number of alternative solutions, with a range of non-functional properties.

Unfortunately, there is still a long way to go before this scenario can be realised. Tools and techniques have been developed for creating Pareto-optimal landscapes of non-functional properties [3]. There are also metrics available for evaluating how difficult the optima are to achieve [4]. Yet, little attention has been given to understanding the landscapes in terms of the relationships between non-functional properties. This is important, as it would allow developers to decide which properties they are most interested in and hence where to focus the optimisation efforts. We propose to characterise the landscape of non-functional properties by applying techniques commonly used in spatial analysis for ecology.

2 Spatial Analysis

Spatial analysis techniques have been applied to understand the behaviour of various natural phenomena, ranging from the number of species a landscape can support [5], through to the rate at which a disease is able spread [6] and the likelihood that a species will recover after a major disturbance (such as a fire [7]). The spatial properties of a landscape have a significant effect on the behaviour of these natural phenomena, such that it is not sufficient to assume that conditions are the same everywhere in the landscape. Similarly, changes made to the program code of a computer system are likely to have a much greater effect on its non-functional properties when made in some regions of the Pareto-optimal landscape than others. In ecology, spatial analysis is used to predict where things are likely to happen, why and what will change in the future. In modelling the non-functional properties of a system, spatial analysis can be used to determine the likely effect of decisions made during development and give some idea of what needs to be done to achieve desirable performance.

Spatial analysis techniques measure differences between values in one part of a landscape and values in another [8]. Metrics can be applied to determine composition (how much of each property the landscape has), or configuration (what spatial patterns occur in the data). They can take into account the structural properties of the landscape (e.g. actual distances between features) or its functional properties (e.g. the distance that a particular organism is able to travel). The configuration of a landscape is typically assessed in terms of its auto-correlation (the similarity of nearby values), complexity (the way its shape changes with scale) and connectivity (the likelihood that different regions will influence each other). All three of these properties are useful for characterising and exploring landscapes of non-functional properties.

3   Characterising the Landscape

Auto-correlation may be measured using metrics such as Moran's I [8], which is based upon Pearson's correlation coefficient. Applied globally, it measures clustering across the entire landscape. A positively auto-correlated landscape, which has the high values for a non-functional property clustered into one region and the low values in another, has a Moran's I value around 1. By contrast, a negatively auto-correlated landscape, which has patches of high and low values alternately interspersed, has a Moran's I value around -1. Applied locally, it identifies regions that are clustered (with similar values) or anti-clustered (with different values). In Eq. 1, z_i and z_j are the values at each point, whilst w_{ij} is the distance weighting between them and n the number of points. Another local metric, the Getis and Ord G_i^* statistic [8], highlights regions of particularly high or low fitness compared to the rest of the landscape. This is useful for identifying rapid changes in the trade-offs between non-functional properties.

$$I_i = \frac{n z_i \sum_j w_{ij} z_j}{z_i^2} \qquad G_i^* = \frac{\sum_j w_{ij} z_j}{\sum_j z_j} \qquad (1)$$

The complexity of a landscape may be interpreted in terms of its fractal dimension [8], which measures the slope of the Pareto surface's perimeter (for each dimension) at different scales. The slope will be linear for a smooth landscape, but the perimeter of a rugged landscape is much larger at finer scales. The fractal dimension can be used to suggest how much the landscape values are likely to change in-between the points we have data for. The values of a rugged landscape (high fractal dimension) change between nearby points more often than a smooth landscape (low fractal dimension). Other techniques, such as Kernel Density Estimation and Cox Processes can be used to predict missing values [9]. These techniques are useful for visualising the landscape, as they help to fill in points for which we do not yet know the non-functional properties. By interpolating between programs with known non-functional properties, they might also be used to suggest programs that could achieve the properties desired.

Connectivity is typically assessed by representing the landscape as a network of connected regions. Network representations are used in ecology to model the flow or migration of organisms from one patch of habitat to another [8]. Yet, it is also possible to use them to divide the landscape into natural segments. We can represent points on the Pareto surface as nodes in the network and set the connectivity of the edge between each node to be some measure of similarity between the non-functional properties. A clustering technique, such Normalised Graph Cuts for image segmentation [10], can then be used to divide the landscape into distinct regions that are effective for different sets of non-functional properties. This helps to represent the landscape of trade-offs between non-functional properties in a way the developer can easily understand, as it reduces the problem of presenting a continuous landscape in multiple dimensions as a discrete set of options for the developer to choose from. As well as making it easier for the developer to visualise, it might also be used to suggest new targets for optimisation in order to achieve a particular set of non-functional properties.

4 Worked Example

We demonstrate some of the ways in which spatial analysis can characterise landscapes of non-functional properties, by means of a simple worked example. Token passing is often used to provide mutually exclusive access in distributed systems: a processor is only allowed access to the shared resource whilst it holds a token. Millard et al. [11] investigated the fairness and stabilisation time of token passing schemes on unidirectional ring networks, in which mutual exclusion can only be guaranteed if there is exactly one token. Stabilisation time measures the average time it takes to eliminate any additional tokens introduced by transient failures. For successful operation, stabilisation time must be less than the failure rate. However, it may also be important for each processor to have equal access to the shared resource — this is known as fairness. We use spatial analysis to illustrate some of the trade-offs between these two non-functional properties.

The experiments were performed using the Non-dominated Sorting Genetic Algorithm II (NSGA-II) to perform multi-objective optimisation on the non-functional properties of a ring network with three processors (n1, n2 and n3). The policy of each processor is determined by its probability of holding onto a token or passing it along to the next processor. A processor which has a high probability of holding on to a token is said to be selfish, whereas a processor which has a low probability is said to be selfless. We applied spatial analysis to understand more about the policies that were explored by the algorithm. The Getis and Ord statistic indicates stabilisation time is shortest when some of the processors are selfish and others are selfless (see Fig. 1), whereas token passing is fairest when the probabilities are more similar (see Fig. 2). Millard et al. [11] explain that selfless processors pass tokens along to selfish processors which are still holding onto theirs, thus eliminating the additional tokens more quickly.

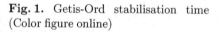

Red indicates high values, blue indicates low values.

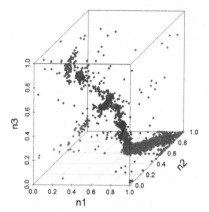
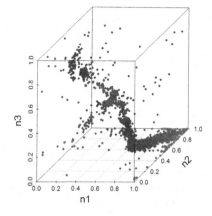

Fig. 1. Getis-Ord stabilisation time (Color figure online)

Fig. 2. Getis-Ord fairness (Color figure online)

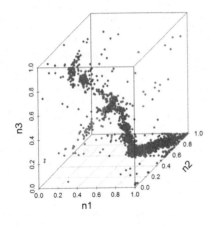

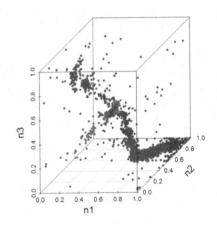

Fig. 3. Moran's i stabilisation time (Color figure online)

Fig. 4. Moran's i fairness (Color figure online)

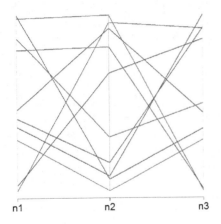

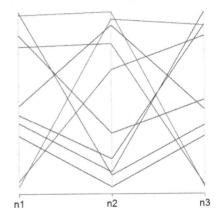

Fig. 5. Segment stabilisation time (Color figure online)

Fig. 6. Segment fairness (Color figure online)

NB: The graphs are not symmetric due to the path followed by the NSGA-II

The Moran's i statistic shows strong auto correlation in the centre of Fig. 4, where solutions are fairest: once a fair probability assignment has been found, exploring around this area is unlikely to bring significant further improvements. The area of highest auto correlation in stabilisation time also occurs in the centre of the graph (see Fig. 3). However, this is the region where stabilisation time is longest. It suggests that multiple restarts might be necessary to optimise networks for stabilisation time, so as to escape this plateau in fitness. Overall, the Moran's i statistic is useful for revealing how the fitness landscape change across the input domain and indicating areas where issues may occur in optimisation.

Finally, Figs. 5 and 6 show parallel coordinates for the median values of 10 distinct segments (partitions of points on the fitness landscape), created using the

Normalised Graph Cuts procedure and coloured according to median fitness. The results support Millard et al.'s findings that fair networks have similar probabilities of holding on to tokens for each processor, whereas networks that contain a greater number of selfish processors stabilise more quickly. The segments with shortest stabilisation time have high probabilities of holding on to tokens for two of the three processors (see Fig. 5); these segments also have the worst fairness (see Fig. 6). The segment with low probabilities for all processors is fairest, but it also has the longest stabilisation time.

5   Conclusion

It can be difficult for developers to optimise the non-functional properties of a program and as a result this tends to be done towards the end of development or not at all. Research has been conducted into automatic optimisation techniques. Yet there remains a divide between this and the tools needed for developers to be able to explore and select their preferred non-functional properties. We propose to bridge this divide by applying spatial analysis techniques used in ecology to help developers understand the fitness landscape. We can identify particular input regions that have important properties, estimate properties not yet explored and guide exploration towards potentially useful regions. Spatial analysis techniques were shown to be effective at characterising the fitness landscape for a simple example involving token-passing. We encourage other researchers to take advantage of the techniques offered by spatial analysis in their own work.

References

1. Rosa, N.S., Justo, G.R.R., Cunha, P.R.F.: A framework for building non-functional software architectures. In: 16th ACM Symposium on Applied Computing, pp. 141–147. ACM, New York (2001)
2. Harman, M., Langdon, W.B., Jia, Y., White, D.R., Arcuri, A., Clark, J.A.: The GISMOE challenge: constructing the pareto program surface using genetic programming to find better programs. In: 25th IEEE/ACM International Conference on Automated Software Engineering, pp. 1–14. IEEE Press, New York (2012)
3. Langdon, W.B., Harman, M.: Optimising existing software with genetic programming. IEEE Trans. Evol. Comput. **19**, 118–135 (2015)
4. Lu, G., Li, J., Yao, X.: Fitness landscapes and problem difficulty in evolutionary algorithms: from theory to applications. In: Richter, H., Engelbrecht, A.P. (eds.) Recent Advances in the Theory and Application of Fitness Landscapes. ECC, vol. 6, pp. 133–152. Springer, Heidelberg (2014)
5. Imad, C., Slaheddine, S., Jihen, B., Rguibi-Idrissi, H., Dakki, M.: Factors affecting bird richness in a fragmented cork oak forest in Morocco. Acta Oecologica **35**, 197–205 (2009)
6. Gilligan, C.A., van den Bosch, F.: Epidemiologial models for invasion and persistence of pathogens. Annu. Rev. Phytopathol. **46**, 385–418 (2008)
7. Wittenberg, L., Malkinson, D., Beeri, O., Halutzy, A., Tesler, N.: Spatial and temporal patterns of vegetation recovery following sequences of forest fires in a mediterranean landscape, Mt. Carmel Israel. CATENA **71**, 76–83 (2007)

8. Fortin, M.-J., Dale, M.R.T.: Spatial Analysis: A Guide for Ecologists. Cambridge University Press, Cambridge (2005)
9. Diggle, P.J.: Statistical Analysis of Spatial and Spatio-Temporal Point Patterns, 3rd edn. CRC Press, Boca Raton (2013)
10. Shi, J., Malik, J.: Normalized cuts and image segmentation. IEEE Trans. Pattern Anal. Mach. Intell. **22**, 888–905 (2000)
11. Millard, A.G., White, D.R., Clark, J.A.: Searching for pareto-optimal randomised algorithms. In: Fraser, G., de Souza, J.T. (eds.) SSBSE 2012. LNCS, vol. 7515, pp. 183–197. Springer, Heidelberg (2012)

Graduate Student Papers

Interactive Software Release Planning
with Preferences Base

Altino Dantas[✉], Italo Yeltsin, Allysson Allex Araújo, and Jerffeson Souza

Optimization in Software Engineering Group, State University of Ceará,
Doutor Silas Munguba Avenue 1700, Fortaleza 60714-903, Brazil
{altino.dantas,allysson.araujo,jerffeson.souza}@uece.br,
italo.medeiros@aluno.uece.br
http://goes.uece.br

Abstract. The release planning is a complex task in the software development process and involves many aspects related to the decision about which requirements should be allocated in each system release. Several search based techniques have been proposed to tackle this problem, but in most cases the human expertise and preferences are not effectively considered. In this context, this work presents an approach in which the search is guided according to a *Preferences Base* supplied by the user. Preliminary empirical results showed the approach is able to find solutions which satisfy the most important user preferences.

Keywords: Release planning · Interactive Genetic Algorithm · SBSE

1 Introduction

The decision about which requirements should be allocated in a set of releases is a complex task in any incremental software development process. Thus, release planning is known to be a cognitively and computationally difficult problem [1]. This problem involves many aspects, such as the customers needs and specific constraints [2].

The current SBSE approaches to the software release planning fail to effectively consider the users preferences. Therefore, the users can have issues accepting such results, given that their expertise was not properly captured in the decision process. On the other hand, when human expertise might be considered, Interactive Optimization can be applied. The main idea of this approach is to incisively incorporate the decision maker in the optimization process, allowing a fusion of his preferences and the objective aspects related to the problem [3].

Given this context, the Interactive Genetic Algorithm (IGA) arises. This algorithm is derived from the Interactive Evolutionary Computation (IEC) and is characterized by the use of human evaluations in the computational search through bioinspired evolutionary strategies [3]. However, repeated user evaluations can cause a well-known critical problem in IEC, the human fatigue [4]. This problem may result in a direct quality reduction of user evaluations, given the cognitive exhaustion.

© Springer International Publishing Switzerland 2015
M. Barros and Y. Labiche (Eds.): SSBSE 2015, LNCS 9275, pp. 341–346, 2015.
DOI: 10.1007/978-3-319-22183-0_32

Regarding to the application of search based techniques to release planning, in [5] was proposed a method called EVOLVE based on GAs to decision support, which was extended in [1] considering diversification as a means to approach the uncertainties. Moreover, in [6] was proposed an approach aimed at maximizing the client satisfaction and minimizing the risks of the project. Recently, Araújo and Paixão [7] propose an interactive approach with machine learning to NRP.

This paper proposes an interactive approach to software release planning which employs an IGA guided through a *Preferences Base* supplied by the user.

2   Proposed Approach

The proposed interactive approach is comprised of three components (Fig. 1).

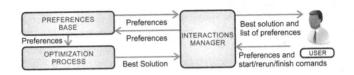

Fig. 1. Proposed approach components and their relations.

The *Interactions Manager* supports the user interactions, enabling the manipulation of the preferences, solutions visualization and control (start and finish) of the search process. The user preferences are stored in the *Preferences Base*. The *Optimization Process* is responsible to search solutions considering the *Preferences Base*.

Initially, through the *Interactions Manager*, the user defines his preferences, which are stored in the *Preferences Base*, and starts the *Optimization Process*. The best solution is shown after each execution of the search algorithm and the user can manipulate the preferences, rerun or stop the search process.

2.1   Release Planning Model

Consider a set of requirements $R = \{r_1, r_2, r_3, ..., r_N\}$ available to be selected for a set of releases $K = \{k_1, k_2, k_3, ..., k_P\}$, where N and P are the number of requirements and releases, respectively. Each requirement r_i has a implementation cost and risk defined by $cost_i$ and $risk_i$, respectively. Each release k_q has a budget constraint s_q. Thus, the requirements with highest risk should be allocated earlier and the sum of the costs of all requirements r_i allocated in k_q cannot exceed the s_q.

Consider $C = \{c_1, c_2, c_3, ..., c_M\}$ as the set of clients, where M is the number of clients and each client c_j has a degree of importance for the company that is reflected by a weight factor w_j. A requirement r_i might have a different value for each client defined by $importance(c_j, r_i)$ which represents how important the requirement r_i is to the client c_j. Finally, the solution representation is a vector $S = \{x_1, x_2, x_3, ..., x_N\}$ where $x_i \in \{0, 1, 2, ..., P\}$, where $x_i = 0$ implies that requirement r_i is not allocated, otherwise it is allocated in release k_q for $q = x_i$.

2.2   Model of User Preferences for Release Planning

The *Preferences Base* contains a set of preference assertions and their respective importance level, explicitly described by a user. A *Preference Assertion* represents a requirement engineer's preference, defined by propositional predicates, as described in Table 1. Thus, consider $T = \{t_1, t_2, t_3, ...t_Z\}$ the set of all preferences, where Z is the number of preferences. Each t_i is a tuple which contains the corresponding preference assertion and the importance level $L_i \in [1, 10]$. This modeling is provided to favor the process of preferences manipulation.

2.3   The Interactive Formulation for Software Release Planning

Considering the definitions in Sects. 2.1 and 2.2, the fitness function is defined as:

$$Fitness(S) = \begin{cases} score(S), & if \ Z = 0 \\ \frac{score(S)}{penalty(S)} & otherwise \end{cases}$$

where $score(S)$ is defined as:

$$score(S) = \sum_{i=1}^{N} y_i \times (value_i \times (P - x_i + 1) - risk_i \times x_i)$$

where $y_i \in \{0, 1\}$ is 1 if requirement r_i was allocated in some release, that is, $x_i \neq 0$, and 0 otherwise. The $value_i$ contains the weighted sum of importance specified by each client c_j for a requirement r_i, calculated by:

$$value_i = \sum_{j=1}^{M} w_j \times importance(c_j, r_i)$$

Therefore, the $score(S)$ function is higher when the requirements with highest *value* and *risk* are allocate in earlier releases.

When there are preferences, which are obtained by user interaction, the $Fitness(S)$ is penalized according to the importance level of each preference which was not satisfied, as follow:

$$penalty(S) = 1 + \mu \times \left(\frac{\sum_{i=1}^{Z} L_i \times violation(S, T_i)}{\sum_{i=1}^{Z} L_i} \right)$$

where the parameter $\mu \in \mathbb{R}_0^+$ defines the weight of the user preferences in the penalty, L_i is the importance level of preference T_i and $violation(S, T_i)$ returns 0 if solution S satisfies the preference T_i and 1 otherwise. Therefore, the higher the number of not satisfied preferences the higher penalty value.

Thus, the proposed interactive formulation for release planning is:

$$\text{maximize} \quad Fitness(S),$$

$$\text{subject to} \quad \sum_{i=1}^{n} cost_i \times f_{i,q} \leqslant s_q, \forall q \in \{1, 2, ..., P\}$$

Table 1. Set of preference assertions for Release Planning

Representation	Basic Interpretation
Arguments	Formal Interpretation
$coupling\_joint(r_i, r_j)$	Two distinct requirements should be placed in the same release.
Requirements r_i and r_j.	$coupling\_joint(r_i, r_j)$ is $satisfied$ iff $x_i = x_j$.
$coupling\_disjoint(r_i, r_j)$	Two distinct requirements should be placed in different releases.
Requirements r_i and r_j.	$coupling\_disjoint(r_i, r_j)$ is $satisfied$ iff $x_i \neq x_j$.
$positioning\_precedes(r_i, r_j, [distance])$	One requirement should precede another by some distance.
Requirements r_i, r_j and a distance between requirements ($[distance]$), always higher than zero.	$positioning\_precedes(r_i, r_j, [distance])$ is $satisfied$ if at least one of the following conditions is met: i $x_i, x_j \neq 0, x_j - x_i \geq distance$, ii $x_i \neq 0, x_j = 0$.
$positioning\_follows(r_i, r_j, [distance])$	One requirement should follow another by some distance.
Requirements r_i, r_j and a distance between requirements ($[distance]$), always higher than zero.	$positioning\_follows(r_i, r_j, [distance])$ is $satisfied$ if at least one of the following conditions is met: i $x_i, x_j \neq 0, x_i - x_j \geq distance$, ii $x_i = 0, x_j, \neq 0$.
$positioning\_after(r_i, k_q)$	One requirement should be placed after a certain release.
Requirement r_i and a release $k_q \neq 0$.	$positioning\_after(r_i, k_q)$ is $satisfied$ if at least one of the following conditions is met: i $x_i \neq 0, x_i - k_q \geq 1$, ii $x_i = 0$.
$positioning\_before(r_i, k_q)$	One requirement should be placed before a certain release.
Requirement r_i and a release $k_q \neq 0$.	$positioning\_before(r_i, k_q, [distance])$, is $satisfied$ iff $x_i \neq 0, k_q - x_i \geq 1$
$positioning\_in(r_i, k_q)$	One requirement should be placed in a certain release.
Requirement r_i and a release $k_q \neq 0$.	$positioning\_before(r_i, k_q)$ is $satisfied$ iff $x_i = k_q$.

where $f_{i,q}$ indicates whether the requirement r_i was allocated in the release k_q.

3   Preliminary Empirical Study

A preliminary empirical study was conducted to evaluate the proposed approach over two distinct instances composed by real data with 50 and 25 independent requirements obtained from [8], named as dataset-1 and dataset-2, respectively.

The implementation risk of each requirement was randomly assigned. The number of releases for dataset-1 and dataset-2 was fixed to 5 and 8, respectively. The budget for each release was defined as the sum of all requirements costs divided by the number of releases. The instances and results are available on-line[1].

Regarding to the search algorithm, the IGA was applied with 100 individuals per population, 1000 generations, 90 % crossover rate, 1 % mutation rate and 20 % elitism rate. These parameters were empirically obtained. The IGA was executed 30 times for each instance and μ variation.

To simulate a user, for each instance, a set of preference assertions, without conflicting, was randomly generated and included in the *Preferences Base*. The number of preferences was 50 and 25 for the dataset-1 and dataset-2, respectively.

The experiments aimed at answering the follow research question:

RQ: How effective is the approach in finding solutions which satisfy a high number of important preferences?

3.1   Results and Analysis

Table 2 shows average and standard deviation for the percentage of number of *Satisfied Preferences* (*SP*), *Satisfaction Level (SL)* and *score* values of the solution for each instance when μ varies. *SL* is a percentage of how much was reached of the total importance of all preferences.

Table 2. Results of *SP*, *SL* and *score* with μ variation for each instance. The symbol $\triangle$ means this result is not significantly higher than the previous one, considering the μ variation, $\triangledown$ (not significantly lower), $\blacktriangle$ (significantly higher) and $\blacktriangledown$ (significantly lower), considerering a 0.05 significance level

μ	dataset-1			dataset-2		
	SP	*SL*	*Score*	*SP*	*SL*	*Score*
0	0.40±0.03	0.40±0.02	25074.8±58.33	0.37±0.05	0.36±0.05	38561.3±154.8
0.1	0.54±0.01 ▲	0.57±0.02 ▲	24889.8±80.55 ▼	0.58±0.03 ▲	0.58±0.04 ▲	38359.9±168.4 ▼
0.2	0.62±0.02 ▲	0.66±0.02 ▲	24591.2±104.23 ▼	0.64±0.04 ▲	0.66±0.04 ▲	37871.7±425.9 ▼
0.3	0.65±0.02 ▲	0.71±0.02 ▲	24312.2±152.30 ▼	0.71±0.05 ▲	0.73±0.05 ▲	37218.1±583.9 ▼
0.4	0.74±0.02 ▲	0.77±0.03 ▲	23862.6±292.98 ▼	0.73±0.04 ▲	0.76±0.05 ▲	36954.5±624.9 ▼
0.5	0.75±0.03 ▲	0.80±0.02 ▲	23568.0±270.29 ▼	0.77±0.05 ▲	0.81±0.05 △	36332.8±646.7 ▽
0.6	0.77±0.02 ▲	0.83±0.02 ▲	23173.3±288.83 ▼	0.80±0.03 ▲	0.85±0.05 ▲	35774.0±873.3 ▼
0.7	0.80±0.03 △	0.86±0.02 △	22867.4±315.07 ▽	0.83±0.04 △	0.88±0.05 △	35211.4±999.6 ▽
0.8	0.81±0.02 △	0.87±0.01 ▲	22804.4±287.04 ▼	0.86±0.05 ▲	0.91±0.04 ▲	34630.7±902.4 ▼
0.9	0.82±0.02 ▲	0.87±0.01 △	22731.9±315.73 ▽	0.86±0.04 △	0.93±0.03 △	34459.7±802.9 ▽
1	0.83±0.02 △	0.88±0.01 △	22494.3±477.97 ▽	0.88±0.04 △	0.94±0.04 △	34052.5±674.0 ▽

With $\mu = 0$, that is, without considering the user preferences during the search process, the solutions satisfied in average 40 % and 37 % of all preferences, reaching 40 % and 36 % of *SL* respectively for dataset-1 and dataset-2. Using $\mu = 0.2$,

---

[1] http://goes.uece.br/altinodantas/pb4isrp/en.

SP reached 62 % and *SL* raised to 66 % for dataset-1, 64 % and 66 % for dataset-2. Comparing the results from $\mu = 1$ to $\mu = 0$, dataset-1, *SP* and *SL* increased 43 % and 48 % respectively, with a scoring loss of only 10.3 %. For dataset-2, the increments were 51 % and 58 % and score loss of 11.7 %.

So, given the number of user preferences equals to the number of requirements, it is possible to satisfy more than 80 % of preferences and get about 90 % of *Satisfaction Level* losing a maximum of 11.7 % of *score*. Therefore, these results answer the *RQ*, showing that the approach can satisfy the most the preferences with high importance level. Besides, *Wilcoxon Test* showed that, for lower values of μ, there was significant increase in *SP* and *SL*, specially, but, with significant loss of *score*. For values of μ near 1, there was no significant variations in *SP*, *SL* and *score*. These results can indicate the more appropriate μ configuration.

4   Conclusions

In any iterative software development process, the decision about which requirements will be allocated in each software release is as complex task.

The main objective of this work was to propose an interactive approach using a preferences base for release planning. An IGA was employed, guided by a *Preferences Base*, which provided a final solution able to satisfy almost of all user preferences, prioritizing the most important ones, with little loss of *score*.

As future works, it is expected to implement a mechanism to identify logical conflicts between user preferences; assess the proposal with other interactive metaheuristics and consider interdependences between requirements.

References

1. Ruhe, G., Ngo-The, A.: A systematic approach for solving the wicked problem of software release planning. Soft. Comput. **12**(1), 95–108 (2008)
2. Ruhe, G., Saliu, M.O.: The art and science of software release planning. IEEE Softw. **22**(6), 47–53 (2005)
3. Takagi, H.: Interactive evolutionary computation: fusion of the capabilities of ec optimization and human evaluation. Proc. IEEE **89**(9), 1275–1296 (2001)
4. Harman, M., Mansouri, S.A., Zhang, Y.: Search based software engineering: a comprehensive analysis and review of trends techniques and applications. Department of CS, King College London, Technical report. TR-09-03 (2009)
5. Greer, D., Ruhe, G.: Software release planning: an evolutionary and iterative approach. Inf. Softw. Technol. **46**(4), 243–253 (2004)
6. Colares, F., Souza, J., Carmo, R., Pádua, C., Mateus, G.R.: A new approach to the software release planning. In: XXIII Brazilian Symposium on Software Engineering, SBES 2009, pp. 207–215. IEEE (2009)
7. Araújo, A.A., Paixão, M.: Machine learning for user modeling in an interactive genetic algorithm for the next release problem. In: Le Goues, C., Yoo, S. (eds.) SSBSE 2014. LNCS, vol. 8636, pp. 228–233. Springer, Heidelberg (2014)
8. Karim, M.R., Ruhe, G.: Bi-objective genetic search for release planning in support of themes. In: Le Goues, C., Yoo, S. (eds.) SSBSE 2014. LNCS, vol. 8636, pp. 123–137. Springer, Heidelberg (2014)

Software Defect Classification with a Variant of NSGA-II and Simple Voting Strategies

Emil Rubinić[(✉)], Goran Mauša, and Tihana Galinac Grbac

Faculty of Engineering, University of Rijeka, Vukovarska 58, 51000 Rijeka, Croatia
{erubinic,gmausa,tgalinac}@riteh.hr

Abstract. Software Defect Prediction is based on datasets that are imbalanced and therefore limit the use of machine learning based classification. Ensembles of genetic classifiers indicate good performance and provide a promising solution to this problem. To further examine this solution, we performed additional experiments in that direction. In this paper we report preliminary results obtained by using a Matlab variant of NSGA-II in combination with four simple voting strategies on three subsequent releases of the Eclipse Plug-in Development Environment (PDE) project. Preliminary results indicate that the voting procedure might influence software defect prediction performances.

Keywords: SDP · SBSE · Multi-objective optimisation · NSGA-II

1 Introduction

Software *Verification and Validation* (V and V) became an important aspect of the software life cycle and one of the key issues is developing an effective V and V strategy based on early fault detection and *Software Defect Prediction* (SDP). The verification space is huge and strategy may be based on numerous objectives. Therefore, it is of big importance to find the best "trade-off" solutions among multiple, and often conflicting objectives. Such optimisation problems are known as *Multi-objective Optimization Problems* (MOP) and are a common case in *Search Based Software Engineering* (SBSE). Performance of machine learning approaches may vary significantly in relation to data imbalance and numerous approaches have been developed to address this problem. Within the SDP several approaches have already been studied [13] and AdaBoost.NC resulted with the best overall performances in terms of the measures such as balance, G-mean and AUC. A multiobjective genetic programming (MOGP) has been proposed to evolving accurate and diverse ensembles of genetic program classifiers [3] and has shown that this approach outperforms its individual members. Actually, the MOGP approach has shown promising results when applied to fault prediction [10] and in software reliability growth modeling [2]. As part of our project [7] we study performance stability using different machine learning methods over different levels of imbalance for SDP. We partialy replicated study [3] and identified that voting procedure may have significant influence on classifier performances

© Springer International Publishing Switzerland 2015
M. Barros and Y. Labiche (Eds.): SSBSE 2015, LNCS 9275, pp. 347–353, 2015.
DOI: 10.1007/978-3-319-22183-0_33

that actually motivated our further experiments that we present in this paper. In this paper, we experiment with a Matlab variant of NSGA-II [5] to create a classification model, and four simple voting strategies to elect one solution from a set of NSGA-II solutions.

Pareto Optimality. The concept of optimality was primarily proposed by Edgeworth and generalized by Pareto [4]. The individual x is said to be Pareto optimal if there does not exist another individual y from a set of individuals which would improve any optimisation objective without aggravating at least one other objective, i.e., there is no y from set of individuals that dominates x [12]. MOP algorithms tend to minimise or maximise two or more objective functions subjected to several equality and/or inequality constraints. Several *Genetic Algorithms* (GA) have been proposed [4] based on the Pareto optimality.

Elitist Non-dominated Sorting GA II. (NSGA-II) is one of the most representative second generation *Multi-Objective Evolutionary Algorithms* (MOEA) [1]. After the initialization, the individuals are sorted based on Pareto dominance and several fronts are created. The individuals on the first front dominate the individuals on the second and so on. Rank is assigned to each individual regarding to the front they belong to (first front rank 1, second rank 2 etc. - the lower the better). Ensuring diversity is important so that algorithm does not get stuck at a local optima and is able to explore unexplored fitness landscape for better solutions [8]. Crowding distance is the measure which helps to ensure diversity among neighboring individuals (the higher the better). Binary tournament selection based on rank and the crowding distance is used to select the parent population. Crossover and mutation are used to create offspring population. Then, the next generation is selected from the parent population and the offspring population. The elitist strategy is implemented so that fitter individuals have a greater probability to pass on to the next generation [1,5].

2 Empirical Study

Data Sets Description. In this article the data from three subsequent releases of the Eclipse *Plug-in Development Environment* (PDE) project is used: 2.0 ($PDE_{2.0}$), 2.1 ($PDE_{2.1}$), 3.0 ($PDE_{3.0}$). Datasets are created using the Bug-Code Analyzer tool [9] each containing 48 different attributes for .java source files and number of bugs linked to the file. A file is classified as *Fault Prone* (FP) if contains at least one fault and otherwise it is classified as *Non Fault Prone* (NFP). Each dataset is 50 times randomly divided into training and test datasets of equal length, as shown in Table 1.

GA Configuration. The configuration of our approach is motivated by several articles [3,6,11]. A Matlab R2014a implementation of NSGA-II, further refered to as mNSGA-II[1] is used for minimising multiple objective functions which has

---

[1] http://www.mathworks.com/help/gads/gamultiobj.html.

Table 1. PDE release datasets, and the training and test sets summary

Name	Whole set						Training sets				Test sets			
	Attributes		FP		NFP		Total	FP		NFP		FP		NFP	
	No.	Type	No.	(%)	No.	(%)	No.	mean	std	mean	std	mean	std	mean	std
$PDE_{2.0}$		Integer	111	(19%)	465	(81%)	576	54.0	4.5	234.0	4.5	57.0	4.5	231.0	4.5
$PDE_{2.1}$	48	decimal	124	(16%)	637	(84%)	761	62.2	4.8	318.2	4.8	61.8	4.8	318.8	4.8
$PDE_{3.0}$			275	(31%)	606	(69%)	881	137.2	6.7	303.3	6.5	137.8	6.7	302.7	6.5

the ability of using a number of sub-populations. Each sub-population is separated from each other to achieve a wider Pareto front. Individuals can migrate at a predetermined rate and generation interval from one sub-population to another. mNSGA-II was set to 3 sub-populations each a size of 200. Migration was set to every 20th generation with fraction of 20%. The initial population was randomly created using a random function with uniform distribution. A single point crossover with a rate 60%, adaptive feasible mutation because of bounded constraints, binary tournament selection and distance crowding in the function space was used. A fraction to keep on the first Pareto front while solver selects individuals from other fronts, called the *Pareto fraction*[2], was set to 0.1 and 0.35 respectively. Regarding the Pareto fraction, six task are used, which are defined: $PDE_{2.0}$-0.10, $PDE_{2.1}$-0.10 and $PDE_{3.0}$-0.10 and $PDE_{2.0}$-0.35, $PDE_{2.1}$-0.35 and $PDE_{3.0}$-0.35. The algorithm terminates if a solution with optimal fitness is found or when a maximum of 100 generations is reached. In total we used 97 *decision variables* X and three different bounded constraints. The first 48 variables are weight factors $w_1 - w_{48}$ in a range of $[-100, 100]$ assigned to dataset attributes a_1 - a_{47}. An arithmetical operator is placed between attributes, depending on the next 47 variables o_1 - o_{47} from set $\{+, -, *, \% \}$. In case of division with zero, the zero is changed to one and algorithm continues. The last two variables are the last operator o_{48} and the noise ϵ in range $[-1000, 1000]$. X and one classifier C can be defined as:

$$X = [w_1, w_2, ...w_{48}, o_1, o_2, ..., o_{47}, o_{48}, \epsilon] \qquad (1)$$

$$C = [(w_1 \cdot a_1)o_1(w_2 \cdot a_2)o_2...(w_{48} \cdot a_{48})]o_{48}w_{49} \qquad (2)$$

During the training process mNSGA-II produces (at each generation) a population of decision variables which is tested on a given training set. If $C > 0$ the file is classified as FP, otherwise it is classified as NFP. This approach were used in article [3]. The objectives to be maximised are the ratio of correctly classified files that actually belong to FP files, the *True Positive Rate* (TPR), and the ratio of correctly classified files that actually belong to NFP files, the *True Negative Rate* (TNR) [3]. Our objectives are:

$$minimise(1 - TPR) \text{ and } minimise(1 - TNR) \qquad (3)$$

---

[2] http://www.mathworks.com/help/gads/examples/multiobjective-genetic-algorithm-options.html

For each run mNSGA-II returns a set of solutions located on the *Pareto approximated* (PA) front. The term PA front is used to indicate that there may be a better Pareto front which our algorithm did not evolve [3]. We obtained 50 PA fronts for each task. For a given task, the *Pareto optimal* (PO) front and the median Pareto front is derived. PO solutions (on the PO front) are calculated as non-dominated solutions among the union of all evolved PA solutions. To evaluate the quality of developed fronts, a trapezoidal numerical integration was used (*hyperarea*) [4].

Making Use of Population. The individuals with the best fitness on training sets do not guarantee best results on test sets. Four voting strategies are used to make one classifier from a set of solutions, similar as Bhowan et al. [3]. The first strategy is a majority vote of the individuals on the *PA Front* (PF-vote) of the evolved population. The second one simply *Removes* solutions from the *PA Front* (RPF-vote) that have a TPR or TNR rate of less than 0.5. The third one is similar to the first and the fourth one is similar to the second, with a difference of using the whole *Final Population* to select the final solution (FP-vote and RFP-vote). In case of equal votes the file is classified as FP. A comparison between the performances of ensemble methods is made by calculating the distance z of the results from the *zenith* point[3] (TPR $= 1$ and TNR $= 1$):

$$z = \sqrt{((1 - TPR)^2 + (1 - TNR)^2)} \qquad (4)$$

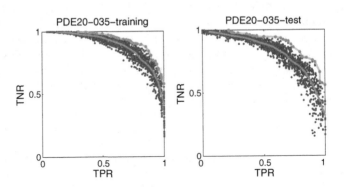

Fig. 1. TPR and TNR of evolved solutions on $PDE_{2.0}$-0.35 at training and test sets (Color figure online)

3   Results

Figure 1 displays TPR and TNR of evolved solutions during 50 mNSGA-II runs for the $PDE_{2.0}$-0.35 task, each time with a different combination of a training and test set. The obtained PA front solutions are represent by blue dots, the

---

[3] http://en.wikipedia.org/wiki/Zenith.

Table 2. Hyperarea of evolved PA fronts and training execution times

Task:	Hyperarea training					Hyperarea testing					Training time(s)		
	mean	std	min	max	PO	mean	std	min	max	PO	total	mean	std
$PDE_{2.0}$-0.10	0.89	0.02	0.84	0.93	0.94	0.81	0.02	0.77	0.87	0.89	2901.6	58.0	10.9
$PDE_{2.0}$-0.35	0.89	0.02	0.84	0.93	0.94	0.81	0.03	0.76	0.87	0.91	2401.9	48.0	11.5
$PDE_{2.1}$-0.10	0.82	0.02	0.77	0.86	0.87	0.74	0.03	0.66	0.77	0.83	3577.8	71.6	1.4
$PDE_{2.1}$-0.35	0.82	0.02	0.76	0.89	0.89	0.74	0.02	0.66	0.78	0.83	3294.6	65.9	12.2
$PDE_{3.0}$-0.10	0.78	0.02	0.73	0.82	0.83	0.74	0.01	0.71	0.78	0.80	3806.4	76.1	13.9
$PDE_{3.0}$-0.35	0.80	0.01	0.76	0.82	0.84	0.74	0.02	0.71	0.78	0.81	3548.0	71.0	14.5

PO solutions by blue dots, the PO front with green line and the median Pareto front calculated from the PA solutions is displayed with a red line. The test results are more dispersed compared to the training results, which is natural because the model was created on training sets. Table 2 reports *average* (mean), *standard deviation* (std), *minimal* (min), *maximal* (max) and PO hyperarea of evolved PA fronts during all mNSGA-II runs for each task. The best fronts have been evolved on $PDE_{2.0}$ (smallest set) and the worst on $PDE_{3.0}$ (biggest set). Training durations are also given in Table 2 with the purpose of comparing the duration of -0.10 and -0.35 tasks. Training time can vary depending on the computer configuration used. As it can be seen from Table 2, the -0.35 tasks are carried out more quickly compared to the -0.10 tasks, and training time increases as the size of dataset increases.

Table 3. Voting results summary using different strategies on the test datasets

Task:	PF-vote						RPF-vote					
	TPR		TNR		z		TPR		TNR		z	
	mean	std	mean	std	mean	std	mean	std	mean	std	mean	std
$PDE_{2.0}$-010	0.618	0.106	0.848	0.049	0.420	0.080	0.744	0.091	0.760	0.058	0.363	0.052
$PDE_{2.0}$-035	0.583	0.097	0.870	0.042	0.442	0.085	0.685	0.088	0.796	0.044	0.383	0.059
$PDE_{2.1}$-010	0.563	0.095	0.791	0.069	0.495	0.057	0.650	0.075	0.702	0.060	0.469	0.035
$PDE_{2.1}$-035	0.538	0.106	0.824	0.061	0.503	0.083	0.625	0.077	0.741	0.054	0.462	0.049
$PDE_{3.0}$-010	0.600	0.081	0.752	0.064	0.480	0.041	0.679	0.056	0.676	0.045	0.461	0.025
$PDE_{3.0}$-035	0.612	0.067	0.740	0.057	0.474	0.040	0.655	0.052	0.693	0.050	0.466	0.032
Task:	FP-vote						RFP-vote					
	TPR		TNR		z		TPR		TNR		z	
	mean	std	mean	std	mean	std	mean	std	mean	std	mean	std
$PDE_{2.0}$-010	0.703	0.083	0.796	0.044	0.369	0.053	0.764	0.062	0.741	0.039	0.356	0.034
$PDE_{2.0}$-035	0.628	0.080	0.847	0.031	0.405	0.066	0.718	0.078	0.773	0.040	0.369	0.044
$PDE_{2.1}$-010	0.665	0.077	0.696	0.060	0.462	0.036	0.674	0.071	0.685	0.059	0.461	0.034
$PDE_{2.1}$-035	0.590	0.083	0.778	0.054	0.473	0.058	0.642	0.077	0.716	0.055	0.464	0.044
$PDE_{3.0}$-010	0.704	0.059	0.651	0.051	0.464	0.025	0.684	0.055	0.672	0.045	0.460	0.027
$PDE_{3.0}$-035	0.643	0.054	0.711	0.044	0.463	0.032	0.663	0.047	0.686	0.039	0.464	0.031

Table 3 presents the voting methods results. TNR is greater than TPR in most tasks. We suppose this is because the dataset is imbalanced. RPF-vote and RFP-vote strategies have produced more balanced and less dispersed results compared to the PF-vote and the FP-vote. From the results we can assume that border solutions, created by mNSGA-II, do not contribute much to the improvement of the software defect classification model for imbalanced datasets (like $PDE_{2.0}$ and $PDE_{2.1}$). The results of voting strategy performances indicate that the use of the whole final population in voting (FP-vote, RFP-vote), instead of just the first front (PF-vote, RPF-vote) with a smaller mNSGA-II Pareto fraction can produce more dense results towards the zenith point and therefore improve the classifier performance.

4   Conclusion and Future Work

This study has shown that using the whole final population instead of just the first front of Matlab variant of NSGA-II together with removing border solutions from voting process (RFP-vote) can lead to the creation of a better model for software defect classification. However, in this study only one MOEA was used on only three datasets. Moreover, a recent study has found that SPEA-II can evolve a better Pareto front compared to NSGA-II on some tasks and that SPEA-II tends to locate more results on the middle region of the Pareto front [3]. In our study, the middle region solutions are more desirable than the edge region solutions. Therefore, our future work will perform a more detailed study on this subject, exploring other models and including test of statistical significance.

Acknowledgments. The work presented in this paper is supported by the University of Rijeka Research Grant 13.09.2.2.16.

References

1. Abraham, A., Goldberg, R.: Evolutionary Multiobjective Optimization: Theoretical Advances and Applications. Springer, Heidelberg (2006). Science & Business Media
2. Afzal, W., Torkar, R.: A comparative evaluation of using genetic programming for predicting fault count data. In: ICSEA 2008, pp. 407–414 (2008)
3. Bhowan, U., Johnston, M., Zhang, M., Yao, X.: Evolving diverse ensembles using genetic programming for classification with unbalanced data. IEEE TEC **17**(3), 368–386 (2013)
4. Coello Coello, C., Lamont, G.: Evolutionary Algorithms for Solving Multi-Objective Problems. Genetic and Evolutionary Computation Series. Springer, Berlin (2007)
5. Deb, K., Pratap, A., Agarwal, S., Meyarivan, T.: A fast and elitist multiobjective genetic algorithm: NSGA-II. IEEE TEC **6**(2), 182–197 (2002)
6. Ferrucci, F., Gravino, C., Oliveto, R., Sarro, F.: Genetic programming for effort estimation: an analysis of the impact of different fitness functions. In: SSBSE 2010, pp. 89–98 (2010)

7. Galinac Grbac, T., Mauša, G., Dalbelo Bašić, B.: Stability of software defect pre-
    diction in relation to levels of data imbalance. In: SQAMIA (2013)
8. Harman, M., McMinn, P.: A theoretical and empirical study of search based testing:
    local. global and hybrid search. IEEE TSE **36**(2), 226–247 (2010)
9. Mauša, G., Galinac Grbac, T., Dalbelo Bašić, B.: Software defect prediction with
    bug-code analyzer - a data collection tool demo. In: SoftCOM 2014 (2014)
10. Sarro, F., Di Martino, S., Ferrucci, F., Gravino, C.: A further analysis on the use
    of genetic algorithm to configure support vector machines for inter-release fault
    prediction. In: SAC 2012, pp. 1215–1220
11. Sarro, F., Ferrucci, F., Gravino, C.: Single and multi objective genetic programming
    for software development effort estimation. In: ACM SAC 2012, pp. 1221–1559
    (2012)
12. Shin, Y., Harman, M.: Pareto efficient multiobjective test case selection. In: ISSTA
    2007, pp. 140–150 (2007)
13. Wang, S., Yao, X.: Using class imbalance learning for software defect prediction.
    IEEE Trans. Reliab. **62**(2), 434–443 (2013)

Author Index

Printed in the United States
By Bookmasters